THE BOOK OF THE
LABRADOR RETRIEVER

THE BOOK OF THE
LABRADOR RETRIEVER

by Anna Katherine Nicholas
with special sections by Janet Churchill,
Mhyra Stapf, Joseph P. Sayres, and Lionel F. Rubin

ISBN 0-87666-748-5

Distributed in the UNITED STATES by T.F.H. Publications, Inc., 211 West Sylvania Avenue, Neptune City, NJ 07753; in CANADA by Rolf C. Hagen Ltd., 3225 Sartelon Street, Montreal 382 Quebec; in ENGLAND by T.F.H. (Great Britain) Ltd., 11 Ormside Way, Holmethorpe Industrial Estate, Redhill, Surrey RH1 2PX; in AUSTRALIA AND THE SOUTH PACIFIC by Pet Imports Pty. Ltd., Box 149 Brookvale 2100 N.S.W., Australia; in SOUTH AFRICA by Multipet (Pty.) Ltd., 30 Turners Avenue, Durban 4001. Published by T.F.H. Publications Inc. Ltd., The British Crown Colony of Hong Kong.

Contents

In Appreciation

There will never be adequate words with which to express my appreciation for the warmth, cooperation, and friendly enthusiasm I have enjoyed from the Labrador Retriever fancy ever since I first mentioned the possibility of my writing this book. As plans took shape, and the book got under way, I felt this even more strongly, with the result that every word and every moment of time and effort that I have expended on attempting to do full justice to Labradors and the Labrador fancy truly turned into a labor of love.

You all have been just great—collecting interesting photographs for use among the illustrations, supplying kennel histories and facts about your dogs and kennels, and helping me to obtain important historical information. You have helped with all the things needed to comprise a worthwhile book, and my gratitude is boundless.

To Jan Churchill, for the time you've spent here with me working on the manuscript, your suggestions, the people you have contacted for valuable material, and all the ways in which you have been helpful, my heartfelt thanks. To Ben Bond, the first to offer assistance by the use of his telephone and with the lists which were so useful, I am endlessly grateful. Many thanks also to Julie Brown Sturman for the thoughtful generosity in sending me the latest issue of your Labrador pedigrees which aided tremendously, and to Nancy Martin for the kind and generous gift of a copy of your interesting and informative book, *Legends in Labradors*—a wonderful source of historical facts. The pedigrees and the book were referred to many times along the way. To Frank Jones, who was so great about gathering important historical notes for me from both Canada and the United States and who made such helpful suggestions of other people for me to contact; Joy Quallenberg, who really "went to town" rounding up her clients' kennel histories and photos for me; to Lisa Weiss, who was instrumental in reminding some of the breeders of our deadline, which they had overlooked; in fact, to ALL of you who have supported the idea of this book so marvelously, I only hope that it will live up to all expectations and that it will be as great a credit to Labradors as the Labrador fancy is to our dog show world.

As usual with these books, Dr. Joseph P. Sayres' "The Veterinarian's Corner" is presented with particular pride. And Marcia Foy deserves an award of merit for the time and careful scrutiny she gave to proof reading, checking copy, and helping in general with gathering material and smoothing out countless details as they arose.

—Anna Katherine Nicholas

Ch. Ashur Deacon, a founding sire for Barbara Barty-King's Aldenholm Kennels, has descendants today in our rings, among them Barbara Barfield's Scrimshaw Labs, and Mary Swan's Chebacco Labradors. Photo courtesy of Mrs. Curtis Read.

Can., Am. Ch. Casadelora's All Spice, by Keating's Kleansa Kita ex Ch. and O.T.Ch. Trollheimen's Golden Sol, is owned by Mr. and Mrs. W.E. Brown, Ladysmith, B.C., Canada.

About the Author

Since early childhood, Anna Katherine Nicholas has been involved with dogs. Her first pets were a Boston Terrier, an Airedale, and a German Shepherd dog. Then, in 1925, came the first Pekingese, a gift from a family friend who raised them. Now her home is shared with a Miniature Poodle and a dozen or so Beagles, including her noted Best in Show dog and National Specialty winner, Champion Rockaplenty's Wild Oats, one of the world's truly great Beagle sires, who, as a show dog, was top Beagle in the nation in 1973. She also owns Champion Foyscroft True Blue Lou and, in co-ownership with Marcia Foy who lives with her, Champion Foyscroft Triple Mitey Migit.

Miss Nicholas is best known in the dog fancy as a writer and as a judge. Her first magazine articles were about Pekingese, published in *Dog News* magazine around 1930. This was followed by a widely acclaimed breed column, "Peeking at the Pekingese," which appeared for at least two decades, originally in *Dogdom* and, when that magazine ceased to exist, in *Popular Dogs*. During the 1940s, she was Boxer columnist for the *American Kennel Gazette* and for *Boxer Briefs*. More recently, many of her articles of general interest to dog show fanciers have appeared in *Popular Dogs*, the Pure-Bred Dogs *American Kennel Gazette*, and *Show Dogs*. She is a featured columnist for *Kennel Review, Dog World, Canine Chronicle*, and *Dog Fancier* magazines. Her *Dog World* column, "Here, There and Everywhere", was the Dog Writers Association of America's winner of the "Best Series In A Dog Magazine" for 1979. And for 1981, her feature article, "Faster Is Not Better," published in *Canine Chronicle*, was one of the four nominees for the Best Feature Article award from the Dog Writers Association of America. She also has written for *The World of the Working Dog*.

It was during the late 1930s that Miss Nicholas's first book, *The Pekingese*, appeared, published by the Judy Publishing Company. This book completely sold out two editions and is now an eagerly sought after collector's item, as is her *The Skye Terrier Book*, published through the Skye Terrier Club of America in the early 1960s.

In 1970, Miss Nicholas won the Dog Writers Association of America award for the Best Technical Book of the Year with her *Nicholas Guide to Dog Judging*. In 1979, the revisions of this book again won the Dog Writers Association of America Best Technical Book Award, the first time ever that a revision has been so honored by this association.

In the early 1970s, Miss Nicholas co-authored with Joan Brearley five breed books for T.F.H. Publications. These were *This is the Bichon Frise, The Wonderful World of Beagles and Beagling, The Book of the Pekingese, This is the Skye Terrier*, and *The Book of the Boxer. The Wonderful World of Beagles and Beagling* won a Dog Writers Association Honorable Mention Award the year that it was published.

Successful Dog Show Exhibiting and *The Book of the Rottweiler* are two of Miss Nicholas's recent releases from T.F.H.; both are being received with enthusiasm and acclaim. The latest of her works, *The Book of the Poodle*, is hailed by many as the greatest breed book of all time. *The Book of the English Springer Spaniel* will be released shortly and is eagerly awaited by fanciers of that breed.

In addition to her four Dog Writers Association of America awards, Miss Nicholas has also been awarded the *Kennel Review* "Winkies" as Dog Writer of the Year on two occasions. And, in 1977, she was winner of the Gaines "Fido" as Journalist of the Year in Dogs.

Miss Nicholas began her career as a judge at the First Company Governors Foot Guard in Hartford, Connecticut, in 1934. Since then, she has officiated at major dog shows throughout the United States and Canada. In 1970, she was the third woman ever to judge Best in Show at the Westminster Kennel Club event at Madison Square Garden in New York (Westminster now has held more than 100 dog shows); she has officiated at this event on some sixteen other occasions as well. She has judged in almost every one of the mainland United States and in four Canadian provinces, where her assignments have included such prestigious events as Santa Barbara, Trenton, Chicago International, the Sportsmans in Canada, the Metropolitan in Canada, the Parent Specialty Clubs of at least several dozen breeds, both here and in Canada.

A lovely drawing of a Lab, sent to us by Laurell Jenny, Mandigo Kennels, West Bountiful, Utah.

CHAPTER ONE

Origin and Development of the Labrador Retriever

Champion Bramshaw Bob LABRADOR RETRIEVER owned by Lorna, Countess Howe

This very famous Labrador Retriever is Eng. Ch. Bramshaw Bob, a dual champion owned by Lorna, Countess Howe. Bred by Mrs. Soper Witburn, Bob won his first field trial award in 1931, followed this award with six field trial wins and ten Challenge Certificates, and then, in 1932, gained his show championship. The following year he completed his field trial title, thus becoming a dual champion.

The Labrador Retriever is a native of Newfoundland, although not of Labrador itself (which is a part of Newfoundland). The Labrador is actually from the St. Johns area where St. Johns water dogs, which bear a strong resemblance to modern Labs, are known to have flourished over many decades. Colonel Peter Hawker is said to have seen these dogs in Newfoundland in 1814, writing of them as "best for every kind of shooting; generally black, no bigger than a Pointer, very fine legs, smooth short hair, does not carry his tail so much curled as the other (*i.e.* Newfoundland), and is extremely quick running and swimming .... We rarely see a Pointer, however expert in fetching, that will follow up the scent and find the wounded ones half so well as the St. John's Newfoundlands."

Another historian, W.E. Cormack, calls the St. Johns Labradors "small water dogs, admirably trained for fowling," adding a comment that their short coat is preferred to the long-coated dogs who become encumbered with ice coming out of the water. Although almost always black, yellows were seen upon occasion and even, though rarely, a chocolate. Their medium size and short, water-repellent coats made them ideal dogs for working with the fishermen.

Newfoundland has a rough coast, extremely perilous for fishing boats to approach closely. For this reason, water dogs were trained to haul in the catch, towing the nets laden with cod by catching the corners in their strong jaws and then swimming ashore. The retrieving instincts of the dogs were also useful to the fishermen because the dogs could fetch articles accidentally dropped overboard by members of the crew. The dogs were also talented at rounding up stray cod which escaped on the surface.

A fairly constant run for the fishing boats was between Newfoundland and Poole Harbor, England, where they delivered salted cod. Of course, some of the dogs made the trip, too. The earliest Labradors are said to have arrived in the Poole Harbor area around the 1820s, and some of them remained after the boats left on their return runs. The English sporting gentry welcomed them with open arms, being quick to appreciate the potential of these fine retrievers and the possibility that they could be developed as gun dogs. The new arrivals were probably bred into the already existing English retriever lines, perfecting and producing the Labradors we know today. (No one seems quite certain when the breed was dubbed "Labrador" Retriever, but it evidently took place sometime after the breed arrived in England.)

A black dog named Buccleuch Avon would seem to be the ancestor of all important black Labrador strains. We have read some glowing descriptions of this dog, who would very definitely seem to have been a most outstanding representative of what is looked for even today in finest type of this breed. Avon was bred by Lord Malmesbury, who was noted for the purity of his Labrador breeding strain, and presented to the sixth Duke of Buccleuch along with two other Labs, Ned and Nell. He also presented Dinah, June, and Smut to Lord Home. Buccleuch Avon was sired by Tramp ex Lord Malmesbury's June, and there are those who firmly believe that this dog's birth was one of the most important events in all Labrador history.

The earliest breeders of excellent Labradors were the Earl of Malmesbury and his son; the Duke of Buccleuch; and the Earls of Home and Verulan. Dogs of exceptional importance in shaping the future of the breed, in addition to Avon, included Sam and Diver owned by the Duke of Hamilton, Keilder owned by Sir Frederick Graham, and Sankey owned by Mr. Montague Guest.

Sir Richard Graham was an early breeder concentrating heavily on Labs, and in 1884, the Hon. A. Holland Hibbert, later Viscount Knutsford, became associated with the breed, continuing his activities without interruption for about half a century at his Munden Kennels near Watford.

The famous artist Ward Binks did this beautiful portrait of, left to right, Ch. Pride of Somersby, Ch. Drinkstone Gyp, Ch. Drinkstone Dan, and Ch. Drinkstone Peg. Pride is the sire of the other three. He was bred by Mr. R. Sharpe, was born in April 1920, and became a champion in 1925.

Munden Sixty and Munden Scotty were the outstanding dogs behind the Munden strain and it was Munden Single, from this kennel, that became the first Labrador to run in a field trial, in 1904. Munden Single's remains were preserved and displayed in the Natural History Museum. We have heard this described sadly as a "rather pathetic object to those who knew of its former glories."

Major Portal's Field Trial Champion Flapper, a widely admired worker, contributed greatly to the breed's prestige (it is said this dog turned the trend of popularity among shooting men from Flatcoats, the former favorite, to Labs). And the Whitmore Kennel of Major Twyford was distinguished as the home of Champion Brayton Swift, another highly admired dog.

In 1904, Labradors were listed by the Kennel Club as a separate breed. The seven which were registered at that time were owned by Munden Kennels, and one of the seven was a Buccleuch-bred bitch. Prior to this time, all retrievers had been grouped together under a single heading.

An outstanding Labrador of the early part of this century was Field Trial Champion Peter of Faskally. Captain A.E. Butler owned him and, working together in what has been described as "perfect unison," they won stake after stake, climaxed by a championship in 1911. Historians tell us that a large number of Labs of the 1930s with an important influence on the future of the breed traced back to this dog, who was the third generation in direct male line descended from Munden Sixty and Munden Scotty.

The Duchess of Hamilton and Brandon owned the Dungavel strain, from which came noted producing bitches, probably the best known of which was Champion Pride of Somersby, the dam of four champions and beloved companion of Dr. H. Munro-Home. He was the owner of the very famous Drinkstone Kennel. The Withington strain of Mr. Hulme, along with the Kinmount, Kirkmahoe, Murrayfield, and Brocklehirst kennels, were also famous for producing dogs of superior working talent. Champion Manor House Belle and Champion Abbess of Harpotts are two early bitches I have heard widely acclaimed.

To everyone who has loved this breed for any length of time, and followed its progress over the years, the names Banchory and Lorna, Countess Howe will always be outstanding. The Banchory dogs have attained literally thousands of honors.

Lorna, Countess Howe, probably the most famous Labrador breeder in history, is pictured here with three of her important winners. They are Champion Bramshaw Bob, Champion Ingleston Ben, and Champion Banchory Trucman.

It was in 1913 that Lady Howe saw, and lost her heart to, Labrador Retrievers. By the following year, she had decided that she must own this breed. In 1916, she and Lord Knutsford, of Munden fame, joined forces and founded the Labrador Club, with Lord Knutsford as president and Lady Howe (then Mrs. Dick) as secretary. The Labrador Club ran its first field trial in 1920.

Dual Champion Banchory Bolo, a son of her first Labrador, Scandal, was probably the best-known of all Lady Howe's dogs, although considering their number and achievements, this is a difficult and possibly debatable statement. During his first season out, he completed his field trial championship, and then shortly thereafter he added a bench show title, becoming the first dual champion in the breed. This dog is credited with being the individual who did the most to further Lady Howe's deep love of Labs. He was her constant companion, nursed back to health from serious illness by her personally prior to the onset of his career and a dog to whom she was completely devoted.

13

Dual Champion Banchory Bolo sired more champions than any other Labrador prior to or during his day (1920s - 1930s), along with a large number of field champions.

Another very famous dog owned by Lady Howe was Champion Ilderton Ben (who, she was quoted as saying, was the "best Labrador ever bred"), the sire of Dual Champion Banchory Sunspeck, Dual Champion Titus of Whitmore, and Dual Champion Flute Flodden.

Then there was Lady Howe's Dual Champion Bramshaw Bob, Best in Show at Crufts in 1932 and 1933 (Bob attained this honor at twelve other championship shows as well); Champion Banchory Danilo, a Best in Show winner of 1925; and Dual Champion Banchory Painter, to name just a few of the other great Labradors bearing this prefix.

Lady Howe passed away in 1960, but she will certainly live forever in the memory of the

Ch. Ilderton Ben, owned by Lady Howe in about 1914, was a great early winner and widely admired.

Labrador fancy because of her tremendous interest and contributions to the progress of this breed.

Bramshaw Bob, a top-flight Labrador of the 1930's, was an important English winner, including a Championship Certificate for the breed and the award of Best Dog in Show at Crufts in 1932.

Labrador.
Champion "Bramshaw Bob"

5858/K.

Four of the splendid Labradors from Lorna, Countess Howe's famed Banchory Kennels. These dogs are probably of the 1920s.

Two more of Lady Howe's Labradors—Field Trial Champion Balmuto Jock and Field Trial Champion Bryngawr Flute.

Great Britain's royal family have always been great lovers of dogs, and one of the most favored breeds with them has been the Labrador Retriever. King George VI exhibited his dogs at leading shows and did nice winning with them. Formerly known as Wolverton, the royal kennels more recently have been identified as Sandringham. Among those known in dog show circles were Wolverton Jet, Wolverton Dan, and Wolverton Ben. We are proud to present to our readers a head study of the King's brace which was shown at Crufts in 1932.

King George was patron of the Labrador Club at the time of his death, and Queen Elizabeth later honored the club by accepting the position. I am sure that all of us at one time or another have seen charming pictures of the royal family with their Labs. Queen Elizabeth has entered into competition with them, too, having run dogs of her own in field trials.

This handsome brace of Labradors belonged to His Majesty King George, who maintained a large kennel of the breed at Sandringham. This brace was exhibited at Crufts in 1932.

The imported Ch. Lockerbie Goldentone Jensen, bred by Graham Morley, Lanes, U.K., came to join the Lockerbie Labradors at Briarcliff Manor, New York. By Australian Ch. Jaysgreen Jasper ex a daughter of Eng. Ch. Sandylands Tandy. Owned by Mrs. James Warwick.

16

CHAPTER TWO

Labradors in England

Ch. Sandylands Mark, probably the most influential stud dog to be found in all Labrador Retriever history, is pictured informally with his owner, Mrs. Gwen Broadley.

While doing research on Labradors for this book, I was tremendously impressed by the impact made on the breed in all parts of the world by one particularly important English kennel. This is, of course, the Sandylands Kennel owned by Mrs. Gwen Broadley, and this kennel's prefix can be found somewhere in the pedigrees of a vast majority of leading Labs.

Mrs. Broadley started with Labradors (she has owned several other breeds as well) back in the 1920s as a very young girl. Her first Lab was a black bitch which she named Juno of Sandylands. This was a daughter of Darky Dan ex Laund Linky; the latter traced her ancestry to Champion Ilderton Ben and Field Trial Champion Peter of Faskally. The first Sandylands litter was by Mrs. Broadley's first champion, Champion Jerry of Sandylands, from Jono. Mrs. Broadley's dogs are now in the eleventh and twelfth generation of her line.

The earlier Sandylands Labs all were black. Then Champion Sandylands Bob sired a yellow pup.

We have read in Nancy Martin's delightful and informative book, *Legends in Labradors*, that, as of 1980, at least sixty-three British Labradors bearing the Sandylands identification not to mention all those that have finished elsewhere around the world. Even during World War II the line was kept active, with June of Sandylands coming out at the war's close to win Best Bitch at the first Labrador Club show.

At the time of this writing, there are twelve champions in residence at Mrs. Broadley's, as well as what she describes as "the best lot of up and coming youngsters for a long time." Unfortunately, Mrs. Broadley has had to limit her breeding, showing, and judging activities as she has recently undergone surgery for her second hip replacement, but nothing will ever dim her interest.

The three most dominant of the Sandylands sires have been Champion Sandylands Mark, Champion Sandylands Tandy, and Champion Sandylands Tweed of Blaircourt. Mark's litter-brother, English and American Champion Sandylands Midas, has also been important. Mark and Midas, a black and a yellow, came from a 1965 breeding of Sandylands Truth to Champion Reanacre Mallardhurn Thunder, a son of Champion Sandylands Tweed of Blaircourt and grandson of Champion Poppleton Lieutenant, Truth's great grandsire. Again quoting Mrs. Martin's book, "No dog has ever sired more British title winners, and there are three dual Challenge Certificate winners and several younger dogs who may yet elevate Mark to the position of Supreme Sire."

Champion Sandylands Tandy was sired by Sandylands Tan (an Australian champion) ex Sandylands Shadow. Champion Sandylands Tweed of Blaircourt was bred by Mr. and Mrs. Grant Cairns, out of Champion Ruler of Blaircourt ex Champion Tessa of Blaircourt.

A group of Labradors with their handlers at the Labrador Retriever Club (England) twenty-fifth trial.

Mrs. Broadley judges all of the Variety groups and Best in Show (which she has done at Crufts); her services are in great demand. She has officiated at several shows in the United States, including a Lab Specialty on the Cherry Blossom Circuit in Virginia and Maryland.

A member of the General Committee, the Executive Committee, and the Show Regulations Committee of the Kennel Club, Mrs. Broadley is also involved with numerous championship and club dog shows. She is indeed a lady who has contributed vastly to her breed and to the fancy in general!

Sandylands Croftspa Stardandy, a Reserve Challenge Certificate winner bred by Mr. and Mrs. Chapman, by Show Ch. Sandylands Storm Along ex Champion Sandylands Geannie. Owned by Mrs. Gwen Broadley and Mr. Garner Anthony. Photo by Thomas Fall courtesy of Mrs. Broadley, Sandylands Labradors, Northants, England.

Ch. Sandylands Newinn Columbus, by Ch. Sandylands Mark ex Newinn Amber (by Ch. Sandylands Tandy) is owned by Mrs. Gwen Broadley and Mr. Garner Anthony. Photo by Thomas Fall courtesy of Mrs. Broadley.

Sandylands Rosy, born May 12th 1979, by Show Ch. Sandylands My Rainbeau ex Show Ch. Sandylands Sparkle. Owned by Mrs. Gwen Broadley and Mr. Garner Anthony. Photo by Thomas Fall, courtesy of Mrs. Broadley.

Show Ch. Sandylands My Rainbeau, by Ch. Sandylands Mark ex Show Ch. Sandylands Longley Come Rain. Owned by Mrs. Gwen Broadley and Mr. Garner Anthony. Photo by Thomas Fall, courtesy of Mrs. Broadley.

This is "Binky," or more formally Ravencamp Grebe, with her litter by Ballyduff Keeper. There was only one other puppy in the litter which included "Binky," and this other puppy, "Bunky," went to Australia while the subject of this photo came to Canada. The breeder was Col. George Craster, a colonel in the Bengal Lancers (India) for 19 years and a great friend of Mahatma Gandhi. "Binky" was the great-granddaughter of Field Trial Ch. Font of Flodden, who in 1936 and 1938 was first in the British Field Trial National and second in 1937, after which there were no trials for a period of years owing to the war. Photo and information courtesy of Frank Jones, Ontario.

Mrs. H. B. Woolley's Follytower Fudge, Ch. Follytower Silsdale Old Chelsea, and Follytower Fiona—three beautiful representatives of the famous Follytower Labradors at Devon, England.

Follytower Labradors, owned by Mrs. Margot Woolley in Axminster, Devon, have achieved a great deal through the remarkable once-in-a-life-time dog, Champion Follytower Merrybrook Black Stormer. This dog's mother, Champion Follytower Silsdale Old Chelsea, was purchased when eight weeks old by Mrs. Woolley as her first venture into the dog show world, back in 1962. Prior to that time, the Woolleys "always had Labradors and had bred a few litters, supplying our friends and relatives with pets." When she decided that it might be fun to do some showing, Mrs. Woolley contacted Mrs. Broadley and Mrs. Wynyard. The former had only a dog puppy for sale at the time, but the latter knew of a litter in Yorkshire by Champion Braeduke Joyful in which there were five black bitches. Mrs. Woolley was fortunate enough to be given choice of the two best bitches picked by her husband and Margaret Ward. As she remarks, "my husband always says I owe my success in Labs to him, as it was he who chose Old Chelsea." What fun Mrs. Woolley had with this bitch!

Ch. Follytower Merrybrook Stormer photographed on his twelfth birthday in 1980. Stormer won his fifteenth Challenge Certificate when seven years old in a record entry at a Labrador Specialty judged by Mrs. Gwen Broadley, where he was also Best Champion in Show. A dominant, highly successful stud as well as show dog. Owned by Mrs. Margot Woolley, Axminster, Devon, England, who has loaned us this photo by Anne Roslin-Williams.

In her first litter, sired by Show Champion Hollybunch of Keithray, Chelsea had two beautiful pups: Fudge, who won a Challenge Certificate, and Fiona, who was the dam of Follytower Cressida (Cressida's name is found in so many pedigrees in Marjorie Brainard's Briary Kennel).

The second time Mrs. Woolley bred Old Chelsea, the sire was the litter-brother of Hollybunch, Champion Ballyduff Hollybranch of Keithray. By this time, Mrs. Woolley's husband was counting heads, so all of these puppies were sold, one of them going to David Hoare in Dorset, who eventually mated her to Champion Sandylands Tandy and ran on two black pups. A third from this litter is Dual Champion Black Duke in Denmark.

When the puppies were about six months old, David Hoare moved from Dorset to Cumbria, stopping off at Follytower en route north. Mrs. Woolley was greatly impressed with the puppies, to the extent that she later bought "Sam," as Stormer is known at home. He was tremendous fun to show, a complete extrovert, but his principal claim to fame, and a most interesting one, is that he is the sire of three of the only four chocolate Labs to have gained championship in Great Britain! He carried the genes for all three colors, which surprised Mrs. Woolley, although Old Chelsea's mother's sister was chocolate. This color is not as popular in England as it is in the United States, so the dogs have to be really super to make the grade.

The other bloodlines at Follytower are, to quote Mrs. Woolley, "due to the kindness of Bridget Docking, who invited me to come to see the last litter sired by Champion Ballyduff Seaman before he left for America." This was the

Follytower Bandbox, a fine Labrador owned by Mrs. Margot Woolley, Follytower Labradors, Axminster, Devon, England. Photo by Anne Roslin-Williams, submitted by Mrs. Woolley.

famous litter bred by Mrs. Butchart from Electron of Ardmargha. Mrs. Butchart kept the pick of the litter, who became Bridget of Tuddenham and Ballyduff. Bridget Docking chose two dogs for herself, and for Joyce Harrison, she chose a bitch who became Champion Curnafane Seamansal; another black pup was sold locally, and Mrs. Woolley chose Follytower Spindrift. The one bitch that was left eventually became Champion Ballyduff Marina.

Spindrift never completed her championship, although she has two Challenge Certificates and four Reserve Challenge Certificates. The reason for this was that she came in season only once a year, in March. The English show calendar is so constituted that when Spindrift was bred each March, there were very few championship shows left during the year for her to compete in. Two of her grandaughters, Bandbox and Bunty, are in the Follytower Kennels now; of course they also are grandchildren of Black Stormer.

British dog shows give cards for their awards rather than ribbons as in the United States. First prize is denoted by a red card (rather than by the color blue as in the U.S.). Photo by Janet Churchill.

Here we show you a British Challenge Certificate, of which three are needed to become a champion, and a Championship Certificate denoting that the dog has completed title. Photo by Janet Churchill.

Mrs. D.I. Gardner, owner of Novacroft Kennels, started with Labradors in the late 1950s, concentrating mainly on working-bred dogs. Her first winner was Novacroft Sampson, out of a working-bred bitch sired by Show Champion Sandylands Sam. This dog did considerable winning, but unfortunately he left no progeny.

Next Mrs. Gardner acquired Novacroft Litchencroft, by Champion Sandylands Tandy. This dog was a good winner and sired well; his descendants include American Champion Novacroft Carlos and American Champion Novacroft Classicway Come Dancing.

Champion Jayncourt Truly Fair, also by Tandy, is considered by Mrs. Gardner to be one of her most versatile Labradors. Although entirely of show breeding, she has been Mrs. Gardner's best worker (she has just completed another season at nine and a half years age), and she also has winning and working progeny in many places.

Currently "pride of place" at Novacroft goes to Mrs. Gardner's young Show Champion

Novacroft Gay Rhapsody, the dam of Novacroft Chorus Girl and Novacroft Charles, is owned by Mrs. D.I. Gardner who has submitted this photo made for her by Anne Roslin—Williams.

Novacroft Chorus Girl and her litter-brother Novacroft Charles, who is probably also a champion by now as he had two Challenge Certificates and one Reserve when this was written. Homebred by Sandylands Charlston ex Novacroft Gay Rhapsody, Chorus Girl and Charles have been a source of much pleasure to their owner. The best bitch from Chorus Girl's most recent litter was sent to the United States, and Mrs. Gardner is looking forward to Chorus Girl's next litter, which will be sired by Champion Sandylands My Rainbeau. Charles, too, is proving himself as a producer; he has numerous winning youngsters in the ring.

Novacroft Litchencroft, 1967–1979, was owned by Mrs. D.I. Gardner, Shropshire, England, who sent us this photo by Anne Roslin-Williams.

Show Ch. Novacroft Chorus Girl (above) and Novacroft Charles (below), who had two Challenge Certificates when this picture was taken. Both photos by Anne Roslin-Williams, courtesy of Mrs. Gardner.

Ch. Novacroft Jayncourt Truly Fair, a lovely bitch of Sandylands' breeding, is owned by Mrs. D.I. Gardner, Novacourt Labradors, Shropshire, England.

The late Mrs. Bridget Docking lived in Norfolk with her Ballyduff Labs. This lady was active with Labradors for more than forty years, having bought her first one, Holton Opal, a daughter of Champion Cheverells Ben of Banchory in 1938. She had many famous winners through the years, dogs of good type that won in both bench and field. Ch. Squire of Ballyduff was one of her most famous. Mrs. Docking also supplied foundation stock for others.

The Heatherbourne Labradors were established in 1966 with the purchase of two yellow bitches sired by Champion Sandylands Tandy. However, their owner, Mrs. Heather Wiles, did not start showing seriously until the purchase of a dog and a bitch in 1971; these two became her first champions, namely Champion Heatherbourne Lawnwood's Laughing Cavalier and Show Champion Heatherbourne Harefield Silver Penny.

Ballyduff Spruce, shown after having won qualifying round for "Puppy of the Year." The judge is R.M. James, at Edinburgh Kennel Club in 1978. The late Bridget Docking considered Spruce to be one of her very best Labs. Photo courtesy of Janet Churchill.

Silver Penny had an enormous effect on the Heatherbourne breeding program. She produced a champion herself, Show Champion Heatherbourne Silver Czar, and was the grandmother of four champions. She was the dam of Heatherbourne Moira who in turn has produced three champions: Show Champion Heatherbourne Statesman, Show Champion Heatherbourne Fisherman, and Fisherman's sister, International Champion Heatherbourne Forget Me Not owned by Mr. and Mrs. Beattie in Canada.

Show Ch. Copperhill Lyric of Heatherbourne, owned by Heather Wiles, Bourne Farm, Harefield, Middlesex, England. Photo by Sally Anne Thompson.

Show Ch. Heatherbourne Statesman (above) and Show Ch. Heatherbourne Fisherman (below), owned by Heather Wiles, Harefield, Middlesex, England. Photos by Sally Anne Thompson.

Mrs. Wiles' top winning bitch was Show Champion Heatherbourne Top Tune who gained nine Challenge Certificates and ten Reserve Certificates. She is the dam of American Champion Heatherbourne Pioneer.

The latest of Mrs. Wiles' champions is Show Champion Copperhill Lyric of Heatherbourne, sired by Show Champion Heatherbourne Silver Czar, who, at the Midland Counties Championship show in October 1981, won the Gun Dog Group. She is a most charming bitch, always eager to please and so like Silver Penny, her grandmother, who, incidentally, had won the Gun Dog Group at the Three Counties show in 1973.

England's Blackpool Championship Show 1977. Eng., Am. Ch. Lawnwoods Hot Chocolate at the head of the line, winning his fourth Challenge Certificate and Best of Breed. Now owned by Janet Churchill, at Spenrock Labradors.

Mary Roslin-Williams (Mansergh Labs) purchased her first Labrador in 1939, which unfortunately developed "night blindness," eventually leading to total blindness; this Lab had to be put to sleep when four years old. Her next Labrador was Carry of Mansergh, a lovely dual-purpose bitch who became the foundation for Mansergh Labs, which are now in their 16th and 17th generation! This highly dedicated breeder of outstanding dogs has contributed an inestimable amount of quality to her breed through such dogs as Champion Mansergh Midnight and his son, Champion Mansergh Bumblikite, and their descendants.

Lisdalgin Live and Learn owned by Mrs. D.I. Gardner, sadly died at only four years of age after some good wins and producing quality progreny. Photo by Anne Roslin-Williams sent to us by Mrs. Gardner.

was by Darkie of Elmbank ex Craigluscar Black Gem, while Tauna was bred by Harry Smith and was a daughter of Knaith Boomerang ex Tomboy of Treesholme. Both of these bitches were splendid producers and are to be found in the background of Blaircourt dogs right up to the present day. Champion Sandylands Tweed of Blaircourt and the fabulous American winner, Champion Sam of Blaircourt, are two of the Labs that have made this kennel justly famous.

Breeder-judge Mary Roslin-Williams, in the United States, awards points to Ch. Pollywag Conic of Chidley, by Castlemine Mask ex Yarrow's Pollywag Sabrina, co-owned by Beth Sweigart and Mrs. Curtis Read.

Eng. Ch. Balrion King Frost, by Eng. Sh. Ch. Sandylands Clarence of Rossbank ex Balrion Loyale Princess. This famous English dog is the winner of 22 Challenge Certificates and is a multiple Best in Show winner, including the Scottish Kennel Club Show in 1978 in an entry of over 9000. Photo courtesy of the Beatties, Shadowvale Labs, Rigaud, Quebec, who imported a beautiful bitch in whelp to this dog.

As we study the background of important members of the breed, we see many references to Blaircourt Labradors. This kennel was founded by Mrs. Margie Cairns and her late husband with the purchase of Tauna of Treesholme, followed shortly thereafter by Craigluscar of Blaircourt purchased from Donald Reid. The latter black bitch, holder of a Field Certificate,

FRASIE

Ch. Dark Star of Franklin contemplates his first Best in Show trophy, won at Rock River Valley in 1954, when he was one-and-a-half years old. We believe that Dark Star still remains the top winning American-bred black Labrador today, in a career distinguished by only 18 months in competition. Mr. Martin owned this dog, bred by his daughter, Mrs. Bernard Ziessow.

CHAPTER THREE

Labradors in the United States

Frank Jones has sent us this photo, captioned "Dorothy Howe's dogs." Mrs. Howe had been owner of the famous Rupert Labradors, an outstanding kennel in the United States.

Labradors had started to gain recognition in the United States even prior to World War I. Still classified, along with the others, merely as "retrievers," these dogs were being imported and used for shooting by at least several Long Islanders who were active in the sport, some of the earliest of whom included Harry T. Peters, Sr., Mr. and Mrs. Guest, Mr. and Mrs. Phipps, and Mrs. A. Butler Duncan.

Full recognition of the Labrador Retriever as a breed came at the end of the 1920s, when the American Kennel Club approved the separation of "retrievers," according each its own classification.

The Labrador Retriever Club was founded at the beginning of the 1930s, largely through the interest and efforts of Mrs. Marshall Field (its first President, 1931-1935), Franklin B. Lord and Robert Goelet (Vice-Presidents), Wilton Lloyd-Smith (Secretary-Treasurer), and a Board of Directors consisting of Marshall Field, William J. Hutchinson, and Paul C. Pennoyer.

1933 was the year of the first Labrador Retriever Club Specialty show, superintended by George F. Foley, with 34 entries. The Best of Breed winner was Boli of Blake, owned by Franklin B. Lord. Mrs. Marshall Field was the judge.

In 1935, Charles L. Lawrence, Jay F. Carlisle, Alfred Ely, Benjamin Moore, and Mrs. E. Roland Harriman stepped into positions of im-

portance in the club, and Jay F. Carlisle became President, serving until 1938. This gentleman, through his Wingan Kennels on Long Island, was a dominant influence in the early history of the breed here—through his personal contributions, his importation of the finest bloodlines, and his active breeding program. The alumni of Wingan, the important dog people who started out at this kennel, are indeed impressive! David Elliott, who brought the bitch Whitecairn Wendy from Scotland, was this kennel's first manager and trainer; Clint Callahan was the first of Wingan's kennel men, in charge of Labradors while Gil Mathisson, also from Scotland, was in charge of Pointers, Mr. Carlisle's other breed.

Among the importations to Mr. Carlisle's kennel were Drinkstone Mars and Drinkstone Pons, along with Banchory Jetsam and Banchory Trump of Wingan. But probably the most important was Drinkstone Peg who arrived in whelp to Lady Howe's great English Dual Champion Bramshaw Bob. From this litter, Mr. Carlisle got Champion Bancstone Ben of Wingan, Champion Bancstone Countess of Wingan, Champion Bancstone Lorna of Wingan, and Champion Bancstone Peggy of Wingan, all of which did well for him. From this litter also came Champion Bancstone Bob of Wingan, one of the fine and successful Labs owned by Mrs. Curtis Read, who was Joan Redmond at that time.

The J.P. Morgan family were great Lab enthusiasts, too. Mr. Morgan himself owned what may well have been the first yellow in the United States, Banchory Snow. His sons and their wives, the Junius S. Morgans and the Henry Morgans, who preferred blacks and yellows respectively, were also great devotees—especially Mrs. Junius Morgan with highly outstanding dual-purpose dogs owned under the West Island banner.

Dr. Samuel Milbank acquired his first Labrador, a dog named Raffles, in the late 1920s. Raffles was selected for him in Scotland by a friend, who in turn had a mutual friend escort the dog to the United States. So excited was Sam Milbank over the acquisition of Raffles that he could hardly wait to get him into the ring, and advance entry was made in the important Labrador Specialty coming up in conjunction with Westbury Kennel Association's all-breed show—within days, Raffles went from the ship to the ring. In a very auspicious manner, Raffles swept the boards that day, even over the Specials entries, to gain Best of Breed and then wound up second in the Sporting Group. He followed through with similar aplomb in his next two shows and became an American Show Champion after a whirlwind three-show ascent to the title. Raffles of Earlsmoor became a successful field dog, too, being usually in the money (which quite literally was the case in those days; betting was a part of the sport, particularly in the Open Stakes).

The Labrador Club Specialty in 1948. Left to right: Jim Cowie handling the Best of Breed, Ch. Stowaway of Deer Creek for Mrs. Kathleen Poor; Club President, J. Gould Remick presenting trophies; Dr. Samuel Milbank judging; and Mrs. Joan Read with Ch. Chidley Spook, Winners Bitch and Best of Opposite Sex. An Evelyn Shafer photograph loaned to us by Mrs. Curtis Read.

Champion Raffles of Earlsmoor proved himself a fantastic sire, particularly when bred to The Honorable W. Averill Harriman's Field Trial Champion Decoy of Arden. These two Labs combined to produce such fabulous dogs as Dual Champion Braes of Arden owned by Mrs. J.R. McManus, Dual Champion Gorse of Arden owned by Mrs. Morgan Belmont, and Dual Champion Shed of Arden owned by Mr. and Mrs. Paul Bakewell. The puppy that Dr. Milbank selected for himself grew up to become Champion Earlsmoor Moor of Arden, the trailblazer of Best in Show Labs; he was the first to gain the award, which he then built up to a multiple record of five times All Breed Best in Show (a record that held for many years), plus 12 times first in the Sporting Group, 27 Group placements, and 40 times Best of Breed (including this win at the Morris and Essex show and, in 1938, '39, '40, '41, and '43—he did not compete there in '42—at the Labrador Specialty). Considering the fact that dogs competed on a far more limited basis in those days than now when number of appearances annually are concerned, Moor's was a truly remarkable record. Best in Show at Greenwich was one of Moor's most exciting all-breed victories. He won the National Bench Show Challenge Cup outright three times over a three year period and then proceeded to win the one which replaced it. Moor was handled throughout his career by James A. Cowie, now a noted dog show judge.

So successful had the breeding been of Field Trial Champion Decoy of Arden to Champion Raffles of Earlsmoor that it was repeated by Mr. Harriman. From this litter, Dr. Milbank got the lovely bitch Champion Earlsmoor Marlin of Arden, and Paul Bakewell of St. Louis, Missouri got a dog he made famous, Champion Shed of Arden, who won the National Championship two years consecutively and then later took it again for a third time. Shed of Arden became an American and Canadian Champion, American Amateur Field Champion, American Field Champion, and National Retriever Champion in 1942, '43, and '46. Mr. Bakewell completed a number of Dual Championships on his dogs, including Dual Champion Matchmaker for Deer Creek, Dual Champion Hello Joe, Dual Champion Little Pierre of Deer Creek (Best of Breed at the National in 1947), and Dual Champion Double Deal. Double Deal accomplished the completion of both field and bench titles on the

Dorothy Howe, author of *This is the Labrador Retriever* and a very famous breeder.

same day, winning the trial in the morning and the conformation show later that afternoon. Mr. Bakewell was the first amateur handler to win an Open Stake and a National Championship, defeating all the leading professionals.

The Honorable W. Averill Harriman's importance in the development of Labrador Retrievers in the United States should be obvious from the information already divulged regarding the Labs bred at his Arden Kennels in upper New York State. This gentleman really started the breed off on the right foot when he imported a black daughter of Ronald of Candahar ex Genta of Sigeforda, namely Peggy of Shipton (descended from Banchory stock), who arrived here in whelp to Duke of Kirkmahoe (Withington Banner ex Kirkmahoe Dina). From this litter Sam of Arden was kept, a valuable working dog with trial placements to his credit.

A dog named Odds On (The Favorite ex Jest) owned by Mrs. Marshall Field was selected as the sire of Peggy's second litter. Born in March 1933, the litter included Field Champion Decoy of Arden and Field Champion Blind of Arden, both of which became "greats" in breed history. So pleased was everyone concerned with this litter that the breeding was repeated, this time producing Mrs. Morgan Belmont's Joy of Arden, a successful field trial winner.

Then Peggy was bred to the English import Hiwood Risk, by Field Trial Champion Hiwood D'Arcy (Ch. Banchory Danilo from a daughter of Dual Champion Titus of Whitmore) ex Hiwood Betty (daughter of Champion Ingleston Ben from Field Champion Hiwood Chance). It was from this litter that Field Trial Champion Tar of Arden, the first Labrador to win a national championship, was acquired by Paul Bakewell III.

Between 1937 and 1944, Mr. Harriman bred four Labs which attained dual championship. They were Dual Champion Braes of Arden and Dual Champion Gorse of Arden (littermates by Champion Raffles of Earlsmoor ex Field Champion Decoy of Arden) owned respectively by Mrs. J.R. McManus and Mrs. Morgan Belmont; Dual Champion Shed of Arken, whom we have already discussed at length; and Dual Champion Bengal of Arden (Good Hope Angus ex Burma of Arden) owned by Mrs. A.P. Loening.

The death of Tom Briggs, the kennel manager and trainer, brought to an end the interest in active participation in field trials and dog shows at Arden Kennels. The Harriman dogs went to a new home in Sun Valley, Idaho, at the beginning of World War II, where they remained to live out their lives with their new owners.

When Mr. Harriman became Governor of New York, his pale yellow Labrador named Brun became a popular favorite with the public.

Some excellent Labradors were owned and raised by Mr. and Mrs. David Wagstaff at Ledgelands, their Tuxedo Park, New York, residence and kennel, where they also enjoyed the ownership of Chows and Springers. David Wagstaff was one of the judges for the first Labrador Retriever Club field trial, which was held on Robert Goelet's estate in New York, in December 1931 (Dr. Milbank shared this judging assignment). Famous Labs owned by the Wagstaffs included Champions Ledgelands Bridesmaid and Maid of Honor, and a splendid bitch, Solwyn Duchess, that placed in important Amateur Stakes.

Other active participants in those days, with large successful kennels, were Mrs. Edmund W. Poor with her Wardwyn Labradors, the Gerald Livingstons with Kilsyth Kennels, Mrs. Howes Burton with How Hi, and Mrs. James M. Austin with Catawba.

It is interesting to thumb through a Westminster Kennel Club catalogue for 1937 to see what was doing with Labradors as that decade drew to a close. Hubert A. Doll was the Lab judge that year, drawing 30 dogs. Jay Carlisle had five in competition. Squirrel Run Kennels, owned by Mrs. S. Hallock du Pont of Wilmington, Delaware, had four. Franklin B. Lord, the Bentley Kennels, and Elsie Stewart each had several, while other entries in the breed came from Miss Jean G. Hinkle, Joan Redmond (who became Mrs. Curtis Read), J.W. Caballos, C.B. Murnan, Mrs. J.F. Frost, Mrs. Belmont, H.V. and Mrs. Chitton, Dr. Lloyd Hoffman, Ledgelands Kennels, and Eugene Brennan. There were six Labs in for Best of Breed competition at this show: Bentley Kennels' Champion Bentley Dina, Squirrel Run's Champion Towyriver James, three of Jay Carlisle's (Champion Banchory Trump of Wingan, Bancstone Lorna of Wingan, and Bancstone Countess of Wingan), and Franklin B. Lord's Champion Middlecote Endeavor (by Bramshaw Bob) bred by Lady Howe.

World War II knocked down the Westminster Labrador entry sharply. In 1943, Charles L. Lawrence judged only six there, two belonging to Mrs. Poor (including the only Special, Champion Michael of Wynward by Champion Earlsmoor Moor of Arden ex Bright of Blake) and one each from Mr. and Mrs. James Harris, Miss Dorcas Lockwood, Mr. and Mrs. James Souter, and Mrs. David Wagstaff (Tattler of Morehouse, bred by Maggie Belmont).

The following year, 1944, it was Dr. Milbank on the woolsack with nine entries coming before him. Mrs. Poor had four, including the same Special as the previous year, while the Wagstaffs, Arthur Hillhouse, Jr., Fred A. Rohn, Virginia H. Pearce, and Mrs. John H. Denison were also represented.

A barely perceptible rise occurred in 1947, when the entries numbered eleven. Mr. U.B. Fishel was the judge. Gerald M. Livingston's Kilsyth dogs were in this year, as were two owned by Joan Redmond. L.H. Faidley, Major H.W. Cochran, and Dela-Win Kennels were represented, and Mrs. James M. Austin had Shell of Catawba. The four entries for Specials were E.J. Shaffer's Champion Ebony Buc, Mrs. Poor's Champion Wardwyn Whiskers (Champion Earlsmoor Moor of Arden ex Champion Buddha of Arden), Joan Redmond's Champion Hugger Mugger, and Mrs. Harley Butler's Champion Miss Dela Winn.

Skipping over to 1952, we find numerous familiar names. Dr. Mitten, so respected by the Sporting Dog fancy, was the judge. Exhibitors included John Graham, Alfred E. Johnson, Jr., Mrs. Frank Ginnel, Mrs. John L. Graham, Mrs. Barbara Barty-King (her entry was Champion Ashur Deacon), Miss Hinkle, E.W. Fisher, Julius Chandler, Thomas Moseley, Mrs. Theodore Gould, Redledge Kennels, Mr. and Mrs. Richard T. Wharton, Mr. and Mrs. Frank Crowe, and Mrs. Anne Cooper Moore with class entries, while the Specials were Champion Whichway David D owned by Missquoque Kennels and Champion Hobbimoor Merganser owned by Townsend Horner.

There were 23 Labs at Westminster in 1954, with Mrs. Winifred Heckman the judge. Lockerbie Kennels were entered, as were Land Fall Kennels, Miss Hinkle, Joan Redmond, B.K. Erdoss, Mrs. Eric Wood, Mrs. Johnson Smith, Anthony Sano, Ruth Williams (professional handler and Lab breeder), Dorothy Howe with Rupert Brookhaven Angel, Paumanok Kennels, Mr. and Mrs. George Doherty, Michael Stevens Nagy, Downsbragh Kennels (Mr. and Mrs. Brainard with Bob Braithwaite handling), and Helen Ginnel.

1956 seems to have been an especially exciting year in Westminster Labs so far as competition was concerned. There were 32 of the breed for Albert E. Van Court to judge, the largest entry coming from Mrs. Junius Morgan's West Island Kennels which had seven on the benches. Dolly Marshall showed Chidley Bounder; Joan Read had Chidley Ducat; and Mrs. Lambert, who became so famous in this breed, had two: Rupert Eight Ball and Rupert Channel Point. Joan Blount, Amory H. Bradford, D.R. Hayes, Mr. and Mrs. Julius Chandler, Mrs. Eric Wood, Lockerbie Kennels (Mrs. Warwick), Mr. and Mrs. Jack L. Doolen, Mrs. Neil Tuttle, and Ruth Williams had the dogs making up the Class entry, while the following were those in to try for Best of Breed: Fred Martin's Champion Dark Star of Franklin, the Tuttles' Champion Cider of McKintosh, Mrs. Wood's Champion

Am., Can. Ch. Dark Star of Franklin, top sporting dog winner in the United States, 1955. Owned by Mr. Fred Martin, Franklin, Michigan.

A head-study of Champion Whygin Gold Bullion taken in 1961. Owned by Helen Ginnel, Whygin Labradors.

Wildfield Mickey Finn, Dorothy Howe's Champion Rupert Brookhaven Angel, C.D., Louise C. (Mrs. Junius) Morgan's Champion West Island Cakes Baby, Helen Ginnel's Champion Whygin Poppit and Champion Whygin John Duck, George W. Brown's Champion Lockerbie Spook, Tyrell M. Ingersoll's Champion Duke of Linden, and Mrs. Joseph J. Haggerty's Invill's Pogey Bait.

What a class of Specials Westminster drew in 1957 for Mrs. Howes Burton! Eleven of the total entry of 30 were Specials. Listed were Mrs. Lambert's Champion Rupert Eight Ball and Champion Golden Chance of Franklin, Mrs. Wood's Champion Wildfield Mickey Finn, Miss Hinkle's Champion Port Fortune Smoke Screen, Mrs. Haggerty's Champion Invill's Pogey Bait, Mr. and Mrs. William Ziegler III's Champion Hay Island Nellie Bimbus, Mr. and Mrs. Brainard's Champion Cherrie of Heatheredge, three of Helen Ginnel's Whygins—Rob Roy, John Duck, and Poppit, and Ruth Williams' Champion Whygin Nerissa. Mrs. Lambert had Harrowby Gordon and Champion Golden Chance of Franklin. This year Mrs. A.B. de Garis of the Abracadabra Kennels was represented by three Specials: Champion Abracadabra Red Bracken and two of her others. (Mrs. de Garis has been a leading breeder of sporting dogs over several decades.)

Most of the foregoing were on hand for Westminster in 1959, with Percy Roberts judging the 36 entries. Here we take particular note of three of the Best of Breed competition entries: Mr. and Mrs. Frank Jones had their Champion Lisnamallard's Tarantella, Mr. Martin had Champion Dark Star of Franklin, and Edward Jenner and Ralph Logan had Champion Kinley Comet of Harham, bred by Fred Wrigley and handled by Dick Cooper.

We shall now let the description of the development of Labrador Retrievers in the United States be continued in our "Kennel Stories," which will bridge for you the period from 1960 to the present day (some will carry you back to the earlier days as well). Probably the most noticeable change in Labrador activities over the decades has been the gradual decrease of dual champions. During the period we have just discussed, the earlier years for Labs in competition in the United States, the same dogs won in both field trial and bench show competition. Such is no longer the case. Breeders now specialize in "field type" and "show type" almost as though they were working with different breeds. This is common with most sporting dogs today. How nice it would be to again see many dual champions appearing on the records! It is our hope for the future! Modern Labrador breeders place great emphasis on their show dogs also working in the field, which is as it should be; but the incentive to aim for dogs excellent in BOTH capacities, so taken for granted during the first half of this century, no longer seems alive.

Ch. Novacroft Jayncourt Truly Fair at work in 1981. Owned by Mrs. D.I. Gardner, Sambrook, Shropshire, England.

Ch. Lockerbie Stanwood Granada, an imported grandson of Ch. Sandylands Tandy, is the sire of six champions as of March 1982. Owned by Mrs. Helen Warwick, Lockerbie Labradors, Briarcliff Manor, New York. Judge, Miss Gwladys R. Groskin.

Ch. Sandylands Morningcloud. Owned by Nancy Martin. Bred by Gwen Broadley, England. The judge is George Bragaw.

Opposite, above: An informal photo of Ch. Ballyduff Lark, an English import from Bridget Docking's famous kennel. This bitch was sired by English Ch. Timspring Sirius ex Spark of Ballyduff and is owned by Mary Wiest and Chris Kofron. **Below:** Eng., Am. Ch. Sandylands Midas, a tremendously important sire and show dog, owned by Mrs. Grace Lambert and handled by Ken Golden. Photo courtesy of Janet Churchill.

Left: Ch. Lawnwoods Fame and Fortune, owned by Marjorie Satterthwaite, is a grandson of Eng., Am. Ch. Lawnwoods Hot Chocolate. This photo, by Jan Churchill, was taken at Lilac Cottage, Markfield, England.

Below: Ch. Lawnwood's Tamster Trust, by Ch. Lawnwood's Fame and Fortune ex Ch. Tamster Glenfield Mischief. Bred by Marjorie Satterthwaite. Imported and shown by Janet Churchill, owned by Mrs. Richard C. du Pont.

Eng., Am. Ch. Lawnwood's Hot Chocolate winning the Sporting Group under Mrs. Kitty Drury. Bob Forsyth handled for owner Janet Churchill, Spenrock Labradors.

English and American Ch. Kimvalley Crispin winning the Gun Dog Group at Blackpool. Bred and owned by Diana Beckett.

Am., Can., Mex. 1978 World and Int. Ch. Franklin's Golden Mandigo, C.D., Am. W.C., is owned by John and Laurell Jenny of Mandigo Labradors, West Bountiful, Utah.

Ch. Briary Brendan of Rainell, en route to the title, going Winners Dog at Westchester 1976. Bred by Ceylona and Marjorie Brainard, by Ch. Lockerbie Brian Boru, W.C., ex Ch. Lockerbie Shillelagh. Owned by Lorraine and Barbara Getter.

Ch. Sandylands Markwell of Lockerbie, an English import by Eng. Ch. Sandylands Mark ex Eng. Ch. Sandylands Waghorn Honesty, was bred by G. Broadley and G. Anthony and whelped on March 21, 1975. Hips x-ray rated excellent at three years, eyes clear of all hereditary defects at six years. Owned by Helen Warwick and Diane B. Jones, Mt. Holly, New Jersey. An outstanding show Lab and producer.

Ch. Cedarhill Autumn Sunday, bred by Thomas J. Feneis and owned by Terry M. De Pietro.

Right: The late Dorothy Howe with her daughter of Ch. Killingworth's Thunderson. Mrs. Howe was for many years a successful Lab breeder and exhibitor under the Rupert prefix.

Below: The handsome Ch. Amberfield's Beach Boy, bred and owned by Amberfield Labradors (Dennis Livesey), Ramsey, New Jersey.

WINNERS
DOG

ASHBEY PHOTO

44

Ch. Broad Reach's English Muffin, U.D.T., W.C. An example of the combined beauty and brains to be found at Broad Reach Kennels (Martha Lee K. Voshell), Charlottesville, Virginia.

Opposite: Ch. Killingworth's Ben, well-known winning son of Blacmor's Chucklebrook Angus ex Chucklebrook Chami of Banner, belongs to Mrs. Nancy W. Story, Guilford, Connecticut. Handled here by Bob Forsyth.

Best of Winners, Am., Can., Bda. Ch. Groveton's Apollo Moondust shown by Eileen Ketcham. Best of Opposite Sex, Ch. Springfield's Cheddar Cheese shown by Tom Ketcham. Groveton Labradors, West Lebanon, New York.

Opposite: Ch. Briary Bonnie Briana, by Ch. Lockerbie Brian Boru ex Ch. Lockerbie Shillelagh, one of the Finchingfield Labs belonging to Dick and Marilyn Reynolds, Herndon, Virginia.

Highlands Bronze Chieftain, by Grovetons Koko Khalif ex Highlands Egyptian Queen, bred and owned by George and Lillian Knobloch. Handled here by Paul Slaboda.

CHAPTER FOUR

Labrador Retriever Kennels in the United States

The foundation bitch at Agber Kennels, left, Tudor's Spring Dandelion with her lovely daughter Ch. Agber's Clover Honey. Both owned by Agnes Cartier, Jackson, New Jersey.

There is no better way to describe the progress of a breed than by telling you of the individual breeders and kennels that have contributed along the way. On the following pages, we are proud to present many important Labradors and summaries of the background from which their success was attained. Not all of the kennels described are still active, but each has contributed to the well-being and development of these splendid dogs. Study these pages well and you will come away with an increased knowledge of where the best Labrador Retrievers have been bred, the care and forethought expended towards their progress and improvement generation after generation, and the exciting results of the efforts of these breeders.

Along with the brief descriptions of long-time breeders, we also pay tribute to the comparative newcomers. On their shoulders squarely rests the task of carrying on and preserving what has already been accomplished and the responsibility for the future well-being of the breed.

Agber

The Agber Labradors, Reg., began in 1970 when owner Agnes S. Cartier of Jackson, New Jersey, purchased the yellow bitch Tudor's Spring Dandelion. From her initial litter came the kennel's first homebred champion, Agber's Clover Honey, whose latest win as of this writing was of the Veteran and Brood Bitch Classes at the 1980 Mid-Jersey L.R.C. Specialty.

Shortly after "Lion" arrived at Agber, she was joined by Champion Whiskey Creek's Lisa and Spenrock Baroke Buffet who was shown to her championship. Then, with the purchase of another bitch, this one from Franklin Kennel, the project was under way.

By breeding carefully and sparingly and combining the best bloodlines in her foundation stock, Agnes Cartier has managed so far to produce thirteen champions in less than ten years. Two of her males, American and Canadian Champion Agber's Daniel Aloysius, W.C., and Champion Agber's Bionic Banana, are Sporting Group winners. The lovely bitch, Champion Agber's Daisy of Campbell Croft, has won Best of Opposite Sex and Winners Bitch at the Golden Labrador Retriever Club Specialty. In addition to these, there have been numerous exciting class wins at Specialties, many more pointed dogs, and many dogs bearing the "Agber" prefix recently finished.

In 1977, Agnes Cartier imported a young black male, Lawnwood's Brands Hatch, from England. As luck would have it, Brands Hatch won his American championship with a Best of Winners at the Labrador Retriever Club of Southern California and a Best of Breed and a second in Group at the Baltimore all-breed show along the way. After a very brief period as a Special, and the winning of a Sporting Group First award, Brands Hatch was retired from competition and is now at stud in the kennel. His youngsters would seem already to be following in his pawprints, with a Group-placing daughter and a Sweepstakes-winning son.

Probably this kennel's proudest achievement to date has been the success of American and Canadian Champion Agber's Daniel Aloysius, W.C. (Ch. Spenrock Cardigan Bay ex Ch. Whiskey Creek's Lisa), a fine example of a yellow dog, who was handled by Joy Quallenberg, an amateur at that time. "Danny's" career began with three Best Puppy in Show victories on the Bermuda circuit. He then went on to complete his American championship with four majors and his Canadian title in one weekend. Together, Joy and "Danny" accumulated sixty Bests of Breed, four of them in entries supported by the Labrador Retriever Club, and fifteen Group placements, putting "Danny" in the National Top Ten ranking. "Danny" was retired from show competition in 1978, after winning the Stud Dog Class at the National Specialty. Shown again in 1980, he won the Veteran Dog Class at the Mid-Jersey Labrador Retriever Club Specialty and Best of Breed at the Kennel Club of Philadelphia. In 1981, at eight years of age, he won the Veteran Dog Class at the Potomac Labrador Retriever Club Specialty and Best of Breed at Sussex Hills Kennel Club, over an entry supported by the Mid-Jersey Labrador Retriever Club. But perhaps more important than any accolade is the happiness he brings at home with his super disposition and eagerness to please.

Am., Can. Ch. Agber's Daniel Aloysius, W.C., here is winning the Veteran Class at Mid-Jersey Labrador Retriever Club Specialty, September 1980. Handler, Joy Quallenberg. Breeder-owner, Agnes Cartier, Agber Kennels, Jackson, New Jersey. The judge is Joan Reade Chidley.

Am., Can. Ch. Agber's Daniel Aloysius, W.C., is a fine example of the Labs from Agnes Cartier's Agber Kennels. He is a Sporting Group winner, has multiple Group placements, and has been sixty Bests of Breed, including two such wins when he was eight years old. He also was winner of the Stud Dog Class at the 1978 Labrador Retriever Club, Inc., Specialty and the Veteran Class in 1980 at the Mid-Jersey Specialty and in 1981 at the Potomac Specialty. Handled by Joy Quallenberg.

Agnes Cartier's goal for the future is the same as her standard has been in the past—to breed typical, sound Labradors who are as comfortable in the show and obedience ring as they would be at home. For her, success has been determined not only by the ribbons from the ring but also by the number of excellent dogs serving so well as companions, gun dogs, and guide dogs for the blind. All Agber Labs are broken to gun and are excellent retrievers. The Cartiers have recently moved to their new location, which is on property affording them the opportunity to train the dogs on a more or less regular basis.

An eight-day-old litter of yellow Labs getting a bit of lunch. Owned by Agber Kennels.

Ahawahnee

Ahawahnee's Labradors are located at Bakersfield, California, and are owned by Robert and Mary Manuel. Although this is a young kennel, it nonetheless is sincerely dedicated to preserving the Labrador with the true, correct type and temperament.

The foundation bitch here is Killingworth Lady B of Ahawahnee, by Champion Ballyduff Marketeer ex Champion Follytower Bradking Lady Jane. Lady B is expecting a litter, by the Manuels' young dog, Spenrock Bearcat (Champion Spenrock Heatheredge Mariner ex Champion Spenrock Brown Bess), in early 1982.

Spenrock Bearcat, by Ch. Spenrock Heatheredge Mariner ex Ch. Spenrock Brown Bear, was bred by Janet Churchill and is owned by Mary Manuel, Bakersfield, California.

In partnership with Janet Churchill, Mr. and Mrs. Manuel own a lovely young black male representing the finest bloodlines. He is a son of Spenrock Argonaut, littermate to Champion Spenrock Anthony Adverse ex Spenrock Spitfire, a daughter of English and American Champion Lawnwoods Hot Chocolate from English and American Champion Swift of Ballyduff and Spenrock.

The Manuels also have a young black puppy bitch, Spenrock Bamboo Bomber (from the two excellent English importations, Summer Sun II and English Champion Swift of Ballyduff and Spenrock), for which hopes are high.

Aldenholme

Aldenholme Labradors were located at Medfield, Massachusetts, and was a hobby kennel owned by the late Barbara Baxter Barty-King, who passed away in June of 1979. Born in the United States in 1909, this lady was educated in the United States and then attended a finishing school in England, where she married and remained until after World War II.

Since early childhood, Mrs. Barty-King loved animals. As a granddaughter of H.H. Baxter, who raised trotting horses and Morgans at Grove Hall in Rutland, Vermont, she grew up an excellent horsewoman and had great enthusiasm for fox-hunting. Her interest in Labs was probably instilled during childhood, as we read mention of the massive larger-than-life bronze dogs, which strongly resembled Labradors, that "guarded" the gates to her grandfather's estate. And she had known some splendid specimens of the breed while shooting on the great estates of England and Ireland, numbering among her friends Lord Joicey, owner of the Flodden Labs to be found in the background of even our present-day winners.

Upon her return to the United States following the war, Mrs. Barty-King really started to take an active interest in Labradors, and it was then that the foundation stock for Aldenholme Kennels was selected. The three first dogs were Chidley Robber, Champion Ashur Deacon, and Champion Hobbimoor's Patricia.

Chidley Robber was bred by and purchased as a puppy from Mrs. Curtis S. Read, a well-known breeder and judge. He was sired by the multiple Best in Show dog, Champion Stowaway at Deer Creek from Dawn II, a sister to Mrs. Read's famous winning stud, Champion Hugger Mugger. Robber, whelped in 1949, was a well-balanced dog of good type, a splendid gun dog, and a Lab that should have become a champion, except that he much preferred home life to that of a show dog. And so, although he did have points, he never fulfilled his potential in the ring. He was, however, his owner's greatest favorite and lived to be 14, sharing his old age with his litter-brother, Champion Chidley Rackateer.

Champion Ashur Deacon was purchased as a puppy from Mrs. Johnson Smith. He was a son of Champion Hugger Mugger ex Champion Rupert Desdemona, bred by Dorothy Howe.

Ch. Ashur Deacon, black male, by Ch. Hugger Mugger ex Ch. Rupert Desdemona, one of Aldenholme's two foundation sires. He is the sire of champions and was Best of Opposite Sex at the 1952 National Specialty. Breeder, Mrs. Johnson Smith. Owner, Barbara Baxter Barty-King, Aldenholme Labradors.

While still a puppy, he won a five-point major, and at the Labrador Retriever Club Specialty in 1952, he was Best of Opposite Sex to his half-sister, Champion Chidley Spook (Champion Hugger Mugger ex Wendy Jinx), a Canadian bitch. Hugger Mugger was also the sire of Ashur Cameron and won the Stud Dog Class with Deacon and Spook. Deacon was an outstanding stud dog and lived into his sixteenth year.

Champion Hobbimoor's Patricia came from the Redledge Kennels, owned by Consuelo Hill, and was purchased as a mature bitch by Mrs. Barty-King. Patricia was a daughter of Champion Chidley Blakso (half-brother to Champion Hugger Mugger) ex Queen Patricia. She was a prolific producer of both quantity and correct type, with litters averaging fourteen puppies.

The pedigrees of these three Labs are of particular interest as they represent some of the finest Labs in the breed's history.

From this foundation, Mrs. Barty-King made a proud record with her homebreds. Among them were Champion Aldenholme's Robbie Son, a Group winner with numerous Bests of Breed and other Group placements to his credit; Champion Aldenholme's Witching Hour; Aldenholme's Magic Spell and Aldenholme's Robbina, both pointed (the above by Chidley Robber ex Champion Hobbimoor's Patricia and whelped in 1953); Champion Aldenholme's Tonga Queen, who finished with four majors and Aldenholme's Gunga Din, pointed (both littermates by Champion Ashur Deacon ex Champion Hobbimoor Patricia, whelped in 1953); Champion Aldenholme's Gremlin and Aldenholme's Hennessey, litter-brothers by Champion Ashur Deacon ex Aldenholme's Robbina, whelped in 1954; Champion Aldenholme's Mumbo Jumbo, a Group Winner, whelped in 1956 by Champion Aldenholme's Robbieson ex Champion Aldenholme's Tonga Queen; and Champion Aldenholme's Juno, by Champion Aldenholme's Robbieson ex Jean's Jet, whelped in 1957.

Champion Ashur Deacon also sired the noted stud dog Champion Chebacco Smokey Joe, from Champion Redledge Waldo, owned by Mary G. Swan of Chebacco Kennels.

Barbara Barty-King preferred black Labradors and kept only this color at the kennel. When yellows were occasionally produced, they were quickly sold or given away; and chocolates, in those days, were not yet looked upon with favor.

Mrs. Barty-King was a truly involved fancier, and all of her dogs were cared for, trained, and shown in both field and bench competition by her personally. All homebreds were finished from the Bred-By Exhibitor Class.

In the 1960s, poor health forced Mrs. Barty-King to end her showing and breeding Labs. All of the dogs remained with her, however, living out their lives happily.

In 1970, seeking a milder climate, Mrs. Barty-King closed Aldenholme, sold her home, and moved to Ireland. There she settled in County Wicklow and raised Smooth Fox Terriers and Irish Wolfhounds, showing them when her health permitted. She left one Lab bitch, Aldenholme's Chota Peg, by Gunga Din, in the United States with her friend, Barbara Barfield, who later founded her own Scrimshaw Kennel.

Amberfield

Amberfield is another of the relatively young Labrador kennels which has nonetheless been highly successful. Owned by Robert Livesey of Ramsey, New Jersey, it began in 1975 with the purchase of a bitch, Agber's Darlyn, from Agber Kennels.

Darlyn started off well, and in her first year of showing amassed 13 points and took Reserve Winners Bitch at Westminster. Then she came in season and her owner, being a novice, bred her, bringing her show career to a halt and not finishing this worthy bitch.

All was certainly not lost, however, for out of this very first breeding came Champion Amberfield's Beach Boy, who finished with four majors and two Bests of Breed from the classes. He went on to win Best of Breed at Westminster in 1980 and in 1981, the latter over 35 Specials—certainly an imposing achievement, and we understand that it was the first time in the show's history that the same Lab took Best of Breed there in two consecutive years. Beach Boy compiled over 25 Bests of Breed his first year out as a Special to finish in the Top Ten of 1980.

Jonte Nantucket Sleighride, by Jonte's King Cole ex Jonte's Camala, is a grandson of Aldenholme's King Coal and Aldenholme's Robber. Barbara Barfield, Scrimshaw Labradors, Meredith, New Hampshire.

We are told that Beach Boy is a controversial dog because of his size. He is 24½ inches at the shoulder and weighs 95 pounds. He is an aggressive retriever who has the strength to lift the largest goose or hare, and he moves with ease. It has been said that his head, although large, is a typical standard for the breed. He is certainly a magnificent dog to see in the ring!

Following in Beach Boy's paw-prints is his son, Beechcomber, who has both majors and a Best of Breed from the Puppy Class over Specials.

Champion littermates, Magnolia and Beach Boy, homebred by Amberfield Labradors from their foundation bitch, Agber's Darlyn.

Agber's Darlyn, the foundation bitch for Amberfield Labradors, at three months of age.

Ch. Amberfield's Beach Boy in the Sporting Group at Westminster handled by Joy Quallenberg, for Robert Livesay.

Also from Darlyn's first litter came Beach Boy's winning sister, Champion Amberfield's Sugar Magnolia, who finished with a Best of Breed from an entry of 50 Labs. Through Magnolia, Amberfield will continue its foundation, building on a bitch excelling in head, front, and movement.

A second bitch was purchased from Agber Kennels, with a totally new outcross. This was Agber's Promise of Devonwood who finished her championship in two months.

Robert Livesey certainly has started off in Labs in a most impressive manner. He gives great credit to his expert handler, Joy Quallenberg, for presenting the dogs so well and for her contributions to Amberfield's breeding program. With the foundation on which they are working, one can foresee much more excitement for this kennel in the future.

Amberfield Kennels' lovely foundation bitch, Agber's Darlyn, going Best of Opposite Sex for a four-point major. Joy Quallenberg is handling this fine daughter of Ch. Agber's Daniel Aloysius, W.C. Darlyn is the dam of the big winning young dog, Ch. Amberfield's Beach Boy.

Ambersand

Although the kennel is a very small one, with only two litters raised there each year, Ambersand Labradors and their owner, Jan Stolarevsky, have accounted for some very exciting records in the Lab world and some dogs of rare quality and distinction.

Located at Dexter, Michigan, Ambersand's "headman" is the handsome yellow dog, Champion Timmbrland Golden Star, a son of Champion Royal Oaks V.I.P. O'Shamrock Acres ex Champion Starline Mecca of Timmbrland, bred by R. and F. Timm. As of the close of 1981, "Psy," as he is called, is the Top Point Winning Yellow Labrador in the history of the breed, having defeated more than 25,000 dogs on the Group and Best in Show level. His grandsire, Champion Shamrock Acres Light Brigade, remains the Top Best in Show Winner as well as the Top Producing Labrador Sire.

Golden Star was Number Three Labrador in 1976, Number One in 1977 and 1978, and Number Three in 1979, although he was shown only six times that year. He was also Number Nine Sporting Dog in 1977 and Number Eight Sporting Dog and Number Thirty-nine All Breeds in 1978.

Ch. Timmbrland Golden Star winning Best in Show at Lima Kennel Club, May 1978. Jan Stolarevsky, owner, Ambersand Labradors, Dexter, Michigan.

tificate holders, two Best in Match winners and four Match Group winners. One son finished his championship by winning a Sporting Group. His get also seem stamped with a strong desire to work in the field, and one of his sons, Champion Ambersand's Shooting Star, will be field-trained during 1982.

Then there is another handsome dog, American and Canadian Champion Rorschach's Royal Flush, by Champion Shamrock Norton of Burywood ex Champion Royal Oaks Rorschach's Libido; Royal Flush was #39 Labrador Retriever in 1974 with six Group placements and 56 Bests of Breeds. Royal Flush has two champions to date, with several more that are pointed; he was bred by Jan and Jay Stielstra.

The total show record for Golden Star stands at eight Bests in Show including a Specialty, 90 Group placements including 34 Group firsts, and 133 times Best of Breed. These wins were attained under 84 different judges.

Used sparingly at stud, Golden Star has produced well, with seven champions, two Companion Dog title holders, two Working Cer-

Ch. Timmbrland Golden Star adding another Best in Show to his laurels for owner Jan Stolarevsky, this time at Lexington Kennel Club, 1977.

Ch. Ambersand Electra whose puppies are now gaining prominence in American and Canadian show rings.

The bitch Champion Ambersand Electra, by Champion Timmbrland Golden Star ex Missy's Easter Dawn, was campaigned briefly as a special, during which time she attained a Group placement, six Bests of Breed over multiple male Specials including Group winners, and four Bests of Opposite Sex. Her pups started out during the 1980-81 season. One daughter, Wendy's Patty of Ambersand, by Royal Flush, had four American points and two Canadian points from the Puppy Classes.

This Royal Flush puppy is a "young hopeful" at Ambersand Kennels.

Hollidaze Medea of Ambersand, by Champion Wrenwell Ramrod ex Champion Could Be's Black Angus Heifer, was bred by Barbara Holl and Barbara Hogan.

Ambersand's Lady Godiva was Best Puppy in Specialty Match and a litter-brother was Best of Opposite Sex at the age of ten weeks. Ambersand's Double Trouble, by Golden Star, was Best Sporting Dog at a Match, also at just ten weeks of age.

Ambersand's Electrolyte, six months old (by Champion Franklin's Whirlaway Barbela ex Champion Ambersand's Electra) and Ambersand's A Star Is A Star, five months old (by Champion Ambersand's Shooting Star ex Beaver Creek's Honey Bee) are two Lab pups being carefully watched for the future.

Ch. Ambersand Electra, by Ch. Timmbrland Golden Star ex Missy's Easter Dawn, in a brief Special career has a Group placement. Six Best of Breeds over multiple male Specials, including Group winners, and four Bests of Opposite Sex.

Ambleside

Although Ambleside Kennels did not produce their first litter of Labrador Retrievers until 1980, their owner, Julie Brown Sturman of Melrose Park, Pennsylvania, has been involved with the breed for quite a lengthy period of time, having purchased her first one back in 1964, a splendid bitch that grew up to become Champion Walden's Blackbird, C.D. Shortly thereafter, Harrowby Todd, a son of the famed Champion Sam of Blaircourt, joined the family and quickly gained his championship.

Ch. Walden's Blackbird, C.D., one of the fine Labs owned by Julie Brown Sturman, Melrose Park, Pennsylvania, and the foundation bitch of her kennel.

It was a breeding of the above two that produced Julie Brown's first homebred Labs. Among these puppies was a beautiful black bitch that was sold to Mrs. Faiella of Bermuda and which was to become Bermudian Champion Amanda of Mandalay.

For her second litter, Blackbird was bred to English and American Champion Sandyland's Midas. American and Bermudian Champion Jo-Dean's Dreamdust Daiquiri was one of the resulting puppies. A bitch dearly loved and widely admired, Daiquiri lived all of her twelve years with Julie Brown. She is, incidentally, one of the Labs pictured on the cover of at least the first printing of the earlier T.F.H. book on this breed, *This is the Labrador Retriever*, by Dorothy Howe.

Am., Bda. Ch. Jo-Dean's Dreamdust Daiquiri, by Eng., Am. Ch. Sandyland's Midas ex Ch. Walden's Blackbird, C.D., a bitch that was well known and loved by everyone, lived with her breeder, Julie Brown Sturman, until she was 12 years old.

A repeat of the Midas-Blackbird breeding produced a litter of seven, all bottle-raised by Mrs. Brown as, sad to say, Blackbird died immediately following a Caesarean section. One of these puppies was the future American and Bermudian Champion Tawny Tim of Mandalay, another Lab owned by Mrs. Faiella of Bermuda, who won well, being piloted by Ken Golden to become #3 Labrador in the United States for 1972.

Am., Bda. Ch. Tawny Tim of Mandalay, bred by Julie Brown Sturman, owned by Mrs. John Faiella of Bermuda.

Throughout this period, Julie Brown's Labrador breeding was done on a very limited basis, and although she remained "in" Labradors continuously, personal matters finally necessitated a complete hiatus from her breeding program for several years.

Then came a most enjoyable trip to England in 1980, plus the acquisition of Novacroft Carousel, and Julie Brown Sturman got back into full swing with her favorite breed and the brand-new kennel name, "Ambleside," after a lovely little fishing village in the beautiful lake district of England.

This lovely photo, taken in 1968, is of Julie Brown Sturman's two sons, Steven and Peter Brown, with Am., Bda. Ch. Jo-Dean's Dreamdust Daiquiri and Brownline's Midnight Cowboy.

The future looks bright at Ambleside, where the first litter, produced in 1980, included the two puppies, Ambleside Marcoal and Ambleside Maraschino, who should make their presence felt in both the conformation classes and in obedience. This is also true of a second litter, from Novacourt Carousel, which has recently arrived.

Mrs. Sturman has made a tremendously valuable contribution to the Labrador Retriever world through her publication of *Julie Brown's Directory to Labrador Retriever Pedigrees*. Here, for a nominal cost, breeders can list their well-known producers, complete with photograph, pedigree, O.F.A. (hips) and C.E.R.F. (eyes) ratings, and description of their accomplishments. This directory is a great help in the selection of studs for one's bitches and is also an aid to students of pedigrees who wish to learn all about the backgrounds of quality Labs.

Ayr

Nancy (Mrs. John E.) Martin of Spring House, Pennsylvania, started the Ayr Labradors back in 1959 when she acquired a Lab as a pet and companion for her family. The Martin children were young then, and the whole family felt that Black Buttons was just the greatest dog that this family had ever owned. Horses had always been Mrs. Martins' principal interest, but her husband,

John, suggested that she buy a Labrador bitch and get involved in breeding. To quote Nancy, "The poor man's been biting his tongue ever since."

The first litter was whelped in 1963, and from it came the beginning of Ayr Labradors. A sweet yellow, Amberlite of Ayr, was the foundation, and Mrs. Martin is now working on the sixth generation—which is not easy when over the years one has kept only five or six dogs at a time.

Champion Black Scot of Ayr was the last choice black male puppy from Mrs. Dorothy Francke's famous litter by Champion Lockerbie Sandylands Tarquin ex Champion Sandylands Spungold, but how fortunate Mrs. Martin was to get him and how tremendously this lovely dog has contributed not only to Mrs. Martin's kennel but also to his breed! From this same litter came Mrs. Francke's Champion Lovat Annie Laurie, Mrs. Janet Churchill's Champion Spenrock Banner and Champion Lewisfield Spenrock Ballot, and Champion Great Scot of Ayr!

Labrador Retriever Club, Inc., National Specialty show, Ox Ridge Kennel Club, 1966. Judge, Percy Roberts. Brood Bitch Class won by Ch. Sandylands Spungold, owned by Mrs. Dorothy Francke and handled by R. Stephen Shaw. On the left is Mrs. Janet Churchill with Lewisfield Spenrock Ballot and Spenrock Banner. On the right is Nancy Martin with Great Scot of Ayr (also Winners Dog). The latter three Labs are the progeny who won the class for their dam and made such spectacular records in the Lab world on their own!

Champion Great Scot's black daughter, Champion Meadowrock Angelica of Ayr, co-owned with Diana Beishline, produced a litter in which there were all three colors. The sire was Champion Dickendall's Flip Flop, C.D.X., and Mrs. Martin takes particular pride in this litter. From it came two winners of the Waterland Retriever Club All-Around Retriever Award, one Seeing Eye dog, one winner of the Dog World Award in Obedience, and her particular "pride and joy," chocolate Champion Meadowbrook Fudge of Ayr, C.D.T., W.C., who, aside

Ch. Great Scot of Ayr, by Ch. Lockerbie Sandylands Tarquin ex Ch. Sandylands Spungold, photographed in 1970. Bred by Mrs. Dorothy Francke and owned by Mrs. Nancy Martin, Ayr Labradors.

Ch. Meadowrock Fudge of Ayr, C.D.T., W.C., who in addition to her show wins has won first and placed in Gun Dog trials, has been honored with the Annual All Around Retriever Award from the Labrador Retriever Club of the Potomac in 1980 and 1981, and also from the Mid-Jersey Labrador Retriever Club in 1981. In 1979, she won Top Show Dog of the Year—Owner-Handled—Award of the Waterland Retriever Club. Since then she has added a Tracking Degree to her title. Nancy (Mrs. John E.) Martin, owner, Ayr Labradors, Spring House, Pennsylvania.

from her show wins, had won first and placed in Gun Dog Trials and has been honored with the Annual All-Around Retriever Award from the Labrador Retriever Club of the Potomac in 1980 and 1981; this award was also given to Fudge by the Mid-Jersey Labrador Retriever Club in 1981. In 1979 she won the Top Show Dog of the Year—owner-handled—from the Waterland Retriever Club. Since these wins, Fudge has added a Tracking Degree to her other accomplishments—all achieved by the age of eight and a half.

The Martins keep their dogs as pets and house dogs, much spoiled and dearly loved; therefore, they can only do justice to and enjoy a few at a time, with an occasional litter. They have owned or co-owned the following seven champions: Champion Lockerbie Olivia, Champion Great Scot of Ayr, Champion Meadowrock Angelica of Ayr, Champion Meadowbrook Fudge of Ayr, C.D.T., W.D., Champion Dickendall's Bear of Ayr, C.D., W.C., Champion Dickendall's Flapper of Ayr, and Champion Sandylands Morningcloud, W.C.

Mrs. Martin is a charter member of the Waterland Retriever Club, Inc., the Labrador Retriever Club of the Potomac, and the Mid-Jersey Labrador Retriever Club in the United States and is also a member of the Labrador Retriever Club and the Mid Counties Labrador Retriever Club, both of England.

In 1979, Mrs. Martin began judging, and after doing several regional Specialties, she was honored with the assignment to judge the Labrador Retriever Club National Specialty in 1981.

In 1980, Mrs. Martin was chosen the Breeder of the Year by the Pennsylvania Federation of Dog Clubs, which pleased her enormously. To breed good dogs that are typical, smart, and full of natural retrieving instinct has always been her goal—a goal which we must say she has reached admirably!

Mrs. Martin is the author of a most interesting and delightful book entitled *Legends in Labradors* which I recommend as interesting, informative reading for all who love the breed.

Beechcrofts

It was some ten years ago, walking along a beach on Long Island, that Michael and Mary Wiest first became acquainted with a Labrador. This was a handsome black dog whose master was throwing a stick into the water for the dog, and so impressed were they with this handsome dog that they decided right then that the Labrador was the breed for them. Shortly thereafter, Beechcrofts Kennels was established, with the purchase of a bitch named Gia, at Wilmington, Delaware.

This was a nicely line-bred bitch, who, in her second litter, produced Mr. and Mrs. Wiest's first champion, a yellow dog named Champion Charlie Tite, about whom his owners remark "still has first rights to the bed."

This handsome drawing by Jacqueline Adams is of Ch. Charlie Tite, the first homebred to finish for Beechcrofts Labs, Michael and Mary Wiest, Wilmington, Delaware. Sired by Forecast Princeton ex Jennifer Gia.

In 1978, the Wiests took a trip to England, during which they met and visited Bridget Docking. To quote Mrs. Wiest, "It was truly an honor to know this lady. Visiting her kennel was an enlightening experience. She was extremely gracious and gave us invaluable advice learned through her many years in the breed. Her dogs looked like clones of each other, very much the type we were seeking." One of her bitches, Spark of Ballyduff, by English Champion Ballyduff Marketeer ex Sparkle of Tuddenham, was soon to be bred to English Champion Timspring Sirius, by English and American Champion Ballyduff Seaman ex Timspring Myrtle, so the

Ch. Ballyduff Lark, by Eng. Ch. Timspring Sirius ex Spark of Ballyduff, bred by the late Bridget Docking in England. Mary Wiest and Chris Kofron, owners, Wilmington, Delaware.

Wiests reserved one from the expected litter.

Late in 1978, the puppy, Ballyduff Lark, emigrated to the United States. At an early age, she was in the ring and winning, taking large classes at numerous Specialty events. She completed her championship in early 1980, the same year that she took Best of Opposite Sex at Westminster.

Lark's first litter was whelped October 14th, 1980; the sire was Champion Jayncourt Ajoco Justice, a son of English Champion Ballyduff Marketeer ex English Champion Jayncourt Star Performer. By one year of age, four puppies have placed in Specialties and one has a Working Certificate.

The Wiests have established a definite line, grounded in the English tradition. They are looking forward to many more years of pleasure with their four-footed friends, as well as with the many two-footed friends they have made through them.

Valleywood's Kannon Ball Kate, a daughter of Ch. Jayncourt Ajoco Justice from Ch. Ballyduff Lark, bred and owned by Beechcrofts Labs, Michael and Mary Wiest.

Broad Reach

Mr. and Mrs. Allen F. Voshell, Jr., owners of the Broad Reach Labradors at Charlottesville, Virginia, became involved with dogs in the late 1960s when Martha Lee (Mrs. Voshell) was presented with a Lab as a gift. Her first interest centered around obedience, and she is proud of the fact that during the past twelve years she has had five U.D. Labs, with three of them being champion U.D.T.'s with Working Certificates. As of late 1981, Mrs. Voshell believes that there are still only eight Labrador champion U.D.T.'s in the history of the breed. Of these, five are living and three of them belong to the Voshells! There is another Lab with a C.D.X. at Broad Reach, but she is of field breeding and will not be shown in the conformation ring. Mrs. Voshell hopes to achieve an obedience trial championship with her.

One of the champion U.D.T.s is Champion Zipper's Hustlin' Wahoo, whose sire was a field champion. Zipper was also the Voshells' first champion, and he was Best of Winners at Westminster in 1973.

Martha Lee K. Voshell, owner of Broad Reach Labradors, with her yellow bitch, Ch. Broad Reach's English Muffin, U.D.T., W.C., and her black male, Ch. Zipper's Hustlin' Wahoo, U.D.T., W.C.

Ch. Yarrow's Broad Reach Psaphire, U.D.T., W.C., with owner, Martha Lee K. Voshell. This bitch was bred by Beth Sweigart of Yarrow Kennels and is by Ch. Poolstea Peer ex Yarrow's Astarte of Windfall.

The second champion U.D.T. was Broad Reach's English Muffin, a yellow bitch who was the first bitch to achieve that status, doing so in 1976. The third champion U.D.T. was Yarrow's Broad Reach Psaphire, a black bitch who has been the Voshells' best producer, having to date three litters with five champions, two other offspring already pointed, and her last litter just over a year old. Two of those offspring won and placed at the National Lab Specialty in October 1981 in Ohio and have won other Puppy Classes and Reserve Winners on several occasions. One of Psaphire's daughters from her first litter, Champion Broad Reach Bittersweet, has produced one C.D. so far with three others pointed. More handsome puppies are anticipated from Psaphire's fourth litter, due in January 1982.

From Psaphire's second litter, Champion Broad Reach Black Magic has her C.D.X. and is now working toward her U.D. degree. She also received her Working Certificate at the National Specialty in October 1981. Psaphire is a lovely bitch who has produced both top show dogs and also top working dogs. She was bred by Beth Sweigart and is a daughter of Champion Poolstead Peer (Reanacre Sandylands Tarmac ex Braeduke Julia of Poolstead) from Yarrow's Astarte of Windfall (Rivermist Banner ex Ch. Follytower Glenarem Dusky Debutante).

Ch. Broad Reach Bittersweet, owner-handled by Martha Lee K. Voshell, taking Group Two at Thronateeska Kennel Club 1980, Mr. Tipton judging.

Ch. Broad Reach Bittersweet finishing title at one year of age. Martha Lee K. Voshell, owner-handler.

Ch. Black Magic of Broad Reach, C.D.X., W.C., by Eng., Am. Ch. Lawnwood's Hot Chocolate ex Ch. Yarrow's Broad Reach Psaphire, U.D.T., W.C., bred by Martha Lee K. Voshell and owned by Cathie Parris, Chattanooga, Tennessee.

The Voshells are among the few Lab owners who have campaigned their dogs in breed, obedience, tracking, and field trials. At the present time, there are two additional black bitches on their way to championship, with two others working in obedience.

Taking second place, Brood Bitch Class, National Labrador Retiever Specialty 1981, is Ch. Yarrow's Broad Reach Psaphire with nine-to-twelve-month-old puppies from her third litter, Broad Reach Psaphire's Sinder and Saunders Broad Reach Brook. Martha Lee K. Voshell owner-handles Psaphire.

Campbellcroft

Campbellcroft Labradors, now located at Soquel, California, came into being one winter's night in 1964, in Caithness (north of Scotland), with a phone call at 11:30 P.M. from Sir Ralph Anstruther, who was the Laird of Lanergill Schoolhouse Master's Cottage where Donald and Virginia Campbell were living. Sir Ralph and his mother had decided that the Campbells needed a dog, as they had left their Dalmatian in the United States because of the British quarantine, and that the dog they needed was "Queenie," a yellow Labrador Retriever bitch owned by Sir Ralph but kept and trained by the gamekeeper, Mr. McGregor. Nothing would do but the Campbells must, despite the lateness of the hour, drive out immediately that bitterly cold night to meet "Queenie." They did, and she became the Campbell's first Lab, Lady Caithness. "Caithy," as she became known, was with the Campbells until 1973 when she died at the ripe old age of 13. Although they still had one of her puppies, the Campbells decided that upon returning to the United States they wanted to become serious breeders and trainers of Labs and that they wanted to start fresh with the best that they could find with English-Scottish bloodlines.

In 1974, at San Francisco Airport, the Campbells eagerly opened the door to a certain very special airline crate, and out bounced ten-week-old Agber Daisy of Campbellcroft. They knew right then that here they had their foundation bitch! According to Virginia Campbell, thanks go to Agnes and Bernie Cartier (Agber) and Jan Churchill (Spenrock).

Daisy grew up to become a bench champion, in the process taking Winners Bitch and Best of Opposite Sex at the Labrador Retriever Club of Southern California Specialty when 20 months of age and earning her Labrador Retriever Club Working Certificate (having met her first duck in the Campbells' driveway the previous day) and her C.D. degree in three straight shows. As Virginia Campbell comments, "Daisy taught us everything she wanted us to know about Labs."

Daisy's first breeding was to Champion Briary's Trace of Brian, C.D., W.C., who was sired by Champion Lockerbie's Brian Boru, W.C. The match was a good one and produced Champion Nivred's Pendragon and Champion Campbellcroft's Pede, C.D., W.C., along with Campbellcroft's Piper, C.D.X., and a brood bitch, Pitten, who went to Guide Dogs for the Blind in San Rafael.

For her second litter, Daisy's mate was Champion Wildwing's McDuff; this mating produced Champion Campbellcroft's Mindy O'Aspin and one close to the title, Campbellcroft's Megan. Daisy was a daughter of Champion Spenrock's Cardigan Bay (Champion Lockerbie Goldentone Jensen ex American and Canadian Champion Spenrock's Banner, W.C.) from Champion Whiskey Creek's Lisa, by a son of Champion Sandylands Tweed of Blaircourt ex a daughter of Champion Shamrock Acres Dapper Dan. Truly the Campbells had succeeded well in obtaining what they had hoped for from Daisy as a foundation bitch!

Ch. Agber Daisy of Campbellcroft owned by Donald and Virginia Campbell, Soquel, California. By Ch. Spenrock's Cardigan Bay ex Ch. Whiskey Creek's Lisa.

From the first litter, Daisy with Trace, Champion Campbellcroft Pede was kept and eventually bred back to her grandsire, Brian Boru. A wonderful litter resulted which included American and Canadian Champion Campbellcroft's Andrew, a yellow dog with placing in Derby; and Campbellcroft's Anticipation, Winners Bitch at the Golden Gate Labrador Retriever Club Specialty in 1981. At that Specialty, under breeder-judge Nancy Martin, not only did "Annie" earn a five-point major but Daisy also took the Veterans Class and, as she

Ch. Campbellcroft's Pede, C.D., W.C. By Ch. Briary's Trace of Brian, C.D., W.C., ex Agber Daisy of Campbellcroft, from the first litter bred by Donald and Virginia Campbell.

made the final cut for Best of Breed, remained in there to watch her other grandchild, Angus, *win* the Best of Breed. As a very small kennel with only one or two litters a year, it is easily understandable that the Campbells feel they have contributed some excellence to the breed in conformation, working ability, temperament, and soundness.

Angus' record is extremely distinguished. He was Best in Futurity at eight months at the Labrador Retriever Club of Southern California Specialty in 1978 and Winners Dog at the Golden Gate Labrador Retriever Club Specialty in 1979 at 15 months; he completed his American Championship at 19 months and his Canadian Championship in five straight shows while his owners were there on vacation; and he was Best of Breed at the G.G.L.R.C. Specialty at three years old. Sharing equally with the excitement of his show career are the successes of his puppies at shows, field trials, and obedience tests. Although the pups are all very young as this book is written, the Campbells have glowing reports of J.A.M.'s (Judges Award of Merit) in Derby, high scoring in Obedience, and show wins at Specialties, including a four-point major on a yellow boy at six months! The nice part is that these are from a number of different bitches. Angus is, indeed, a fine dog, a joy for his owners to live with, and it is hoped that he will continue to produce progeny even better than himself.

This baby Lab seems to be saying, "I love you, Mommie" to her dam, Ch. Agber Daisy of Campbellcroft, C.D., W.C. Campbellcroft Labs, Donald and Virginia Campbell, owners.

Ch. Campbellcroft Mindy O'Aspin at a puppy match. Note the quality and promise of this fine youngster, bred by the Campbells.

Campbellcroft's Piper, C.D.X., belongs to Campbellcroft Labradors.

Meanwhile, the girls at Campbellcroft are getting special attention, and the Campbells are importing some of the British lines they love, including Sandylands (Gwen Broadley) and Lawnwood (Marjorie Satterthwaite). With luck they hope to bring back a lovely black bitch from England during the summer of 1982.

The Campbells sell many puppies as family pets and gun dogs and constantly receive messages and photos of these dogs; this sort of

Daisy and Woofie, two of the Labs at Campbellcroft relaxing together at the home of Donald and Virginia Campbell, Soquel, California.

Another view of Campbellcroft's Piper, C.D.X., from the first litter bred by Donald and Virginia Campbell, by Ch. Briary's Trace of Brian, C.D., W.C., ex Ch. Agber Daisy of Campbellcroft, C.D., W.C.

communication is one of the greatest pleasures of breeding Labradors. It means a great deal to them to hear that these pups are having a wonderful time enriching the lives of their owners—"How could you have known that she is absolutely perfect for our family?"—and enriching the larders of their owners—"70 dove for 4 shooters opening day, and 52 duck, 1 goose and 4 pheasants in 5 trips."

Sir Ralph was quite right, it seems to me, when he felt the Campbells needed a Lab, because certainly knowing "Queenie" has led to a hobby which I am sure will long continue for this couple!

Sprigger's Choice at eight weeks of age, already "doing what comes naturally" to Campbellcroft-bred Labs. By Am., Can. Ch. Campbellcroft's Angus, C.D., W.C.

Bda. Ch. Cedarhill Briton Rock Candy, Am., Bda. C.D., bred, owned and handled by Thomas J. Feneis, Cedarhill Labradors, Freehold, New Jersey, pictured winning under Alva Rosenberg, dean of dog-show judges.

Cedarhill

Cedarhill Labradors, at Freehold, New Jersey, had their start in July 1963, when Tom and Barbara Feneis purchased a seven-week-old yellow Lab bitch puppy, Binta's Stellar Honey, as a house pet and to be trained for duck hunting.

At six months of age, Honey was taken to an obedience school, and after a ten-week beginner course, she graduated fourth out of 50 dogs! She would have been first, Tom tells us, had he not made several handling errors which lowered her score. After another ten weeks of training in the Novice Class, Honey graduated first with a score of 199½ (almost perfect). Members of the training club of course encouraged Tom and Barbara to start entering her in trials.

Honey was entered and gained both her C.D. and C.D.X. She was all trained and ready to try for her U.D. when she injured her rear leg while retrieving in the ocean; this prevented further jumping and ended her obedience career.

In 1965, Honey was bred to the excellent yellow male, Champion Harrowby Lightening, and produced eight puppies, her only litter. Two were kept, a dog and a bitch, Cedarhill Briton Rock Candy and Cedarhill Amber Dawn. The dog, "Brit," was handled by Tom to his Bermuda championship and had seven points, including a four-point major on his American championship, when he decided that he did not care for dog shows and was retired. He earned his American and Bermudian C.D. titles when handled by Barbara. Amber, owner-handled by Tom, won her American Championship, won both an American and Bermudian C.D., and gained several championship points in Bermuda.

The biggest thrill with "Brit" and Amber was when Alva Rosenberg, dean of all-breed judges, awarded them Winners Dog and Winners Bitch each for a four-point major at Elm City Kennel Club in 1968. Amber went on to Best of Winners.

Ch. Cedarhill Amber Dawn, Am., Bda. C.D., was bred and owned by Thomas J. Feneis.

A third puppy from this litter, owned by a neighbor who trained him for obedience, distinguished himself by gaining his American U.D., placing in the ribbons in almost every trial, before he was three years old. At one of his appearances, he was Highest in Trial with 199 in the Open Class, and he also obtained U.D. degrees in Canada and Bermuda. This was Cedarhill Snow Blaze, or "Tawny."

After finishing her championship, Amber was bred in 1969 to Champion Lockerbie Golden-tone Jensen, by whom she whelped six puppies. The three that were kept grew up to become Champion Cedarhill Autumn Haze, American and Bermudian Champion Cedarhill Misty Morn, both bitches, and American and Bermudian Champion Cedarhill Golden Sunset, a dog. The latter had his first win, a four-point major, at nine months of age from the Bred-by Ex-hibitor Class at Burlington County Kennel Club under John Rementer and was finished by the time he had reached 14 months of age. He was also shown in Bermuda, where he finished his title in two shows, both five-point majors and a second in the Sporting Group. Shown in the United States as a Special, he had numerous Best of Breed wins.

In 1971, Amber was bred to Jensen for a second time and produced four puppies. The bitch and two dogs that were kept became Champion Cedarhill Champagne Heather, Champion Cedarhill Gold Dust, and Champion Cedarhill Sundance Kid, the latter two both dogs. Sundance Kid completed his title in a most auspicious manner by taking Winners Dog at the Labrador Retriever Club of America's National Specialty in 1976 at Ox Ridge, following this up with an exciting career as a Special.

Tom and Barbara are justly proud that, out of ten puppies in two litters from Champion Cedarhill Amber Dawn, American and Bermudian C.D., all six which were kept and shown finished.

In 1975, Champion Cedarhill Autumn Haze was bred to Champion Sandylands Midas (English import), producing eight puppies.

Am., Bda. Ch. Cedarhill Golden Sunset at nine months of age gaining a five-point major at Burlington County. Barbara A. Feneis, owner, Tom Feneis handling.

Above: Ch. Cedarhill Champagne Heather, bred-owned-handled by Thomas J. Feneis. **Below:** Ch. Cedarhill Gold Dust, another of the handsome Labs from Cedarhill Kennels.

Cedarhill's Autumn Sunday from this litter was sold to Mrs. Terry DePietro of Colt's Neck, New Jersey, for whom he gained championship. Another from this litter, Cedarhill Golden Ciara, was kept and bred to Champion Briary Bracken, producing a litter of eight. Cedarhill Ciara's Sandstorm, a dog from this litter, gained his title under two years age with four majors and has numerous Best of Breed and Group placements to his credit. In 1981, he was one of the Top Ten Labradors in the country, and Tom and Barbara Feneis are hoping for and anticipating an even better year for him in 1982.

Another dog from this same litter, Cedarhill Ciara's Sandpiper, is started toward championship. While a sister, Cedarhill Ciara's Serenade, took first in Sweepstakes at the 1979 Labrador Retriever Club of the Potomac Specialty; since then, due to hormone imbalance, she has had problems holding a show coat, which we hope will eventually be overcome.

Above: Cedarhill Ciara's Serenade winning the Sweepstakes at the Labrador Retriever Club of the Potomac Specialty in 1979. **Below:** Thomas J. Feneis smiles proudly as Ch. Cedarhill's Ciara's Sandstorm, by Ch. Briary Bracken ex Cedarhill Golden Ciara adds another Best of Breed victory, at Wallkill Kennel Club 1980.

Cedarhill Ciara's Sandpiper, a home-bred belonging to Thomas J. and Barbara A. Feneis, Cedarhill Labradors.

In October 1981, Mr. and Mrs. Feneis purchased a twelve-week-old yellow bitch puppy, out of American and Canadian Champion Coalcreek's Briary Breakthru and Briary Bisque. And in November 1981, two seven-week-old pups, a dog and a bitch out of Allegheny Eclipse and Sandylands Radiance, were also added, co-owned by Mrs. Terry DePietro.

Unfortunately, Rock Candy died in 1976 and Amber, as well as Honey and Golden Sunset, died in 1980, the latter three within two and a half months of each other, making it a very unhappy year for their owners. All the others are still well and happy as show dogs and house pets.

Ch. Cedarhill Autumn Haze, by Ch. Lockerbie Goldentone Jensen ex Ch. Cedarhill Amber Dawn, Am., Bda. C.D., is one of the impressive Labradors bred and owned by Thomas J. and Barbara A. Feneis.

Cedarhill Misty Morn, owned by Barbara A. and Thomas J. Feneis.

Cedarhill Kennels also has a black dog, Buckie, which they rescued from the pound, and also several mixed breeds. Tom and Barbara live in a densely wooded area and people abandon dogs in that area; if homes can't be found for the waifs, Tom and Barbara wind up keeping them, as they will not turn the dogs in to the pound. In 1972, they obtained an Irish Setter in this manner, and they finally tracked down the original owners of the dog and got its papers. This one was good enough to be a show dog except for a hereditary eye problem. She thought she was a Labrador and loved swimming and retrieving with them. Very clearly Tom and Barbara are the type of dog fanciers I most greatly admire, who truly love dogs and have a heart for those abandoned!

Cedarhill consists of forty wooded acres of land, which include a ten-acre pond where the dogs can swim. Several years back, Tom and Barbar built a heated and air-conditioned kennel, which contains an office, grooming room, bathroom, kitchen, and bedroom. The kennel runs are twenty feet long, divided by three-foot concrete walls with three-foot chain link on top. All runs are covered. The kennel does not get too much use, however, as Tom and Barbara keep the dogs in the house most of the time.

The breeding policy at Cedarhill is to limit the number of litters produced, striving always for quality and being absolutely certain that all puppies produced go to really good homes. Since 1963, they have had only five litters for a total of thirty-three puppies.

Ch. Hugger Mugger, by Ch. Bancstone Bob of Wingan ex Marsh (Ch. Earlsmoor Moor of Arden ex Wingan's Maid of the Mist), was a great show dog, an outstanding shooting dog, and a sire of tremendous importance in American Labrador history. Owned by Mrs. Curtis Read, Oyster Bay, New York.

Chidley

The Chidley Labradors were founded in the early 1930s, the result of Joan Redmond (Mrs. Curtis S. Read) having received a six-month-old Labrador bitch puppy as a gift from her uncle. This was Cinders, from imported Scottish gun dogs Diver of Liphook and Ridgeland Black Diamond, who for fourteen years remained her owner's constant and devoted companion.

In 1935, Cinders was bred to Champion Bancstone Ben of Wingan. This mating produced Bender, who sired Champion Star Lea Sunspeck, important in the establishment of Helen Ginnel's famous Whygin dogs.

In 1944, Mrs. Read bred one of the most influential and important Labradors on the east coast of the United States, Champion Hugger Mugger, who won the 1946 Specialty from the classes under Alva Rosenberg and went on to be a leading influence through his descendants.

Mugger was a grandson of the English Dual Champion Bramshaw Bob, who twice won Best in Show at Crufts. His other grandsire, Champion Earlsmoor Moor of Arden, was the breed's first American Best in Show All Breeds winner, and Moor also held field awards.

Mugger's sons and daughters included Champion Chidley Spook, a daughter that took Best of Opposite Sex at the National in 1948, Best of Breed there in 1949, and Best of Breed again in 1952. Champion Chidley Racketeer, Mugger's nephew, was Best of Winners at the National in 1951. Mugger's son, Champion Ashur Deacon, was Best of Opposite Sex in 1952 (to Spook's Best of Breed), on which occasion another son, Champion Ashur Cameron, was Best of Winners. In 1953, Mugger's daughter, Champion Chidley Genie, was Winners Bitch; then in 1954, she took Best of Breed, while Mugger's son, Champion Wildfield Mickey Finn, was Reserve Winners Dog. In 1955 Champion Chidley Goldfinch, Mugger's granddaughter, was Best of Opposite Sex. In 1960, a double great-grandson, Champion Kirkside Royalist, was Winners Dog. In 1961, Champion Whygin's Campaign Promise, a granddaughter, was Best of Breed. And in 1964, Champion Hibeau's Royal Punch, a great-great-granddaughter, was Best of Winners.

It is highly significant that Mugger's sons and daughters helped to found kennels still active at the present time. His daughter, Champion Chidley Spook, provided founding descendants for the Kurt Unklebachs' Walden Kennels in Chidley Twoshakes' son, Champion Ashur Deacon, a founding sire for the late Barbara Barty-King's Aldenholm Kennels in Massachusetts. Today Deacon's descendants are winning with the prefixes of kennels owned by Barbara Barfield (Scrimshaw) and Mary Swan (Chebacco). Ch. Chebacco J. Robert is double descended from Mugger, on both his sire's side and his dam's.

Mugger's son, Champion Wildfield's Mickey Finn, was a field trial winner and the sire of champions. Mickey's daughter, Champion Whygin Campaign Promise, was one of the

Ch. Chidley Spook, by Ch. Hugger Mugger, Best in Show in Mid-west Specialty during the early 1950s, shown by Dolly Marshall. Photo courtesy of Mrs. Curtis Read.

founding dams for Shamrock Acres Kennels. Birchbriar Labradors have Mugger descendants behind their dogs, as do those of Audrey Wolcott's Blackmor Kennels.

The yellow Champion Chidley Almond Crisp was the first champion yellow Labrador bitch in the United States. She was a granddaughter of Mugger's litter-sister.

Aside from being the owner of a fine kennel, Mrs. Read is a tremendously popular judge and enjoys officiating.

Chilbrook

Chilbrook Labradors at Reston, Virginia, belong to Debby Kobilis who, having been associated with her father's Beagles since childhood, established the kennel with her own first Beagle in 1969. This Beagle was a field trial bitch. When space permitted, Debby acquired her first Lab, in 1972, from George Bragaw's Shooktown Kennel. This event proved to be fortunate for the future of the Labrador Retriever Club of the Potomac, which was not in existence

Ch. Chidley Almond Crisp, the first Yellow Champion Bitch, in 1950, and Ch. Chidley Spook at six months of age— two very famous names in Labrador history, from the kennels of Mrs. Curtis S. Read.

CH·CHIDLEY ALMOND CRISP
CH·CHIDLEY SPOOK AS A PUPPY

Briary Joy For Ever, one of Tarquin's great daughters, is an excellent example of the type of Lab at Chilbrook Kennels. Owned and photographed by Debby Kobilis.

set about the long, arduous task of breaking the ice to have her dogs accepted at the Seeing Eye School.

The first puppy she sent to them was "Susie" in 1974. Since that time, a long succession of Chilbrook puppies has followed. Although by the standards of most people, Chilbrook has bred a large number of puppies each year, sixty to eighty of them, less than 10% have been sold to outside sources, with the remainder going as guides for the blind or being retained for Ms. Kobilis' own breeding program.

Endless experimentation in breeding was done at Chilbrook to learn the mode of inheritance for various traits, and Ms. Kobilis has compiled thousands of pages of notes on the subject. Nearly fifteen years after first visiting the Seeing Eye School, Debby Kobilis realized her greatest achievement with a litter whelped on Christmas Eve in 1979. The sire was the great Champion Lockerbie Brian Boru, W.C., and the dam was one of her early bitches, Chilbrook Hurricane Heather, C.D. Every puppy in the litter sent to the Seeing Eye School graduated to become a guide, and one of the bitch puppies was selected for the school's breeding program. This bitch, after producing several litters at the Seeing Eye School, went with a blind owner, and the bitch's puppies are now serving as guides for the blind.

at that time. Mr. Bragaw and Ms. Pilbin, along with others, worked hard to get the club, now so successful, "off the ground." Later Mr. Bragaw served as the first President of this club; Debby Kobilis was its charter Secretary; and their friend Liz Clark (Mrs. Robert D. Clark, Jr.) was Vice-President. This club has set many precedents, such as holding the first Labrador Tracking Trial and being responsible for the split in the Open Classes at the dog shows (i.e., black, chocolate, and yellow).

Although Debby Kobilis has been successful in showing her Labs in conformation, obedience, tracking, and field trials, her lifelong ambition has been to breed Seeing Eye dogs. A visit to the Seeing Eye School in Morristown, New Jersey, in 1967 convinced her that it is the greatest honor a dog can achieve. Although she owned two Shepherds and was fully appreciative of their talents, she was convinced that a Labrador was certainly an equal choice, so she

"Hunting box turtles" Douglas Point Research Project, N.E.R.F. funded. Photo by Debby Kobilis, owner of Chilbrook Labradors, Reston, Virginia.

One of the fine Labradors owned by Debby Kobilis is seen here advertising National Conservation Week.

Ch. Chilbrook Brannigan at two years of age. Photo by breeder-owner Debby Kobilis.

The dog from this litter, which had been retained at Chilbrook for breeding, earned his Canadian championship in four days at four shows with four majors and needs only one major to complete his championship in the United States. He has taken Best in Match at a very large show and Best of Breed from the classes en route to finishing his title. He has sired many guides for the blind as well.

Today there is very little breeding done at Chilbrook, but the kennel carries an unbroken four-generation line from its foundation.

Chilbrook Sea Raven, C.D., T.D. Owned by Debby Kobilis.

Chucklebrook

Chucklebrook, Reg., was established in 1967 as a Golden Retriever kennel. By 1973, however, it was well on its way to becoming exclusively Labrador.

Probably the biggest factor influencing the decision to change breeds was "Chamey," Champion Spenrock's Bohemia Champagne, who was originally owned by John G. Martin. At the time when Mr. Martin decided to give up his kennel, Mrs. Leslie G. Pilbin, who, with her husband, owns Chucklebrook at Burlington, Connecticut, offered to assist Mr. Martin with the proper dispersal of his dogs. From the time that "Chamey" and Diane Pilbin first came to know one another, "Chamey" constantly tried to divert Mrs. Pilbin's attention from the other dogs by running big circles around her or by taking her wrist gently in her mouth and trying to lead Mrs. Pilbin away. Gradually Mrs. Pilbin became very attached to this lovely dog, and the realization grew that either she must buy "Chamey" for herself or lose a very devoted friend. She reasoned, too, that "Chamey" would not look too out of place among the Goldens. After all, she certainly was the right color (yellow)—maybe a little short-coated, but that seemed all right.

"Chamey" seemed to bring good luck to Chucklebrook. The second time she and Diane Pilbin went into the show ring together (Westminster) "Chamey" went Best of Opposite Sex; then she repeated that win at the National a few months later. In 1979, she was rated Top Producing Labrador Bitch by *Kennel Review*.

"Chamey," at 12 years of age, enjoying a nap.

Ch. Spenrock's Bohemia Champagne (above) at Westminster in 1973 with owner Diane Pilbin, and (below) in the Parade of Champions at the National Specialty in 1981. Owned by Chucklebrook Labradors, Reg., Mr. and Mrs. Leslie G. Pilbin, Burlington, Connecticut.

Chucklebrook now has progressed four generations from "Chamey" with, of course, many champion progeny to carry on the line. The goals there are to continue to produce the quality that "Chamey" brought to them as the base of their original Lab breeding program.

The background at Chucklebrook has relied heavily on Sandylands, Ballyduff, and Lockerbie lines. In 1980, the English import Champion Follytower Singalong was added to the kennel to be used as an outcross.

To date, Chucklebrook has produced numerous Labrador champions holding obedience titles, working titles, Working Certificates, and placements in licensed field trials.

In addition to the pleasure the Labs give them on a daily basis, the Pilbins' greatest satisfaction is derived from handling their own dogs in the show ring as well as in the field.

Ch. Follytower Singalong was selected Best of Opposite Sex in this judging of the finals at the Potomac Labrador Specialty in 1981. Mr. and Mrs. Leslie G. Pilbin, owners.

Mrs. Nancy Story's Ch. Killingworth's Ben, a head study showing beautiful male head and lovely expression.

Croysdales

The Croysdales Labradors have been in existence since the mid-1970s when Mrs. Nancy W. Story of Guilford, Connecticut, decided that she would like to start a kennel of this breed.

In 1975, Mrs. Story purchased Killingworth's Ben, a son of Blacmors Chucklebrook Angus from Chucklebrook Chami of Banner, with the intention of having an enjoyable family pet that was also a quality representative of the breed. With Ben, Mrs. Story became involved with attending American Kennel Club Match Shows "for fun and relaxation." As so frequently happens, the wins at the matches spurred Mrs. Story on to try the point shows, with the result that, in 1978, Ben became an A.K.C. Champion of Record.

Croysdales Sara of Ludlowe, by Kalons Thistle ex Ch. Ludlowes Topaz Pride has been an outstanding producer for Mrs. Nancy W. Story's Croysdales Kennels at Guilford, Connecticut.

Meanwhile, as she was finding the shows fun and exciting, Mrs. Story decided to look for another Lab, this time a bitch to breed to Ben. After much study and research she finally selected a bitch from Ludlowe Kennels, Croysdales Sara of Ludlowe, by Kalons Thistle ex Champion Ludlowes Topaz Pride, bred by Nancy Edmonds.

Owner-handled, Sara's show career has been a bit "spotty" due to her maternal duties. Even so, she has reached the stage, as this is written, of needing only one three-point major with which to complete her championship. With Ben, Sara has produced three litters of quality Labradors, many of which are pointed toward their championships.

Croysdales Sara of Ludlowe taking Winners Bitch at Carrol County in 1980, Mrs. Anne Rogers Clark judging. Owned and handled by Mrs. Nancy W. Story.

Recently Sara's and Ben's children have reached the age when they can be bred. Mrs. Story has been so fortunate as to sell the majority of the puppies to excellent homes both as pets and as show prospects. As they have matured to breeding age, the owners of the pups have come back to Mrs. Story for assistance in the choice of stud dogs for their bitches, with the result that Mrs. Story was recently complimented by another breeder with the remark "you should be very proud to see your dogs producing even better than themselves." This is what breeding is all about!

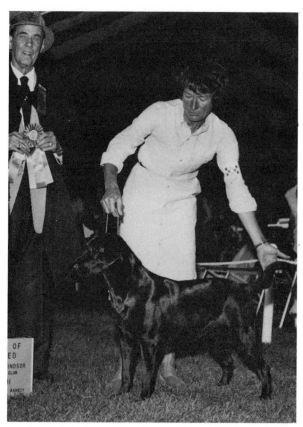

Croysdales Black Velvet, by Ch. Killingworth's Ben ex Croysdales Sara of Ludlowe, pictured going Best of Breed from the classes at 16 months of age, South Windsor Kennel Club, 1981. The judge is the late James W. Trullinger. Mrs. Nancy W. Story owner-handler.

An informal pose of Mrs. Nancy W. Story's Croysdales Victoria, by Ch. Killingsworth Ben ex Croysdale Sara of Ludlowe.

Winning the Stud Dog Class at the Labrador Retriever Club of Central Connecticut Specialty, Ch. Killingworth's Ben with his "get," Croysdales Royal Jester and Croysdales Victoria.

Ben has produced well not only with Sara, but his progeny from other bitches are also now in the ring and doing well. Many of his offspring have also proven themselves in the field (this is so important to the Labrador breed).

Mohawk Valley in 1981 was the first ring appearance for the six-month-old Croysdales Blue Creek Julie, by Ch. Follytowers Singalong ex Croysdales Victoria. Owned by Mrs. Nancy W. Story.

Croysdales Blue Creek Julie at eight months age. Mrs. Nancy W. Story, owner.

This head study of Ch. Follytower Singalong, a well-known Labrador importation, was made by Debby Kobilis, Reston, Virginia.

Mrs. Story has lately acquired a puppy bitch by Champion Follytower Singalong ex Croysdales Victoria (Champion Killingworths Ben ex Croysdales Sara of Ludlowe) who has started off well with some prestigious wins in the Puppy Classes. At the supported entry of the Labrador Retriever Club of Central Connecticut, this puppy, Croysdales Blue Creek Julie, was the top puppy bitch in an impressive entry, and she has aroused much favorable comment among judges, breeders, and exhibitors. Mrs. Story is looking forward to an exciting show career for this bitch as well as, eventually, some fine future winners from her.

Driftwood

Driftwood Labradors came about as a result of Mrs. Pam Kelsey's decision to purchase a Labrador as a pet, back in 1968. Now located at Bayville, New Jersey, the kennel is going strong, and Mrs. Kelsey can well review with satisfaction the success her Labs are enjoying.

The Kelseys named their first Lab Driftwood's Sea Bee. She was never shown, but she was bred—just once. The dog to whom she was mated was a top sire of his day, Champion Lockerbie Kismet, owned by Helen Warwick, who was Mrs. Kelsey's "mentor" during the early days. This litter produced the black Champion Driftwood's Gypsy, who is the bitch on which Driftwood has been built.

Gypsy was bred to Champion Mijan's Corrigan, the sire of at least eleven American champions, and produced Mrs. Kelsey's lovely and well-known yellow bitch, Champion Driftwood's Limited Edition. She, in turn, was bred to Champion Sandylands Markwell of Lockerbie, producing Mrs. Kelsey's first male, Champion Driftwood's Celebration. Now Mrs. Kelsey has just acquired a yellow Celebration daughter, which makes a fifth generation Driftwood Labrador.

To summarize the thirteen years of Driftwood, five litters have been bred which have produced five champions and several more Labs which are pointed. Mrs. Kelsey owns five dogs which constitute five generations. All champions finished easily and were entirely owner-handled. Limited Edition was never topped for Best of Opposite Sex, and she was Best of Breed at the Meadowlands. Celebration was Reserve Winners Dog from the 6th - 9th Month Puppy Class at the Labrador Retriever Club of the Potomac Specialty, Best of Breed from the classes at Kennel Club of Philadelphia under breeder-judge Ken Golden, Best of Winners at Westminster under breeder-judge George Bragaw, Best of Winners at Boardwalk, and Best of Breed at the latter the following year.

But probably the accomplishment giving Mrs. Kelsey the greatest pleasure is that of having bred Champion Driftwood's Honeysuckle (Champion Sandylands Midas ex Champion Driftwood's Gypsy) who is the dam of Champion Mijan's Corrigan, a current Top Producer who is being used extensively. Many of today's pedigrees include this dog and thus the Driftwood line.

Ch. Driftwood's Gypsy, by Ch. Lockerbie Kismet ex Driftwood's Sea Bee, is the bitch upon whom Pam Kelsey's Driftwood Labradors are founded.

Ch. Driftwood's Celebration taking Best of Breed from the Classes, Kennel Club of Philadelphia, 1979, under breeder-judge Ken Golden. Pam Kelsey, owner, Bayville, New Jersey.

Basically, Mrs. Kelsey has line-bred on Kismet and Midas, and it seems to have been an excellent combination. She has endeavored, successfully, to follow the old adage "quality, not quantity" and feels that a dog must be able to win easily on type, movement, and that very elusive quality known as "style."

Best of Breed campaigning, Group wins, Best in Show, and other such accomplishments are not what interest Mrs. Kelsey. Breeding quality Labs that can produce successive quality generations is the thing she finds exciting; for her, the fun is in the breeding, very aptly labeled an "art."

Ch. Driftwood's Celebration as a promising five-month-old puppy. Mrs. Pam Kelsey, owner.

Ch. Driftwood Limited Edition, never beaten for Best of Opposite Sex and a Best of Breed winner, too. Owned by Driftwood Labs, Mrs. Pam Kelsey. Photo by Vince Serbin.

Eireannach

Although in the future it will be located in Ireland, as owners Nancy and Walter Rutter have recently moved there on a permanent basis, Eireannach Labradors have been actively bred and shown in the United States in the past and are so well-known here that we feel their kennel history belongs with the others in this section.

The foundation of this kennel was Powhatan Sable, purchased in England from Major and Mrs. Aikenhead in 1971. This bitch proved herself to be not only the standard for which the Rutters would strive in their breeding program, but she also was one of those rare bitches that produced excellent progeny no matter to what dog she was bred. She was by the Aikenheads' dog, Powhatan Chief, from their bitch Powhatan Corn. These two, in turn, were out of Champion Powhatan Solo and Champion Braeduke Joyful respectively. At the same time a yellow dog puppy, Timspring Lucky Star, by Champion Kingsbury Nokeener Moonstar and Timspring Landyke Venus, was purchased from Mrs. Joan Macan in England.

The Rutters bred Sable to Lucky Star, thus producing their yellow dog, Canadian Champion Eireannach Irish Grouse. Although he had major points toward his American championship, his sad death from a rare lung disease at a young age prevented this title's completion. Other dogs in the kennel's early stages were two black bitches: Black Bliss of Powhatan, also imported from the Aikenheads, and Eireannach Moosehead, out of Champion Mansergh Moose, an English import bred by Mary Roslin-Williams.

During the course of their early involvement with Labs, the Rutters spent many hours with the late Dorothy Howe, of Rupert Labradors, and the Rutters speak of the knowledge and guidance she gave them. From her they purchased Rupert Cara.

Starting to show, the Rutters became quickly impressed with a dog then recently imported, Champion Mansergh Moose. He represented everything they looked for in a black Lab. His breeder, Mary Roslin-Williams, had bred only blacks for over 35 years. They loved this dog so much that it was decided to breed Sable to him; and in 1976, she whelped six black puppies, a litter which was going to prove of tremendous importance to Walter and Nancy Rutter. Much as they would have liked to do so, they could not keep all of the puppies. Mr. and Mrs. Richard Oster, their good friends and the owners of Moose, took the pick dog puppy of the litter,

Timspring Lucky Star, by Ch. Kingsbury Nokeenek Moonstar ex Timspring Landyke Venus, owned by Nancy and Walter Rutter, Eireannach Labradors.

Champion Eireannch Black Coachman, which the Rutters bought back when they moved to Ireland in 1981; the Osters also purchased the pick bitch, Champion Eireannach Black Angel, which also wound up going to Ireland with the Rutters. The other dog puppy went to Mary Ellen Pfeifle of Hampshire Kennels and is Eireannach Black Gnat, now pointed. Mrs. Pfeifle also purchased another daughter of Sable, Eireannach Shandy Gaff, a yellow by Maestro of Suddie (Champion Sandylands Mark ex Mosca of Suddie).

Left to right are Can. Ch. Eireannach Irish Grouse, Eireannach Moosehead, and Powhatan Sable, the background for Eireannach Labradors, Walter and Nancy Rutter, County Tipperary, Ireland.

Can. Ch. Eireannach Irish Grouse on first show appearance at six months of age. It takes a bit of time for puppies to build up ring confidence and showmanship. Nancy and Walter Rutter, owners.

Four magnificent Labs belonging to Eireannach Kennels—Black Bliss of Powhatan, Powhatan Sable, Eireannach Moosehead, and Can. Ch. Eireannach Irish Grouse.

At that time, the Rutters were living in Standfordville, New York. They decided to breed Sable one last time and they chose as the sire Helen Warwick's black import, Champion Lockerbie Stanwood Granada, by Ch. Sandylands Tandy ex Longley Gipsey. Then later they bred Angel to Champion Sandylands Markwell of Lockerbie. A black dog, Eireannach Black Corker, from the Granada-Sable combination is now with the Buchanans in Canada.

Angel and Coachman, as mentioned, returned to Ireland with the Rutters. They will be out of quarantine in February 1982, and there are plans to show them at the St. Patrick's Day Show in Dublin. Angel will be bred during spring 1982 to a top dog that is line-bred along the lines the Rutters admire. From the Hepworths' Poolstead Kennels, the Rutters have recently purchased a young black bitch puppy, Poolstead Pick Me Up, by English Champion Fabracken Comedy Star and Champion Poolstead Pictorial, all going back to the great Sandylands dogs, Mark, Tandy, and Tan.

Both Coachman and Angel left progeny in the United States and Canada, and they should make their mark in the show ring and in the field. Angel had a litter in 1981 by Maestro of Suddie, and Coachman has many get close to finishing, sons and daughters of his being with Janet Churchill at Spenrock, Mr. and Mrs. Oster at Ajoco, Claire Senfield at Allegheny, Kendall Herr at Dickendall, Diane Jones at Jollymuff, Rosalind Moore of Moorwood, and the Buchanans at Apoquai.

The Rutters will continue to breed and show Labs in Ireland and in England, remaining true to the type they have owned and love.

Elden

Elden Labradors belong to Elden Williams of Portland, Oregon. Among the famous dogs to be found there are some extremely distinguished Labs that have brought fame and numerous important show honors home to their owner.

American and Canadian Champion Apollo's Silver Mist, or "Misty the Character," was the Westminster winner in 1976. This lovely bitch became the dam of American and Canadian Champion Elden's Tigger Too, America's Number One Lab for 1980, whose wins included Best of Breed at the Rose City Labrador Specialty.

American and Canadian Champion Elyod's Macbeth of Canterbury, known as "Tigger," was America's Number One Lab in 1979 and Canada's Number One Lab in 1977-1978. He now holds the position of Number Five Labrador in the history of the breed.

American and Canadian Champion Elden's Elyod The Bear Facts, "Bear Bear," finished his title in six shows with four majors, placing in Groups from the classes. He was America's Number One Lab for 1981.

American and Canadian Champion Elden's Cadillac Kid was a Best of Breed winner from the classes en route to the title.

Am., Can. Ch. Appollo's Silver Mist, the dam of Am., Can. Ch. Elden's Tigger Too, America's Number One Lab in 1980. Both owned by Elden Williams, Portland, Oregon.

Now retired, and lying on his very own bench, is Am., Can. Ch. Elyod's MacBeth of Canterbury, Number Five Labrador in the History of the Breed (Phillips Points System). Owned by Elden Williams, Elden Labradors.

Am., Can. Ch. Elyod's MacBeth of Canterbury, "Tigger One."

Am., Can. Ch. Elden's Tigger Too, America's Number One Labrador Retriever in 1980. Owned by Elden Williams.

American Champion Elden's Mona Baby finished in four shows, among her successes being Winners Bitch, Best of Winners, and Best of Opposite Sex at the Rose City Labrador Retriever Club Specialty. Like Cadillac Kid, Mona Baby was a Best of Breed winner from the classes. Mona has had two excellent litters, one by "Bear Bear" and one by Champion Briary Bell Buoy of Windsong.

Ch. Elden's Elyod The Bear Facts, "Bear Bear." America's Number One Labrador Retriever in 1981. Owner, Elden Williams.

Ch. Elden's Mona Baby finished in four shows, with four majors. Owned by Elden Williams, Elden's Labradors.

Mr. Williams is, of course, proud of the fact that his dogs have been America's Number One Labradors for 1979, 1980, and 1981. In addition to Roses, there are several other especially nice-looking youngsters by the current winners that would seem destined to continue in the family tradition.

All of the Elden's Labradors are worked daily in the field and in water.

Am., Can. Ch. Elyod's MacBeth of Canterbury playing with his son, Elden's Tigger of Canterbury. Tigger is nine years old here, the puppy three months.

American Champion Elden's Sparkle Farkle, "Sparkie," had a five-point major to her credit at eight months and finished with four majors, three of them five-pointers.

A young daughter of "Bear Bear," Elden's Stop n' Smell The Roses, already has a four-point major from the Puppy Classes, so an exciting future is anticipated for this one, too.

Am., Can. Ch. Elyod's MacBeth of Canterbury at three weeks old.

Fantasy

Fantasy Labradors was founded by René J. and Debra Lynn Krier of Salisbury, North Carolina, on the belief in the triple-purpose Lab (stressing temperament, enthusiasm, and type) and focusing attention on the improvement of the chocolate Lab in all the essential aspects. It has been successful in producing a number of obedience and show champions who can run equally as well in the field.

The first of the Kriers' Labradors was Count René De Coco, a son of Champion Great Scot of Ayr, a chocolate male who was purchased mainly as a gun dog. He was a lovely dog and a marvelous worker in the field. He lived eight

Ch. Elden's Sparkle Farkle, a new youngster with a good future. Elden Williams, owner, Portland, Oregon.

years and produced only two litters before going sterile, leaving his owners not a single pup with which to carry on the line. When "Mud," as he was called, was four years old, the Kriers became interested in pursuing field training in a more serious manner, so they introduced to their family a black bitch carrying chocolate lines, Tal Vez Tara's Rosie, C.D., W.C., a super typey and aggressive hunter. She was the granddaughter of Irish, Canadian, and American Champion Castlemore Shamus. Rosie is still with the Kriers and is one of their favorites, teaching all the young dogs field manners and introduction to water. She has been bred to field and show champions and has produced obedience champions, show-pointed puppies, and dogs running in the field.

The Kriers' first real introduction in the show ring was with a chocolate bitch, Selamats Wagg'ontails Gal, a Champion Castlemore Bramble daughter. At her first show, in Puppy Sweepstakes, she took her class and went on to gain Best in Sweeps. At that time, the Kriers became "hooked" (as don't we all with the first taste of winning!), and showing became Debra Krier's first love and interest. This bitch, "Thumper" to friends, produced a very handsome chocolate bitch when bred to Mexican, American, and Canadian Champion Gunfield's Super Charger, C.D., W.C. The chocolate grew up to become Champion Fantasy's Rikki Tikki Tava, C.D., and is probably Debra Krier's favorite of all the dogs. "Tik" has true type,

temperament, and kindness; she is also a superb marker and a thoroughly enjoyable dog in the field. "Tik's" grandfather is Dual Champion Shamrock Acres Super Drive, giving her the qualities her owners very rightly consider to be so important and what the Labrador is really all about.

"Tik" recently had a litter from Shenandoah Ebon Express, a black with an impeccable linebred English pedigree. Among the litter was Fantasy's De'Ja Vu, a black male that at ten months of age looks extremely exciting; he already has points from the Puppy Class, and expectations for his fulfilling his triple potential are high.

The sire of Fantasy's Bit of Broad Reach, C.D., is Eng., Am. Ch. Lawnwoods Hot Chocolate, shown here at a Specialty Show in Virginia. Note the manner in which this dog strikes a natural pose, as they are taught to do in England. Janet Churchill owner-handler.

Also among Fantasy's Labradors is Fantasy's Bit of Broad Reach, C.D., a daughter of English and American Champion Lawnwood's Hot Chocolate ex Champion Yarrow's Broad Reach Psaphire, U.D.T., a lovely black bitch who has taken the breed from the classes from Group-winning Specials and is proving herself a marvelous Labrador who should be a great asset to the Kriers' breeding program later on.

The Kriers have very definite ideas about breeding the highest quality chocolate Labradors. They try to breed their chocolates to chocolates and blacks of American and English lines to complement their existing lines, and they never sacrifice the quality of their Labs just to maintain the chocolate color. It is planned that Fantasy Labradors will be around well into the future! Recent breedings from there are to Swedish and American Champion Puh's Superman and to Champion Follytower Singalong.

Ch. Fantasy's Rikki Tikki Tava, C.D., by Mex., Am. Ch. Gunfield's Super Charger, C.D., W.C., ex Selamats Wagg'ontails Gal. Bred and owned by Fantasy Labradors, Rene J. and Debra Lynn Krier, Salisbury, North Carolina.

Ch. Lockerbie Shillelagh, with Ch. Lockerbie Brian Boru, were the basis of the Briary Line, and both were bred by Helen and James Warwick of the Lockerbie Kennels. This is Shillelagh.

Finchingfield

The Finchingfield Labradors, owned by Richard and Marilyn Reynolds of Herndon, Virginia, are based upon the Briary breeding of Marjorie and Ceylone Brainard, which goes back to Champion Lockerbie Brian Boru and Champion Lockerbie Shillelah bred by Helen and James Warwick of the Lockerbie Labradors. The Reynolds were introduced to the Brainards, and Briary, by Jean and Don Prior who have been line-breeding Labradors of similar type and nature.

The first brood bitch owned by the Reynolds, Champion Briary Bustle, by Champion Spenrock Anthony Adverse ex Champion Briary Bonnie Briana, was a Top Producer in the Sporting Group for 1980, according to *Kennel Review*. Her two breedings to Champion Briary Brendan of Rainell, owned by Lorraine and

Jean Prior owns this magnificent Labrador, Ch. Briary Bonnie Briana, the dam of three champions. Briana was Top Show Lab Bitch in 1976. Photo taken by and courtesy of Debby Kobilis.

Eugene Getter of Rainell Labradors, have produced seven champions that have finished to date: three in the United States, three others in Canada, and the most recent a single-circuit Bermuda champion. Recently, Bustle's breeding to Jayncourt Ajoco Justice, owned by Janet Farmilette and Tony Huble, produced the Best Puppy in Show at the 1981 National Labrador Club Specialty.

Ch. Briary Bustle going Best of Breed at the Wilmington Kennel Club, 1978. Damara Bolte handling for Richard and Marilyn Reynolds, Finchingfield Labs, Herndon, Virginia.

The Reynolds keep the kennel small, with four or five adults, and breed about one litter annually.

Richard and Marilyn Reynolds own Ch. Finchingfield Fascination, by Ch. Briary Brendan of Rainell ex Ch. Briary Bustle, who is a great-granddaughter of Champion Lockerbie Shillelagh.

An informal pose of Ch. Briary Bustle owned by Richard and Marilyn Reynolds, Herndon, Virginia. Daughter of Ch. Spenrock Anthony Adverse ex Ch. Briary Bonnie Briana.

The philosophy of the Finchingfield breeding program has focused upon obtaining and maintaining a line of highly substantial, sound Labradors. The Reynolds strive to keep the lovely expression and personality so typical of the Champion Lockerbie Brian Boru ex Champion Lockerbie Shillelagh line on which their own is based (the foundation bitch, Bustle, is a granddaughter of these two), and they hope to maintain a consistency of type through preserving a directly descending bitch line which will, in turn, enable them to continue a strong linebreeding program.

Forecast

One bitch dominates the background of the Forecast Labradors, owned by Elizabeth K. Curtis and Ann and Samuel Cappellina at Litchfield, Connecticut. This bitch is Mallows Fanfare, purchased as a five-and-a-half-month-old puppy from Mr. and Mrs. R.J. Hennessy of Weston, Connecticut. Born on January 29th, 1969, Fanfare was a daughter of Canadian and American Champion Annwyn's Jack O'Diamonds (Canadian and American Champion Annwyn's Shedrow ex Canadian and American Champion Lisnamallard Tarantella) from Champion Goldsboro Velvet of Hallow (by Champion Harris Tweed of Ide ex Champion Kimvalley Deborah). Fanfare followed Forecast's first Lab, Trucker, that had come there as a pet, and so completely sold Elizabeth Curtis and the Cappellinas on the breed that they wanted more of his kind and they also planned to raise some.

On the good advice of Mrs. Kurt Unklebach, Fanfare was bred to Champion Blacmor's Buckie and produced three champions in the

Mallow's Fanfare, by Can., Am. Ch. Annwyn's Jack O' Diamonds ex Ch. Goldsboro Velvet of Mallow, was purchased by Forecast Kennels in 1967 and is the dog behind their current winners, now five generations later.

Ch. Mallow's Fanfare with her first two champion sons, Am., Can. Ch. Forecast Beloit and Am., Can. Ch. Forecast Hofstra. Forecast Labradors, Elizabeth K. Curtis and Ann and Samuel Cappellina.

first litter, making Fanfare a Top Producer, according to the Phillips System, for 1970. The breeding was twice repeated, adding three more champions to Fanfare's record. The five champions she produced, all by Buckie, were American and Canadian Champion Forecast Beloit, American Champion Forecast Hofstra, Champion Forecast Wheaton, Champion Forecast Skidmore, C.D., and American and Canadian Champion Forecast Keuka.

Ch. Forecast Keuka, by Ch. Blocmor's Buckie ex Mallow's Fanfare. Forecast Labradors.

Ch. Forecast Beloit, Best of Breed. Forecast Hofstra (finishing his championship) Winners Dog. Forecast Wheaton (finished at the next show) Winners Bitch. Littermates, the first three champion progeny of Mallow Fanfare. Owned by Forecast Labs.

A charming young Labrador owned by Forecast Kennels, Litchfield, Connecticut.

Beloit and Hofstra were both Top Ten Winners, Beloit in 1971 and Hofstra in 1974, when each attained the Number Eight breed position. Beloit and Hofstra, shown together, also had many Best Brace in Show awards in both the United States and Canada.

Forecast boasts approximately seventeen breed champions and ten or more obedience champions. Among the best known winners are American and Canadian Champion Terriwood's Forecast Friends, Champion Summit Lane's Forecast Heller, Forecast Scrippes, C.D., American and Canadian Champion Terriwood's Forecast Witchita, Champion Forecast Charleston, Champion Forecast Atlanta, American and Canadian Champion Forecast Rockefeller, American and Canadian Champion Forecast Cascade, American and Canadian Champion Tamarack's Forecast Outlaw, and Tamarack's Forecast Jaysun, now nearing championship. These represent five generations of breeding, and all go directly back to the original bitch, Mallow's Fanfare.

Am., Can. Ch. Terriwood's Forecast Friends, by Am., Can. Ch. Forecast Beloit ex Merry Go Round Cinderella, is owned by Forecast Labradors.

Ch. Summit Lane Forecast Heller, by Am., Can. Ch. Forecast Hofstra ex Summit Lane's Rambling Rose. Forecast Labradors.

Tamarack's Forecast Jaysun (by Am., Can. Ch. Fredwell Silver Dollar ex Can. Ch. Forecast Atlanta), great-grandson of Mallow's Fanfare. Forecast Labradors.

Franklin

Franklin Labradors were founded in 1951 and are still active at the locality for which they were named, Franklin, Michigan, the home of their owners, Mr. and Mrs. Bernard W. Ziessow.

It all came about through a lovely Labrador bitch who grew up to become Champion Pitch of Franklin. Madge Ziessow had been planning to purchase a Weimaraner as a gift for her husband. When she mentioned this fact to a friend, she was promptly told that a Labrador was the breed Bernard should have as a companion and shooting dog and that he (the friend) would give one to Mrs. Ziessow for him. Thus it is that Pitch arrived to join the family, eventually to become one of her breed's most famed and successful producers.

Ch. Pitch of Franklin was the first Labrador owned by Mr. and Mrs. Bernard W. Ziessow whose Franklin Kennels became so justly famous. Pitch to this day will be found in the pedigree of every Lab that has Franklin in its background.

Pitch was sired by Field Champion Pickpocket of Deer Creek and was a granddaughter of Dual Champion Shed of Arden, Best in Show-winning Champion Earlsmoor Moor of Arden, and Champion Buddha of Arden. With so outstanding a background, she was surely destined to make history—which is exactly what happened. Finishing her championship in less than two months was easy, with Bests of Breed and Group placements from the Classes, despite this being at the period when Labs were still considered to be a "rare breed." Her excellence of conformation and quality, plus a certain brilliance of demeanor, were passed on to her offspring with the result that she became the dam of seven champions, two of them Group winners and one a great and noted Best in Show winner. Additionally, she produced an amateur field champion and field champion, Discovery of Franklin, and numerous qualified Open All Age dogs. Pitch became the grandam of fifteen champions and more champion great-grandchildren than the Ziessows have been able to keep count of.

Fld. Ch. and Am. Fld. Ch. Discovery of Franklin, a National Field Trial Finalist, out of Ch. Pitch of Franklin. Owned by John Olin, whose Nilo Kennels was probably the top field trial kennel of that period. Handler, T.W. Pershall.

Pitch was bred through the line of the greatest dual champion of all time, Shed of Arden. The Ziessows credit this fact with responsibility for the success of Franklin dogs not only in the show ring but also in the field. Today, all champion Labs bearing the Franklin prefix trace their ancestry back to this truly remarkable bitch.

To date (early 1982) Franklin has bred 53 champions and two field and amateur field champions despite a very limited but extremely carefully planned breeding program. Only between two and four litters are raised annually here, all bred to look as a Lab *should* look and work as a Lab *should* work. The Ziessows' philosophy is that by breeding only the best to the best, one has the greatest chance of producing the best, which is certainly good thinking and has worked out well.

Pride of place among all Franklin Labs goes to American and Canadian Champion Dark Star of Franklin, top American-bred black of all time and 1955's Top Sporting Dog in the United States. For over ten years, this magnificent dog was top winner in the breed, and in 18 months of active campaigning, he won 116 Bests of Breed, 93 Group placements, 40 firsts in the Sporting Group, and 8 Bests in Show. He also was winner of the Labrador Retriever Club Working Certificate; he excelled as a gun dog. At eight years of age, in 1960, he came out of retirement to pay his first visit to the National Specialty. He won Best of Breed, defeating all the top young Labradors of the day and then, in triumph, retired permanently from future show ring competition. This 1960 Specialty, incidentally, was quite an occasion for the Ziessows, as Dark Star's brother, American and Canadian Champion Troublemaker of Franklin, won the Veteran and the Stud Dog Classes there as well.

American and Canadian Ch. Dark Star of Franklin, one of the great American Labs, top winner in the breed for over ten years. Dark Star was bred by Mrs. Bernard W. Ziessow, then sold to her father, Mr. Martin.

Above left: A very youthful picture of Ch. Dark Star of Franklin. **Above Right:** Ch. Franklin's Troublemaker at the National Specialty in 1960, where he won first in both the Veteran's Class and Stud Dog Class. This was Barney Ziessow's hunting and field trial dog and was the sire of Golden Chance of Franklin. **Below:** Ch. Dark Star of Franklin (Ch. Labcroft Master Chips ex Am., Can. Ch. Pitch of Franklin, granddaughter of Ch. Earlsmoor Earl of Arden) is shown here by Mrs. Bernard W. Ziessow for her dad. Dark Star is winning under the famous Hollis Wilson.

Troublemaker of Franklin when he was a baby. Sire of the top yellow bitch, Ch. Golden Chance of Franklin. Mrs. Bernard W. Ziessow, owner, Franklin, Michigan.

Another particularly noteworthy Lab at Franklin is Field and Amateur Field Champion Franklin's Tall Timber, who qualified for both the National and Amateur National trials. This was the very first Michigan-owned and Michigan-bred dog that ever became a field champion. Sired by Field Champion Del Tone Buck from Champion Franklin's Gold Charm (Champion Kinley Comet of Harham ex Champion Sunset Road of Franklin), Tall Timber was amateur-trained and amateur-handled, a source of pride to his owners.

Mr. Ziessow has been a Sporting Dog judge for more than twenty-five years and feels strongly that a show dog should be put together as described in the standard and at the same time should look able to perform his job in the field.

The Ziessows' first yellow Lab, Champion Golden Chance of Franklin, was a Dark Star granddaughter and Troublemaker's daughter. She was purchased by Mrs. Grace Lambert when 13 months old, following her Best of Breed win at Chicago International. Later she went on to win the National Specialty on two occasions and take Best of Opposite Sex there on two others. She was a multiple Group winner with numerous placements as well.

This is one of many Franklin Labs, now with blind masters, that were trained at the Leader Dog School in Rochester, Michigan.

The Ziessows' first yellow Lab, Ch. Golden Chance of Franklin, shown winning Best of Breed at Chicago International from the classes at 13 months.

The first litter at Groveton Kennels, by Lady Tinkerbelle of Groveton ex Ch. Lockerbie's Sandylands Tarquin. Tom and Eileen Ketcham, owners, West Lebanon, New York.

Groveton

Tom and Eileen Ketcham, of West Lebanon, New York, were avid bird hunters who worked over friends' Labradors for several years. They enjoyed these dogs, not only for their retrieving skills but also for their personalities and their "smarts."

When they were able, the Ketchams acquired their first Labrador, Rebel. He was strictly gun dog breeding. He was smart and was a good retriever, but he was a very poor specimen of the breed.

Realizing the latter, the Ketchams studied what they could find in books, at dog shows, and at field trials until they located a bitch they felt would make a suitable foundation for a breeding program. This was Lady Tinkerbelle of Groveton. Groveton, the identification that "Belle" and all of the Ketcham Labs carry, was selected by the Ketchams because it was the name of the village in northern Virginia where they formerly lived. "Belle" was trained for the field, and the Ketchams also practiced dog showing on her. She did win some championship points, but Mrs. Ketcham says, "We were terrible handlers and are still not all that great."

When "Belle" came of age, she was bred to Champion Lockerbie Sandylands Tarquin. That litter was born on April 2nd, 1967 and included Champion Groveton's Copper Buck Shot (chocolate), Groveton's Copper Penny (chocolate), Groveton's Sir Lancelot, Why Cinnamon, and Groveton's Maid Guinevere who was winning Bred-by Exhibitor Classes at Specialties and supported entries up to six months before her un-

timely death in 1974. She went to her grave with eleven points, lacking a major to finish. She was happier having puppies than smiling in the ring. The Ketchams are still looking for another bitch like her, as she passed on grand quality to her puppies.

When Mrs. Ketcham first started showing Champion Groveton's Copper Buck Shot, she was excused from the ring several times by judges because she had "the wrong breed," as chocolates were never seen and barely heard about. Ken Golden finished this good dog later on.

Ch. Groveton's Copper Buck Shot at nine years of age—one of the early champions at Groveton Kennels.

For her second litter, "Belle" was bred to English and American Champion Kimvalley Crispin and produced Groveton's Affable Andora, the Ketchams' very best water retriever. At the same time, "Chessy" was purchased at fifteen months of age; she became Groveton's first champion, Springfield's Cheshire Cheese.

"Chessy" was bred to Champion Shamrock Acres Light Brigade and produced American, Canadian, and Bermudian Champion Groveton's Apollo Moondust and Champion Groveton's Apollo Countdown, so named because the Ketchams were watching the moon shot while whelping the puppies.

Groveton's Copper Penny was bred to Champion Carefree of Keithray, who Mrs. Robert V. Clark, Jr., gave to Mrs. Ketcham in a co-ownership several years later.

These are the bloodlines on which the Ketchams have built their present success, always aiming for a Labrador that not only looks like a Labrador but also has intelligence. They are very proud of their Labs, and justifiably so, for their dogs are honest, willing workers. They have become "narcotics dogs" (working to locate narcotics, I hasten to explain!), working tracking dogs, field dogs, show dogs, and obedience dogs; they herd sheep and cattle; they also, to put it simply, just provide love; and Mrs. Ketcham is especially proud of her activities with the Guiding Eyes, as several of her Labs are doing this work while others are training and participating in the breeding program.

Champion Springfield's Cheshire Cheese (yellow) was the first champion that Eileen Ketcham finished, in 1968. Ch. Groveton's Copper Buck Shot (chocolate) gained his title in 1970. Champion Nahauto Tara (chocolate), Ameri-

Guiding Eyes Millie, by Groveton's Lindys Challenge ex Groveton's Valencia, bred by Mrs. Eileen Ketcham, West Lebanon, New York.

Ch. Springfield's Cheshire Cheese, born October 1966, by Ch. Harris Tweed of Ide (Ch. Sandylands Tweed of Blaircourt ex Cindy Sue of Ide) from Ch. Kimvalley Cinderella (Ch. Sandylands Tandy ex Kimvalley Guildown Cassandra). Bred by Mrs. Robert V. Clark, Jr., Springfield Kennels; owned by Mrs. Eileen Ketcham, Groveton Kennels.

can, Canadian, and Bermudian Champion Groveton's Apollo Moondust (yellow), and Champion Groveton's Apollo Countdown (yellow) finished in 1971. Three more champions were added in 1974: Champion Groveton's Lucky Lindy (black), Champion Groveton's January Jill (yellow), and Champion Groveton's Kid Kolt (black). In 1975 came Champion Groveton's Copper Adventurer (chocolate), who, at 14 months, finished with

four majors from both the Puppy and Bred-by-Exhibitor Classes. For 1976, it was Champion Groveton's Shashane (yellow) and Champion Groveton's Moon Valley Gwen. A black, Champion Groveton's Windjammer, and a yellow, Champion Groveton's Fun n Folly, finished in 1977. In 1979, the black Champion Groveton's To Be or Not To Be joined the list, and the latest addition is another black, Champion Groveton's Velvet Tiger, who finished in 1981. This is certainly an imposing list!

The Labs' playmates at Groveton Kennels, Mrs. Eileen Ketcham, owner.

Ch. Groveton's January Jill, by Ch. Carefree of Keithray ex Grovetons Maid Guenevere. Owned by Mrs. Eileen Ketcham.

Ch. Groveton's Lucky Lindy, by Ch. Groveton's Copper Buck Shot ex Springfield's Cheshire Cheese, also belongs to Eileen Ketcham.

Mrs. Ketcham's Ch. Groveton Copper Adventurer.

These ten-month-old babies grew up to become Am., Can., Bda. Ch. Groveton's Apollo Moondust and Groveton's Apollo Astronaut. By Ch. Shamrock Acres Light Brigade ex Ch. Springfield's Cheshire Cheese. Eileen Ketcham, owner.

Champion Briary Barley at one year. A son of Ch. Lockerbie Brian Boru ex Briary Allegra owned by Hart Lake Labradors, Bob and Kaye Peltonen.

Hart Lake

The Hart Lake Labradors are owned by Bob and Kaye Peltonen and located at McHenry, Illinois. The kennel is named after a lake in Michigan, near where Bob Peltonen grew up.

The first litter of Labs owned by the Peltonens was whelped in 1976 and came about through the encouragement of Kaye Peltonen's family, who had owned the breed since the late 1960s. This litter of blacks and yellows was sired by the black Champion Briary Sure Shot Boru Too, a dog with which the Peltonens were much impressed, and they have had the Briary bloodlines ever since.

In early 1978, Mr. and Mrs. Peltonen purchased Champion Briary Barley as their stud dog. In addition to being Winners Dog at the 1976 Labrador Retriever National Specialty, he

Left to right: Ch. Briary Barley wins the Stud Dog Class with his progeny, Ch. Hart Lake Moon Magic (center) and Hart Lake Bart Maverick. Bob and Kaye Peltonen, owners. Mrs. John Patterson is the judge of this Lab Specialty.

has won the Stud Dog Class at various Specialties and has sired several champions and Working Certificate holders.

At present there are nine Labs in residence at Hart Lake Kennels: three pets; two studs, Champion Briary Barley (by Champion Lockerbie Brian Boru, W.C. ex Briary Allegro) and his son, Hart Lake Bart Maverick, who is out of Spenrock Miranda; and four brood bitches, Champion Hart Lake Moon Magic (a Barley daughter), Spenrock Amanda (Champion Lockerbie Stanwood Granada ex International Champion Spenrock Banner, W.C.), Killingworth's Caviar (Champion Ardmargha So Famous ex Champion Rupert Caviar), and Hart Lake Abby O'Windsong (Champion Briary Brendan of Rainell ex Briary Maeve). Abby is co-owned with Betty Dunlop of Windsong Labradors. Bart Maverick won Best in Sweepstakes at the Miami Valley Labrador Retriever Specialty in May 1981.

Mrs. Peltonen is showing in conformation, but all of the Hart Lake dogs are also worked in the field and have had their novice obedience training.

Hart Lake Abby O'Windsong, by Ch. Briary Brendan of Rainell ex Briary Maeve, is co-owned by Betty Dunlop with Bob and Kaye Peltonen.

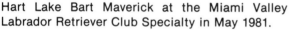

Hart Lake Bart Maverick at the Miami Valley Labrador Retriever Club Specialty in May 1981.

Hart Lake Bart Maverick winning Best in Sweepstakes at the Miami Valley Labrador Retriever Club Specialty.

Highland

Highland Kennel is a very young Labrador Retriever kennel which specializes in chocolate Labs. It is owned by George and Lillian Knobloch of Howell, New Jersey.

The Knoblochs have always been dog lovers, with a special emphasis on Labs ever since they first acquired one some years back, a field-trained black male named Hedidit. Owing to his intelligence and natural working instincts, this dog really sold the Knoblochs on the breed.

This is Hedidit, Lillian Knobloch's first Lab, all field breeding. He is the dog that taught her to love the breed and made her choose to raise Labradors.

In 1974, Mr. and Mrs. Knobloch discovered that Labradors come in chocolate, and they bought their first bitch, a chocolate named Sambeau's Cam. They had a lot of fun with field work, even entering Cam in non-contention Derby for a short while.

Then they discovered the breed ring and decided that by breeding Cam, they would be able to create their own champions. To date, Cam has several pointed progeny, but it is her grandchildren that are fast becoming champions. Soon after acquiring Cam, the Knoblochs rescued her full aunt, Betty Lou, known as "Cindy" to her many friends. In 1977, this bitch was bred to Eileen Ketcham's homebred Champion Grovetons Lucky Lindy. From a litter of six, Champion Highlands Moon in Pisces gained her title; Highlands Ace of Aries has points; Highlands Hershey Kiss, C.D. gained his obedience degree; and with great pride, the

Knoblochs saw Highlands Onyx go into harness for Second Sight, Guide Dog Foundation for the Blind, at Smithtown, New York. The Knoblochs still donate puppies to this foundation and will continue doing so as long as they breed.

Mr. and Mrs. Knobloch note that they were fortunate in starting with dogs that were hip-and eye-clear. They certify all of their dogs to be so, and through selective breeding, they attempt to stay with proven, clear lines.

Specializing in chocolate sometimes becomes a problem, the Knoblochs mention, because it is not easy to find compatible bloodlines in a chocolate dog or a black carrying the chocolate gene for their breeding program. It is their personal belief that a chocolate should not be bred to a yellow because if each carries the gene for the other's color, the result can be liver-pigmented yellows and poorly pigmented chocolates. A chocolate breeding program should be free of the yellow gene, these breeders believe; then chocolate can be bred to chocolate forever with no loss of coat color or eye color.

Sambeau's Cam, chocolate bitch, a line-bred granddaughter of Ch. Lockerbie Sandylands Tarquin, bred by Jean Curtis, owned by Lillian Knobloch, Highland Kennels. This is the Knoblochs' foundation bitch, the mother of pointed get, the grandmother of champions.

A beautiful example of the three Labrador Retriever colors! The black is Ch. Highlands Moon in Pisces. The chocolate is Betty Lou. The yellow is Ch. Cedarhill Goldust. The black and the chocolate are owned by Lillian and George Knobloch, the yellow by B. Fenets. Photo by Vince Serbin.

Highlands Ace of Aries, by Ch. Groveton's Lucky Lindy ex Betty Lou, shown going Winners Dog at New Brunswick Kennel Club, owned and handled by George Knobloch, Jr., for his first points. Mr. John Laytham is judging.

The Knoblochs have had "top chocolate" four times at Labrador Specialties, and their home-bred chocolate, Highlands Egyptian Queen, took Brood Bitch first at the 1981 Labrador Retriever Club's National Specialty in Macon, Ohio, over an entry of twelve lovely bitches and their get. Egyptian Queen's two exciting seventeen-month-old sons, Highlands Bronze Chieftain and his littermate, Highlands Bronze Starbuck, stood with her. These boys, both of which will probably become champions, were sired by a chocolate son of the English import, American Champion Carefree of Keithray, owned by Eileen Ketcham, Groveton Kennels. This Keithray breeding blends beautifully with the Knoblochs' favorite breeding combination, Champion Lockerbie Sandylands Tarquin and his litter-sister, Lockerbie Sandylands Tidy, who were owned by Helen Warwick. The Knoblochs

Highlands Egyptian Queen and her son Highlands Bronze Chieftain pictured taking Open Chocolate firsts at the New Jersey Labrador Retriever Club Specialty in 1981. Breeder-owner handled by George and Lillian Knobloch, Howell, New Jersey.

Highland's Bronze Starbuck taking Winners at Great Barrington 1981. Breeder-owner-handler George W. Knobloch, Jr.

feel that Tarquin and Tidy had the greatest influence on today's American Labrador, and it was this combination that produced Champion Lockerbie Brian Boru who has proved himself an outstanding sire. Unfortunately, Brian did not carry chocolate. So, wanting to add his bloodline in chocolate to their breeding program, Mr. and Mrs. Knobloch recently acquired a line-bred Brian grandson, Ravenwood Highland Sentry, from Kay Fesekas of Washington, sired by her homebred dog, American and Canadian Champion Ravenwood Brigadier, Best of Breed at the 1979 Labrador Retriever Club National Specialty.

Hywater

Being very young as a Labrador kennel, Hywater, owned by Brenda and Bob Matthews of Elmira, New York, is just beginning to enjoy the fruits of its labors with its second generation now making appearances in various parts of the country.

Bob Matthews purchased the foundation bitch, Champion Van Lee's Pot O'Chocolate, W.C., while avidly pursuing the field trial game. She was to be Brenda Matthews' personal companion while Bob continued his trialing. "Pot-C" developed into an exceptional conformation dog, however, and the decision was reached that she should be shown. With her conformation and field breeding, it was felt that she would become an outstanding foundation bitch, which certainly has proved to be the case.

During "Pot-C's" show career, she won multiple Bests of Breed from the Classes and placed in the Sporting Group. Although never campaigned as a Special, her debut as a champion at the Newton Kennel Club was a smashing success. She led a "chocolate sweep" of the show prizes from a large Specials entry, winning the purple and gold. English Champion Lawnwood's Hot Chocolate was Best of Winners and Best of Opposite Sex, with Spenrock's Brown Bess taking Winners Bitch. This rare event became especially significant, Bob Matthews points out, when Hywater's Rufus Brown and Hywater's Peanut Colada, by Champion Lawnwood's Hot Chocolate ex Champion Van Lee's Pot O'Chocolate, swept the Suffolk County Kennel Club event from the Classes, with Winners Dog, Winners Bitch, Best of Breed and Best of Opposite Sex in 1979. Another indication that the chocolates had really arrived!

Champion Van Lee's Pot O'Chocolate is a daughter of American and Mexican Champion Gunfield's Super Charger, W.C. (by Dual Champion Shamrock Acres Super Drive ex Ironwood Two Bits) from Whiskey Creek Chocolate Chip (Field Champion Troublemaker of Audlin II ex Champion Whiskey Creek's Brown Bruina). She is proving herself to be outstanding as a producer, with some very handsome progeny coming into competition. Sired by English and American Champion Lawnwood's Hot Chocolate, she is the dam of Champion Hywater's Rufus Brown, Hywater's Peanut Colada, Hywater's Prince Chocolate, Hywater's Pride O'Whisper Oaks, and Hywater's Toast to

Pattengale, all born in May 1978. She was then bred to Champion Ravenwood Brigadier, and her June 1979 get included Champion Lostacres Hywater Limerick, Canadian Champion Cedarwood's Instant Replay, Hywater's Demi-Tasse, and Hywater's Mandy O'Mine. Her next litter, whelped July 1980, was by Champion Williston Brown-Smith, with five youngsters among those who will be heard from shortly. Nine of "Pot-C's" get are now in competition, and six others, still only babies, from a repeat breeding to Brown-Smith, will be heard from in the future.

Champion Van Lee's Pot O'Chocolate retired in September 1981 and spends her autumns as a gun dog for the master. She has always been, and will remain, "best friend and confidante" to her mistress; and of course, she will always be loved.

Hywater chocolates have had the good fortune to have competed equally with blacks and yellows. Many are used in marsh and in field as gun dogs. Most have become family members owing to the kind dispositions and exceptional intelligence acquired from their sires and dam.

Ch. Lostacres Hywater Limerick, by Ch. Ravenwood Brigadier ex Ch. Van Lee's Pot O'Chocolate, from the Hywater Kennels, Bob and Brenda Matthews, Elmira, New York. Pictured taking Winners at Albany Kennel Club in 1981.

Hywind

Hywind Labradors are a fairly new venture as far as being a kennel is concerned, for although Mrs. Barbara B. Gill of Sherwood, Michigan, has owned and loved the breed for more than twenty-five years, she has done so on a strictly personal basis over the majority of those years.

"Pride of place" currently goes to Champion Donnybrook's Shillelagh, a son of the famous Champion Shamrock Acres Donnybrook, C.D., but hopes are high for the future of an exciting youngster, a puppy of exceptional potential known as Hywind's Yellow W of Windsong. This young fellow is from Champion Brendan of Rainell ex Briary Maeve, and his show career started off well when on his first time out he won the Puppy Class under George Bragaw at Grand Rapids.

These two, along with three brood bitches, including a Winroc Picasso daughter, complete the Hywind Kennels. Plenty of bone and substance, even disposition, and show, field, and obedience promise are emphasized in this kennel's breeding program; and Mrs. Gill also works to preserve the hunting instinct in her Labs, feeling that, as she says, "that's what the critter is all about."

Ch. Donnybrook's Shillelagh en route to the title. Mrs. Barbara B. Gill, owner.

Jollymuff

The kennel name "Jollymuff" was derived from a combination of the names of the owner's first two Labradors, Jolly Old Blackjack, U.D., and Marilyn, U.D., the latter always called "Muffin." Located at Mt. Holly, New Jersey, and owned by Diane B. Jones, Jollymuff Labradors are noted for quality and for prestigious accomplishments.

An informal shot of a lovely young Lab. Hywind's Yellow W of Windsong belongs to Mrs. Barbara B. Gill, Sherwood, Michigan.

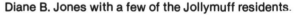

Diane B. Jones with a few of the Jollymuff residents.

Blackjack (1967 - 1978) was well-known in the obedience ring. His scores were high, and he attained his C.D., C.D.X., and U.D. with ease, often placing in the ribbons. Marilyn (1968 - 1980), a yellow bitch sired by English import Champion Kirbyhall Gunsmith, was a very good worker and earned her C.D., C.D.X., and U.D. in nine consecutive shows. She won three first places for her three legs in Novice and the same for her three legs in Open. Utility was a bit more difficult, and she won a first and two seconds. Along the way, she gained three Highest Scoring in Trial awards and managed to whelp two litters between degrees. Marilyn's second litter, which was by Champion Tudor Lincolnshire Poacher, produced a lovely yellow

This is Marilyn, U.D., the first generation of Jollymuff Labradors, a daughter of the imported Ch. Kirbyhall Gunsmith. A very good worker, she earned her C.D., C.D.X., and U.D. in nine consecutive shows. Marilyn was the dam of Ch. Jollymuff Merry Mindy, C.D., W.D., the foundation bitch for Jollymuff Kennels.

bitch who became the foundation bitch for this kennel. Her name is Champion Jollymuff Merry Mindy, C.D., W.C., and she was whelped in 1971. Mindy is the dam of three champions and granddam of many more.

Bred to the noted English import, English and American Champion Sandylands Midas, Mindy produced Champion Jollymuff Question Mark, C.D., W.C., and Champion Jollymuff Honey Pot, C.D., W.C. Bred to Ch. Dickendall's Flip Flop, C.D.X., a Midas son, she produced Champion Jollymuff Little Bull II and Jollymuff Holly D, who in turn produced Champion Jollymuff Chips Ahoy when bred to Sandylands Markwell of Lockerbie.

Ch. Jollymuff Merry Mindy, C.D., W.D. Foundation bitch, second generation, by Ch. Tudor Lincolnshire Poacher ex Marilyn, U.D.

In 1973, Diane Jones purchased a black bitch by Champion Tudor Lincolnshire Poacher. She was Champion Tudor's Renege of Breakwater and when bred to Midas, she produced Champion Jollymuff Bicentennial. After that she was bred to an English import, Champion Lockerbie Stanwood Granada, and produced Champion Jollymuff Salina, who is now co-owned by Diane Jones and Helen Warwick.

Diane B. Jones making a good win with her Ch. Jollymuff Salina.

At about this time, Diane Jones formed a very good friendship with Helen and Jim Warwick, owners of the famed Lockerbie Labradors. Helen Warwick offered a co-ownership in her three-year-old black import, Sandylands Markwell of Lockerbie, which was instantly accepted. Markwell came to live with Diane Jones, and after several months of training, he was entered in a few shows. He finished in a matter of six weekends, taking Best of Breed from the Open Class, several times defeating champions. He went on later in 1978 to win Best of Opposite Sex at the largest National Labrador Specialty ever held, and it is interesting that the only Lab who defeated him that day was his half-sister, English and American Champion Kimvalley Picklewitch, who was also sired by English Champion Sandylands Mark. "Mark," as Markwell is known at home and by his friends, has sired many outstanding litters of black, yellow, and chocolate puppies. By the end of 1981, he had ten champions to his credit, with many more on the way. Gwen Broadley is the breeder of this splendid, well-admired dog.

When Champion Jollymuff Honey Pot, C.D., W.C., was bred to "Mark," the litter contained two exceptional yellow bitches, Champion Jollymuff Orange Blossom and Jollymuff Northwind Crystal; the latter is on the way to her title. Blossom gained most of her points from the Bred-by-Exhibitor Class. She was Best of Breed over champions all three times that she was entered in the Open Class, and she won Bred-by-Exhibitor in the 1981 National Specialty. She was bred last year to Champion Eireannach Black Coachman and has a lovely black daughter, Jollymuff My Amanda, in her owner's kennel. In 1982, Blossom will be bred to Jollymuff's new black English import, Jollymuff Fly Away. "Flyer," with points toward his title, represents the best characteristics resulting from the crossing of the finest English field breeding with the noted Sandylands show breeding of today and yesterday. He will be used on the Jollymuff tightly line-bred bitches, including Sandylands Margie of Lockerbie, who is co-owned by Helen Warwick, with the aim of producing *true* Labradors.

Diane B. Jones of Mt. Holly, New Jersey, on horseback is happily accompanied by a group of the Jollymuff Labs. This is part of the daily routine at Jollymuff.

Killingworth

Killingworth Labrador Retrievers, in the words of their owner, Lorraine Robbenhaar of Washington Depot, Connecticut, have "occupied almost half of my life."

Lorraine Robbenhaar worked at Yale in the late 1950s, during which time everyone seemed to own a Labrador. Since she was working in medical research, she was constantly in touch with veterinarians, and at a certain moment she was offered a black dog puppy who had been given to one of the vets. She promptly bought the puppy, and he became Rolf of Killingworth.

Rolf endeared himself to his human family, but he was not so endearing to other animals and people. He had a certain intractable nature; he hated puppies, cats, and woodchucks; and he had probably the hardest mouth a dog could possess. After weighing his desirable qualities against his faults, it was decided to abandon any thoughts of breeding Rolf and to acquire another Labrador for this purpose.

It was then that Benjy's Wendy of Killingworth was selected, a bitch with Squirrel Run ancestry. The intention had been to breed her to a Lab that was staying with Lorraine, a dog of Shed of Arden bloodlines with other "greats" in his pedigree, who flatly refused to service this bitch. Then the matter was taken out of the owner's hands; Wendy and Rolf got together on their own, with a resulting family of 11 black pups, all of which became lovely pets for their subsequent owners.

Next time around, Wendy was bred to Champion Annwyn's Jack O'Diamonds and produced Champion Killingworth's Judith, who was Winners Bitch at the National Specialty in 1955 under Mrs. Mary Scott of the Bramhope Kennels in England.

Around this same period, Lorraine Robbenhaar leased a bitch named Champion Windrows Samantha, by Champion Sam of Blaircourt from a bitch that went back to Champion Diant Jupiter and Americal Field Trial lines. She, also, was bred to Champion Annwyn's Jack O'Diamonds, who had been imported from Frank Jones in Canada. This produced Killingworth's Snipe who ultimately produced Champion Killingworth's Thunderson, one of the breed's great sires. Of Champion Annwyn's Jack O'Diamonds, Mrs. Robbenhaar says:

> I had a number of dogs at that time, but none were what I really wanted

Ch. Annwyn's Jack O'Diamonds, the famous "Nobby" that was so influential in the establishment of the Killingworth Labradors, snapped at 12 years of age. A son of Ch. Annwyn's Shedrow ex Ch. Lisnamallard Tarantella from Frank Evan Jones' famous kennel.

until I met "Nobby" (Jack O'Diamonds). What a sweet old dog he was. Loved water, loved his family, loved life, and most of all loved to retrieve. I determined to breed a line of "Nobbys," and I realized that I needed a good bitch line from him in order to do so. Samantha, unfortunately, had only one litter, as did Thunder's dam, Dinah (Killingworth Snipe). But from these matings in the 60s and from these two bitches I have continued to produce many of the original characteristics of "Nobby." I see them in the eyes of all my Killingworth dogs that I have that are descended from Thunder through Samantha and Dinah.

Champion Killingworth's Thunderson was whelped July 27th, 1970. He was a beautiful puppy and a remarkable puppy in that he never did anything wrong. "Thunder" was another "Nobby" so far as temperament was concerned. "Thunder's" great loves, from puppyhood on, were the swimming pool and the three Robbenhaar children. The youngest of these, John, was three years old when "Thunder" was born, so they grew up together, neither ever causing five minutes of trouble and both endearing themselves to everyone.

Ch. Killingworth's Thunderson, a most outstanding Lab dog owned by Killingworth Kennels, Lorraine Robbenhaar, Washington Depot, Connecticut.

Ch. Killingworth's Thunderson at a field trial. "Thunder" was an excellent field dog.

As Thunderson was growing, so was the Killingworth Kennel and its reputation. Mrs. Robbenhaar also owned a lovely black male, "Thunder's" uncle and Snipe's brother, Killingworth's Black Brant. This dog loved to hunt, work and retrieve. He had 13 points toward his title, two majors and three reserves, but never finished as he hated showing and refused to do so for his owner or anyone else. He did, however, produce some extremely worthwhile puppies, among them the dam (bred to Harrowby Penny) who produced Dual Champion Phantonshire Howar.

Thunderson completed his title at 14 months of age and then decided that he did not enjoy showing; he lacked that ring presence necessary to do well in Specials. But since Mrs. Robbenhaar has never particularly wished to campaign a dog past the title, she did not really care.

"Thunder" left a legacy of 25 American champions, many obedience degree holders, and a large number of progeny that have gone to other breeders to incorporate into their bloodlines. A few of these should be mentioned because of the historical impact they have had on some of the newer kennels.

Champion Augustin Degregorio was one of four champions from the same dam by Thunderson. He was Number Six Labrador in the United States in 1977.

Champion Ludlowe's Topaz was a litter-sister to the above and has been the foundation bitch for Ludlowe and Croysdale Kennels, two of the newer small hobby kennels.

Champion Killingworth's Valiant Lady and Champion Rupert Caviar provided the foundation for Winterset Labs. Dorothy Howe, who was an extremely well-known Lab breeder and the author of *This is the Labrador Retriever*, bred two bitches to "Thunder" shortly before she became incapacitated, and Caviar was from one of these.

Champion Winrock's Thunderstruck was a two-time winner of Specialty Shows and a bitch that was widely admired. She was a "Thunder" daughter and was bred and owned by Marion Foote.

Forecast Kennels bred many bitches to Thunderson, and their owner, Bette Curtis, had three champions from these litters: Champion Forecast Dodge City, Champion Forecast Thunderking, and Champion Forecast Cascade.

Mrs. Robbenhaar's favorite son of Thunderson, she tells us, is Champion Chucklebrook Perrybingel, U.D., who was bred by Diane Pilbin from Champion Spenrock's Bohemia Champagne (a Banner daughter) and was sold to Marilyn Miller and Pat Perriello. Perry finished his bench championship in between field trials. He was entirely amateur-handled and has been run in licensed and sanctioned trials with placings. He also finished his U.D. He is an excellent marker and a beloved pet—all in all the epitome of the dual-purpose dog.

Progeny of Thunder have had many, many placings at Specialties, including Winners Bitch and Best of Winners at three Regional Specialties and Best of Winners and Best of Opposite

Killingworth The Black Brant is the grandsire of Dual Ch. Warpath Macho. Mrs. Lorraine Robbenhaar, owner.

Above: Ch. Augustin Degregorio, owned by Lorraine Robbenhaar. **Below:** Am., Can. Ch. Forecast Dodge City. By Ch. Killingworth Thunderson ex Am., Can. Ch. Naiad's Promising Forecast (a grandson of Mallow's Fanfare), owned by Elizabeth K. Curtis and Ann and Samuel Cappellina, Forecast Labradors, Litchfield, Connecticut.

Sex at the National. Thunder was a Top Producer in 1977 and 1978.

As so often in life, Killingworth seems to be divided into eras. There was the time pre-Thunderson, about ten years when Mrs. Robbenhaar searched and found what she wanted. Then there was what she considered to be her best time, with "Thunder." Now, since his death in June 1980, it is post-Thunderson. She has been to England and imported a number of dogs, with the intention of following what has been successful in the past, combining these Labs with her Killingworth dogs descended through Annwyn's Jack O'Diamonds, his daughter Samantha, her daughter Snipe, and her son Thunder. She has imported Ballyduff, Kypros, Follytower, Bradking, and Novacroft breeding, and also has Mansergh and Sandylands.

It is Mrs. Robbenhaar's intention to attempt to breed and produce a good-looking Labrador that will work. She has always bred for soundness, and this will continue to be the case. She takes great pleasure in her show wins, but like a true dog lover, she takes even greater pleasure in the treasured family pets that she has sold. She would also very much like to own a field trial dog descended from Killingworth and has bred a black daughter of Thunder's from Super Chief bloodlines to her young chocolate Champion Clemson of Killingworth.

As this is written, Mrs. Robbenhaar has a lovely trio of stud dogs, a source of tremendous pride. They are Champion Shadowlands Schuyler, a yellow eight-year-old son of Thunder; Killingworth Sum O'Thunder, a year and a half old, Thunder's last son; and a chocolate, Champion Clemson of Killingworth.

Ch. Killingworth's Thunderson playing ball with a granddaughter. Mrs. Lorraine Robbenhaar, Killingworth Labs.

Ch. Clemsen of Killingworth with a friend.

Mrs. Diana Beckett handling Ch. Springfield's Rule Brittania for Mrs. Robert V. Clark, Jr.

Kimvalley

The Kimvalley Labradors, owned by Diana and Don Beckett, were started in England during 1957. The Becketts' eldest son had an imaginary dog called "Mick" who was so real to the youngster that people were not permitted to sit next to any of the family until "Mick" had been lifted up. The Becketts decided that the time had come for their son to have a *real* dog. This was by no means Mrs. Beckett's first dog. She had owned a Smooth Fox Terrier bitch and an English Cocker prior to World War II; and as a thirteen-year-old, she had owned a black Labrador called "Sweepy," but at that time she had not yet become interested at all in showing or breeding.

The Becketts selected a black bitch called Kimvalley Maid, and as her name had not been registered as a prefix, they adopted "Kimvalley" for their own kennel and registered it as such. Kim was a lovely Lab and did a good deal of winning for the Becketts, including a first at Crufts which was only her third show.

Kimvalley Guildown Cassandra, Kimvalley Maid and Kimvalley Imp, the three earliest Labs at Kimvalley, owned by Diana and Don Beckett. Cassandra, on the left, is the dam of Eng., Am. Ch. Kimvalley Crispin and Eng. Ch. Kimvalley Crofter. Maid, in the center, is the original Kimvalley Lab, from whose name the Kimvalley prefix was selected.

Don Beckett decided he would like to own a yellow Lab, and so the next purchase was a bitch of this color from Miss Tompkins of Guildown Kennel fame. The bitch was called Kimvalley Guildown Cassandra, and she is now in the background of a great number of pedigrees, both in England and in the United States, through her children. Her son, English and American Champion Kimvalley Crispin, was the Becketts' first homebred English champion, shortly thereafter followed by his brother, English Champion Kimvalley Crofter. Her daughter, American

Eng. Ch. Kimvalley Crofter, litter-brother to Crispin, bred and owned by Don and Diana Beckett, Kimvalley Kennels.

Champion Kimvalley Deborah, was the Becketts' first American export; and although she only had one litter, she is behind numerous American Labs—seven of the litter finished, and these included such famous dogs as Champion Goldsboro Kim and Champion Goldsboro Tweed.

Three English champions were bred at Kimvalley, and as the co-owner of English and American Champion Kimvalley Picklewitch, Diana Beckett finished another one.

Diana Beckett became an open show judge of Labs in England in 1968. She judged Labs twice in America before coming here to live in 1973.

Mrs. Beckett came to the United States to manage Springfield Kennels, one of the largest Lab kennels in America, and has co-owned many famous dogs with Mrs. Clark. Some of the best known of those that she bred are American Champion Kimvalley Warrenton and American Champion Kimvalley Swingin Lizzie.

Eng., Am. Ch. Kimvalley Crispin, first homebred champion bred by Diana and Don Beckett.

In January of 1982, Don and Diane Beckett returned to England to live; there they are going to try their hand at a new career, that of being grandparents. With them they took a beautiful bitch, American Champion Kimvalley Oakstone Seamist, to enable them to carry on with their old career, that of being Labrador breeders. They look forward to showing and judging again.

During their eight years in the United States, Diana Beckett made up sixteen champions. She left behind some outstanding stock to carry on the Kimvalley name. We hope that she will come to visit frequently, as she made a host of friends here in our dog show world!

Labradese

Labradese Labradors came into existence shortly after their owners, Dr. and Mrs. William A. Hines of Kittredge, Colorado, spoke those famous last words: "We're through with dogs." This state of mind had been brought about by misfortunes with three successive dogs of another breed: one was hit by a car after accidentally slipping out the front door and thinking it great sport for the Hines to try to catch him; the second died of a malignancy at six years of age; and the third one had a temperament problem. Since their children were maturing rapidly, the Hines felt that they didn't need any more dogs and preferred to avoid future heartaches.

Three years later, their future daughter-in-law got Kirstyn, a yellow bitch Lab puppy, for the birthday of the Hines' eldest son. The Hines' daughter and youngest son also fell in love with the puppy, and although Mrs. Hines did not really want her, since she had big plans for that summer which did not include training a puppy, yet, when the puppy became sick with coccidiosis, her heart melted and the youngster stayed. Bill, the eldest son, planned to take her to college with him; and the Hines found that the decision to have no more dogs had been too hasty. The youngest son, who would be at home for several years more, was heartbroken at the puppy's leaving with his brother. So a black Lab puppy was added to the household and given the impressive name of Hines' Royal George.

Hines' Golden Kirstyn (right) with her son by Sandy Andy, Hines' Roaf Beest, litter-brother to Labradese Princess SaraSu.

Kirstyn was the daughter of American Field champion Columbine Loran and The Duchess of Crestmoor. She was extremely intelligent and very sound. George was a Ralston Valley dog with strong Shamrock Acres and Avandale lines, possibly the prettiest dog the Hines have owned. Kirstyn was bred to Sandy Andy, son of an Irish import, Princeps Regni ex Miss Deb of Pleasant Hill (a California kennel) who belonged to a school friend of young Bill Hines. It was an unscientific breeding, with no line-breeding for guidance, but it resulted in a good-looking litter, from which Dr. and Mrs. Hines kept Labradese Princess SaraSu to be bred to their George. Unfortunately, George developed a problem necessitating his being castrated, so plans had to be

Some of the Labradese Labradors of all ages owned by Dr. and Mrs. William A. Hines, Labradese Kennels.

116

changed. A nice dog in their area was selected, and SaraSu had a litter that was line-bred, although not closely. Two dark yellow bitches were kept from that litter, and the Hines immediately started looking for a suitable sire for SaraSu's next family. He appeared in the form of Shamrock Acres Gentle Ben, owned by Don and Leslie Cheyne of Arvado, Colorado. (Although he was very young, Ben was already on the way to his championship.) That litter produced 11 puppies who, although they possessed show quality, had little opportunity to make their presence felt in the ring. Soon after SaraSu's puppies were born, the Cheynes had a litter by Ben's son, Longbow's Arbor Acres Andy ex Shamrock Acres Wayward Angel, a Light Brigade daughter. The Hines purchased a male from that litter specifically to breed to their Ben-SaraSu daughter, Labradese Bluebelle Bouquet. This dog puppy grew up to become Champion Labradese Lancelot O'Longbow, the Hines' pride and joy. To date, these two Labs have produced five champions, with more on the way and others who are equally handsome but not being shown. Those that have finished are Champion Labradese Tylance Brigade, Champion Labradese O'Sunshine, Champion Labradese Misty Morn, Champion Labradese Sundance Kid, and Champion Labradese Came The Dawn. Dr. and Mrs. Hines also owned a litter-sister to Bluebelle who was bred to Lancelot, but since they were not pleased with what this bitch produced, they had her spayed. Lance and Blue-belle had three litters, with only three puppies in the last one. Bluebelle seemed to object to being bred to her kennel-mate, so it was finally decided to try her with another stud, for which a Shamrock Acres line-bred dog was selected: American, Canadian, Mexican, and 1978 World and International Champion Franklin's Golden Mandigo, C.A., American W.C. Again only three puppies resulted, but at age six months, they looked very promising and beautiful. The Hines are expecting Bluebelle to become a Top Producer and feel that two or three of her daughters, Labradese Sweet Spice, Champion Labradese Misty Morn, and Champion Labradese O'Sunshine, will do likewise.

Spice was bred to her uncle, Labradese Singer, who is Bluebelle's litter-brother. The puppies from this litter matured into excellent dogs, and Bearfoot Gypsy is being shown. They all seem to be English type. Spice next was bred to the

Ch. Labradese Lancelot O'Longbow, by Longbow Arbor Acres Andy ex Shamrock Acres Wayward Angel, handled here by Stuart Rogell for Dr. and Mrs. Wm. A. Hines.

Labradese Misty Morn, by Ch. Labradese Lancelot O'Longbow ex Labradese Bluebelle Bouquet, a homebred bitch from the Labradese Kennels.

Labradese Buck Bluebeard and Labradese Spice's Black Ben, by Ch. Ham's Surfire Winston ex Labradese Sweet Spice.

Hines' Champion Ham's Surfire Winston who they had obtained from Robert and Thelma Ham of Hi-Tide Kennels in Illinois. He is a double American and Canadian Champion Shamrock Acres Sonic Boom grandson and a son of Champion Shamrock Acres Dark Cloud ex Champion Ham's Queen of Spades. Three of these offspring, at eleven months of age, are doing well in the show ring: Labradese Black Pearl, Labradese Buck Bluebeard, and Labradese Spice's Black Ben. Spice has recently had a litter of seven by American and Canadian Field Champion Trieven Thunderhead, a Top Producer of Field Champions.

Mrs. Judith Fellton here is awarding Best of Winners to Labradese Tylance Brigade (Ch. Labradese Lancelot O'Longbow ex Labradese Bluebelle Bouquet).

LABRADESE BLUEBELLE BOUQUET, his mother, 1st in Bred-by-Exhibitor. Girls breeder-owner handled.

LABRADESE TYLANCE BRIGADE (Ch.Iabradese Lancelot O' Longbow X Labradese Blue-belle Bouquet)
BOW by Judge Judith Felton
Handled by Stuart Rogell
Owned by Dr. Dick L. Brown
Bred by Dr. & Mrs. Wm.A.Hines

and his litter sister, LABRADESE MISTY MORN 3rd in Open Bitches

Ch. Ramblins' Seven and Seven, W.C., owned by Mrs. Billie Hines and Laurell Jenny, handled by Karen Case. Yellow male, whelped January 1976.

Misty was bred to Champion McGeorge's Baron Zena of Dija, W.C., who combined the Hines' Shamrock Acres lines and the Irish Princeps Regni ex Miss Deb of Pleasant Hill lines. Labradese Sweet Georga Black and Labradese Bianco Buck are from that breeding. She has recently been bred again, this time to her kennel-mate, Champion Ramblin's Seven and Seven, W.C., co-owned by the Hines with Laurell Jenny of Mandigo Retrievers.

Sunny had an exceptional litter by Champion Sunnybrook Acres Solitaire, whose background is half Shamrock Acres and half English bloodlines.

The Hines kept a Mandigo-Bluebelle yellow bitch puppy and at that same time acquired a black dog puppy from Champion Labradese O'Sunshine, who is owned by Jim and Karen Case of Casador Labs and who was sired by Champion Sunnybrook Acres Solitaire. These are Labradese Ingot O'Gold and Labradese Matador of Casador. They are a striking combination at five and six months of age. Mrs. Hines remarks that their third and fourth generation Labradese litters look even better than their second generation ones did. Other lines which should be compatible with their own and which at the same time would carefully preserve the good qualities already being maintained are now being considered for future breedings.

From SaraSu's first litter a bitch was kept, Labradese Valiant Doll, C.D., and another was placed with a co-owner. These sisters were line-bred, although not closely, on the field trial side of the pedigree. The puppies were good-looking, but Mrs. Hines tells us that the most outstanding thing about them was their color, ranging from an apricot color to one nearly as dark as an Irish Setter. Later, the Hines regretted not keeping one of the dark red puppies, but when one of the bitches was bred to Lancelot in 1980, this time the darkest bitch was kept. Her half-sister was bred to the Hines' Champion Ramblin's Seven and Seven, and they plan to keep a male from that litter in an effort to develop a line of Labs of this rarely seen color. It is hoped that a breeding of Labradese Autumn's Glow, Lancelot's daughter, to Cisco's son will produce good type as well as the dark reddish color because both Lancelot and Cisco are strongly Shamrock Acres line-bred. This is a challenge that intrigues Dr. and Mrs. Hines.

Although they are pleased with the progress they have made, Dr. and Mrs. Hines are still striving for perfection, as are all dedicated breeders. They feel that a Lab should be capable of good performance in the field as well as be a beautiful dog to look at; and they are combining both top field and top show bloodlines in their program, with the dream of someday becoming the breeders of a dual champion or, perhaps, several dual champions—quite a long way from the "no more dogs" state of mind!

Labradese Autumn's Glow and Labradese Spice's Black Ben are owned by Dr. and Mrs. Wm. A. Hines. Autumn Glow is an example of the attractive fox-red color which the Hines are hoping to establish in show type.

Can you stand it *not* to own a baby Lab? This one belongs to Lobuff Kennels, Jerry and Lisa Weiss.

Lobuff

Lobuff Labradors belong to Jerry H. Weiss and Lisa E. Weiss of Huntington, New York. Their first Lab, the breed with which Jerry's wife had grown up (Jerry himself had owned Collies as a youngster), was acquired in 1960.

The first dog was Lobo of Logeros, and he was followed a couple of years later by Goldfish of Logeros, known as "Buffy." Logeros was the kennel of Anne N. Carpenter, a noted German Shepherd breeder and judge, as well as a Lab breeder. Mrs. Carpenter did a lot of field training; her Labs have good field strains behind them as well as a lot of Mrs. Curtis S. Read's Chidley dogs.

With the help of Mrs. Carpenter and Mrs. Read, the Weiss family started showing these dogs. Mrs. Carpenter always had a pup around that Lisa and her four sisters could take to the shows, which helped get their interest underway by giving them experience in the show ring. They, of course, also showed their own two.

Unfortunately, "Buffy" and Lobo were killed in an accident. It was in their honor that the kennel prefix "Lobuff" was coined to carry on their memory. By this time Lisa's sister, Patti, had acquired and was showing a Newfoundland. But Jerry and Lisa "had to have a Lab."

The week after the accident in which "Buffy" and Lobo were killed, Jerry and Lisa received a telephone message from the Metz family, close friends and owners of the Waldschloss Kennels, so famous for superb Sporting dogs of several different breeds. The message was, "Your new puppy is ready. Come and get him." So Jerry and Lisa went to New City and awaiting them there was a little yellow pup sired by Champion Lewisfield Gunslinger, the 1969 Specialty winner. This became Champion Gunslinger's Tawny Boy.

Ch. Gunslinger's Tawny Boy, born October 1969, bred by Anna Metz, owned by Jerry H. Weiss, Lobuff Kennels, Huntington, New York. This yellow dog was sired by Ch. Lewisfield Gun Slinger ex Littlemore Rose of Traile.

Soon after that, Jerry and Lisa acquired their black foundation bitch from Janet Churchill of Spenrock Kennels. This bitch was future Champion Spenrock's Cognac, a daughter of the top-winning Champion Spenrock Banner by Bill Metz's Champion Lockerbie Goldentone Jensen, the latter imported by Mrs. Warwick. Tawny and Cognac produced the first of the Weiss homebred champions, Champion Lobuff's Dandy Lion. Both Tawny and Dandy have won many Best of Breed awards, and Tawny and Cognac have produced some outstanding Labs, including Group and Specialty Sweepstakes winners. At 13 years of age, Tawny and Cognac are still the busiest mischief-makers among the Labs at Lobuff!

Banner's sister, Tequila Sunrise, or "Tiki" as she is called, did some nice winning as a young bitch, gaining points and going on to Best of Breed from the Puppy Class over Specials. She has won the breed several times since starting out as a Special herself and was Best of Opposite Sex at Westminster 1982. She has also taken time out for a beautiful litter by Champion Mardas Brandleshome Sam's Song which will be in the ring during 1982.

There have been some lovely new additions at Lobuff recently. A young black dog, Mardas Grand Marquis, has come from Mr. and Mrs. Hepper's kennel in England; he is a son of Show Champion Martin of Mardas (Champion Ballyduff Marketeer ex Mardas Vivette) from Mardas Moonglow (Mardas Brandleshome Sam's Song ex Mardas Mardi Gras). Spenrock Tempest, a handsome chocolate bitch by Champion Lawnwood's Hot Chocolate ex Spenrock Citation, has come to them from Janet Churchill's in Maryland, as has Champion Swift of Ballyduff and Spenrock.

Lisa Weiss with Ch. Spenrock's Cognac, by Ch. Lockerbie's Goldentone Jensen ex Ch. Spenrock's Banner. Lobuff Labradors.

Champion Spenrock Heatheredge Mariner (imported and owned by Janet Churchill) and Champion Spenrock's Cognac produced Champion Lobuff's Seafaring Banner and Champion Lobuff's Tequila Sunrise. Banner was a Labrador Retriever Club of Potomac Specialty Sweepstakes winner as a young dog, as well as a Group winning Special when fully mature. In addition to his many promising show prospect progeny, Banner is being used as a stud dog for the Guide Dog Foundation for the Blind, which primarily uses Labs for this work.

Ch. Lobuff's Tequila Sunrise (by Ch. Spenrock Heatheredge Mariner ex Ch. Spenrock's Cognac), Best of Opposite Sex at Westminster 1982, belongs to Jerry and Lisa Weiss.

Ch. Lockerbie Blackfella, the first homebred champion from Mrs. James Warwick's Lockerbie Labradors, is a dog whose strong influence on the breed is still felt today, nearly 30 years after his birth. Sired by Ballyduff Treesholme Terryboy ex Am. Ch. Ballyduff Candy, the imported foundation bitch at Lockerbie by Dual Ch. Staindrop Saighdear from Ballyduff Venus.

Lockerbie

There is no more famous or respected prefix in all Labrador history than Lockerbie, made so by the enthusiasm, talents, and efforts of Mr. and Mrs. James Warwick of Briarcliff Manor, New York.

The Warwicks grew up with dogs that were a far cry from retrievers. Helen Warwick had German Shepherds; and James had various terriers and, on his station in the Australian outback in Queensland, many sheepdogs. One summer in her early teens, Helen Warwick visited in England with her uncle, who owned a testy old bronze curly-coated Retriever and a lovely flat-coated bitch. These old buddies were his pride and joy, and annually he would enjoy grouse shooting with them in Scotland during August. Had she been able to accompany him, Mrs. Warwick feels sure she would have learned much about retrievers at work, and she also would have seen many Labradors! As it was, the Warwicks saw their first Labrador in 1947. He was a double grandson of Champion Raffles of Earlsmoor, imported by Dr. Samuel Milbank, a great Lab enthusiast who later became a good friend and mentor to the Warwicks.

An introduction to Mrs. Curtis Read, owner of the Chidley Kennel located on Long Island, gave the Warwicks the fortunate opportunity to learn about the breed. Mrs. Warwick comments, "If it had not been for Mrs. Read's criticism, warranted and accepted, I doubt that we would have made the progress we did." The Warwicks' first bitch came from Mrs. Read's kennel and became their first champion. She was Champion Chidley Hocus Pocus, by a well-known import of the day, Champion Zelstone Duke.

In 1950, the Warwicks asked Harry Pound, a veteran Terrier man who came to this country with the famous professional handler and later respected all-breed judge Percy Roberts, if he knew anyone in the old country from whom they might purchase a good bitch. He said he knew "just the man" and sent off a letter. Weeks passed. Then one day up the road came Harry, waving a letter he had received in reply. It rambled on for several pages about the old days, and at the end were the hoped-for words "I think I have the bitch for you." A photo was enclosed, and it was that of a yellow, Ballyduff Candy, with two reserve Challenge Certificates to her credit and "a lineage equal to that of the old Queen." The letter was from H.S. Lloyd of Ware Cocker Spaniel fame, who subsequently came over and judged a Labrador Specialty here. Shortly after Lloyd wrote this letter, he brought to the United States three Ballyduff Labs from Dr. Acheson: Treeshome Terryboy, Ballyduff Reilly, and the bitch Candy. The two dogs went to Mrs. S. Hallock du Pont of Squirrel Run Kennels in Delaware, who had already some excellent Labradors chosen by Percy Roberts. (He also handled them and many of her English Cockers from Ware Kennels.) The Warwicks were at the docks to meet Lloyd's ship, and down the gangplank came Candy, attached to a chain big enough to moor the huge liner on which she had been travelling.

Soon afterwards, the Warwicks became friends with Mrs. du Pont and chose Terryboy as the mate for Candy. This combination was used for six litters and set the Warwicks on the road to a sound and happy breeding program. From it came the Warwicks' first homebred champion, the great Champion Lockerbie Blackfella whose influence is still felt today, and at least ten other Labs who completed their titles in the show ring.

A few other imports followed over the years. They included Champion Lockerbie Golden-tone Jensen, a wonderful dog who dominated the breed as a producer for a decade or more; Sandylands Tidy, the dam of Champion Lockerbie Kismet, Number One Labrador of 1967; and Sandylands Tarquin, a highly influential dog in Labrador progress in the United States.

It was through these Sandylands lines that Champion Lockerbie Kismet and Champion Lockerbie Brian Boru were produced, some of the Warwicks' "best efforts and the nucleus of many kennels today, including Mrs. Marjorie Brainard's Briary prefix in California." Mrs.

Above: Ch. Lockerbie Sandylands Tarquin was an important dog in the history of Lockerbie Kennels. Imported from Mrs. Gwen Broadley, this fine dog was a son of Ch. Sandylands Tweed of Blaircourt (Ch. Ruler of Blaircourt ex Ch. Tessa of Blaircourt) from Sandylands Shadow (Ch. Sam of Blaircourt ex a daughter of Ch. Peppleton Lieutenant and Ch. Diant Juliet). His influence on the breed in the United States has been tremendous. **Below:** One of the greats in Labrador history, Am. Ch. Lockerbie Kismet, shown winning Best of Breed at Westchester in 1966. Courtesy of Frank Jones who was a tremendous admirer of this dog and is here making the Westchester award.

Brainard purchased Brian Boru at the age of four months, along with a Tarquin daughter who grew up to become Champion Lockerbie Shillegah. To quote Mrs. Warwick, Mrs. Brainard has been "changing the face of Labradors in California with an innate eye and skill." Brian is gone now, but he left, as of early 1982, 59 champion sons and daughters who continue to maintain the proper breed type and character. Brian Boru's grandson, Champion Briary Bellboy of Winsong, was Number One Labrador in early 1982, while a granddaughter won Winners Bitch at Westminster 1982, representing the breed at its best.

Ch. Lockerbie Kismet, Number One Labrador Retriever of 1967, at the Labrador Retriever Club Specialty Show that year. Mrs. James Warwick, owner, Lockerbie Kennels, Briarcliff Manor, New York.

Both Mr. and Mrs. Warwick started to judge in 1959, and they have officiated many times in England and on the Continent. Until recently, Mr. Warwick was Show Chairman for the parent club, and he was also the parent club's faithful A.K.C. Delegate for twenty years. The Warwicks have always believed that breeding and judging should not be taken lightly. Show wins are fine if taken in proportion, but the Warwicks' goal has always been to *breed* the best, whether or not the dog would ever be shown. The type and quality of Lockerbie Labs, and the influence they have had on breed progress over the past several decades to the present day, are impressive indeed!

Sharon Simon with Glenarem Crusader owned by Denny and Sue Simon, Lyric Labradors, Westfield, New Jersey.

Lyric

Lyric Labradors, at Westfield, New Jersey, got their start in 1973 (as "Devonwood"), when Denny and Sue Simon purchased their first pup from Harvey and Judy Sanderson, prefix "Caballero." Soon after that, the Simons were fortunate enough to acquire their first bitch, an English import, from Glenarem Kennels.

Today, Lyric Labradors can look back on an active, diverse, and interesting period. During this time, the Simons have bred and finished several champions, and they are proud of the number of dogs that they have sent to the Seeing Eye School. Their two latest English imports are

The first Seeing Eye Labrador from Lyric Kennels, "Sharon" is a daughter of Ch. Springfield's Apricot Whip and went to The Seeing Eye from Dennis and Sue Simon.

Sharon and Jennifer Simon with Ch. Follytower Glenaren Dusky Debutante owned by Dennis and Sue Simon.

a black bitch named Marketlane Superior and a yellow dog named Glenarem Crusader.

Unfortunately, the years have not all been bright. There were some somber moments when one of Lyric's original bitches produced a champion who later was diagnosed as suffering from P.R.A. But the good times have made up for the less happy ones.

As they continue to enjoy their Labradors, the Simons strive to breed healthy, sound Labs that not only look good in the show ring but also can do a good job, whether working in the field or leading a blind person.

A recent English import at Lyric Kennels, the black dog Marketlane Superior.

Mandigo

Mandigo Kennels have recently moved to West Bountiful, Utah, where Laurell Jenny and her husband John are continuing to carry on the high standard of quality for which these Labs are famous. Gene Hand, himself a Golden and Lab breeder, is the trainer here, and he gives tremendous credit to Mrs. Jenny for the outstanding success of these dogs.

The Jennys acquired their first show Labrador bitch, in 1971, from Nancy Chargo of Banner Labradors; then they decided that they very much wanted a good male. Mrs. Chargo referred them to Mrs. Madge Ziessow of Franklin Kennels in Michigan, which Mrs. Jenny describes as "probably the luckiest thing that ever happened to our kennels."

Am., Can., Mex. 1978 World and Int. Ch. Franklin's Golden Mandigo, C.D., W.C., A.W.C. Owned by John and Laurell Jenny, West Bountiful, Utah.

From Mrs. Ziessow, the Jennys purchased a yellow male puppy who later became American, Canadian, Mexican, and 1978 World and International Champion Franklin's Golden Mandigo, C.D., American W.C. Mandigo is now a multiple Group placer in the three countries and the most titled Labrador in the United States. He is a two-time Outstanding Producer, according to the *Kennel Review* system, in 1978 and again in 1981. Mandigo himself is from a breeding sired by Champion Shamrock Acres Light Brigade, the sire of 93 champions, and out of Champion Franklin's Tally of Burywood, the dam of 16 champions. Mandigo's four grandparents are Champion Shamrock Acres Casey Jones, C.D., Champion Whygin Busy Belinda, Champion Franklin's Sun Star, and Champion Franklin's Spring Dawn.

Am., Can., Mex. 1978 World and Int. Ch. Franklin's Golden Mandigo, C.D., Am. W.C., doing what comes naturally to his breed—bringing in the bird. Mandigo is head man at the kennels of John and Laurell Jenny.

Am., Can. Ch. Concho's Chivas Regal, W.C., by Ch. Shamrock Acres Donnybrook C.D. ex Ch. Concho's Black Molasses, is the dam of ten champions. Mandigo Labradors, owners, John and Laurell E. Jenny.

At nine years of age, Mandigo won Best of Breed from the Veteran's Class at the Houston Labrador Retriever Club Specialty.

In 1975, the Jennys acquired American and Canadian Champion Concho's Chivas Regal, W.C., who became an outstanding producer in 1978 and the Top Producing Labrador Bitch in the United States for 1978. A daughter of Champion Shamrock Acres Donnybrook, C.D. ex Champion Concho's Black Molasses, she was bred to Mandigo with results which included American, Mexican, and 1978 World Champion Mandigo's Annabel Lee, C.D.X., W.C., a top-winning bitch of the past several years, which the Jennys kept for themselves; other littermates were Champion Ramblin's Tequila 'n' Lemon, Champion Mandigo's Simerdown Destiny, C.D., and Champion Mandigo's Golden Nugget, W.C.

The entire Mandigo Kennel is based on American, Canadian, Mexican, and 1978 World and International Champion Franklin's Golden Mandigo, C.D., American W.C., and the two bitches the Jennys acquired as adults, American and Canadian Champion Concho's Chivas Regal, W.C. and Wildways Penny Ante, W.C.

Am., Can. Ch. Banner's Cole Younger, Am. and Can. C.D., by Ch. Killingworth's Thunderson, W.C. (grandson of Eng. and Am. Ch. Sandylands Midas and Am., Can. Ch. Annwyn's Jack O'Diamonds) ex Am., Can. Ch. Hillsboro Charisma of Oz (Ch. Baroke's Yellow Jacket ex Ch. Goldsboro Toto of Oz) won Best of Breed at the Houston Specialty in 1980, Best of Breed Canadian National Lab Specialty in 1978, and Best of Winners at Maimi Valley Specialty in 1978. John and Laurell Jenny, owners.

Later another male was purchased from Mrs. Nancy Chargo, who has also done well by the Jennys. This one has become American and Canadian Champion Banner's Cole Younger, American and Canadian C.D. and W.C. Cole is a multiple Specialty winner in both Canada and the United States.

Both Annabel Lee and Champion Mandigo's Windriver Amber, C.D. are Specialty winners, and both are sired by Mandigo.

The Jennys have been breeding Labs since 1975, during which time they have produced fifteen champions—certainly an exciting record.

Am., Mex. 1978 World Ch. Mandigo Annabel Lee, C.D.X., W.C., an outstanding bitch from the Jennys' Mandigo Kennels.

This head study is of Nancy Scholz's imported foundation bitch, Threepear's Nightshade, C.D.

Threepear's Nightshade, C.D., foundation bitch at Manora Kennels, imported from England by Nancy M. Scholz, Ballston Lake, New York.

Manora

Manora Labradors, bred at a small kennel located at Ballston Lake, New York, are owned by a most enthusiastic fancier, Nancy M. Scholz.

The kennel was founded late in the 1970s with the purchase of a lovely black bitch, imported for this purpose from England. Her background combines English field trial champions with the finest English bench champions, and she has produced some lovely sound puppies which are doing well in the United States. This bitch is Threepears Nightshade, C.D., and despite time out for maternal duties, she is within a point of her A.K.C. championship, as of early 1982.

A Nightshade daughter, Manora's Robin, C.D., is co-owned by Nancy Scholz with her thirteen-year-old nephew, Steven. Steven has worked her in the 4-H program, in obedience; and in the summer of 1980, she earned a

Manora's Robin, C.D., photographed at 13 months, belongs to Nancy Scholz and her nephew Steven.

Companion Dog degree with Steven in three consecutive shows. Needless to say, Nancy is very proud of them both. Steven is looking forward to Robin's next being campaigned in point-show competition.

Ma-Pat-Ma

Ma-Pat-Ma Labradors started approximately in the mid-1950s when Robert C. Heaney, whose daughter Margaret owns the kennel today, brought to his home at Derby, New York, his first of the breed, a black bitch. At the time his interest was solely in owning a first-class all-around family dog. It was not long, however, before he was introduced to field trialing, and in short order Mr. Heaney had become known as an excellent field trainer of retrievers and other sporting breeds.

The first bitch, Heaney's Ma-Pat-Ma Midget, was an outstanding field trial dog. She was well on her way to a field championship when Mr. Heaney was taken ill and thus became unable to continue the rigorous work inherent to field training and trialing.

The kennel records, all of Mr. Heaney's Labradors, and their papers were destroyed following Mr. Heaney's death, so his daughter has little to go on in researching background. Through the years she has tried to obtain as much information as possible from his friends in and out of New York State who have found the Ma-Pat-Ma name in their pedigrees, and through them she is rebuilding the history.

Three very handsome Labs, Croysdale's Ma-Pat-Ma Tru Chanc, Heaney's Ma-Pat-Ma Dream Cum Tru, and Heaney's Ma-Pat-Ma M'Boy Fitzgo, all owned by Margaret D. Heaney, Ma-Pat-Ma Kannels, Derby, New York.

Robert A. Heaney and Margaret D. Heaney with their first Labrador, Heaney's Ma-Pat-Ma Midget, following a training session.

It was Margaret Heaney's dream, after the death of her father and the destruction of his stock, to begin again with Labs and to follow in his footsteps. She began, as did her father, with an interest only in field work. While looking for her own first Lab, she was introduced through obedience and field training clients to the A.K.C. licensed dog shows and subsequently found the Lab she was looking for; at the same time, she began to develop an interest in the dog show world. The black Labrador bitch she purchased was Heaney's Ma-Pat-Ma Dream Cum Tru, the daughter of Champion Shamrock Acres By Jiminy and Champion Willowmount Sundown Sandy, bred by Margaret A. Watson of Sunstorm Kennels.

Around 1970, Margaret Heaney started showing Labs. When she began with Dream, pride and determination kept her from placing this beautiful bitch with a handler; and so, due to circumstances, lack of know-how, and bad breaks, Dream was never finished. Although she won numerous reserves with four- and five-point majors, she still remains one three-point major away from her championship. She is still, at nearly eleven years old, an exceptional representative of the breed; just recently she won the Veteran Bitch Class at the Labrador Retriever Club of Central Connecticut's supported entry, and she is still able to put in a full and productive day hunting upland game and waiting in a blind for the chance to retrieve a felled bird.

Margaret D. Heaney owner-handles Heaney's Ma-Pat-Ma M'Boy Fitzgo to Best of Opposite Sex, Wyoming Valley Kennel Club, May 1975.

Heaney's Ma-Pat-Ma Dream Cum Tru, by Ch. Shamrock Acres By Jiminy ex Ch. Willowmount Sundown Sandy, taking a three-point major from the classes. Bred by Margaret A. Watson, owned by Margaret D. Heaney. Mrs. Anne Rogers Clark is judging.

Dream was bred to Champion Shamrock Acres Benjamin, the progeny from which included some mighty respectable representatives of the breed, among them Heaney's Ma-Pat-Ma M'Boy Fitzgo who has done some worthy winning.

A run of really bad luck with her bitches has kept Margaret Heaney practically without puppies during the past five years. Fitzgo, however, is being used by other breeders with very satisfactory results.

All of the Heaney dogs have been and will be field dogs. Margaret Heaney feels it especially important that each Lab develop its potential to be a dual-purpose dog, excelling in health, temperament, brains, and conformation.

MiJan

MiJan Labradors, bred at a comparatively young kennel, have been proudly exhibited throughout the Eastern United States, where they have done well in competition as they conform to type, temperament, and soundness. They are owned by Joan and Tony Heubel of Little Ferry, New Jersey, and by Mike and Janet Farmilette of Hillsdale, New Jersey.

These breeders wisely started out by concentrating on good bitches, one of whom was Champion Driftwood's Honeysuckle (English Champion Sandylands Midas ex Champion Driftwood's Gypsy) who became one of their best producers; she was the dam of Champion MiJan's Corrigan, sire of eleven champions, and of the Specialty-winning MiJan's Frisket.

Twillingate Duchess, by Champion Lockerbie Kismet ex Lockerbie Tuckety Boots, produced Champion Lockerbie Cinda Samantha and Lockerbie Torborlina.

Champion MiJan's Corrigan has been a true asset to the kennel, both as a winner and as a stud dog. His progeny include, from Champion Lockerbie Cinda Samantha, the well-known Champion Lockerbie MiJan's Britannia, Champion Lockerbie Brass Tack, and Champion Lockerbie Samantha's Striker.

Two fine English imports were eventually added to the kennel, both males, and they have worked in well. They are Champion Jayncourt Ajoco Justice, a black dog by Champion Ballyduff Marketeer ex Champion Jayncourt Star Performer, and Champion Marbra Guardsman, a chocolate dog by Waltham Galaxy of Condor ex Marbra Rhapsody. Bred to Champion Lockerbie Cinda Samantha, Ajoco Justice has sired MiJan's Rocky Mountain High, MiJan's Mindy, and MiJan's Summer Sun, a black dog, black bitch, and yellow bitch respectively; all three of these Labs have points toward their titles.

Best of Winners at Queensboro in 1981. Ch. Jayncourt Ajoco Justice, by Ch. Ballyduff Marketeer ex Ch. Jayncourt Star Performer, imported from England and owned by Mijan's Labradors, Joan and Tony Heubel and Mike and Janet Farmilette.

Champion Marbra Guardsman, with Champion Lockerbie Cinda Samantha, produced MiJan's Bewitched of Westwood, a lovely black bitch with major points.

Corrigan (yellow), Ajoco Justice (black), and Guardsman (chocolate) are making their mark in other kennels as well as at MiJan; they are popular with breeders because of the type and temperament they produce.

Ch. Driftwood Honeysuckle, by Eng., Am. Ch. Sandylands Midas ex Ch. Driftwood's Gypsy, owned by Janet Farmilette, Hillsdale, New Jersey.

Ch. Lockerbie Cinda Samantha, by Ch. Lockerbie Stanwood Granada ex Twillingate Dutchess, is the dam of Ch. Lockerbie Mijan's Britannia, Ch. Lockerbie Brass Tack, and Ch. Lockerbie Samantha's Striker. Owned by Mijan Labradors.

Moorwood

Moorwood Kennel is rather young, the first litter there having been whelped in 1976. It is also small, by necessity; the dogs go back and forth between Indian Lake, New York, and Crystal River, Florida, with their mistress, Mrs. Rosalind D. Moore, who divides her time between these two places each year.

The puppy who was to become Moorwood's foundation bitch was acquired in 1972. The great pleasure that both Mrs. Moore and her husband derived from this bitch's delightful, assertive personality, from her compulsive retrieving, and from her beauty led them to show her to her championship and then eventually to breed her.

Moorwood Beaver's Brewstar, born June 1979, taking Best of Breed at Brookhaven in 1981 under judge Bob Braithwaite. By Ch. Sandylands Markwell of Lockerbie ex Ch. The Black Baroness. Rosalind B. Moore, owner, Moorwood Kennels.

Moorwood Lab puppies around six weeks old. Owned by Rosalind B. Moore, Indian Lake, New York.

Moorwood has finished four champions—its foundation bitch and three Moorwood-bred puppies. Another bred-by-Moorwood now being shown lacks only a major. These five (four bitches and a dog), plus two young bitches to be shown in the spring of 1982, comprise the kennel's breeding stock. Some other Moorwood-bred dogs are being shown by their owners.

Upon resuming breeding in 1979, Mrs. Moore decided to keep only bitches and sold her dogs, but later that year, the foundation bitch whelped a litter which included Brewster, an especially fine puppy, outstanding in personality and conformation. He is giving Moorwood its first experience in "Specialing" a champion, and Mrs. Moore is finding it exciting. In his first appearance as a Special, at Brookhaven in September 1981, he went Best of Breed over 35 Labs and was pulled out as one of the top six in the Sporting Group. This happening was a real thrill.

In planning their first litter, the Moores decided that they would like to breed Labradors along British show lines and to date have bred to Champion Somerset Cider of Kimvalley, Champion Sandylands Markwell of Lockerbie, and Champion Eireannach Black Coachman, with excellent results from all of them.

Showing and training their first litter, and their contacts with field trial people, became an enjoyable and absorbing interest, and plans began to be formulated for a long-range breeding program. Sadly, just after the second litter was whelped in 1977, tragedy struck the Moores' human family, and the entire 1977 litter was sold. As a result of Mr. Moore's illness and death, no breeding was undertaken again until 1979.

Ch. Beaver's Hillary of Moorwood, W.C., photographed in 1980. By Ch. Somerset Cider of Kimvalley ex Ch. The Black Baroness. Rosalind B. Moore, owner.

Two of the Moores' champions, Champion Beaver's Hillary of Moorwood, W.C. and Champion Beaver's Lavinia of Moorwood, W.C. are out of the foundation bitch by Champion Somerset Cider of Kimvalley. Champion Moorwood Beaver's Brewster and Moorwood Beaver's Patience (who lacks one major) are out of the foundation bitch by Champion Sandylands Markwell of Lockerbie.

The two young bitches to be shown in the spring of 1982 are by Champion Eireannach Black Coachman out of Lavinia.

Mother is on guard while the puppy room is being cleaned! Seven of the five-week-old puppies from Ch. Beavers Hillary of Moorwood W.C. by Ch. Sandylands Markwell of Lockerbie. Beautiful baby Labs from Moorwood Kennels.

Moorwood's foundation bitch, Champion The Black Baroness (call name "Beaver"), is a granddaughter of Champion Shamrock Acres Light Brigade through her sire, Champion Shamrock Acres Top Brass who was Best of Breed at Westminster in 1972. On her dam's side, she goes back to a combination of English champion stock and some outstanding American-bred field trial dogs.

"Beaver" has been bred only twice, whelping a total of nine puppies (litters of five and four) of whom three are champions and one needs only one more major. In addition, "Beaver" has transmitted to her puppies unusually strong retrieving instincts which they, in turn, are passing on to their offspring.

Ch. Beaver's Lavinia of Moorwood, W.C., born February 1976, by Ch. Somerset Cider of Kimvalley ex Ch. The Black Baroness. Rosalind B. Moore, owner.

Mrs. Moore's breeding program includes a plan to breed back to "Beaver's" line, possibly with two young bitches she has that are bred from Lavinia and Black Coachman.

Field trial work is, as a practical matter, beyond the scope of Mrs. Moore's small kennel, but she feels complimented that two field trial kennels have purchased young stock, one dog and two bitches, from Moorland for use in their field trial breeding programs. Some of the progeny which was produced from interbreedings with field trial stock have already distinguished themselves in field trial competition. The breedings were undertaken by these field trial breeders in an effort to produce dual-purpose Labs in their lines.

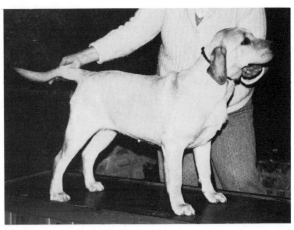

Moorwood bitch puppy at five months of age. By Ch. Eireannack Black Coachman ex Ch. Beaver's Lavinia of Moorwood, W.C.

Another Moorwood dog, one from the Moores' first litter, is a fully trained working gun dog, while a number of others serve their owners as gun dogs; the owners have found the dogs to be exceptionally easy to train.

All five dogs in Moorwood's first litter earned their Working Certificates with high grades and, in one case, the judge noted on his report "Stylish" and "Stylish Throughout." Limitations of time have prevented Moorwood from obtaining Working Certificates since then.

Guiding Eyes for the Blind, Inc. was given three Moorwood puppies, part of a litter of twelve whelped and successfully raised by their dam, in 1980. All these have graduated and are serving their owners as guide dogs.

After dinner nap-time! Baby Labs at Moorwood Kennels owned by Rosalind B. Moore.

Northwood

Northwood Labradors are owned by the Schultze family, Karen and Charles and their daughters, Janet and Patricia, at Middle Island, New York. In 1975, they purchased their first bitch and began to show at the matches. Since they did fairly well, within a short time all were thoroughly enjoying the hobby, and they decided to purchase a dog in 1976, a handsome yellow male named Briary Birch, from Mrs. Brainard. This dog became the first Northwood champion.

Ch. Briary Birch, born in April 1976, bred by Mrs. Brainard, is the first owner-handled champion from Northwood Kennels owned by the Charles Schultze family, Middle Island, New York.

Next, a black male was purchased from Mrs. Jones of Jollymuff Kennels; he became Northwood's second champion, earning Group 1, numerous Bests of Breed, and a Working Certificate.

Now the Schultzes felt that it was time to bring in some bitches. They obtained two yellows, one from Mr. and Mrs. Reynolds (Finchingfield) and the other again from Mrs. Jones (Jollymuff). Finchingfield Fantasia completed her championship at the age of sixteen months and has won Bests of Breed and numerous Best Opposites. Jollymuff Northwood Crystal is pointed and recently won Reserve Winners Bitch at a Labrador Specialty.

Ch. Finchingfield Fantasia, born September 1978, bred by Mr. and Mrs. Reynolds. A lovely young bitch who completed her championship at 16 months and who has Best of Breed and numerous Best of Opposite Sex awards. Owned by Karen and Charles Schultze, Northwood Labradors.

All of the Northwood dogs are entirely owner-handled, which makes the Schultzes very proud of their successes. Both of their teenage daughters, Janet and Patricia, have been active in the breed ring as well as in junior showmanship. Presently, as they are bringing out puppies from their first litter, Northwood has just bred what will be its third litter. The youngsters now in the ring have achieved many nice match show wins and point placings in Puppy Classes at Specialties.

Ch. Williston Jollymuff Jubal, W.C., born September 1976, bred by Mrs. Richardson, is the winner of a Working Certificate, Group One at Elm City, July 1979, and numerous Bests of Breed. Northwood Kennels.

The whole Schultze family is now completely involved in the fancy and looking forward to bringing out many more worthy homebred puppies. Of course, the main objective at Northwood is to breed good representatives of the breed for show, obedience, and pet purposes—dogs to bring pleasure for their intelligence and personality as well as for their looks.

Jollymuff Northwood Crystal, born September 1978, bred by Mrs. Jones. Pointed bitch, Reserve Winners at the Mid-Jersey Labrador Retriever Specialty in 1981.

Mr. and Mrs. Schultze are members of the Riverhead Kennel Club, with Karen holding the office of Treasurer. In 1979, they helped found the Labrador Retriever Club of Long Island; currently Karen is Vice-President of this organization and Charles is Treasurer. They are also members of the Mid-Jersey Labrador Retriever Club, the Labrador Club of South Jersey, and the Labrador Retriever Club in England.

Riverroad

Riverroad Labradors are bred at a small kennel situated on fifteen acres in Gurnee, Illinois, and owned by Mrs. Frank G. Thomas. The first Lab was purchased in 1971, and Mrs. Thomas comments, "Soon this was the only breed we could see."

1981, ten years later, marked the completion of a new kennel building with twelve inside and outside runs and an office on the second floor.

Mrs. Thomas started showing in 1977 with a yellow Light Brigade son who finished quickly at 17 months of age. He is American and Canadian Champion Riverroad's Summerstraw. Shown during 1980, he became the Nation's Number Three Labrador despite having only been campaigned for six months of that year. He also excels as a sire; among his progeny was the youngster that took Best in Sweepstakes at the 1980 National Lab Specialty.

Am., Can. Ch. Riverroad's Summerstraw, Number Three Lab nationally in 1980. Sire of Best in Sweepstakes at the 1980 National Specialty. Owned by Mrs. Frank G. Thomas, Riverroad Labradors, Gurnee, Illinois.

This handsome young hopeful is from the Riverroad Labradors.

Ch. Weklyn's McMark Flite, Best of Breed at both the spring and fall Chicago-International of 1980, is another splendid Labrador owned by Riverroad Labs.

In 1981, another of Mrs. Thomas' Labradors, Champion Weklyn's McMark Flite, won the breed at the Chicago International in both the spring and fall shows. This dog is a black Winroc Picaro son.

There are also some excellent brood bitches at Riverroad, including two daughters of Brian Boru (one a champion producer, the other a Specialty-winner producer) and a young Specialty winner who has recently whelped her first litter.

Rupert

The prefix "Rupert" is one of the best known and most highly respected in the American Labrador Fancy. The kennel was started by the late Mrs. Dorothy Howe in Vermont, who owned it from the 1940s until her death in the late 1970s.

A bitch named Lena was the foundation behind all Rupert breeding stock. Born in 1941, Lena was sired by Field Trial Champion Timbertown Clansman ex Wingan's Primrose, and she was bred by Mrs. Gavan. Among Lena's famous progeny were four blacks sired by Dauntless of Deer Creek: Champion Rupert Dahomey, Champion Rupert Daphne, Champion Rupert Desdemona and Champion Rupert Dusky—one dog and three bitches born in 1947, bred by Dorothy B. Howe.

At the present time, Elinor C. Ayers of the Seaward Newfoundlands, a long-time friend of Dorothy Howe's, is keeping the Rupert prefix in the limelight through littermates which she owns, American and Canadian Champion Seaward's Adonis of Rupert and American and Canadian Champion Seaward's Dr. Watson of Rupert, C.D., which were bred by Dorothy Howe; these two dogs combine some of the outstanding English and American bloodlines. Born on April 26th 1977, they were sired by Champion Ardmargha So Famous, an English import son of English Show Champion Sandylands Storm Along ex English Champion Faith of Ardmargha (from Rupert Goldylocks who descends directly on her dam's side from Champion Rupert Searchon).

"Donny," as Adonis is called, was a champion by fifteen months of age, and he has been one of the Top Labs in the United States for several years, ranking Number Four for 1980 and 1981,

Ch. Seaward's Adonis of Rupert, bred by Dorothy Howe, belongs to the Seaward Kennels, Manchester Center, Vermont, and is handled by Gerlinda Hockla.

according to the *Kennel Review* System. He has multiple Group placements in keen northeastern competition and has sired five litters. He is handled exclusively for Mrs. Ayers by Gerlinda Hockla.

Adonis' litter-brother, "Watson," is not shown as regularly as "Donny" but nonetheless has made his presence felt, even defeating "Donny" a few times. "Watson" is currently being trained for his C.D.X., has a Group placement to his credit, and, like his brother, has sired five litters. "Watson" is handled exclusively for Mrs. Ayers by Phyllis Wright.

This handsome Lab and efficient gun dog is Scrimshaw Holystone, by Ch. Scrimshaw Another Deacon ex Ch. Sandylands Crystal, and he belongs to Barbara Barfield.

Scrimshaw

As are so many of the small, successful kennels in this breed, Scrimshaw, located at Meredith, New Hampshire, is strictly a "hobby project," owned by Barbara and John Barfield. Because John is a career Navy man (Master Chief Petty Officer) and consequently not always at home to help with the dogs and because no kennel help are employed, the Barfields are limited in the number of dogs they can keep and in the number of litters bred each year—usually only one or two.

The Barfields also have a policy of not getting rid of their "old-timers," and they are also "guilty" of keeping a few as "just pets." As Barbara says:

This is, I have been told by saner souls, not the way to operate a successful kennel. And, as I glance around at the recumbent forms draped over our furniture and under my feet, I will admit they *may* be right. However, I would not trade one of my 'old timers' or 'just pets' for their brand of 'wisdom.' I was taught many years ago that success can be achieved, if only on a small scale, without sacrificing the qualities of humanity and compassion.

This writer heartily agrees, and I sincerely admire Mrs. Barfield for her point of view!

This is Barbara Barfield, owner of Scrimshaw Labs, in her favorite picture with Ch. Scrimshaw Blue Nun. As Barbara points out, "She is so full of *joie de vivre*, and this quality comes across in the ring, which judges either love or hate". In a show dog, overenthusiasm is certainly far preferable to a bored, indifferent dog.

Barbara Barfield owes her start in Labs to her dear friend Barbara Barty-King, from whom she learned every aspect of caring for, feeding, training (obedience and field), and showing Labs. In the early fifties, she became an "apprentice" at Mrs. Barty-King's Aldenholme Kennels, and as the years passed, the two became great friends.

Because her parents insisted that she complete her education, it was not until after her marriage that Barbara Barfield was able to start out as a Labrador breeder on her own. Of course she wanted the Aldenholme dogs for her foundation stock. Unfortunately, this was not to be, as Mrs. Barty-King had been forced to discontinue breeding and showing Labs due to her poor health, but Mrs. Barfield did locate a friend whose kennel had been based on Aldenholme (although by then the line had been somewhat diluted due to outcrossing).

Thus, the first Scrimshaw Lab was Jonte Nantucket Sleighride, a son of Jonte Camala who was by Aldenholme's Robber from a granddaughter of Champion Aldenholme's Witching Hour. A male was selected because all the bitches had previously been sold. He was a lovely dog and was shown with moderate success. His greatest talents lay in field work. Before long, Mrs. Barfield decided to lease his dam, Camala, since her pedigree went back to some of the dogs with whom she had grown up, and to line-breed her to Champion Chebacco Smokey Joe, one of the best producing sons of the old Aldenholme foundation stud, Champion Ashur Deacon. The result of this mating was that in 1967 the first Scrimshaw-bred bitch was whelped, Jonte Scrimshaw O'Spindrift.

Although pointed in her brief show career, this bitch was not yet what Mrs. Barfield wanted, since her pedigree contained too many "variables." She was retired from the ring and bred again, in this instance to another Chebacco dog from the Aldenholme line, Chebacco Walter R., a fox-red. This breeding gave the Barfields their first really good bitch, Scrimshaw Mother Carey, a solid black strongly resembling the old Aldenholme bitches. She was whelped in 1969.

At this point, John Barfield was beginning to be transferred from one part of the country to the other, so a three-year moratorium on breeding was declared. As Mrs. Barfield had been brought up with the belief that one only bred to improve the breed, this was no great sacrifice. Somewhere along the way she had

Scrimshaw Mother Carey, eight weeks old, surrounded by some of her playthings.

heard the following adage from a Terrier breeder now long forgotten: "For every litter you breed in the flesh, breed five on paper." Mrs. Barfield has followed this advice through the years, and it has stood her in good stead.

In 1973, Mrs. Barfield again picked up the thread of her breeding program. By this time, hip and eye problems had come to the fore in Labradors. Luckily, all of the Scrimshaw dogs were clear. However, the Barfields were running out of sources of the old Aldenholme lines; therefore, a decision to outcross was necessary. Mrs. Barty-King had advised Mrs. Barfield to turn to England, and so it was decided to try the most successful line ever established there (or perhaps even anywhere!), the combination of

Scrimshaw Mother Carey, 12 weeks, by Chebacco Walter R. ex Jonte Scrimshaw O'Spindrift, on the left. Chebacco Walter R. (Fox-red), bred and owned by Mary Carey, Essex, Massachusetts, on the right. Mother Carey bred and owned by Barbara Barfield, Meredith, New Hampshire.

Ch. Scrimshaw Another Deacon, whelped August 1973, at five years of age. By Whiskey Creek Tweed's Bairn ex Scrimshaw Mother Carey. Bred by Barbara Barfield and owned by Barbara and John Barfield.

best dog we had bred to that point, and he is probably the best male we have ever bred."

In 1976 came the opportunity of a lifetime. The Barfields had the chance to lease Sandylands Crystal (a half-sister to one of the all-time great producers of the breed, Sandylands Charlie Boy) from their dear friend, Marc Hall. The addition of Crystal in 1976 and the addition of another English import, Champion Jayncourt Follow Mee (a Charlie Boy son), from their friend, Dick Oster, in 1977 have been invaluable.

In 1977, Deacon was bred to Crystal for the first time and produced two puppies: Scrimshaw Tipsy Parson, a black male now within a few points of both American and Canadian Championships and a second generation O.F.A. Excellent stud (his sire enjoys the same rating), and a yellow bitch, Champion Scrimshaw Blue Nun. The latter distinguished herself by finishing with four majors and a Group First from the Open Class when not yet two years old. She was the first Lab bitch since March 1977 to win a Group First (April 1979) and was named Number One Labrador Bitch for 1979 by *Kennel Review*.

Sandylands and Blaircourt. Mother Carey was bred to a son of the pillar of the Labrador breed, Champion Sandylands Tweed of Blaircourt. This breeding, the Barfields' third, produced the black male Champion Scrimshaw Another Deacon, which Mrs. Barfield describes as "the

The English import, Ch. Sandylands Crystal (Cliveruth Harvester ex Cliveruth Sandylands Witch) taking Winners Bitch at Westminster 1972 for four points under breeder-judge Joan Read, owner of the Chidleys. Owner-handled by Marc Hall, Crystal was bred by Captain and Mrs. Wilkinson and owned by Marc Hall, Frances Almirall, and Barbara Barfield, Scrimshaw Labradors.

A lovely headstudy of Ch. Jayncourt Follow Mee. Barbara Barfield, owner.

Winners Dog at the age of 18 months at the Labrador Retriever Club of the Potomac Specialty under Irving Eldredge for five points, and he was Reserve Winners Dog a few months later at the Mid-Jersey Labrador Retriever Club Specialty. His sisters are just beginning their show careers and will be bred in the not-too-distant future.

Ch. Scrimshaw My Sin, black bitch, by Ch. Scrimshaw Another Deacon ex Ch. Sandylands Crystal, winning Winners Bitch (four points) under judge Kurt Mueller, Sr., at Scottsdale Dog Fanciers, 1981. Handled by Debbie Sharpsteen and bred by Barbara Barfield, who are the co-owners. This lovely bitch finished with four majors.

The second breeding of this pair, six months later, produced, among others, Champion Scrimshaw My Sin, the black bitch who produced the Number Five Lab in the United States for 1981, according to the *Canine Chronicles* System; Champion Coal Creek's Perish of Char-Don, who finished at the tender age of 13 months and has many Bests of Breed and Group wins to his credit; Scrimshaw Clearly An Angel, C.D.X. and T.D.X., a yellow bitch; Scrimshaw The Devil's Own, U.D.; and Scrimshaw Holystone, a black male who distinguished himself as a gun dog by bringing in, during his first season as a puppy, 26 ducks, 24 pheasant, and three woodcock. The Devil's Own is also credited with making "believers" out of several Fish and Game officials who claimed there was no longer such a thing as a dual line. Of the remaining littermates, Scrimshaw Church Mouse, a yellow bitch, was retained as a brood bitch, and a black male is a family companion. It is also interesting to note that all but one of the litter were O.F.A. Certified (one has not been x-rayed).

Crystal was bred to Champion Jayncourt Follow Mee late in 1978, and at the age of nine, she produced her last litter (her third for the Barfields, her fourth all told). All three pups, Scrimshaw After Me (a male) and Scrimshaw A Hard Act To Follow and Scrimshaw Ondine O'Montifore (both bitches), were yellows. After Mee was

Scrimshaw Labradors currently have leased a black bitch, Eireannach Moose Head, a daughter of the English import Champion Mansergh Moose and Champion Springfield's Mimi, who has been bred to Springfield Kennels' English import, Champion Linershwood Kalan, a son of English and American Champion Kimvalley Kenbara Mr. Softee. This will give the Barfields an important, tightly bred outcross when it is needed. Also in the outcross department, they are running on two stud puppies by Parson, their dam a blend of the finest English and Irish dual lines. Hopes are high for these two promising youngsters.

Ch. Scrimshaw Blue Nun, by Ch. Scrimshaw Another Deacon ex Ch. Sandylands Crystal, bred and owned by Barbara Barfield, is pictured finishing her title with Group One from the Classes at Vacationland Dog Club, April 1979, under Joyce MacKenzie. This outstanding bitch, handled by Norman Grenier, was Number One Lab bitch in the U.S. in 1979, *Kennel Review* system.

Scrimshaw Tipsy Parson, black male, by Ch. Scrimshaw Another Deacon ex Ch. Sandylands Crystal, at two years of age. Bred by Barfield, owned by Barbara and John Barfield.

To date, Deacon is the sire of three champions, the two previously mentioned plus American and Canadian Champion Chief Happy Warrior of Unami, bred by Nancy Martin and Kendall Herr. He has produced other major-pointed get, obedience title-holders, and some excellent working gun dogs. All of these have been produced in only six breedings.

Champion Jayncourt Follow Mee was almost seven years old when he arrived at Scrimshaw. Mrs. Barfield does not know his previous breeding record, except that he is the grandsire of at least one Specialty winner. Since acquiring him, Mrs. Barfield has bred him to four bitches. From the first litter, now just past two years old, he has produced three title-holders so far: Champion McDerry's Midwatch Star Dancer, who finished with several Bests of Breed and Group placements as well as some Specialty wins;

American and Canadian Champion McDerry's Midwatch Starburst, a yellow male who also has Best of Breed and Group placements; and a black bitch, Canadian Champion McDerry's Midwatch Starkist, C.D.

Follow Mee was bred to Blue Nun in January 1981, and the Barfields consider the resulting litter to be the best yet. The puppies from that combination are especially exciting; and all three, Scrimshaw Habit Forming (a bitch) and Scrimshaw Gorblimee and Scrimshaw The Godfather (both dogs) have started out well by winning Specialty Best in Match and Best of Opposite Sex.

The Barfields have shown Follow Mee only at Specialty Shows during the three-and-a-half years that they have had him, and his record includes Best Stud Dog and Best Veteran at the Labrador Retriever Club of Greater Boston under breeder-judge Anne Simoneau and Best Stud Dog at Mid-Jersey Labrador Retriever Club under breeder-judge Joan Read. It is a source of particular pride that the progeny for the stud dog classes were from different litters. Follow Mee has never been unplaced in either the Stud Dog Class or the Veteran Class at any Specialty.

Scrimshaw After Mee, yellow male, by Ch. Jayneourt Follow Mee ex Ch. Sandylands Crystal, pictured winning the dog points at the Labrador Retriever Club of Potomac in 1980, judged by Ted Eldredge with Susan E. Dash handling for breeder-owner Barbara Barfield, Scrimshaw Labs.

Tipsy Parson is just starting out his stud career, and After Mee has not as yet been used. The Barfields prefer not to use either their dogs or their bitches for breeding until they have been O.F.A. certified and eye-cleared, which means they will have to wait until the dogs are at least two years of age before breeding from them.

The Barfields' motto is "*Selectively* breeding for dual-purpose excellence," and they closely adhere to this motto at all times.

The judge in this picture is the late Brigit Docking, whose Ballyduff Kennels in England were world famous for Labradors for over 40 years. Here she is awarding first in the Open Yellow Class at the Labrador Retriever Club to Gordon Sousa's Ch. Maestro's Song, W.C.

Shababaland

Shababaland Labradors belong to Gordon W. Sousa, Jr., of Old Tappan, New Jersey. Although it has been in existence only since the late 1970s, this kennel has certainly made its presence felt and would seem to have a bright future ahead.

"Pride of place" among these Labs belongs to the foundation bitch, Champion Maestro's Song, W.C., who was bred by Patrick Corliss and represents some of the outstanding bloodlines in the breed; her paternal side goes back to such dogs as Champion Sandylands Mark, Champion Reanacre Mallardhurn Thunder, Champion Sandylands Truth, and Champion Sandylands Tweed of Blaircourt, while her maternal side lists such dogs as Champion Cornlands Hamlet, Champion Cornlands Kimvalley

The noted Specialty Show and Westminster winning bitch, Ch. Maestro's Song, W.C., pictured at the Labrador Retriever Club of Potomac Specialty. This is the foundation bitch at Shababaland Kennels, owned by Gordon W. Sousa, Jr.

Mr. Sousa gives much credit and appreciation for his success in Labs to seventy-five-year-old Patrick Corliss, who bred Champion Maestro's Song, W.C. and shared her with him. Mr. Sousa also commends Joy Quallenberg, who so capably handles his Labs.

At Shababaland Kennels, the primary concern is temperament, the aim being to maintain the multi-purpose qualities which have made Labradors the fourth most popular breed in America. "Melody's" littermates include a pointed field trial dog. In addition, "Melody" has produced champions and guide dogs for the blind in the same litter. It is Mr. Sousa's hope to continue along these same lines in the future.

Ch. Shababaland's Creme De La Creme, owned by Gordon Sousa, Jr. Joy Quallenberg is the handler of this splendid Labrador.

Crofter, Champion Kimvalley Crispin, and Champion Brentchase Pompadour in the first three generations.

"Melody," as she is known to her friends, went Winners Bitch, Best of Winners, and Best of Opposite Sex at Westminster in 1979. She gained the Top Winners Bitch Award in 1980 from the Mid-Jersey Labrador Retriever Club for having defeated the most competition en route to her title (286 Labs). When she was five-and-a-half years old, she finished her title at the Labrador Retriever Club of the Potomac Specialty, beating 221 Labs, and having previously won the Open Yellow Class and Reserve Winners there in 1977. She gained her Working Certificate in 1981 at the National Specialty. Needless to say, Mr. Sousa feels very fortunate at having her on whom to found his breeding program.

In addition to "Melody," there are some other quality yellows at this kennel. Currently, Mr. Sousa owns five bitches who have been Specialty winners. In 1981, twelve of the Labs from Shababaland took ribbons at Regional or National Specialties. One of these is Champion Shababaland's Creme De La Creme, a young male who finished his title in only two months, going Best of Breed from the classes. It is hoped that he will be a top contender for Top Ten honors in 1982.

Shamrock Acres

Shamrock Acres Labradors, owned by Sally B. McCarthy at Waunakee, Wisconsin, have been an important influence in this breed since 1955. Sally McCarthy has always loved animals, and as a child she dreamed of the day when she could live in the country and have a kennel. She read every dog book the library offered, and she pored over *Dog World* and other magazines, changing her mind with each issue over which breed was the one for her.

The first purebred dog she owned as an adult was a young, smooth black and tan Dachshund bitch, Badger Hill Marcie, C.D., from one of the top Dachshund breeders in the United States of that period, and Mrs. McCarthy felt fortunate to have acquired her. Several litters were raised from her; thus Shamrock Acres' first homebreds were Dachshunds.

The McCarthys enjoyed their Dachsies but soon realized that their outdoor, hunting-oriented family needed a good retriever. So in 1955 they purchased their first Lab, for $35.00, a six-week-old black female from Martin Julseth, a well-respected local breeder who had produced many fine hunting dogs. The McCarthys were so completely inexperienced at this time that they were terribly impressed when Mr. Julseth's dogs retrieved and even delivered the training dummy to hand. These Labradors sold themselves with their willingness to please, their lovely soft expressions, and their beauty. Right then, Sally McCarthy knew that she had found her breed.

That great little puppy was the introduction to the breed that has held Mrs. McCarthy's ever-growing love and respect ever since. Little did she know what an impact Marlab Gypsy, C.D. would have on her life!

The McCarthys were then only interested in a well-behaved family companion and hunting dog that could be used on both upland game and waterfowl. In their search for someone who could tell them how to train a dog for hunting, they met some very helpful members of the Madison Retriever Club. Sally's husband started training with them, and eventually they encouraged him to enter some A.K.C. sanctioned field trials. The McCarthys joined the club, and their hunting dog became a field trial prospect overnight.

Simultaneously, Sally entered Gypsy in an obedience training class sponsored by the all-

The Labrador Retriever Club, October 1st 1961. Ch. Whygin Campaign Promise making a good win for Shamrock Acres Kennels, Mr. and Mrs. James McCarthy, Waunakee, Wisconsin.

breed Badger Kennel Club of Madison, Wisconsin. There were many good breeders and very knowledgeable members in the club who were willing to help and advise, and Sally was hungry to learn. Thus began an association with a club and some marvelous "dog people" that is still going on nearly three decades later.

Sally had already accomplished the impossible by getting a C.D. degree on her Dachshund who had never been out of a kennel run until the McCarthys got her at eight months of age. Training the Lab was a breeze by comparison, and Sally took her to the C.D. in three consecutive trials— before she was a year old.

The McCarthys bred Gypsy to the State of Wisconsin Open Stake Field Champion, Nemec's Jeff, who had a good solid field pedigree. From that first litter of Labradors, the McCarthys selected one bitch puppy for themselves. She was Shamrock Acres Domino Queen, C.D.X., who later qualified for the National Amateur Retriever Trial and won High in Trial at an A.K.C. licensed obedience trial.

It was at this time that the McCarthys decided they wanted a dual-purpose Labrador that they could show in the conformation ring as well as in field trials and obedience. They selected and bought from Gloria E. Riedinger a black bitch puppy, Champion Glor-Loral Dinah Might, C.D.X., who had a very interesting dual-purpose background. By two years of age she had already completed her championship, gotten her C.D.X. degree, and had a licensed field trial J.A.M. (Judges Award of merit), plus several sanctioned field trial wins and placements. By the age of three she had won a large qualifying stake and the McCarthys were ready to start a serious campaign toward her dual championship. Unfortunately, and very sadly, within a month it was discovered that she had a brain tumor, and within a year she was dead. The McCarthys quickly learned that there are many heartaches as well as many joys in breeding and showing dogs.

In the meantime, Sally had contacted several breeders on the East Coast, and in 1959, the McCarthys bought two unrelated seven-week-old black pups from Helen Ginnel of Whygin Ken-

nels. The bitch, American and Canadian Champion Whygin Campaign Promise, still holds the record, Sally believes, for the Top Producing Labrador Dam—with 17 champion offspring—and her Best of Breed win at the National Labrador Retriever Specialty in 1961 was the first time that a bitch had won that honor. She won many other honors and had some great wins. She never ran in trials, but she was a tremendous hunting dog and was used in the field until she had reached at least 12 years of age. The dog that came with Campaign Promise was Canadian and American Champion Whygin Royal Rocket, C.D., who also had an impressive list of wins.

In 1960, Sally saw a beautiful young black bitch that literally took her breath away at the Labrador Retriever Club National. The bitch, Champion Whygin Gentle Julia of Avec, belonged to an East Coast owner. Within a year her owner died and "Julie" was passed from

Ch. Whygin Gold Bullion, Best of Breed, and Ch. Whygin Campaign Promise, Best of Opposite Sex—at both Chicago-International and Westminster. Helen Ginnel handling Gold Bullion, Sally McCarthy handling Campaign Promise.

family to family, finally ending up as a pet with a nephew in Ohio. He could not tolerate her, and he finally contacted Helen Ginnel to help him find a home for her. Helen remembered Sally McCarthy's great interest in this bitch, so she suggested that Sally be advised of "Julie's" availability. He contacted Sally and told her all the "terrible things" she had done, including such things as learning to turn door knobs and let herself out at will and going down a heavily traveled highway to a turkey farm, where she retrieved turkeys and dutifully took them home.

Despite being appalled by all the details of "Julie's" misdeeds, Sally decided to have the bitch sent out to her, so that she could see for herself how really bad she might be. No time was wasted, and "Julie" arrived the next day. The McCarthys had been prepared for the very worst. However, the bitch was in excellent physical condition and was even more beautiful as a mature bitch than she had been when Sally

had seen and been so favorably impressed by her. She seemed temperamentally none-the-worse for all of her experiences. Upon their return from the airport, "Julie" and Sally had a long discussion about turkeys, door knobs, and all the like. Sally feels certain that "Julie" realized her new owner had rescued her, and she also understood that Sally "had her number" and that life at Shamrock Acres meant discipline, fun, and lots of love. She moved into the house, and from that day on, Sally never had a problem with her. They became the best of friends, and "Julie" was a thoroughly enjoyable companion. She was very smart, was quite perceptive, and had a delightful sense of humor. The two of them had many good times together over the years. This bitch not only became Sally's favorite, but she also was in Sally's opinion the best bitch in conformation that she has ever owned. Sally adored her, and the bitch responded accordingly.

Ch. Whygin Busy Belinda, handled here by Stanley Flowers to a good win under Charles Hamilton, Progressive Dog Club of Wayne County in the late 1960s. Shamrock Acres Kennels, owners, Mr. and Mrs. James McCarthy.

Ch. Whygin Gentle Julia of Avec, one of the famous Labradors owned by Sally McCarthy, Shamrock Acres Kennels.

Within three weeks of her arrival at Shamrock Acres, "Julie" was entered in a show at Dubuque, Iowa, and she went Best of Breed for five points from the Classes over Specials and then finished off the day with second in the Sporting Group. The following week-end, she was Winners Bitch at the International for three points. She was bred to the State of Wisconsin Open Stake Field Champion Brodhead's Bar Booze and was not shown for five months. From that litter came Champion Shamrock Acres Jim Dandy, Champion Shamrock Acres Sugar, and Champion and Amateur Field Champion Shamrock Acres Simmer Down. After the litter was raised and she was back in coat, the McCarthys took "Julie" to two shows in New York and Connecticut. The first day she was Winners Bitch for four points at Suffolk County under James Warwick and the following day she was Best of Winners for five points at the Labrador Retriever Club National Specialty under judge Jerome Rich. She completed her championship with four majors in four consecutive shows. In 1962, she was Best of Opposite Sex at Chicago International.

Sally McCarthy credits "Julie" with "probably being the key to most of my successful breeding, and most everything I have in my show lines today goes back to her." No matter how this bitch was bred, she produced good Labs that finished. One of her offspring, Champion Shamrock Acres Ebony Lancer, owned by James Vercouteren, was sired by the 1965 National Field Champion Marten's Little Smokey. She was a prepotent bitch; her offspring, regardless of their sire, were typey and became splendid field workers.

After successful outcrossings, Helen Ginnel and Sally McCarthy decided to do a bit of experimenting. In those years, little line-breeding was practiced, and inbreeding was almost unknown in Labradors. Their decision to breed "Julie" back to her sire, Champion Whygin Gold Bullion, was made after careful study of the pedigree and the offspring of both proposed parents. It was a daring decision, made with serious and careful thought. The litter of six blacks and three yellows arrived on June 29th, 1962. Each of the ladies kept two puppies from the litter, and then each sold one of these later. All four of them finished. They were Canadian and American Champion Shamrock Acres Sonic Boom, Champion Shamrock Acres Casey Jones, C.D. (Light Brigade's sire), Champion Shamrock Acres Whygin Snow, and Champion Whygin Luck of Shamrock Acres. One bitch, sold to a show home, became Champion Shamrock Acres Twenty Caret. Thus five champions came out of this "experimental" litter. Two were sold as companions, and two were excellent gun dogs. All nine in this litter were very good-looking and probably finishable. In later years, the breeding was repeated twice. The first litter had two puppies in it; both were good-looking, but only one of them was shown and finished, Champion Shamrock Acres Sparkle Plenty C.D. The third litter from these parents was a disappointment; not one of the eight pups finished a championship. Some breeders feel that repeat breedings are never as successful as the original. Sally McCarthy does not believe this always to be true, although in this case it was for sure!

In 1963, another bitch, four-year-old Champion Whygin Busy Belinda, was acquired from Helen Ginnel. She was a well-coordinated Lab who moved beautifully, never putting a foot down incorrectly. She completed her championship in 1965. She was bred to the two littermates, Champion Shamrock Acres Sonic Boom and Champion Shamrock Acres Casey Jones, C.D., and produced eleven champions, including two Best in Show winners, Champion Shamrock Acres Dapper Dan and Champion Shamrock Acres Light Brigade.

The foundation bitches in the Shamrock Acres lines were Champion Whygin Campaign Promise, Champion Whygin Gentle Julia of Avec, and Champion Whygin Busy Belinda. The two original studs that had the most influence were Champion Whygin Poppitt and Champion Whygin Gold Bullion. Out of these five dogs came the first Shamrock Acres Labrador champions, the first seven of which were finished in 1963.

Sally McCarthy's own breeding produced Champion Shamrock Acres Sonic Boom, sire of 32 champions; Champion Shamrock Acres Casey Jones, C.D., sire of nine champions; Champion Shamrock Acres Light Brigade, sire of 94 champions; Champion Shamrock Acres Donnybrook, sire of 31 champions (27 American and 4 Canadian); Champion Royal Oaks V.I.P. O'Shamrock Acres C.D., sire of 31 champions; and Champion Shamrock Acres Dark Cloud, sire of eight champions. These are the dogs behind all of the breeding taking place at Shamrock Acres today. Sonic Boom, Light Brigade, and Donnybrook all belonged to Sally McCarthy. The other three were owned by other fanciers after puppy age, but Mrs. McCarthy used them frequently.

Sonic Boom (black) was as beautiful as his dam, Gentle Julia. Mrs. McCarthy had kept him and Casey Jones (yellow), and as the two pups matured, she felt that she could not properly socialize two littermates and so sold Casey at six months of age to Suzanne Sullivan. "Boomer" reminded his owner so much of his dam that there was never any question as to which she would keep. He accumulated an impressive record in the ring, considering that he was shown owner-handled on a very limited basis. Stan Flowers took him to two shows as a champion and won the Group on both occasions. Other than that, Mrs. McCarthy handled the dog herself. When Sonic Boom was 15 months old, Mrs. McCarthy felt that he was ready to go, and they headed for their annual trip to the Labrador National Specialty. That was in 1963, when "Boomer" won Best of Winners for five points at the Specialty held with the Ox Ridge

Can., Am. Ch. Shamrock Acres Sonic Boom belongs to Mr. and Mrs. James McCarthy.

Kennel Club in Connecticut; then the following day he did likewise at Northwestern Connecticut. He completed his American title in fifteen days with three majors. On his first time out as a Special, when he was 16 months old, he won a Group second. Two weeks later, he won his first Sporting Group. In 1964, he was Best of Breed and fourth in the Group at Westminster, the first time that a Labrador had placed in a Group at that event in more than 30 years. That same spring, he was Best of Winners at the Labrador Retriever Club of Ontario, Canada, Specialty show for five points and on to Best of Breed over 13 champions. He was shown four times in four days at the Canadian National Sportsman shows, winning four five-point majors, three Bests of Breed, and a first in two Sporting Groups, all from the classes. The next month, he was Best of Breed and fourth in the Group at the International Kennel Club in Chicago. Sally McCarthy does not particularly enjoy handling, but of Boomer she says, "he was a joy in the ring and we had fun together. He was a delight." When he was seven-and-a-half years old, this magnificent dog developed a malignant tumor on his jaw, and he was gone before he was eight years old.

Champion Shamrock Acres Light Brigade and Champion Shamrock Acres Dapper Dan were littermates, born on July 6th, 1964. Mrs. McCarthy kept only one of these puppies, "Briggs," as Light Brigade was known. As a very young puppy he travelled with his owner to the shows, as that was the year during which she was showing Sonic Boom. Owner-handled, "Briggs" completed his championship with three majors by the time he was 13 months old. Mrs. McCarthy felt he needed maturity before being shown for Best of Breed competition, so she kept him home for two years to "grow up." Since she was going through a divorce in 1966 and was left with six young children, she made very few shows during that period.

In the spring of 1967, "Briggs" came out to be campaigned. He was co-owned by Sally McCarthy and John W. McAssey for one year, and then in February 1968 John sold his interest in the dog to Mrs. James Getz, who co-owned him with Mrs. McCarthy for the balance of his lifetime. Dick Cooper handled "Briggs" to all of his wins as a Special.

"Briggs" earned 13 Group placements in the five months that he was shown during 1967. He won five Group firsts in January 1968 on the Florida Circuit, his first Best in Show in Louisville, Kentucky, and Best of Breed at Westminster. He was off and running on a career that

Champion Shamrock Acres Light Brigade, the sire of 94 champions, is the Top Producing Labrador Sire for numbers of champions in the United States and in the world. Winner of 12 Bests in Show, Light Brigade is the Top Winning Labrador Retriever of all time in the United States. Owners, Sally B. McCarthy and Mrs. James R. Getz.

brought him a total of 12 Bests in Show, 45 Group firsts, 14 Group seconds, 9 Group thirds, and 7 Group fourths. He was the winner of the Ken-L-Ration Sporting Group Award in 1968, although he was shown only nine months out of that year. Mrs. McCarthy believes this to be the only time to date that a Lab has won that honor. All of "Briggs" Group placings and Bests in Show were gained during a period of 14 months in 1967-68.

To date, Champion Shamrock Acres Light Brigade has sired 94 champions, which is certainly impressive! He died at age 14 in July 1978. Even at that advanced age, he was a handsome-looking dog. He moved soundly and stood square, front and rear—both looked good. He was up on his pasterns and still had beautiful feet. Mrs. McCarthy comments: "Most of the Shamrock Acres dogs mature quite slowly, but age gracefully. They are still active gundogs at 12 years, and do not break down as they grow older." Sally McCarthy further comments:

It always amazes me that dog owners are still coming up to me and saying that they will never forget how beautiful he looked in 1968, winning at International. He always seemed to be the favorite with the 'gate,' which is unusual for a Lab since they are neither so flashy as a coated dog nor so cute as a Toy. They were always curious as to what kind of a dog 'Briggs' was at home. Above all else he was a gentleman—well mannered, polite, and sensitive. He could be kenneled with any dog I owned, male or female. He loved children (was always finding his training dummy for them to show) and enjoyed everyone. he was an easy dog to live with and an easy dog to condition. He just stayed in good shape all of his life and lived here except for the 14 months he was with Dick Cooper. 'Briggs' was known not only for his record-setting wins, and championship, but for his smile. He was quite a smiler, and would do so upon request. It really got to be quite a joke. Unfortunately, he hadn't perfected it during his show career, or he might have smiled at judges and won a few more Bests in Show.

And there you have a picture of the ideal temperament that makes Labradors so dearly loved by all who know the breed.

Mrs. McCarthy adds that "Briggs" was not only the Number One Sporting Group winner in 1968, but he was also the Number Five Group winner of all breeds. The 94 champions he sired include two Best in Show dogs, two dogs with T.D. degrees, four dogs with U.D. degrees, six C.D.X. winners, and 20 C.D. winners in obedience. Nineteen of his champions also have obedience degrees, including two T.D.'s and two U.D.'s. He also sired the Top Winning Labrador in Norway (1971, Mrs. McCarthy believes), Norsk Champion Royal Oak Shamrock Acres Thyme.

In 1968, an Illinois couple bred their Shamrock Acres Tara to Light Brigade while he was down at Dick Cooper's. Mrs. McCarthy had not seen Tara since she was seven weeks old, when she was sold as a family companion, so Mrs. McCarthy had absolutely no idea what she looked like when mature. Shortly after the litter was whelped, the family from Illinois moved to California. The family sold all of the pups except one, which they deposited at Shamrock Acres one weekend while Mrs. McCarthy was away. She was quite upset about this and had no intention of keeping the pup. However, he had a most delightful personality and she quickly found that she was quite taken with him. He grew up to become Champion Shamrock Acres Donnybrook, C.D., named because of the donnybrook he caused upon his arrival. He was definitely not a fighter, just a good-natured, fun-loving guy known as "Mr. Congeniality" at home.

Donnybrook completed his championship at 13 months of age, with three major shows, including Best of Breed over champions. He was Best of Winners from the Puppy Class for five points at the spring 1969 International. He was rarely shown as a Special and never campaigned. Donnybrook was a fine working dog, had several months of professional field training, and was featured in a television documentary on retrievers in the field. As the sire of 31 champions (27 American and four Canadian) and at least 12 offspring with obedience degrees, he played an important role in the Shamrock Acres breeding program. A daughter of his was Winners Bitch at the International in 1971, as was another daughter at the fall International in 1973.

Over the years Shamrock Acres has continued its breeding program with subsequent generations from their original Whygin stock. Most of their breeding in the show championship lines is line-breeding. Occasionally a puppy is purchased from an entirely different line to bring into the program, or one of the field-bred bitches is used to do an outcross; then Mrs. McCarthy keeps a pup from one of these litters to breed back into the original line.

Of particular interest is the fact that in so prominent a show Lab kennel, "field" breeding has by no means taken a back seat; Shamrock Acres is undoubtedly the only Labrador kennel in the United States featuring *both* a show line and a field line. Additionally, Shamrock Acres has, for three years, produced the Top Winning Labrador in the United States (Light Brigade for 1968, Champion Royal Oaks V.I.P. O'Shamrock Acres for 1973, and Champion Shamrock Acres Benjamin, C.D. for 1974) and has *also* bred a National Field Champion, 1979 National Field Champion McGuffy, whom Mrs. McCarthy bred but who does not carry the Shamrock Acres prefix because the novice owner inadvertently omitted it when registering the dog. It is ironic, indeed, to finally achieve this and then have the kennel name left off, as Mrs. McCarthy is very proud of having accomplished this with her breeding program.

Ch. Shamrock Acres One Way Ticket, owned by the Shamrock Acres Kennels of Mr. and Mrs. James McCarthy, pictured at the Greely Kennel Club in 1968.

Ch. Ralston of Shamrock Acres, by Ch. Whygin Poppitt ex Ch. Whygin Campaign Promise, an excellent example of the breeding program at Helen Ginnel's kennel, Bedford Hills, New York.

The Shamrock Acres Kennel population is usually divided evenly between the dogs with show backgrounds and those with field backgrounds, and there are some with a combination of the two. Mrs. McCarthy feels it is always more of a challenge to breed better looking field dogs and better working show dogs, than to see what can be improved by combining the two lines. Basically she feels Labradors should be top-notch workers in the field, beautiful to look at, and easy to live with. To break it down, her ideal Labrador should have a lovely soft expression, have a great sense of humor, and be an eager, hard worker in the field, perceptive, intelligent, loyal, typey, sound, willing to please, and just plain easy to live with on a day-to-day basis. She says, "I haven't bred the perfect one yet, but I'm always hoping I will. I love the breed!"

Shamrock Acres still has bitches that are fifth and sixth generation progeny of their first Labrador, Marlab Gypsy, C.D. This line has "worn well" over the years; thus it is being continued. In addition, Mrs. McCarthy has kept several daughters and granddaughters of National Amateur Field Champion (1968) Super Chief and has bred them to sons and grandsons of the National Amateur Field Champion (1972 and 1975) and Canadian National Field Champion (1971, 1973, and 1974) River Oaks Corky. No males from the field lines are kept at Shamrock Acres; Mrs. McCarthy prefers to send all of their field champion daughters out to be bred to other field champions or occasionally to breed them to one of their show champion studs.

Shamrock Acres has improved the looks of its field lines over the years. Dark eyes, much improved heads, and type are the greatest changes. In retrospect, however Mrs. McCarthy feels they were fortunate that their first Labs were sound in body and temperament and that they were quite representative of the breed. She does some line-breeding in her field lines, but this line-breeding is not quite so tight as in the show lines. The McCarthys are no longer running field trials, but the family members are avid hunters and have their personal hunting favorites among the dogs, using them on pheasants, partridge, geese, and ducks.

It is interesting that several of the more recently finished dual champions have show champion dams and field champion sires. For example, there are Dual Champion Shamrock Acres Super Drive, by National Amateur Field Champion and National Field Champion Super Chief ex Champion Could Be's Mis Erable, bred by Sally McCarthy; Dual Champion Royal Oaks Jill of Burgundy, by Super Chief ex Champion Shamrock Acres Whygin Tardy, C.D., bred by Laurie Allen; and Dual Champion Trumarc's Triple Threat, by Field Champion and Amateur Field Champion Air Express ex Champion Sunburst Blackfoot Nell, bred by Judith Weikel. Air Express and Blackfoot Nell are of particular interest because Air Express is a son of Super Chief and Blackfoot Nell a daughter of Champion Shamrock Acres Sonic Boom, one a top producer in the field area and the other a top producer in the show line.

The first Amateur Field Champion Sally McCarthy bred was Champion and Amateur Field Champion Shamrock Acres Simmer Down, by Brodhead's Bar Booze ex Champion Whygin Gentle Julia of Avec. In some books, she is listed as a dual champion, but according to A.K.C. rules, a dual champion is a show champion and a field champion, which Simmer is not. She is a show champion and an amateur field champion whose owners, because of a divorce, stopped running her in trials when she needed only half a point to become a full field champion, which is a pity.

Shamrock Acres has always been a family operation, thoroughly enjoyed by Sally McCarthy and her sons and daughters. Two of the girls show in conformation, one also in obedience. The three boys live and breathe hunting, and one girl has a "companion Lab."

There are Labs of all three colors at Shamrock Acres, which started with blacks. The first yellow, Champion Whygin Copper Coin, came from Helen Ginnel in 1960. The first homebred yellows were produced in 1961, and the first chocolates were whelped in 1965. Many of the chocolates have a dual background, with both Super Chief and Light Brigade figuring in the picture.

Beautiful Labs owned by Simerdown Kennels, Rob and Linda Vaughn, Arvada, Colorado. Ch. Mandigo's Simerdown Destiny, C.D. (yellow, left), Ch. Simerdown's Rompin' Renegade, C.D.X. (yellow, right), and Ch. Wingmaster's Swiss Ms, C.D. (chocolate).

Simerdown

Simerdown Labradors, at Arvada, Colorado, belong to Rob and Linda Vaughn who became involved with the breed early in the 1970s. They have made it a policy to use only the soundest breeding stock (their dogs are O.F.A. and P.R.A. cleared annually) of superior looks, temperament, working ability, and pedigree. The Vaughns' dogs are entirely owner-trained and owner-handled.

Among the Labs that have been successful for the Vaughns is Champion Mandigo's Simerdown Destiny, C.D., a yellow son of Ch. Franklin's Golden Mandigo ex Champion Concho's Chivas Regal. At five years of age, Destiny has four pointed-offspring, and has produced the 1980 and 1981 L.R.C.G.D. Best Puppy in Match winners. Both Destiny's sire and dam are Top Producers, and the Vaughns are hoping that this dog will follow in their footsteps. Destiny is also a Best of Breed winner, although he is not extensively campaigned.

Champion Simerdown's Rompin' Renegade, C.D.X., by Champion Shamrock Acres Yellow Fella ex Mandigo's Free 'n' Easy, is the granddaughter of the Vaughns' first Labrador. She is a multiple Best of Breed winner and was Reserve Winners Bitch at the 1979 G.G.L.R.C. Specialty. She also is successful in obedience and is now training for her U.D. Renegade's puppies are just now reaching show age, and her pup by Champion Monarch's Black Arrogance, Simerdown's Tedrick, was Best Puppy at the 1981 fall Match show in Denver.

Champion Wingmaster's Swiss Ms, C.D., by Champion Williston's Brown Smith ex Wingmaster's Shenandoah, C.D., was Winners Bitch and Best of Opposite Sex at the 1980 H.L.R.C. Specialty under Mrs. Janet Churchill, and she is also a Best of Breed winner. She has one major-pointed daughter, Johnson's Molly, sired by Champion Ravenwood's Brigadier, and two promising young sons, Simerdown's Charlie Brown and Simerdown's Jackson Brown, sired by Champion Gunfield's Super Charger.

Simerdown's McKenna Kendall (left), by Ch. Coal Creek's Briary Breakthrough ex Ch. Mandigo's Simerdown Destiny, owned by Lee Monez and the Vaughns; Ch. Simerdown's Rompin' Renegade (yellow, lying down), co-owned by the Vaughns and Chris Simons; Wingmaster's Annie Oakley (middle), by Ardmargha Samson ex Wingmaster's Brayhill Noel, owned by the Vaughns; Ch. Mandigo's Simerdown Destiny, C.D. (right); Ch. Wingmaster's Swiss Ms, C.D. (lying down).

Simerdown's McKenna Kendall is co-owned with Lee Monez. At 18 months of age, he has nine points (both majors) and was Best of Breed from the classes and Best in Sweepstakes at a recent Specialty.

Wingmaster's Annie Oakley, 20 months old, has both her majors and her Labrador Retriever Club Working Certificate.

South Gate

South Gate Labradors, owned by Sally P. Jennings of Southport, Connecticut, traces its beginning to a hot, steamy bathroom on Christmas day in 1973. The mistress of the house had dumped soaps and bath salts, gifts found under the tree, into a hot tub and was about to settle herself in when a knock was heard on the door and the master appeared with "one more unopened Christmas gift"—a yellow Labrador puppy in a large red flannel Christmas stocking.

A few Match shows in early 1974, followed by handling classes and some summer A.K.C. local point shows, convinced the puppy's owners that Labradors are, indeed, a worthwhile breed. One beautiful moonlit summer evening, the Jennings, in answer to a Long Island ad for puppies for sale, sped across Long Island Sound in a 14-foot Whaler to purchase not one but two puppies, returning with these additions to a kennel

Ch. South Gate's Beau Geste taking his first points at his first show, Farmington Valley 1979, owner-handled by Edward A. (Ted) Jennings, Southport, Connecticut.

whose name they now proudly display on the side of their van.

The competitive spirit took hold, and three years of trial-and-error breeding followed. The Jennings' mastery of the pitfalls of genetic defects and pedigree welding led to outstanding results.

1977 was a memorable year. It began with a visit from the town's zoning officer, who informed the Jennings that no more than three dogs could be loose in their backyard at one time. In March of that year, future Champion South Gate's Meggin, W.C. was born, an outstanding yellow bitch who distinguished herself in the show ring and as an owner-handled field dog of great acclaim. In the summer of 1977, South Gate Labradors moved to a four-acre farm in Connecticut with complete seclusion, a pond for dogs, and a large swimming pool to accommodate children and dogs. Add to all of this a kennel-barn with horses, chickens, goats, cats, and honey bees and all that is lacking is Noah's Ark!

In 1978, Champion South Gate's Beau Geste (O.F.A. Excellent) joined the kennel, followed in 1979 by the additions of South Gate's Gator, C.D. and South Gate's Stormy Petrol.

As the 1980s begin, South Gate continues to flourish with new breeding designed to establish this name as one of New England's finest dual-purpose Labrador kennels.

Handler-breeder Sally P. Jennings with Ch. Meggin of South Gate, W.C., taking her class, Open Yellow Bitches, at the 1979 Potomac Specialty. Meggin followed through that day by going on to Best of Breed. Her owner is Charles W. Appleton.

South Gate's Serendipity at nine months old was Best Puppy in Sweepstakes at the New Jersey Labrador Club over an entry of 90 puppies. Handled by Ted Jennings for owners, Thomas and Natalie Shawah.

South Gate's Gator, C.D., taking her first points, a three-point major from Bred-by Exhibitor Class at Kenilworth 1981. Owned and handled by Sally P. Jennings.

Spenrock

Spenrock Kennels, Registered, was established in the 1960s. For many years prior to that, Janet Churchill had bred German Shepherds for conformation and obedience, and Aberdeen-Angus cattle were also bred under the Spenrock prefix for many years. While German Shepherds were her childhood breed, Janet became interested in fox-hunting while attending college in Virginia, where she was M.F.H. (master of foxhounds) of the Sweet Briar Hunt for two years, and then in Massachusetts she was M.F.H. at the Groton Hunt for over ten years. At Groton, all hounds in the pack (usually 50 to 60 hounds) were retained, so the breeding program which was necessary gave her a chance to establish the best type of hound to hunt the country as well as an animal with good conformation. For many years, the Groton hounds took top honors in stiff competition at the Foxhound shows. Three to four litters a year were whelped and all puppies were retained for the hunt; thus Janet was given an excellent opportunity to study the results of a breeding program. Uniformity in appearance was desirable, sound conformation and movement were essential, and hunting qualities to provide good sport were also vital.

A move to Maryland's Eastern Shore in 1964 prompted the need for a "water dog" for gunning ducks and Canada geese. Janet decided the Labrador would be the best gun dog and retriever for a family companion and hunting, and knowing nothing at all about the breed, she looked in the *Baltimore Sun* under "Dogs for Sale." Since, at that time, there were ten Foxhounds and several German Shepherds in residence at her kennel, she thought an older pup would be easier; so she purchased a four-month-old black male, advertised as a pet. At the time of the purchase, the owner asked, "Would you like to see his sister?" Not needing any more dogs, Janet gave a reluctant nod, just to be polite. Out came a black puppy bitch who came up to her, tugged at Janet's socks, and looked her in the eye in a manner that demanded, "Buy me, too." Janet did, and she went home with two Labradors, not knowing or caring anything about their pedigrees. When this information finally arrived from the previous owner, Mr. James F. Lewis, who had a surrogate sell the puppies for him, she was pleasantly surprised to find champions and a lot of line-breeding.

Janet Churchill with her first two Labs, Ch. Lewis-field Spenrock Ballot, W.C., and Int. Ch. Spenrock Banner, W.C., when these Lab littermates were eight months old.

When the puppies were six months old, Janet entered them in a show, and the rest is history. Because she was bewildered by the crowds, the bitch placed Reserve Winners at that show, but from there on she finished her championship while still a puppy and that year won Best of Breed at the Westchester Kennel Club under Helen Warwick. The week after the Westchester show, she got the first of many Group placements at a show in Pennsylvania. Janet believes that this bitch, discarded by the breeder as pet quality and purchased by her with no knowledge of the bitch's background, could so easily have been purchased by someone else, and then spayed and forgotten—this would certainly have been a tragic loss to Labradors!

As fate would have it, Champion Spenrock Banner was destined to become an important name in many pedigrees. She lived to be 15 and left behind a legacy of outstanding progeny and descendants. Banner herself was highly successful in the ring. Janet handled her to championships in the United States, Canada, and Bermuda. Bob Forsyth also handled her to many important wins, including an exciting Best of Breed in Beverly Hills, California. Banner was Best of Breed or Best of Opposite Sex 98% of the time she appeared in the ring during her career, accumulating 85 Bests of Breed and 13 Group placements, mostly in tough East Coast competition.

Banner's brother, Champion Lewisfield Spenrock Ballot, finished his championship with a five-point win under Frank Evans Jones and was given to a friend, Elsie Hunteman, who used him as a working gun dog in her goose hunting business near Easton, Maryland.

Banner's dam, Champion Sandylands Spungold, was imported from England by Dorothy Francke, who bred her to Champion Lockerbie Sandylands Tarquin, another English import. Spungold had only one litter, which produced five champions.

Working ability was always important to Janet, so she raised mallard ducks with which to train her labs. Both Ballot and Banner earned Working Certificates and were used during the gunning season. In the winter time, they continued to work—pulling a dog sled. Banner was the lead dog when a team of three was driven, and she really knew her job. Not only could Banner do a day's work, but she also had a style and grace that has yet to be duplicated. A great tribute was paid to her by the late Alva Rosenberg in an incident quoted by both Mrs. Churchill and Frank Jones. Walking across a show ground in New Jersey with Frank one day, Alva spotted Banner from a distance. "Isn't she beautiful," said Mr. Rosenberg, as he and Frank rushed up to go over the bitch. Mr. Rosenberg said she was the best Lab he had ever seen, and Mr. Jones informed him that she was the top bitch the *breed* had ever seen, and one of the greats of both sexes as well. Anyone who knew Alva can recall his excitement and enthusiasm whenever a dog particularly impressed him and thus can picture this occasion quite clearly!

Left, Int. Ch. Spenrock Banner, W.C., and on the right her brother Ch. Lewisfield Spenrock Ballot, W.C., having fun pulling the sled for the children.

Trenton Kennel Club, 1966. Janet Churchill's Ch. Spenrock Banner taking Best of Breed handled by Robert S. Forsyth.

Banner was bred to Champion Sandylands Midas (English import) for her first litter, which produced the outstanding yellow bitch Champion Spenrock Sans Souci who won the National Lab Specialty in 1970. Sans Souci was owned by John Valentine, who never allowed her to be bred as she was too valuable to him as a companion and hunting bitch. This litter also produced Champion Spenrock Phanomshire Amber and Champion Spenrock Spun Candy. Spenrock Statesman, also from this litter, won a five-point major at the Eastern Dog Club show in Boston his first time out, but unfortunately he suffered an untimely death.

Banner's second litter was sired by the English import, Champion Lockerbie Goldentone Jensen. This litter produced some very well-known Labs: Champion Spenrock Cardigan Bay (placed in Groups) an outstanding gun dog; Champion Spenrock Bohemia Champagne, foundation bitch for Diane Pilbin's Chucklebrook Kennels; Spenrock Delta Minnow, foundation bitch for Robert Montgomery; Champion Spenrock Cognac, foundation bitch for Lobuff Kennels, owned by Jerry and Lisa Weiss; Champion Spenrock Cajun; and Spenrock Egyptian Candor, foundation bitch for Sue Powers. Spenrock Kim Huntley, also from this litter, had won points and was to be a foundation bitch for Dr. John Gordon, but unfortunately she was lost in a fire.

Banner's third litter was small, with only four puppies sired by Champion Lockerbie Goldentone Jensen. Champion Spenrock Topaz became a foundation bitch for George and Louise White. Champion Spenrock Topgallant was a good winner in the United States and Canada.

For her fourth litter, Banner was again bred to Champion Sandylands Midas. Spenrock Domino was sold to Mr. A.B. "Bull" Hancock, one of the top breeders of thoroughbreds at his Claiborne Farm in Lexington, Kentucky. Champion Spenrock Hello Dolly was a foundation bitch for Rosalind Paul, and Spenrock Dynamo was a foundation bitch for Jane Babbitt. Spenrock Dragon went without papers to owners in Texas via a friend. He was sent to a field trial trainer and was so good that they wrote to find out his breeding; they were no doubt surprised at what they considered a "show" pedigree. Spenrock has always felt that show Labs could work if given an opportunity.

Champion Rivermist Tweed of Spenrock was the sire of Banner's next litter, from which came the Group-placing bitch Champion Spenrock Boomerang, as well as Spenrock Brandy Snifter, C.D., foundation bitch for Patty Ramey, and Spenrock Bucephalus, owned by Patricia Quinn.

Banner's last litter was sired by another

Janet Churchill, owner of Int. Ch. Spenrock's Banner, W.C., did this beautiful needlepoint which hangs on the wall at Spenrock.

English import, Champion Lockerbie Stanwood Granada. This produced Champion Spenrock Anthony Adverse, who as a puppy was placed Best in Match by Mrs. Gwen Broadley of the Sandylands Kennel. Unfortunately, he was lost to the breed at an early age and sired only a few litters. However, his influence on the breed has been outstanding, mainly through his daughters, Briary Allegra and Champion Briary Abbey Road. Another Anthony daughter, Spenrock Amanda, became a foundation bitch for Thelma Ham. Two good males from this litter were Champion Spenrock Ambassador and Spenrock Argonaut.

Ch. Lawnwood's Tamstar Trust at Spenrock. Winner of Best in Show in England, this handsome Lab by Ch. Lawnwood's Fame and Fortune ex Ch. Tamstar Glenfield Mischief was imported and shown by Mrs. Janet Churchill. Owned by Mrs. Richard C. du Pont.

Because of the predominance of English bloodlines, Janet has made half a dozen trips to England to meet the breeders of the Labs in her pedigrees. Spenrock's first English import was a lovely yellow bitch, Champion Lawnwood's Tamstar Trust, who won several Bests in Show in England.

A search for a suitable black male in England to stand at stud at Spenrock led Janet to Champion Spenrock Heatheredge Mariner. Purchased as a puppy, Mariner stayed in England with Marjorie Satterthwaite, who showed him as a puppy in England and Scotland. At the Manchester Championship show, Mary Roslin-Williams gave Mariner the following critique:

"very promising black Labrador, quality and outline, charming head and expression. Good neck and shoulders, beautiful body for age, excellent coat, legs and feet . . . . should make a lovely quality Labrador." Imported at the age of ten months, Mariner, handled by Janet's daughter Jenny, won a major at his first show a month after his arrival. Used at stud shortly thereafter, Mariner sired all three colors in his first litter, including a chocolate bitch, Champion Spenrock Brown Bess. This gorgeous bitch never lost a class at a Specialty over a span of years, from Puppy to Open, winning under five different English judges.

Janet made a trip to Yorkshire to meet Miss M. Ward, Mariner's breeder, and to see his dam, Seashell of Heatheredge. Janet thought Seashell was a most outstanding bitch. Interestingly, Mariner is the 13th generation of Miss Ward's breeding. Miss Ward explained that she kept only bitches, always sending them to England's best stud dogs. A long time friend of Dr. Keith Barnett's, she tested her dogs for P.R.A. years before most breeders recognized the necessity for this.

Mariner has been a useful stud, siring black, yellow, and chocolate champions in the United States and Canada. His get have good hunting ability. His daughter, Milgrove's Special Amie, U.D.T., was Top Scoring Obedience Lab for several years and was the first Labrador to be Highest Scoring Obedience Dog, All Breeds, in the United States. Amie is owned and trained by Vicky Creamer.

A lovely informal pose of Ch. Spenrock Heatheredge Mariner.

Mrs. Richard C. du Pont owns these two handsome Labs, both from Janet Churchill's Spenrock Kennels. In this picture they are sitting with a canine friend at the entrance to Mrs. du Pont's Woodstock Farm.

Champion Lawnwood's Tamstar Trust, by Champion Lawnwood's Fame and Fortune ex Tamstar's Glenfield Mischief, was imported from England in 1973 from breeder Marjorie Satterthwaite. She produced two almost all male litters for Spenrock and then retired to nearby Woodstock Farm, owned by Mrs. Richard C. du Pont. Trust was later joined by Champion Spenrock Brown Bess, and these two Labs are Mrs. du Pont's constant companions. Trust appeared with Mrs. du Pont on the T.V. show entitled *Greatest Sports Legends*, when Tom Seaver interviewed Mrs. du Pont about the accomplishments of Kelso, her great race horse.

Spenrock next needed a good English male to use on the descendants of Banner, as well as the Mariner daughters, so Janet asked her friend Marjorie Satterthwaite in England to find a son of Champion Follytower Merrybrook Black Stormer. Spenrock wanted a grown dog so that his hips could be X-rayed before leaving England. Mrs. Satterthwaite searched around England, but nothing was available—until one day a pup she had sold was returned to her. She told Janet it was a nice dog, but it was chocolate (liver) rather than black. It was, however, sired by Stormer. Janet decided to buy him, and he soon received a hip dysplasia pass (#3975) from the British Veterinary Association. Marjorie wanted to show the dog, and so it was decided

that "Chock" should remain in England and, if possible, become the first chocolate English champion male Labrador. At that time, liver was not a color that the English favored, but Chock made up for his color with his excellent type and superlative showmanship. This dog is famous for the way he sets himself up, never putting a foot down incorrectly. He is what is referred to as "a showing fool," and Janet notes that one English judge called him a "devil." Chock became English and American Champion Lawnwood's Hot Chocolate. His record in England includes five Challenge Certificates, nine Reserve Challenge Certificates, and two Bests in Show, one of them at the Labrador Club of Northern Ireland. At Blackpool, in June 1977, judge Doris Johnson was lavish in her praise of him, calling him a dog "who has the right build to do a day's work and still go to the top in the show ring." This was on the occasion of Chock's fourth Challenge Certificate, a short time after he had completed his title at the Three Counties Championship show to become, as Janet and his breeder had hoped, the first male chocolate Labrador champion in England. He was shown once more overseas, winning a Challenge Certificate at the Border Union Championship show in Scotland, after which he left for Maryland. His get in England include two Challenge Certificate winners and guide dogs for the blind.

Above: This is Janet Churchill's famous chocolate Lab, appropriately named Lawnwood's Hot Chocolate. The English and American Champion here enjoys a day at Spenrock. **Left:** Handled by Robert S. Forsyth, the great winner and sire takes the Sporting Group at Hatboro Kennel Club in 1977.

Labrador Retriever Club of Potomac 1980. Winning the Stud Dog Class is Eng., Am. Ch. Lawnwood's Hot Chocolate with his progeny Ch. Broad Reach Bittersweet and Ch. Broad Reach Sugar and Spice. Hot Chocolate belongs to Mrs. Janet Churchill, the progeny to Martha Lee K. Voshell.

Champion Lawnwood's Hot Chocolate was four years old when he arrived in the United States. Up until this age, "Chock" had never been in a crate, his first introduction to this confinement having come at Heathrow where officials made him get in one for the short trip from the building to the cargo plane. "Chock" did not come over the way other dogs do. An airline captain who owns a Spenrock Lab went over specifically to pick up "Chock" for his new owner, bringing him back on a cargo plane so that he could ride loose up front with the crew. The crate was just a formality. Janet met "Chock" at Kennedy Airport, and after clearing customs, he was loaded into her small plane where again he had to get in a crate. He spent his first twenty minutes trying to take the crate apart, but when he gave up, that was it—and he never again objected to being crated when it was necessary.

Janet took "Chock" travelling so that people all over America could see the first chocolate English champion. Jane and Bob Forsyth handled "Chock" to his American title and to a Group win shortly after his arrival in the United States.

Janet handled "Chock" at all of the Specialties, and within one year he won three of them—in Texas, in California, and in Virginia. For three consecutive years, Janet and "Chock" won the Waterland Retriever Club's Trophy for the Top Winning Retriever (All Breeds), owner-handled. As all who ever saw him in the ring can attest, "Chock" was a wonderful showman. He looked like he was a handful, but it was all show. Once in the Sporting Group in Lexington, Kentucky, judge Ralph Del Deo asked for a loose lead, but this was no problem for "Chock"—his lead was held as an English handler would hold it and the dog moved like a gentleman on a loose lead. "Chock" enjoyed all the Specialty shows and attended many parties. He is an extrovert who loves a good time.

"Chock" was trained for the field in England, where he passed the necessary tests to be a full champion (instead of just a show champion). When you say "heel" out in the field, Janet notes, you have a different dog with you. Learning to swim among decoys took a little time, but otherwise he found American hunting to his liking, especially the water work.

In the off-season, "Chock" spends hours in the river, swimming around and dragging logs out of the water. His energy knows no bounds,

Eng., Am. Ch. Lawnwood's Hot Chocolate arrives from England on the way to his new home, Spenrock Kennels.

but even so he is a gentleman in the home and he makes a delightful house dog. Acting like an ordinary dog, "Chock" will accompany Janet in the car and sit on the seat for hours while she shops. "Chock" is a remarkable dog, for not only has he made his mark as a sire both here and in England, but he has also brought much pleasure to his owners as a show dog, gun dog, and family dog—another *true* dual-purpose Lab!

Spenrock's most recent English import was the black bitch Champion Swift of Ballyduff and Spenrock, a daughter of Champion Ballyduff Marketeer, purchased from the late Bridget Docking. Swift was purchased as a young pup-

Eng., Am. Ch. Lawnwood's Hot Chocolate gives another example of the fact that great show Labs can be great field Labs, too, as he carries the bird on retrieve. Jan Churchill owns this celebrated and widely admired dog.

py, but she remained in England so that Janet could personally handle her at Cruft's, where she won a large Puppy Class. Swift is a sister of one of England's best Labs, Champion Squire of Ballyduff, of whom it has been said: "he could win at field trials in the morning and top shows in the afternoon." Swift herself is a top gun dog. She won her class at the Labrador Specialty, and owner-handled, she was Best of Winners to finish at the Westchester Kennel Club. Swift has had two litters of all black bitches. One of Spenrock's young hopefuls is her grandson, Spenrock Sea Fury, sired by Spenrock Argonaut, a brother of Champion Spenrock Anthony Adverse. It is unfortunate that Anthony sired only a few litters before his untimely death, but despite this fact, he has been very influential in the breed through his daughters Champion Briary Abbey Road, Briary Allegro, and Champion Briary Bustle.

Young hopefuls are Spenrock Sea Fury, co-owned with Mary Manuel in California, and Spenrock Tempest, co-owned with Mrs. Jerry Weiss in New York. Another of Spenrock's youngsters is Spenrock Gooney Bird, sired by American and Canadian Champion Martin of Ballyduff, a littermate of Swift. The dam is Champion Spenrock Winds Aloft, a grand-daughter of Banner.

Future Ch. Swift of Ballyduff and Spenrock at seven months old while still in England. Spenrock Kennels, owner, Janet Churchill, Chesapeake City, Maryland.

Spenrock has strived to produce dual-purpose Labs who can do a day's work and win in the show ring. English bloodlines have been used to retain good Labrador type. All breeding stock is X-rayed normal, and eyes are examined on a regular basis. While the dog's hunting instinct is very important, its ability to perform other tasks is also appreciated, and some Spenrock Labs have been given to schools that train Labs to be guide dogs for the blind.

Spenrock's latest champion is Champion Spenrock Tweed of Windfields, at one time co-owned with Mr. E.P. Taylor, Windfields Farm,

The lovely puppy Spenrock Sea Fury, co-owned by Mary Manuel of Bakersfield, California, and Janet Churchill of Spenrock Kennels, Chesapeake City, Maryland. The puppy, sired by Spenrock Argonaut (litter-brother to Ch. Spenrock Anthony Adverse) ex Spenrock Spitfire, was bred by Spenrock Kennels and Frederick Johnson and is pictured along-side a painting of one of Mrs. Churchill's famous winners, in whose paw-prints the youngster hopes to follow.

Janet Churchill out shooting with three of her Labs representing all three colors: Eng., Am. Ch. Lawnwood's Hot Chocolate on the right, then Ch. Spenrock Tweed of Windfield, and Ch. Spenrock Heatheredge Mariner, black, on the left.

Ch. Spenrock Heatheredge Mariner, co-pilot in Jan Churchill's airplane.

who is the world's top breeder of thoroughbred race horses.

Labradors travelling to and from Spenrock are often transported in Jan Churchill's twin-engine Skymaster. Jan holds an airline transport license and is an instrument flight instructor and an F.A.A. Accident Prevention Counselor. She is also type-rated in a DC-3 and flies a restored World War II Navy R4D (a military DC-3 or C47) at air shows and open houses at military bases for the Mid-Atlantic Air Museum.

Jan Churchill has been approved to judge Labradors since 1972.

Spenrock Kennels is located on a 150-acre farm on Maryland's Eastern Shore, with about half a mile of shoreline on the Bohemia River, a tributary of the Chesapeake Bay. Ducks and geese are hunted at Spenrock during the gun season.

Spenrock Labradors enjoying the Bohemia River on Maryland's eastern shore. Photo by Jan Churchill, owner.

Springfield

One of the most famous kennels of any breed in the United States is Springfield Labradors, started in 1963 by Mrs. Robert V. Clark, Jr. at Springfield Farm in Middleburg, Virginia. At that time, the kennel was managed by Connie Barton, who has since joined the American Kennel Club as a Field Representative. More recently, Mrs. Diana Beckett has been manager at Springfield, but she and her husband are planning to return to their native England in early 1982.

Ch. Kimvalley Cinderella, litter-sister to Eng., Am. Ch. Kimvalley Crispin, belongs to Mrs. Robert V. Clark, Jr., Springfield Farm, Middleburg, Virginia.

The first show Lab, and the foundation bitch for Springfield, was American and Canadian Champion Kimvalley Cinderella, who was purchased by Mrs. Clark from Diana and Don Beckett in England. She was nicknamed "Barkie" and reigned as "queen" at Springfield until the age of 14½ years. She was loved by all, and anyone who knew Liz Clark also knew "Barkie," as Mrs. Clark and she were inseparable—"Barkie" accompanied her owner everywhere. "Barkie" was the dam of Champion Springfield's Miss Willing, who was the kennel's first homebred champion. The number of champions to Springfield's credit totals at least one hundred, with sixty or more of them homebred! This is, indeed, an exciting record.

Ch. Springfield's Miss Willing taking first in the Veteran's Class at the 1976 Lab Specialty. Owner is Mrs. Robert V. Clark, Jr.; handler is Diana Beckett.

Shamrock Acres Light Brigade ex Champion Goldsboro Toto of Oz); Champion Kimvalley Warrenton (English Champion Sandylands Garry ex Hope of Ardmargha); and Champion Ardmargha Goldcrest of Syrancot, bred by Mr. and Mrs. H.C. Clayton in England, by Champion Sandylands Garry ex Sandylands Komely of Ardmargha.

Among the top winning males produced at Springfield Kennels are Champion Springfield's Faust, Champion Springfield's Cabaret, and Champion Springfield's Jack O'Lantern. The emphasis here is on the homebred bitches, however; Mrs. Clark's policy from the beginning has been to import the finest English bloodlines as stud dogs and to raise her own bitches for breeding to them.

Some of the noted dogs who have helped bring fame and success to Springfield, in addition to those already mentioned, have included Champion Sandylands Midnight Cowboy, English and American Champion Sorn Sandpiper of Follytower, Champion Poolstead Private Member, and, of course, the current "star,"

Eng., Am. Ch. Kimvalley Picklewitch winning the Veteran Bitch Class at the Labrador Retriever Club Specialty, October 1981. This magnificent 11-year-old went on that day to Best of Opposite Sex, defeating 221 bitches in the process. Owned by Mrs. Robert V. Clark, Jr.; handled by Diana Beckett.

Mrs. Clark has won the National Specialty five times. She won twice with Champion Hillsboro Wizard of Oz, once with a homebred bitch named Champion Springfield's Musette, and twice with English and American Champion Kimvalley Picklewitch, whose last Specialty Best of Breed was from the Veterans Class at eight years old and who in 1981, at eleven years old, was Best of Opposite Sex at the National, again from the Veterans Class over a huge entry of bitches. "Pickle" is probably the most famous Lab bitch in America, if not in the world!

English and American Champion Kimvalley Crispin, litter-brother to Champion Kimvalley Cinderella, was another purchase from Don and Diana Beckett and was not only Number One Lab for two years but was also the first Best in Show winner owned by Mrs. Clark. Other Best in Show Labs that have brought honors to Springfield include Champion Hillsboro Wizard of Oz (who was by the great Champion

Champion Mardas Brandlesholme Sam's Song, who was not only Number One Lab two years in a row under D. Roy Holloway's capable handling but is also the Lab who has placed highest of any member of his breed to date at Westminster, when he won second in a recent Sporting Group there.

Left: The highest Group placement to date at Westminster for a Labrador is pictured here. The Best of Breed dog, and Group Two, is Ch. Mardas Brandlesholme Sam's Song, handled by D. Roy Holloway for Mrs. Robert V. Clark, Jr. **Below:** Eng., Am. Ch. Kimvalley Crispin, owned by Mrs. Clark, is pictured winning under the late Alva Rosenberg. D. Roy Holloway, handler.

Mrs. Clark's special favorites are her bitches, most of these winding up as house dogs. The most famous brood bitch at Springfield has to be English and American Champion Kenbara Jill, imported from England, who produced fifteen champions, seven of them by Champion Kenbara Crispin. In the kennel now is Jill's daughter, Champion Springfield's Musette; her granddaughter, Champion Springfield's Rule Brittania; and her up-and-coming great-granddaughter, Springfield's Mulberry Tart. Another bitch that has surely made her presence felt is Champion Springfield's Scottish Reel, known to her friends as "Butter," who has produced such excellent bitches as Champion Springfield's Buttered Toast and the currently winning Springfield's Butter Cream. Then there are Champion Springfield's Prune, Champion Springfield's Maytime, Champion Springfield's Brodich, Champion Springfield's Minis, and numerous others, all assuring a bright future for the kennel.

Eng., Am. Ch. Kenbara Jill, winner of the Brood Bitch Class and Veteran Bitch Class at the National Specialty in 1975. Owned by Mrs. Robert V. Clark, Jr., Springfield Farm. Diana Beckett handling.

Mrs. Robert V. Clark, Jr., with a few of her favorites at Springfield Farm, Virginia.

Although a manager is actually in charge of the kennel, Mrs. Clark is a very interested and involved owner who has a great eye for a dog and a tremendous love for dogs. She likes personally to select from each litter which puppies will be kept and which will go to new homes. She names them all. She also equally enjoys watching her dogs in the ring displaying their best manners, spread out in front of the fire at home, or enjoying life romping and playing on the spacious grounds of Springfield Farm. Mrs. Clark has had some world-famous winners in other breeds as well as Labs, but unquestionably her greatest favorites are, and always will be, the Labrador Retrievers.

Stonecrest

Stonecrest Labradors are owned by George and Louise White of Charlestown, Rhode Island. Through the years, it has been a very family-oriented venture. The dogs were all handled by the Whites and their children. Whelpings, puppy care, and dog care are all shared by the family.

Although the Whites did not buy their first Labrador, Champion Anderscroft Roustabout, until 1968, they finished their first dog, a home-bred Basset Hound, twelve years earlier than that, in 1956.

Stonecrest's foundation bitch was a lovely daughter of Spenrock's Banner, Champion Spenrock's Topaz, who is still the matriarch of the Labs and their Scottie kennel-mates.

Among the well-known Labs owned by the Whites are Champion Stonecrest's Swift Current and Stonecrest's Quissex Rip Tide.

Ch. Stonecrest Swift Current photographed by Claire White-Peterson, daughter of the George Whites, owner of Stonecrest Labs.

From left to right: Ch. Spenrock's Topaz, Stonecrest's Harbour Grace, Stonecrest's Quissex Riptide, and Ch. Stonecrest's Swift Current, some of the outstanding Labradors at Stonecrest Kennels, George and Louise White, Charlestown, Rhode Island.

Sunnybrook Acres Misha, owned by Dr. and Mrs. John Arbuckle, is a typical Lab puppy from the Sunnybrook Acres Kennels owned by Dr. and Mrs. John H. Ippensen, Springfield, Missouri.

Sunnybrook Acres

Sunnybrook Acres Labradors began in 1972 with the purchase, by Dr. and Mrs. John H. Ippensen of Springfield, Missouri, of their first member of the breed, a lovely black bitch who had been selected from champion parents primarily as a family and hunting companion. Mrs. Ippensen was persuaded to show her at six months of age at a local A.K.C. show, and although she did not win the points that day, the judge was so favorably impressed with the bitch that he strongly suggested she continue being shown. Put in professional hands, this bitch, at 19 months of age, finished in one week on the Texas Circuit with four major wins. Needless to say, the Ippensens were "hooked" on Labradors and on dog shows!

A handsome yellow male was purchased as a mate to this first bitch. This dog, Champion Sunnybrook Acres Sandpiper, was the first dog to carry the Sunnybrook Acres prefix. Sandpiper finished his championship at 18 months of age, and the first time he was shown as a special he won first in the Sporting Group at the very large benched show in Kansas City.

Sandpiper, featured as the Ideal of the Standard of the Breed in the 1980 Standards Issue of *Dog World* magazine, has gone on to sire numerous champions, field trial dogs, and obedience dogs. He is still standing at stud at Sunnybrook Acres.

One outstanding daughter of Sandpiper's, Champion Sunnybrook Acres Ray's Honey, U.D., W.C., finished her championship and utility obedience degrees while competing in both conformation and obedience at the same shows. Honey earned the *Dog World* Award for Outstanding Achievement, finishing her Utility Degree just nine months from the first time she stepped into the obedience ring. At 18 months of age, she is the youngest U.D.-titled Labrador in the United States and the youngest Champion, U.D., W.C. Labrador of all time.

Champion Sunnybrook Acres Ray's Honey, U.D., W.C. has also proved to be an excellent producer. Her first litter, sired by American and Canadian Champion Shamrock Acres Ebonylane Ace, C.D.X., W.C., was a huge success, and this cross has produced six champions, two Utility Dogs, four C.D.X. dogs, and four C.D. dogs, plus four Working Certificate and a Tracking Degree—truly all-purpose Labradors who fulfill the objective of Sunnybrook Acres to keep the "workability" in this lovely breed.

An outstanding dog from the Honey-Ebonylane Ace cross is American and Canadian Champion Sunnybrook Acres Ace O'Spades, C.D.,

Ch. Sunnybrook Acres Dandelion, U.T., on an injured goose rescue mission. Owned by JoAnn Kopek; photographed by Mike Kopek.

Am., Can. Ch. Sunnybrook Acres Ace O'Spades, C.D., W.C. with his owner Fran Ippensen.

W.C. Ace was owner-handled to his championship by Fran Ippensen, who also handled him to his Working Certificate and Companion Dog degrees. At two years of age, Ace and Fran won a large Specialty in Ohio, defeating 214 Labradors, including 25 champions. At two-and-a-half years of age, Ace was a Best in Show winner. He stands at stud at Sunnybrook Acres, while he also works on his C.D.X. and T.D. degrees.

American and Canadian Champion Sunnybrook Acres Ace O'Spades, C.D., W.C., a third generation representative of Sunnybrook Acres' breeding, is carrying on the family tradition of siring black, yellow, and chocolate puppies who have superior movement and outstanding personalities. Just three years of age, Ace already has numerous pointed sons and daughters, including a Group II placing daughter.

Mrs. John H. Ippensen (Fran), founding force and manager of Sunnybrook Acres Labradors, has utilized her scientific background (Master's Degree in Biological Sciences from Northwestern University) and that of her husband, Dr. Ippensen, (an M.D.) to formulate a sound breeding program. This program places emphasis on the development of an all-around Labrador capable of competing successfully in conformation as well as in the obedience ring, while retaining the natural instincts which make the Labrador an ideal waterfowl retriever and a fine companion for the upland game bird hunter. All breeding stock at Sunnybrook Acres is certified free of hip dysplasia and inherited eye defects.

Waterdog

The Waterdog Labradors are of particular interest because they have been highly successful in the United States and Canada, dividing their time between Bradford, Rhode Island, and St. John's, Newfoundland.

Michael and Lynn Woods, owners of this kennel, are originally from Newfoundland, and they will be returning there after a four-year stay in the United States.

Since the Labrador is Newfoundland's native dog, the Woods are particularly devoted to the breed, and their aim is to restore Labradors to a place of prominence in the land of the breed's origin, where it had virtually disappeared and where there are no really serious breeders. The Woods imported a nice dog from England in 1969, but unfortunately he was so dysplastic at seven months old that he was unable to walk. Mr. and Mrs. Wood then decided to go to England for a year for the express purpose of endeavoring to find some really good dogs with which to revive the breed in Newfoundland.

After visiting virtually every kennel in England and after experiencing many disappointments, the Woods were fortunate to find two really excellent dogs who eventually became American and Canadian Champion Powhatan Black Badger, C.D.X. and Canadian Champion and Obedience Trial Champion Ballyduff Storm, U.D. (U.S.A.) and W.C.

When they returned to Newfoundland from England, the Woods adopted the traditional Newfoundland name for the breed, "Waterdog," as their registered kennel name and have been showing and breeding under that banner since about 1970. Both of their English imports easily gained their breed and obedience titles and have sired numerous breed and obedience winners as well as dependable hunting companions. Above all, both have passed on their true, gentle, and tractable Labrador temperament to their offspring. Storm is a Best in Show winner and was Number Thirty-nine Sporting Obedience Dog in Canada in 1977 and Number One in 1978. He has 27 High in Trial awards along with multiple Group wins and placements.

The pride of the Woods' kennel is their home-bred bitch, American and Canadian Champion Waterdog's Raine Storm, C.D.X., a Ballyduff Storm daughter. She has multiple breed wins and Group placements and, owner-handled, was Best of Breed at the Mid-Jersey Labrador Specialty in 1981 over an entry of 220. She is also a High in Trial dog, and her first litter has done well in both obedience and breed rings.

Since they have been in the United States, Mr. and Mrs. Woods have tried to bring some of the best U.S. bloodlines into their breeding, and they hope that when they return to Newfoundland they can continue to make a contribution to re-establishing a truly quality Labrador in the land of his origin.

Can. Ch. and Obedience Ch. Ballyduff Storm, U.D., W.C., is a Best in Show winner, has 27 High in Trial awards, is a multiple Group winner, is the sire of multiple breed, obedience, and Specialty winners, and was Number One Sporting Obedience Dog in Canada in 1978. Owned by the Waterdog Labradors, Michael and Lynn Woods, Bradford, Rhode Island and St. John's, Newfoundland.

Am., Can. Ch. Waterdog's Raine Beau, C.D.X., has multiple Group placements, is a High in Trial winner, and was Best of Breed at a Mid-Jersey Labrador Retriever Club Specialty. Owned by Michael and Lynn Woods.

Ch. Whygin Poppitt, by Ch. Rupert Dahomey ex Cedarhill Whygin, is a splendid example of Helen Ginnel's famed Labs at Bedford Hills, New York, photographed in 1961.

Whygin

Whygin Labradors are owned by Helen Whyte Ginnel (the kennel name coined from the first three letters of the last two names), who trained her first dog, an English Setter registered with the Field Dog Stud Book, in 1932. She ran this English Setter in field trials with some small success, but when she had devoured every book on the breed written up to that time she noticed that compared to the Setters being shown, hers certainly did not conform to the standard. She set a goal of producing a dual-type dog. From a careful perusal of the standard, she noted a problem. Her Setter, a tri-color with a very slight amount of ticking on her body, pointed with her white tail sky-high. This made her very easy to locate when she was on point in typical bird cover; when she was getting close to a bird, the fast action of the high tail proclaimed the fact. The show standard, however, demanded that the tail be set low and carried below the level of the topline. After watching a few classes in the ring, Mrs. Ginnel realized that the belton color was the only acceptable marking for a show dog, regardless of the fact that a rusty orange-colored or bluish gray dog would be most difficult to keep track of against typical autumn foliage, and that the size, bone, and general conformation eliminated the possibility of a stylish field dog.

That was the end of her dual-purpose dream so far as English Setters were concerned. She had bred six generations of that breed and produced a lot of useful shooting dogs and collected a few ribbons at the trials, but she had learned to breed for the conformation that would create a stylish, easy-running dog who would be able to last all day in the field rather than a show-type dog.

Everything changed in 1947, when Mrs. Ginnel acquired her first Labrador Retriever, Cedarhill Whygin, known as "Dinah." Just plain luck was involved in the selection of this foundation bitch. In a book of pedigrees of current show Labradors published in 1978, "Dinah" would have appeared in the extended pedigrees of 50% of the dogs pictured. Two sons, at least two great-grandsons, and at least three great-great-great grandsons were awarded Best of Breed at Westminster. Three Nationals and an Amateur National Field Championship have been won by descendants; three individuals have won both field and bench championships, and over 150 have placed in licensed open trials. Possibly this would not have meant so much were it not for the fact that many, many of these noted Labs go back to Cedarhill Whygin's name four or more times! Champion Shamrock Acres Light Brigade, the top winning (12 times Best in Show) and top producing show Lab ever, lists seven crosses to Champion Cedarhill Whygin in his pedigree, and he alone has sired 94 champions!

Mrs. Ginnel comments, "the show and field awards of "Dinah's" (champion Cedarhill Whygin's) offspring are very minor compared to the happiness brought by the hundreds of excellent shooting dogs, family dogs, and working guide dogs descended from her to their owners."

Mrs. Ginnel has always stood firm in her belief that the foremost goal of any breeder should be to produce dogs capable of the above. She abhors the expression, "only a pet," feeling that to be a successful, well-adjusted family and field dog should be among the Lab's most important functions. She further believes that one's goal as a breeder of winners should be dogs that can also reproduce their quality.

Champion Cedarhill Whygin's five-generation pedigree went back to the early English imports that were running in Long Island field trials in the early 1930s. She was bred to Champion Rupert Dahomey who carried a line very similar to her own, being a grandson of Dual Champion Shed of Arden and Field Champion Timber-down Clansman. A dog and a bitch from this litter were kept, Champion Whygin Poppitt and Whygin Dark Magic. The bitch, shown twice, won two five-point majors, going Best of Opposite Sex at Chicago International before she was nine months old. At Chicago, she contracted distemper which left her with a chorea that ended her show career.

Probably Poppitt's two most successful matings were to his sire's littermate and to his own dam. Poppitt's mating to his sire's littermate, Champion Rupert Desdemona, produced Champion Whygin John Duck who won his championship from the Puppy Classes and was undefeated in the breed in 19 straight shows, winning Best of Breed at Westminster at 18 months with his litter sister, Whygin Shia of Southdown, going Best of Opposite Sex. Shia further distinguished this litter by winning Best of Breed at the Labrador National Specialty and then, sad to say, died at only two years of age. Poppitt's mating to his own dam produced Champion Whygin Rob Roy, Best of Breed at Westminster 1957, and Whygin Popsicle, dam of three champions, one of whom, Champion Whygin Gold Bullion, became a very important sire with tremendous influence on the breed. Both of these matings are examples of intensive inbreeding which, under proper circumstances, can be fabulously successful. In order to inbreed and obtain such fine results, one must possess a very thorough knowledge of one's own stock and be aware of possible dangers as well as potential successes.

Three Westminster Best of Breed winners from the Whygin Kennels of Mrs. Helen Ginnel: center, Ch. Whygin Poppitt, 1954; left, his son, Ch. Whygin John Duck, 1956; right, another son, Ch. Whygin Rob Roy, 1957.

Champion Whygin Gold Bullion's most influential mating probably was to Champion Whygin Gentle Julia, his daughter. This produced Champion Shamrock Acres Sonic Boom, sire of a long list of champions, and Champion Shamrock Acres Jim Dandy, sire of nine champions, two of them Best in Show winners, including Champion Shamrock Acres Light Brigade.

Helen Ginnel has never campaigned her dogs very extensively. Gold Bullion beat the best that were in competition at that time by winning the Specialty, Best of Breed at Chicago International, and Westminster. Owner-handled, he made only a few ring appearances each year.

The Whygin line is a consistent, recognizable strain within the breed; it is the result of close inbreeding producing sound, prepotent individuals who have proved themselves on the bench, in the field, and, most important of all, as intelligent, loyal pets.

Ch. Whygin Gold Bullion and son during field practice. Helen Ginnel, owner, handling Gold Bullion.

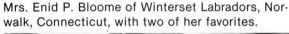

Mrs. Enid P. Bloome of Winterset Labradors, Norwalk, Connecticut, with two of her favorites.

Winterset

Winterset Labrador Retrievers are bred by a small hobby kennel owned by Mrs. Enid P. Bloome and located at Norwalk, Connecticut. She and her husband adopted this hobby due to their great love of dogs, and they are finding it fun, rewarding, and a source of great pleasure. They are meeting their challenging aim of breeding better dogs in each generation, and they look forward, in the future when they retire (Mrs. Bloome is a teacher and Mr. Bloome is an engineer), to going in for field work in addition to raising show dogs. The kennel is based pretty much on the Sandylands bloodlines.

Champion Killingworth's Valiant Lady was the first of the Winterset Labs, purchased from Lorraine Robbenhaar, followed by Champion Killingworth Winterset My Jo. Mrs. Bloome promptly put C.D. titles on both of these bitches, and it was My Jo that produced the first Winterset litter, ten lovely puppies sired by Champion Seaward's Adonis of Rupert. So far, none of these have been shown, but one of them, Winterset Tara, has a C.D. and is working towards C.D.X.

Champion Killingworth's Valiant Lady was bred to Janet Churchill's Champion Spenrock Heatheredge Mariner and she produced eight exceptional puppies, two of which are being shown on a limited basis by the owners to whom they were sold.

Valiant Lady next was bred to Diane Pilbin's Champion Follytower Sing-A-Long and produced eleven gorgeous black pups, six bitches and five dogs. Two of these have been sold to a fancier in Iowa for whom they are doing well, the bitch taking points from the Puppy Class with the dog going Reserve from the Puppy Class.

Mrs. Bloome leased Champion Rupert Caviar for breeding, and she selected Janet Churchill's Champion Lawnwood's Hot Chocolate as the stud for her. Eight puppies resulted this time, only two of which were bitches. Mrs. Bloome kept the black bitch and sold the yellow, which she now regrets because the purchaser is not show-minded and the bitch has turned out exceptionally well.

Winterset Labradors at the Potomac Specialty in Leesburg, Virginia, April 1981. Winterset Blkchoc Cavianne and the current "star" of the kennel, Ch. Chucklebrook Wint'rset Marks, both owned by Mrs. Enid P. Bloome.

Ch. Killingworth Winterset My Jo, C.D., one of the fine Labs owned by Winterset, is en route to the title here, handled by Jane K. Forsyth.

Winterset Hot Tar will probably soon be a champion; he has three majors and is short only one point. Litter-brother Champion Winterset High Jinks finished at eleven months of age, in less than a month of showing, with four majors, and since then he has added his Canadian championship in two five-point shows. Everyone has been most admiring of these two young Labs. Joy Quallenborg is handling Tar, while Kathy Kirk is handling Jinks.

Winterset Blkchoc Cavianne is a young bitch for which hopes are high as a show winner and as a producer, while the "pride and joy" of the Bloomes is their newly finished Champion Chucklebrook Wint'rset Marks who finished his title in October 1981, going Best of Breed from the classes over seven Specials for four points at Albany and Best of Winners the next day at Troy for his fourth major. Already he has Group placements to his credit.

Mark is also distinguishing himself as a stud dog; one of his daughters, from Champion Killingworth Winterset My Jo, has recently been purchased as a foundation bitch for a new kennel, while several others will soon be representing their new show homes.

This handsome Lab is the imported Ch. Poolstead Peer at the age of seven years. Photo courtesy of Debby Kobilis.

Yarrow

Yarrow Labradors are owned by Mrs. Beth Sweigart of Bridgewater, Virginia. Mrs. Sweigart has been highly successful as a breeder-owner-handler of Labs.

Champion Springfield's Ondine, C.D., W.D. is the foundation bitch here, and with her sire, Champion Poolstead Peer, whom Mrs. Sweigart co-owned with Mrs. Robert V. Clark, Jr., of Springfield Kennels, Mrs. Sweigart had five generations of Labs, all of which were owner-handled by her to their titles.

One of the most famous of Mrs. Sweigart's homebred litters was that containing the Group winner Champion Yarrow's Broad Reach Peer, the obedience "star" Champion Yarrow's Broad Reach Psaphire, and Champion Yarrow's Pendragon, who has done good winning in the ring.

Ch. Yarrow's Broad Reach Psaphire, U.D.T., W.C., winning Obedience First Place at Asheville Kennel Club in 1978. Martha Lee K. Voshell, owner.

Champion Yarrow's The Magus, by Champion Sandyland's Midas ex Ondine, is another lovely winner from this kennel.

A most beautiful bitch co-owned by Beth Sweigart and Betty Graham is an import, Sandylands Radiance, daughter of English Show Champion Sandylands My Rainbeau, bred by Mrs. Gwen Broadley. She is a truly excellent yellow bitch who is earning exciting wins while on the way to her title.

On her way to championship, Sandylands Radiance, daughter of English Show Ch. Sandylands Rainbeau, was bred by Mrs. Gwen Broadley and is owned by Betty Graham and Beth Sweigart.

Champion Pollywag Conic of Chidley, by Castlemire Mask ex Yarrow's Pollywag Sabrina, has done well for co-owners Mrs. Curtis Read and Beth Sweigart, including Winners Dog at the National Specialty judged by noted English breeder Mary Roslin-Williams.

These handsome Labs are Telia of Broad Reach, U.D., Bawdy Bear of Broad Reach, U.D., Ch. Zippers Hustlin Wahoo, U.D.T., W.C.; Ch. Broad Reach's English Muffin, U.D.T., W.C., and Champion Yarrow's Broad Reach Psaphire, U.D.T., W.C. All are alive and owned by Martha Lee K. Voshell, Broad Reach Labradors, Charlottesville, Virginia.

Ch. Springfield's Buttered Toast at Agathon Kennel Club. Mrs. Diana Beckett handled for Mrs. Robert D. Clark, Jr., Springfield Farm, Middleburg, Virginia.

Ch. Van Lee's Pot O'Chocolate, W.C., foundation bitch at Hywater Kennels, Bob and Brenda Matthews, Elmira, New York. Although never campaigned as a Special, this splendid bitch has multiple Bests of Breed and at least one Sporting Group placement.

Opposite: Ch. Springfield's Chimney Sweep, owned by Mrs. Robert D. Clark, Jr., and handled by Mrs. Diana Beckett.

Ch. Lobuff's Dandy Lion, by Ch. Gunslinger's Tawny Boy ex Ch. Spenrock's Cognac, bred and owned by Jerry H. and Lisa E. Weiss, Lobuff Labradors, Huntington, New York.

Ch. Shamrock Acres Light Brigade winning the Sporting Group at Saginaw Valley Kennel Club, judged by Bernard W. Ziessow.

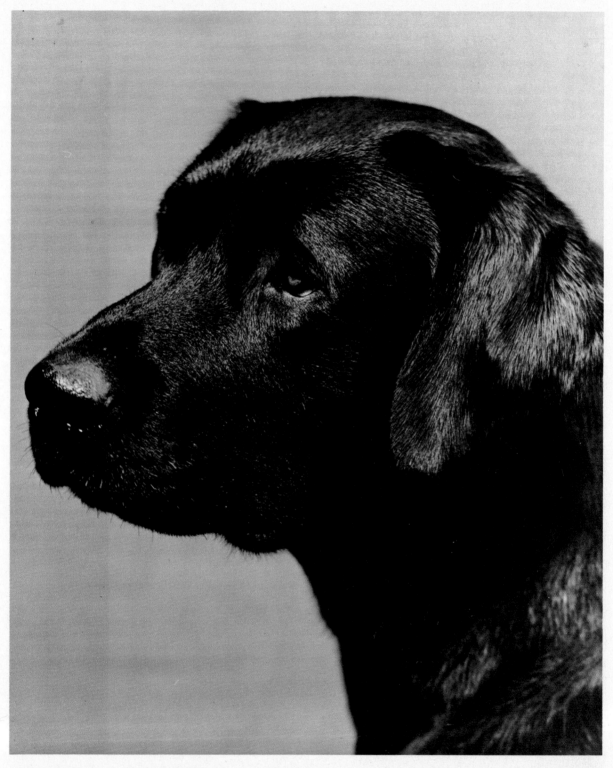

Head study of Ch. Lobuff's Seafaring Banner, by Ch. Spenrock's Heatheredge Mariner ex Ch. Spenrock's Cognac. Owned by Jerry and Lisa Weiss, Huntington, New York.

Left: A lovely head study of the winning dog Heaney's Ma-Pat-Ma M'Boy Fitzgo, by Ch. Shamrock Acres Benjamin ex Heaney's Ma-Pat-Ma Dream Cum True. Bred and owned by Margaret D. Heaney, Derby, New York.

Below: Ch. Spenrock's Cardigan Bay in 1973. Bred, owned and handled by Janet Churchill, Spenrock Labs, Chesapeake City, Maryland. By Ch. Lockerbie Goldentone Jensen ex Int. Ch. Spenrock's Banner, W.C.

Am., Can. Ch. Forecast Rockefeller, whelped May 1972, a grandson of Ch. Lockerbie Kismet and Am., Can. Ch. Forecast Hofstra. Forecast Kennels, Litchfield, Connecticut.

Am., Can. Ch. Tamarock's Forecast Outlaw, great-grandson of Mallow's Fanfare, at Elm City in 1979. Owned by Forecast Kennels.

These handsome dogs are taking Best of Breed, Winners Dog and Best of Winners, and Best of Opposite Sex respectively. They are Am., Can. Ch. Forecast Hofstra; Forecast Stanford; and Am., Can. Ch. Naiad's Prom—each representative of the outstanding quality to be found at Forecast Kennels. Owned by Elizabeth K. Curtis and Ann and Samuel Cappellina.

Calgary, January 1975. Shirley Costigan, breeder-owner-handler, winning Best of Breed under judge Joe Tacker with Ch. Springfield's Fanny Sweet Adams, by Ch. Redsky's Double Or Nothing, C.D., ex Springfield's Constant Elsa.

Opposite, above: Apohaqui Braunayr Sadi, owned by Braunayr Kennels, Bruce and Sandra Derby, Ayr, Ontario. **Below:** On the left, Am., Mex. 1978 World Ch. Mandigo's Annabel Lee, C.D.X., W.C., with her sire on the right, Am., Can., Mex. 1978 World and Int. Ch. Franklin's Golden Mandigo, C.D., Am.W.C. Both of these magnificent yellow Labs belong to John and Laurell Jenny, Mandigo Kennels, West Bountiful, Utah.

Left: Ranchman's Rustic Rustler, bred by Marion Reid, Medicine Hat, Alberta. Owned by Janet Murdock, Barrie, Ontario.

Below: Winners at Winnipeg under judge Robert Wills. The dam is Killingworth's Tarbinavon with Marion Reid, left; the sire, Can., Am. Ch. Rupert Krest of Wallesey with Hugh Crozier; the daughter, Ranchman's Slap - n - Tickle with Hilary J. Reid, right.

Right: This is Romillar's Weaver Triever at two months old. Litter-brother to Ch. Romillar's Ace of Spades, C.D. Bred by Helen and Walter Millar, sold as a puppy to Mr. and Mrs. Edward Nawrot, Oshawa, Ontario.

Below: Keeping a watchful eye on her two-week-old puppy is Can. Ch. Romillar's September Velvet, C.D., by Can. Ch. Gold's Pride of Bonzo ex Can. Ch. Romillar's Jody. The puppy is Romillar's Blaze of Glory, sired by Can. Ch. Barrymar's Adam. Owners are Helen and Walter Millar, Carrying Place, Ontario.

American, Canadian, and Puerto Rican Ch. Heatherbourne Forget Me Not is owned by Shadowvale Labradors, Mr. and Mrs. M. Beattie, Quebec, Canada. Roy Holloway, judge.

On the sign in the photo:

SWEEPSTAKES
FIRST

LABRADOR RETRIEVER
CLUB OF POTOMAC

1980

GILBERT PHOTO

Ch. Ebonylane's Sandy Sunshine with breeder-handler Mike Lanctot. Ebonylane Labradors, Hemmingford, Quebec.

Am., Can. Ch. Ebonylane's Aslan in the summer of 1980 at Delaware County Kennel Club. Owned by Pat and Mike Lanctot of Ebonylane Kennels.

Ch. Springfield's Faust (above) is handled to first in the Sporting Group by D. Roy Holloway for owner Mrs. Robert V. Clark, Jr., Middleburg, Virginia. Ch. Springfield's Scottish Reel (below) is also owned by Mrs. Clark.

Ch. Franklin's Proud Clarion (above), sired by Dual Champion Happy Playboy ex Ch. Sunset Road of Franklin, is owned by Mrs. Bernard W. Ziessow, Franklin, Michigan. Ch. Glenyries Black Diamond (below), sired by Ch. Hindu from Franklin, is also Ziessow-owned.

Pictured to the right is Ch. Ironpride's Pacesetter → at 26 months of age. By Ch. Jagersbo Mr. Mustard ex Spenrock Delta Minnow and owned by Rhonda Thompson of Iowa.

Castlemore Coronet, Irish Dual Champion, Canadian Champion and Group winner, and Winners Dog at Westminster 1961, is owned by Mr. and Mrs. Frank Evan Jones, Annwyn Kennels, Minesing, Ontario.

CHAPTER FIVE

Labrador Retriever Kennels in Canada

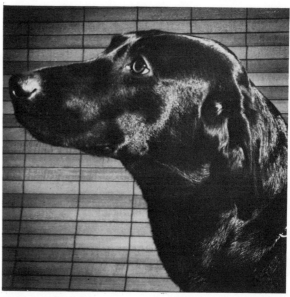

This lovely head study is of Annwyn's Western Fern, C.D., one of Frank Jones's excellent Labradors.

Labradors enjoy great popularity in all parts of Canada, which is easily understandable. Great and famous members of this breed are to be found on the East Coast, the West Coast, and all points in between.

Annwyn

Frank Evan Jones of Minesing, Ontario, is a widely respected authority on Labradors (and on a great many other breeds) in the United States and Canada, where his services as a judge are constantly in demand. Mr. Jones is President of the Labrador Retriever Club, Incorporated, America's National Specialty Club for this breed.

It was in 1949 that Frank Jones, with his wife, started raising and showing Labs, having named their kennel "Annwyn" after Frank's mother, Ann Wynn. From the very beginning they were determined to have only the best, and among their famous winners have been such dogs as Dual Champion Castlemore Coronet and English, American, and Canadian Champion Lisnamallard Tarantella.

Coronet was Winners Dog at Westminster in 1961. He came to Canada as an Irish dual champion and quickly gained his Canadian title, taking Best of Breed nine times, placing in the Sporting Group on each of these occasions. A yellow himself, he was a grandson of Dual

Champion Staindrop Saighdear, the first yellow Lab ever to have gained the dual title.

Tarantella, during the late 1950s and early 1960s, brought home a splendid array of awards from her numerous ring appearances in the United States and Canada, including Best of Opposite Sex against 23 competitors at the Westminster Kennel Club in 1959. It was unfortunate that this outstanding bitch hated the show ring, as she was widely admired and would have undoubtedly made a sizable record had she been more cooperative in competition.

One of the Annwyn Labs of which Frank Jones is proudest is Champion Annwyn's Tric or Treat, owned by Thomas Murphy, whose life the dog saved when Mr. Murphy became stranded in a small boat off Wolfe Island about 1500 yards from shore. He had been hunting with friends and took a small boat, with only a small paddle, out into the channel on the American side to retrieve a duck. When the wind and the currents became too strong, Mr. Murphy was unable to control the boat. He put the tow line around the dog's neck, and the dog jumped into the water and swam ashore, towing the boat with him—truly an outstanding act of canine bravery and intelligence! For this, "Pat," as the dog was known, became the Number One Dog in the Canine Hall of Fame at Clarkstown, Ontario, and received a plaque in honor of the occasion from Mr. Kortwright, who was then President of the National Sportsman Show.

Ch. Annwyn's Tric or Treat, born September 16th 1958, by Am., Can. Ch. Knolltops Cloud of Annwyn ex "Binky" (Ravencamp Grebe) is here receiving a plaque for having saved the life of owner, Thomas Murphy. Mr. Kortwright, President of the National Sportsmen Show, is presenting the plaque to Mr. Murphy, as the dog proudly shakes hands. Tric or Treat is the Number One Dog in the Canine Hall of Fame, Clarkston, Ontario, Canada.

Right: Irish Dual Ch., Can. Ch. Castlemore Coronet ("Roddy"), owned by Mr. and Mrs. Frank Evan Jones, Annwyn Kennels. **Below:** Eng., Can. Ch. Lisnamallard Tarantella, a very famous Lab of the 1950s owned by the Annwyn Kennels.

In speaking of the breed which he dearly loves, Frank Jones comments not only on its ability to do things well but also on its superb disposition. He considers it regrettable, as do many fanciers, that while when he started showing forty years ago, it was not at all unusual to find three or four dual champions in competition, this is no longer the case. Nowadays, although efforts are still being made to bring the two factions together, one sometimes wonders if it will ever again be the usual thing to see dogs bearing the dual title.

Best Canadian-bred at Ottawa in 1962, Ch. Blyth's Comet. Frank Jones, who made the award, comments that "this dog has what we seldom see nowadays, the real otter tail."

Am., Can. Ch. Rupert Crest of Wallasey, owned by Hugh Crozier, winning Best Gun Dog and Best Stud Dog at the Labrador Retriever Club Specialty Show in Winnipeg, Manitoba, December 1980. Judged by Frank Jones.

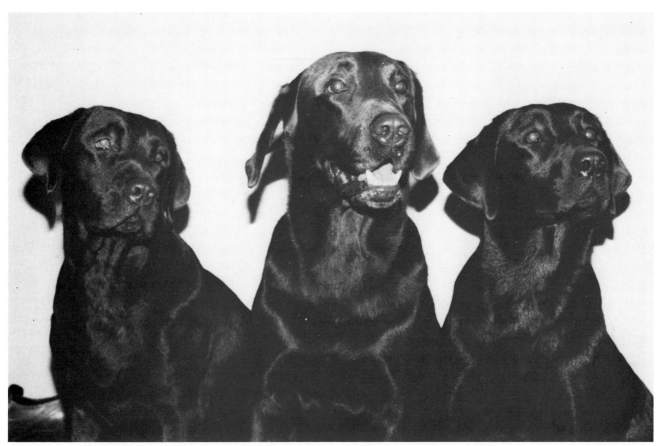

Handsome Labradors at Braunayr Kennels: left, chocolate female Ch. Selamat's Hear the Echo; center, chocolate dog, Ch. Bromac's Brown Derby, C.D.; right, black female, Apohaqui Braunayr Sadi. Bruce and Sandra Derby, owners, Ayr, Ontario.

Ch. Bromac's Brown Derby, C.D., owned by Braunayr Labradors.

Braunayr

Ayr, Ontario, is the location of the Braunayr Kennels, which were started in the mid-1970s by Bruce and Sandra Derby as a result of their infatuation with chocolate Labs. Their good friends Art and Enid MacAlpine, who own and operate Bromac Kennels, introduced the Derbys to their dogs, which included several black Labradors, a mature chocolate male, and a mischievous ten-week-old chocolate female, future Champion Shamrock Acres Little Brown Jug, who would later be the dam of the Derbys' first dog. They fell in love with "Sally" and, through the encouragement of her owners, trained and showed her part way to her championship. The Derbys were "hooked" (as we suspect the MacAlpines knew would be the case). As payment for the time they had spent working with her, they were given the pick of Sally's first litter. They chose a male, future Champion Bromac's Brown Derby, C.D., who finished in three straight shows with majors and who is a source of tremendous pleasure for them.

199

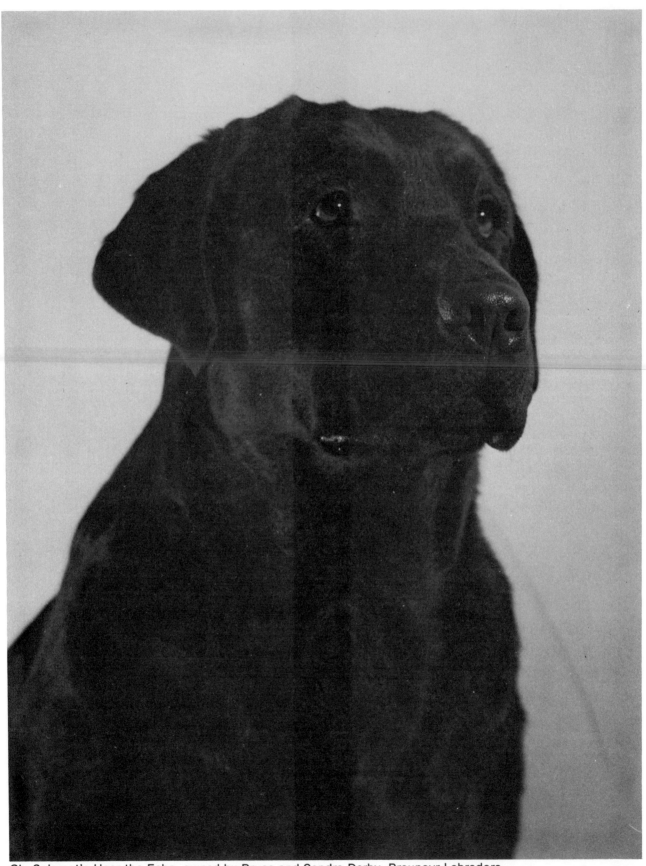

Ch. Selamat's Hear the Echo, owned by Bruce and Sandra Derby, Braunayr Labradors.

Braunayr Li'l Bessy Brown, seven weeks old in August 1981. Owned by Braunayr Labradors, Bruce and Sandra Derby.

Because of a busy schedule, the Derbys keep their small kennel just as a hobby. They purchased a chocolate female, now Champion Selamat's Hear The Echo, because of her Irish background, hoping to get the type and bone they preferred. They were most fortunate in getting a truly lovely example of the breed.

The Derbys line-bred Echo to Champion Castlemore Bramble (an Irish import) and the result was Braunayr's first litter, all good-boned and typey and with promise for future success in the ring.

The Derbys also have Apohaqui Braunayr Sadi, a black Dual Champion Trumarc Triple Threat daughter, who they hope also will produce well for them.

Ch. Winderway's Victory Rocket taking Best Puppy in Show. Carho Labradors, owners, Carole J. Nickerson, Yar County, Nova Scotia.

Braunayr's Zoe Firefly and littermate at seven weeks of age.

Carho

Carole Nickerson has founded her small kennel in Nova Scotia on Canadian and English show and hunting stock. Her dogs include Champion Wimberway's Victory Rocket, by Wimberway's X-hibit, W.C., from Spirit of Miska, a Group winner; "Rocky's" yellow son, Champion Carho's Chip Off The Old Rock (from Treecroft Bamboo Shannon), also a Group

Ch. Treecroft J.B. Storm at Carho going Best of Winners at Evangeline Kennel Club, June 1981. Carole J. Nickerson, owner.

winner; "Rocky's" black daughter, Champion Treecroft J.B. Storm At Carho (from Treecroft Jolly Black Sheena), still another Group winner; and Carho's Captain Kelley, a Best of Breed dog, by Champion Powhatan Black Piers ex Treecroft Jolly Black Sheena II.

Carho's Captain Kelley taking Best Puppy in Group, Pictou County, September 1981. Carole Nickerson, owner, Carho Labs.

Casadelora

The Casadelora Labradors are located at Ladysmith, British Columbia, where they are owned by Mary Brown. Situated in the heart of Vancouver Island, on the west coast of Canada, this comparatively recent kennel, since being registered with the Canadian Kennel Club in 1973, has been breeding one litter a year. Despite the small size of the operation, twenty show championships and over thirty obedience titles, including two obedience championships, have been completed by Casadelora Labs—all with dogs produced in their own kennel!

Ch. and O.T. Ch. Trollheimen's Golden Sol with pups. Mr. and Mrs. W.E. Brown, Casadelora Labradors, Ladysmith, British Columbia.

Champion and Obedience Trial Champion Trollheimen's Golden Sol, a granddaughter of Champion Sandylands Tweed of Blaircourt, was the first Lab at this kennel. Her grandmother, Diant Moonlight, was imported in whelp from England. Sol acquired her show and obedience championships and then whelped three litters, from which eight puppies became champions.

Sol produced two great sons, Champion Casadelora's Duffy Stout, C.D. and Canadian and American Champion Casadelora's Allspice.

Ch. Casadelora's Duffy Stout, C.D., by Can., Am. Ch. Keating's Whiz Boy Nelnors ex Ch. and O.T. Ch. Trollheimen's Golden Sol. Mr. and Mrs. W.E. Brown, owners, Casadelora Labradors.

Duffy Stout, whelped in 1975, was an excitingly handsome dog whose show career ended due to an unfortunate accident when he was very young. Allspice, whelped in 1976, has been a consistent Group and Best in Show winner. He was Number Two Lab in Canada in 1980 and a top contender, as this is written, for Number One in 1981. His potential as a sire has not yet been achieved because there was a non-breeding agreement attached to his being sold as a pet puppy; and it was not until 1979 that the non-breeding agreement was lifted, and Ms. Brown and others could use him at stud. His get are just now starting to appear in the show ring.

Casadelora tries to keep the number of Labs they own to six dogs at a time, thus giving each dog the individual attention he deserves. In addition, they offer obedience and field training for all breeds. Once a year they are hosts to a field trial sponsored by the Vancouver Island Retriever Club. At this time, all the dogs demonstrate their working ability, for although they are not intensely campaigned in the field, they all have an inbred desire to retrieve and a great love of water.

Can., Am. Ch. Casadelora's All Spice with his son Casadelora Dionysus bring Christmas greetings. Mr. and Mrs. W.E. Brown, owners.

Ebonylane Labradors on August 26th 1978. Left to right: Ch. Ebonylane's Shadow at 14 months; Mike Lanctot; Ch. Ebonylane's Amber Lady at 14 months; Jimmy Lanctot; Ch. Shamrock Acres Ebonylane Ace, C.D.X., W.C. at three years; Ch. Ebonylane's Dawn of Rivendell, C.D. at two years; Obedience Trial Ch. Claybank's Black Maria, W.C., at five years; Ebonylane's Tiger at six months; Pat Lanctot; Shamrock Acres Marshland Sari at three years. Ebonylane Labs are owned by the Lanctots and located in Hemmingford, Quebec.

Ebonylane

Ebonylane, a kennel of particular note, was established in August 1974 by Pat and Mike Lanctot in the picturesque apple-growing valley of Hemmingford, Quebec, located approximately 30 miles due south of Montreal, bordering on New York. There are Ebonylane pups placed with serious breeders and fanciers in Austria, Cuba, West Germany, Bermuda, Oregon, Florida, Missouri, Illinois, Maine, New York, the Northwest Territories, British Columbia, Alberta, Manitoba, Ontario, New Brunswick, and Quebec. Ebonylane stud dogs have serviced visiting bitches from many of the United States and many provinces of Canada, resulting in over thirty champion Labrador Retrievers and many others pointed. Ebonylane is one of the top champion-producing Labrador kennels in Canada for 1980 and 1981.

The key dog in the Ebonylane breeding program has been owner-handled, Best in Show winner, and top producer, American and Canadian Champion Shamrock Acres Ebonylane Ace, C.D.X., W.C., who was whelped May 21st, 1975, and bred by Sally McCarthy and Jackie Childs in Wisconsin. Ace was Ebonylane's first breed champion. He completed his Canadian championship amateur-owner-handled in two consecutive show week-ends, just three days after his first birthday, by defeating champions in three of four shows and capturing two four-point wins, a Group placement from the Puppy Class, and a Best Puppy in Group. Ace completed his C.D. degree in August 1976, his W.C. in June 1977, and his C.D.X. in August 1977. He was runner-up in 1977 for the Briggs Trophy awarded by the Labrador Owners Club of Canada to the top Labrador in the breed ring, and in 1978 he won the Briggs Trophy. In 1977, '78, and '79, Ace was owner-handled, mainly in the local shows, and accumulated 43 Bests of Breed, 17 Group placements, and a cherished Best in Show. In 1980, Ace completed his American championship with a Best of Winners award over 111 Labs under breeder-judge Andrew Stewart. When shown in the United States, Ace never placed lower than Reserve Winners Dog with one exception. Also in 1980, Ace won the highest award of the Labrador Owners Club of Canada, the Neville Trophy, awarded to the top all-around Lab in show, field, and obedience in the club that year. So far, Ace has sired 17 champions in Canada and the United States, of which six share multiple Group placements, three share eleven First in

Group awards earned on both sides of the border, and two have each earned a Best in Show, one in Canada and one in the United States. Several of Ace's get have earned Specialty wins in the United States. One of Ace's daughters completed her W.C. and American U.D. before she reached the age of two and she lacks only one major to complete her championship. Many of Ace's get have won other obedience degrees as well. Ace is believed to be the only Best in Show winning Lab in Canada to have both a C.D.X. degree in obedience and a W.C. in the field. He is also the only Best in Show Lab in Canada to have produced two Best in Show winners: multiple Group winning American and Canadian Champion Hollyhock's Sam, Number One Labrador Retriever in breed competition in Canada in 1980, bred by Tom and Sandy Barcomb of Rouses Point, New York, owned by Wayne Peak of Ottawa, and on lease to Ebonylane; and American Specialty Best of Breed and multiple Group winner, American and Canadian Champion Sunnybrook Acres Ace O'Spade, an all-breed Best in Show dog in Canada with C.D. and W.C. degrees, bred by Ray and Ruthie Kleissle of Houston, Texas, and owned by John and Fran Ippensen of Springfield, Missouri.

Ace and Sam comprise the only Best in Show winning father and son Labrador Retriever Stud Team in Canada.

This noted Labrador is Best in Show winner and producer, Am., Can. Ch. Shamrock Acres Ebonylane Ace, C.D.X., W.C., with his co-owner Pat Lanctot.

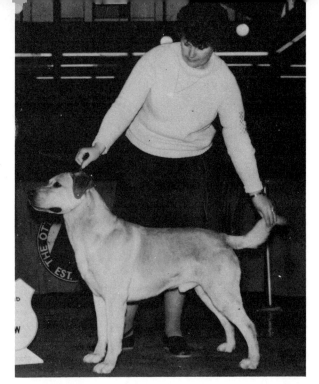

Best in Show winner and the Number One Labrador in Canada 1980, Am., Can. Ch. Hollyhock's Sam, with handler Jennifer McAuley.

Ebonylane's foundation bitch, Champion Ebonylane's Shadow, an Ace daughter bred and handled by Ebonylane, completed her championship at barely a year of age and has produced a total of 11 pups in her three litters. From her first litter came multiple Group winner American and Canadian Champion Ebonylane's Aslan, owned by Dr. Ken Bentley of Westmount, Quebec, and bred, handled by, and on lease to Ebonylane. Aslan was awarded his Canadian championship at 11½ months of age, earning two five-point wins and a three-point win, a second in Group, and two Best Puppy in Group. At 16 months, he completed his American championship with several Best of Breed awards, and as of this writing, he is in the lead for Number One Labrador Retriever in Canada 1981. Aslan is another important key in the Ebonylane breeding program; although he is only two-and-a-half years old, he has already sired four champions. Three of the champions came from his first litter, one of whom finished from the Puppy Class with a Group placing and four Best Puppy in Group awards, and the fourth champion, Ebonylane's Busy Bee, completed her title in two consecutive week-end shows at seven months of age to the day. Another from the first litter won her class in the Sweepstakes and was fifth in the Open Class at the American National Specialty.

Another pup from Shadow's first litter was Champion Ebonylane's Myra at Romillar, C.D., owned by Walter and Helen Miller of Carrying Place, Ontario. She completed her title the second week-end out and was Best of Breed in an entry of 40 at the first Booster held by the Labrador Retriever Club of Canada.

Then there is Champion Ebonylane's Northern Trooper, owned by Bob and Pierette Lanctot of Otterburn Park, Quebec, who was breeder-handled to his title in two consecutive week-ends. Ebonylane's Cavier, owned by Rick Thiel of Huberdeau, Quebec, and bred, handled by, and on lease to Ebonylane, is a multiple Best Puppy in Group winner and American National Specialty Best in Sweepstakes winner. Cavier's first points were won in a five-point major at the Ottawa Retriever Club Booster, where Winners Bitch for five points went to Champion Ebonylane's Black Diamond, owned by Mrs. Fran Peak of Ottawa, and bred, handled, and on lease to Ebonylane. Since that show, Cavier gained another five-point Best of Winners and while he has enough points for his Canadian championship, he still requires the nod from one more judge to complete the title.

Six-week-old Labrador puppies at Ebonylane Kennels with their breeder, Mike Lanctot.

Ch. Ebonylane's Black Diamond with breeder-handler Pat Lanctot. Ebonylane Kennels, Quebec.

The second brood bitch at Ebonylane is Champion Elden's Duchess of Ebonylane, C.D., bred by Elden Williams of Portland, Oregon, owned and handled by Ebonylane. Dutch is the daughter, sister, and half-sister, respectively, of the three Number One Labradors in the United States in 1979, 1980, and 1981. She completed her championship owner-handled at nine months of age with wins over Specials. Her first litter by Ace produced Champion Ebonylane's Black Diamond, and her second litter, by Aslan, produced Champion Ebonylane's Busy Bee.

The third brood bitch (in order of seniority) at Ebonylane is an Ace granddaughter, Champion Ebonylane's Cotton Candy, bred, owned, and handled by Ebonylane. Candy completed her championship at 15 months of age, with two three-points and a five-point win, including Best of Winners and Best of Opposite Sex over Specials from the Bred-by Exhibitor Class at the Labrador Owners Club Booster of the Metropolitan Kennel Club in Toronto. Candy is expecting her first litter in early 1982.

Ebonylane feels itself fortunate, through the cooperation of their owners, to have the following Ace daughters on lease: champion producing Champion Hollyhock's Black Pepper owned by J.Y. McNulty of Laval, Quebec; Champion Hollyhock's Leiley, a champion producer owned by Mr. and Mrs. Bernard Laberge of Quebec; Best Puppy in Group winner, Champion Ebonylane's Black Diamond, a maiden bitch owned by Mrs. Fran Peak of Ottawa; and another maiden bitch, an Ace granddaughter, Champion Ebonylane's Sandy Sunshine, winner of the Open Yellow Class at the 1981 National, owned by Mr. and Mrs. Alain Brazeau of St. Bruno, Quebec.

Mr. and Mrs. Lanctot are justly proud of the success which their dogs have met. Through careful planning, the Ebonylane breeding program is a dedicated effort to produce pups that excel in type, temperament, and trainability. Of prime importance is the original purpose of the breed; that is, a sound hunting companion who typifies the characteristics and temperament of the breed. Many Ebonylane champions have also earned titles in licensed obedience trials and Working Certificates in the field. In just seven-and-a-half years, which is a very short time by breeders' standards, the Lanctots have earned themselves a place of honor in the breed history of the Labrador Retriever in North America.

Best in Show winner and producer, Am., Can. Ch. Shamrock Acres Ebonylane Ace, C.D.X., W.C., owned by Pat and Mike Lanctot, Ebonylane Kennels.

Ch. and O.T. Ch. Wimberway the Zealous Wendy, W.C. winning High in Trial, High in Open B, and High in Utility under Jake Giacomelli, July 1980, at Wendy's last trial of the home club, Newfoundland All Breed Kennel Club, on the occasion of its 50th conformation show. Pictured also is co-owner Alanna Downton.

Okkak

In the Labrador's own home province, Newfoundland, we find the Okkak Kennels, located at Goulds and owned by John and Alanna Downton. The Downtons have made some splendid records with their dogs in conformation competition, but their main interest lies in obedience.

The foundation bitch here is Champion and Obedience Trial Champion Wimberway the Zealous Wendy, W.C., who finished her conformation championship with breed wins and Group placements but has succeeded even more spectacularly in the obedience ring. This is particularly noteworthy because living in Newfoundland limits the Downtons' access to trials, only eight of which are held in the entire province annually. Despite this fact, Wendy, in five years of trialing, has achieved the following: 22 High in Trial awards, 43 High in Class awards, the *Dog World* award for C.D. in 1976, Number Two Lab and Number Three Sporting Dog in Canadian Obedience Trials in 1977, Top Lab and Number Six All Breeds in Canadian Obedience Trials in 1978, Number Two Lab and Number Seven Sporting Dog in Canadian Obedience Trials in 1979, and Top Lab and Number Six Sporting Dog in Canadian Obedience Trials in 1980—a proud list of achievements, indeed!

Additionally, Wendy has won numerous obedience awards from obedience and other clubs and also holds a Working Certificate for retrieving in the field.

In two litters, Wendy has produced three conformation champions and three more are pointed, one obedience trial champion, five C.D. dogs, and six hunting dogs. Wendy is now eight years old and is retired, enjoying perfect health. She is a daughter of Winning Knave of Wimberway, C.D.X., W.C. ex Champion Wimberway the Contessa, C.D. and was bred by Sandy Briggs.

Okkak Labradors, bred at a small kennel, were initially based on Wimberway lines, but now the move is toward English lines. Among the dogs there, in addition to Wendy, are Obedience Trial Champion Wimberway the Winning Sue, W.C., with eight High in Trials, 20 High in Class, and national ranking in the breed and in the Sporting group in Canadian Obedience Trials in 1978, '79, and '80; Champion and Obedience Trial

O.T. Ch. Wimberway the Winning Sue elegantly taking the jumps. This lovely obedience "star" belongs to the John Downtons, Goulds, Newfoundland.

Ch. Okkak's Island Suspense, C.D. and Ch., O.T. Ch. Okkak's Atlantic Clipper, W.C., two fine representatives of the Okkak Labradors owned by Mr. and Mrs. John Downton.

Champion Okkak's Atlantic Clipper, W.C., with three High in Trials and eight High in Class wins; and Champion Okkak's Island Suspense, C.D., with five High in Trials and eight High in Class out of eight trials. "Penny" is also a breed winner in conformation, with a Group placement to her credit. "Penny" is a Wendy puppy sired by Champion and Obedience Trial Champion Ballyduff Storm, W.C., a Best in Show winner and Number One Lab and Number Five All Breeds in 1977 Canadian Obedience Trials. Storm and the Downtons' three bitches, Sue, Wendy, and Clipper, are the only dogs of any breed in Newfoundland that have attained the utility title.

The newest member of Okkak Kennels is a beautiful English-bred black male puppy who, at his first show when he was seven months old, went Best of Breed over four specials, two of which were Group winners and one a Best in Show winner. "Sunny," or Shadowvale Okkak Sundown Frost, was sired by England's Top Show Lab for 1978 and 1979, English Show Champion Balrion King Frost (Best in Show winner) ex English Show Champion Bradking Black Charm (Top Show Bitch in England in 1980). The Downtons are planning to breed "Sunny" and "Penny," gradually establishing solid English bloodlines for their kennel. Having competed only since 1975, during which time they have totalled 38 High in Trials and 80 High in Class awards, with only four dogs in obedience, the Downtons feel that the Okkak Labs, although small in number, have definitely taken a prominent position in the world of obedience Labradors in Canada, and I heartily agree! It is good to see this interest, and success, in the land from which Labradors first came!

Ranchman's

Mrs. R.J. (Marion) Reid of Medicine Hat, Alberta, is a very dedicated and knowledgeable breeder of Labradors at her Ranchman's Kennel, a kennel which has been highly successful in the breeding of fine dogs. The Reids feel strongly that a Lab should be an all-purpose dog, and it is Mrs. Reid's hope that eventually in Canada a Labrador will not be considered a champion until it is issued a Working Certificate from the field, thus retaining the true instinct of this beautiful animal. The ambition at Ranchman's is to breed true to type, good-looking dogs with brains and exceptional hunting ability. Mrs. Reid is firm in the belief that there should *not* be one type of dog for showing and another for the field. To quote Mrs. Reid:

> The snipey, long in the leg, thin-tailed Labrador type which seems preferred in the field trial circles because of its speed is not what the breed was meant to be. A fast dog is not what the Lab was bred to become, but rather a strong, sturdy dog with the staying power and stamina to last a day of continuous hunting, not a speed machine similar in type to a hound. In contrast, the show ring has produced some nice looking specimens with what seems to be a brain the size of a pea, and many times these same dogs are also gun shy. One's goal should be a happy medium between these two, trying always to improve the quality of the dogs in body and mind.

Left to right: Marion and Bob Reid and Vina and Frank Jones snapped informally with two of the Reids' Ranchman's Labradors.

Representative of the handsome Labradors at Ranchman's Kennels, Medicine Hat, Alberta.

Ranchman's is not a large kennel. The bloodlines on all Labradors there are based on those which produced Canadian Champion Lisnamallard Tarantella (Irish Champion Stokestown Duke of Blaircourt and English and Irish Champion Hilldown Sylver). "Tara," who was owned in England by Col. George Craster (known to Mrs. Reid as "Uncle George") of the Ravencamp prefix was sold to Frank Jones of Annwyn Labradors in Ontario, where she so well proved her quality in the show ring and the whelping box. This line was one of the best, consistently proving itself with Labs such as "Tara" and her well-known brother from a later litter, Canadian and Irish Champion Castlemore Shamus.

The Reids' first Labrador in Canada was Annwyn's Glenavon, by Annwyn's Simon the Sweep ex Annwyn's Amanda, who they purchased from Frank Jones as a hunting dog for Mr. Reid and a companion for Mrs. Reid. "Glen" was a lovely black dog with a true Labrador nature, tolerant and loving of people and cautious and alert when danger threatened. He was neither shown nor offered at stud, as Mrs. Reid's time at that period was filled with the care of a small child and a new home.

The second Lab, who came to the Reids some years later, again by way of Frank Jones, was Killingworth's Tarbinavon, by American Champion Killingworth's Thunderson ex Forecast Adelphi. This was a lovely black bitch from Lorraine Robbenhaar's kennel in the United States. With her arrival, and as the children were now older and more independent, Mrs. Reid returned to the interest of her youthful days as a child in England, that of breeding and showing Labs. "Tarbin" is a third generation descendant of "Tara's," and after careful consideration, Mrs. Reid applied for registration of the kennel name "Ranchman's" and set out to raise Labs which would be a credit to the breed and which would upgrade quality in Western Canadian Labs. "Tarbin" was X-rayed clear of hip dysplasia at twenty months of age and was bred to Canadian and American Champion Rupert Krest of Wallesey (Champion Ardmargha Goldcrest of Syrancot ex Rupert Judicious), owned by Hugh Crozier, a long-time leader in the Canadian Lab world. Krest was the top pointed Lab in Canada for the year 1976.

From "Tarbin's" seven puppies in this litter came Canadian Champion Ranchman's Medicine Man, who finished his championship with a Group II award and who is now a leading sire in Ontario; Canadian Champion Ranchman's Gunsmoke, who was a multiple Best of Breed winner and also won a Group II his first time out as a Special; and Canadian Champion Ranchman's Champagne Sparkle, C.D., C.D.X., who finished her championship as a puppy, taking numerous Best Puppy in Breed and two Best Puppy in Group awards, has won Best of Breed honors over Specials of both sexes, and has earned two obedience titles. "Tarbin" now resides with the Reids as a "professional granny" and as an avid and steady hunting dog.

A bitch puppy from Tarbin's first litter was kept by the Reids' daughter, for whom she has made a wonderful companion. Shown sparingly, she nonetheless has points toward her championship and a leg on her C.D. She has proved to be a producer of consistently high quality offspring, as have her littermates. This bitch was bred for her first time in 1980 to Canadian

Killingworth's Tarbinavon taking Best of Opposite Sex at the Manitoba Canine Association in 1979. Mrs. Marion Reid, owner-handler.

Killingworth's Tarbinavon with Bob Reid of Ranchman's Labradors.

Ranchman's Moonwind Dancer at Calgary 1981, Best of Winners and Best Sporting Dog Puppy in Show. Ranchman's Labradors, Marion Reid.

Killingworth's Squire at one year old. Ranchman's Labradors, Marion and Bob Reid.

Champion Rupert Esquire of Barala (Champion Ardmargha So Famous ex Rupert Goldylocks), who is owned by Barala Kennels in Winnipeg. She, like her mother, produced seven healthy puppies. They include Ranchman's Rouge Nero, who has been awarded several Certificates of Merit in field trials as a puppy in Ontario; and Ranchman's Moonwind Dancer, who has three Best Puppy in Breed, a Best Puppy in Group, and Winners and Best of Opposite Sex while still a puppy. The Reids kept a bitch puppy from this litter: Ranchman's Kameo Keepsake, who will be shown in conformation and obedience starting in 1982.

In 1979, the Reids purchased Killingworth's Squire (American Champion Stonewood Killingworth KY KY ex Chucklebrook's L'il Audrey) as a stud dog, having selected him for his overall quality and especially for his magnificent head, "the kind I have not seen since I left England many years ago," to quote Mrs. Reid. Mrs. Reid started Squire's career owner-handled, but she took the advice of the friends who told her that the strength of her dog together with the weakness of her handling skills was holding him back; so Squire was turned over to James Campbell, a professional handler from British Columbia, who finished the dog in short order in both Canada and the United States,

with some splendid Best of Breed and Group placements over top West Coast specials. Now with many Group placements, including a first, behind him, "The Squire" is semi-retired to fulfill his hunting career and stud requirements.

Two more Labradors joined Ranchman's Kennels in 1981. These are a black bitch and a yellow dog, a sister-brother team, by Canadian Champion Springfield Jeeves ex Canadian Champion Follytower Jenny, an English import.

Can., Am. Ch. Killingworth's Squire is handled here by James M. Campbell for Marion R. Reid, Ranchman's Kennels.

Redsky

Grace L. McDonald, of Winnipeg, Manitoba, has been breeding Redsky Labradors since 1965. A very much involved Labrador enthusiast, this lady has belonged to the Labrador Owners Club of Ontario for many years, and she founded the Labrador Retriever Club of Manitoba in October 1971. Additionally, she assisted in the formation of the Labrador Retriever Club of Alberta and is a Charter Member of the newly formed Labrador Retriever Club of Canada. She is a Canadian Kennel Club Licensed Obedience Judge for all Classes, and has judged Obedience in the United States.

The bloodlines of the Redsky Kennels are primarily based on two stud dogs imported from Great Britain by Mr. Hugh Crozier of Crozier Kennels back in the 1960s. He first imported a black from Ireland, Irish, Canadian, and American Champion Castlemore Shamus, and a few years later from England he imported a yellow, Champion Halsinger's Bartonly Rubens. Shamus went back to the Blaircourt and Sandylands lines, and "Sam" (Halsinger's Bartonly Rubens) originated from the Diant lines. Both of these stud dogs did a great deal for the quality of the Labrador Retrievers in the western provinces of Canada.

In 1965, Mrs. McDonald purchased her foundation bitch from Hugh Crozier. Born August 23rd, 1965, she was the product of a Shamus daughter being bred back to Shamus. Her name was Amber Lady of Murdoch Bay, C.D., C.D.X. This bitch lived to be 15 years old.

Due to Amber's tight line-breeding to Shamus, Mrs. McDonald felt that she should outcross her, and so Amber was bred to Champion Halsinger's Bartonly Rubens. The first breeding produced Champion Samber's Don Juan of Redsky, C.D., C.D.X., who was tragically lost at three years and one day of age under the wheels of a car. He would have been the first dog in Manitoba to have both an obedience trial championship and a show championship, and he had two legs to his utility degree at the time of his death.

A repeat breeding of Amber and Sam gave Mrs. McDonald her next brood bitch, Obedience Trial Champion and Champion Redsky's Dandy Little Honey, W.C. Honey was the first dog in Manitoba to have a double championship, and she earned her utility degree in three consecutive trials.

These are some of the famous Redsky Labradors owned by Ms. Grace L. McDonald, Dickens Post Office, Winnipeg, Manitoba, Canada. Lying down is Amber Lady of Murdoch Bay, C.D., C.D.X. Behind are, right to left: Redsky's Dufferin Dutchess; O.T. Ch. and Ch. Redsky's Dynamic Duke, Am. C.D. and C.D.X.; and O.T. Ch. and Ch. Redsky's Dandy Little Honey, W.C.

In order to go back to the Castlemore Shamus lines which Mrs. McDonald felt offered more type, she bred Honey to a Shamus son, Champion Castlemore Brandy of Cordova, and this produced the dog she refers to as "the light of my life," Obedience Trial Champion and Champion Redsky's Dynamic Duke, American C.D. and C.D.X. Duke earned his C.D., C.D.X., and U.D. degrees in under six months, which garnered him a *Dog World* award, and was the Top Obedience Labrador in Canada in 1976.

Mrs. McDonald is careful to keep her breeding operations to one litter approximately every second year and usually breeds only for the purpose of retaining a pup either for breeding or for training.

In 1979, after having been training director for many different dog clubs over the previous ten years, Mrs. McDonald opened her own private obedience school, the Obedience School of Instruction, which she enjoys but which does interfere with an enlarged breeding program and also with travels to the dog shows. She also is employed by the Health Science Centre as a Laboratory Supervisor.

Honey, now 11 years old, "Chance" (Dynamic Duke), now nine years old, and two Chance daughters and two of his granddaughters currently comprise the Redsky Labs. One of the Dynamic Duke daughters is out of a daughter of Honey's litter-brother, Champion Redsky's Dare Devil C.D., and the other Dynamic Duke daughter is out of a granddaughter of his litter-brother, Champion Redsky's Double or Nothing

Ch. Springfield's Fanny Sweet Adams during the training season. Springfield Kennels, the Costigans, Calgary, Canada.

C.D. That pup's dam was the product of Springfield's Fanny Sweet Adam being bred to Brian Boru. Mrs. McDonald notes that Champion Springfield's Fanny Sweet Adam, who is a fantastic producer, is a daughter of Dynamic Duke's litter-brother, Double or Nothing.

The two Dynamic Duke granddaughters come from a strong outcross and a close line-breeding. The first line-breeding was the mating of Champion Redsky's Double Dynasty (the product of Dynamic Duke bred back to his mother, Honey) to a Dynamic Duke daughter. The outcross was the mating of Champion Redsky's Double Dynasty's litter-sister, Double Destiny, with a lovely black male, Canadian and American Champion Shamrock Acres Chief Invader. "Angus," as Chief Invader is known, belongs to Richard and Jeri Delaliaux of Loonbay Kennels in Dugold, Manitoba. He was Winners Dog and Best of Winners at the American National in 1977. This is the only occasion on which Mrs. McDonald has ever bred to a black, but she felt that Angus could offer her line something that no readily available yellow could at the time. As it worked out there was just one puppy—a yellow bitch.

Romillar

Romillar Labradors, at Carrying Place, Ontario, were started with a rather unique goal: raising college funds for Helen and Walter Millar's sons. In 1963, this family purchased a dark yellow bitch from Blackgold Kennels. She was Golden Glory II, by Canadian Champion Gift of Gold from Blackgold Juno. She had championship points when the Millars bought her, but being complete novices at the time, they were not interested in showing her to complete the title, although they since have regretted not doing so. "Goldie" gave the Millars four litters, from which they kept one outstanding black male, Champion Gold's Pride of Bonzo, sired by Bonzo of Blyth. The latter dog, by Canadian Champion Bonnie's Ace, was a grandson of Dual Champion Blyth's Knave of Spades, Canadian Champion Black Mina, Dual Champion Blyth's Ace of Spades, and Dual Champion Blyth's Queen of Spades.

Since the Millars' original purpose was to breed quality hunting dogs with good conformation, up until 1970 their exhibiting experience had been brief. But all that changed when, in June 1970, they purchased a beautiful two-year-old bitch, Champion Rosedale's Daisy. She was a light yellow Best Puppy in Show winner, and she was the beginning of Romillar Kennels' show-producing line. Born in 1967, Daisy was sired by American and Canadian Champion Murrayville Benefactor ex Riverside Midnight Majic and she was bred by Denice Hayes.

Ch. Gold's Pride of Bonzo, whelped December 1968, grandson of Ch. Bonnie's Ace and Ch. Gift of Gold. Bred by Helen and Walter Millar, this dog belonged to their son, Glenn, who hunted with him. This marvelous family companion and field dog as well as a conformation winner gained his championship in four shows handled by another of the Millars' sons, Chris.

Daisy was bred to Champion Caledonia Great Heart, becoming the dam of Champion Romillar's Jody. The latter bitch was a Best of Breed winner and an excellent producer. Among her progeny, sired by Champion Gold's Pride of Bonzo, was Canadian Champion Romillar's September Velvet, C.D., who completed her championship on her first birthday. She was handled by Helen Millar in conformation and by her son Chris in obedience.

September Velvet has been an invaluable producing bitch for the Millars. Among her best-known get is Canadian Champion Romillar's Chelsea, C.D., by Romillar's Golden Boy Sam,

Can. Ch. Romillar's Chelsea, C.D., born June 1978, by Romillar's Golden Boy Sam ex Can. Ch. Romillar's September Velvet, won a five-point major at a Labrador Specialty in 1979 and became a champion on her first birthday. Owned by Helen and Walter Millar.

Can. Ch. Romillar's Jody, born March 1970, by Can. Ch. Caledonia Great Heart ex Ch. Rosedale's Daisy. A Best of Breed winner and excellent producer owned by Helen and Walter Millar, Carrying Place, Ontario, Canada.

Can. Ch. Ebonylane's Myra at Romillar, C.D., by Ch. Astroloma Joshua (imported from Australia) ex Can. Ch. Ebonylane's Shadow. Purchased at six weeks of age from the Lanctots, this lovely bitch became a Canadian Champion at ten months of age. Pictured winning the Labrador Retriever Club of Canada Booster Show at Credit Valley, December 1980. Also was awarded the Red Dawn Trophy for Highest Scoring Champion Labrador in obtaining her C.D. in three trials in one weekend. Owned by Helen and Walter Millar.

who won a five-point major at the Labrador Specialty in 1979, became a champion on her first birthday, and then earned her C.D. in four trials. Chelsea, in turn, is the dam of the up-and-coming young male the Millars are campaigning in 1981, Canadian Champion Romillar's Ace of Spades, C.D., who is by American and Canadian Champion Shamrock Acres Ebony Lane Ace, C.D.X., W.C.

The Millars also own a lovely bitch bred by the Lanctots, Canadian Champion Ebonylane's Myra at Romillar, C.D., sired by an Australian import, Champion Astroloma Joshua from Canadian Champion Ebonylane's Shadow.

If you think it is not hard to get this many puppies all to pose in the same picture, just try it! These adorable babies are from Ro-Shan Labradors, owned by Tom and Phyllis Philip, Crysler, Ontario.

Ro-Shan

Ro-Shan Labradors, at Crysler, Ontario, are owned by Tom and Phyllis Philip, who have been breeding Labs since 1965. They raise all three colors and maintain a kennel of between 12 and 15 dogs.

Ro-Shan has made a very proud record. Fifty litters have been produced there in the past 16 years, and so far there are 30 champions bearing the Ro-Shan prefix.

One of Ro-Shan's early important winners was Runroy, a son of Irish, Canadian, and American Champion Castlemore Shamus (Champion Stokestown Duke of Blaircourt ex International Champion Hilldown Silver) from Willou's Red River Belle (Glengarvin's Rookie ex a daughter

Can. Ch. Runroy, by Irish, Am., and Can. Ch. Castlemore Shamus ex Willou's Red River Belle, was Canada's Top Labrador and Third Top Sporting Dog in 1972. Photo by Robert Philip. Owned by Ro-Shan Labradors.

of Field Champion Sandburr Pete). This fine dog was purchased by Mr. and Mrs. Philip in March of 1972. He started out in Open Class, and by November 30th had become Top Labrador in Canada with two Bests in Show and many Group placements. He also was Number Three Sporting Dog in Canada in 1972. Runroy was retired after one year of showing, and he proceeded to make himself an outstanding stud dog with 13 champions to his credit.

In 1975, a Runroy son was Top Labrador in Canada, the black Champion Barrymar's Domino. Another of his sons, Champion Ro-Shan's Runjess Mr. Bones (a yellow) was Number Two.

In 1974, Champion Barrymar's Domino was Number Two Lab. In 1976, Champion Ro-Shan's Runjess Mr. Bones was Number Two Lab and Domino was Number Three. Champion Barrymar's Domino was bred by Margaret and Barry Hartford, Barrymar Kennels.

Ch. Trelawney's Jolly Roger at 11 years of age in May 1981. Handled by his friend Samuel Cappellina; owned by Ro-Shan Labradors, Tom and Phyllis Philip.

Ch. Trelawney's Jolly Roger, by Ch. Lockerbie's Sandylands Tarquin ex Trelawney's Beck and Call, was born April 1970, and is owned by Ro-Shan Labradors.

A pure black dog, Champion Trelawny's Jolly Roger, was purchased by Ro-Shan in December 1973, from the Trelawny Kennels of Mrs. Clifford E. Clarke. To date he has sired 11 champions for Ro-Shan, with his latest litter of ten sired at 11½ years. The Philips consider Roger the best investment they have made so far, and Phyllis Philip says of him, "He has a tail like a 2 x 4 that never stops wagging, a very dense heavy coat, and a fantastic temperament." Ro-Shan combined Roger's line in the breeding program

with Champion Driftwood's Rusty of Ro-Shan's line to improve Ro-Shan's chocolates, which they have been placing special emphasis on since the mid-1970s. Roger is now almost twelve years old, and although he is a little stiff, he is in the best of health. Mrs. Philip says, "He now spends his winters inside in a big blanket."

The Philips have two sons, Robert and Shane, whom we are sure share their parents' enthusiasm for Labs. Ro-Shan consists of a house, a kennel, and a very large pond on 50 acres of land; the pond is well used by both adult and puppy Labs.

Seven-week-old Labrador puppies trying out the pond at Ro-Shan Kennels.

Head study of English Show Ch. Bradking Black Charm owned by the Beatties at Shadowvale Labradors in Rigaud, Quebec, Canada.

Shadowvale

Shadowvale Labradors, in Rigaud, Quebec, are bred at a kennel which was started in 1974 by Michael and Huguette Beattie with the purchase of their first member of the breed as a family pet. This bitch, "Penny," was later to become Canadian Obedience Trial Champion Marshland Penny, and she is responsible for the Beatties' love of Labradors. Because of "Penny," the Beatties joined clubs and made friends and became interested in conformation. It was then that they learned that "Penny" was not quite "typey," and they set about studying the show points of the breed.

After several false starts with puppies from both Canadian and American kennels, Mr. and Mrs. Beattie went to England to buy an older bitch. Mr. Beattie had been born in England and had owned Labradors for shooting, so they had an idea of where to begin. They fell in love with a beautiful bitch who was not for sale, but an agreement was made that they could buy a bitch puppy from her first litter. Heatherbourne Moira was bred to English Show Champion

Balrion King Frost and produced the Beatties' foundation bitch, American, Canadian, and Puerto Rican Champion Heatherbourne Forget Me Not. "Faye" was Canada's Top Winning Labrador Puppy in 1980, with seven Best Puppy in Group awards, one Best Puppy in Show (All Breeds), and one Best Puppy in Show at the Labrador Owners Club Specialty. "Faye" was bred, late in 1981, to American Champion Jayncourt Ajoco Justice.

While the Beatties were in England, they attended two dog shows and had the good fortune to meet Mr. Arthur Kelley of Bradking fame. When they asked him if he had any older bitches for sale, he asked in turn if they would be interested in an English show champion. Needless to say, the Beatties were thrilled at the prospect! They went off to Mr. Kelley's home, where they saw English Show Champion Bradking Black Charm. To quote Mrs. Beattie, "Vicky is the stuff Labrador dreams are made of," and it was arranged that she would remain in England to be bred to English Show Champion Balrion King Frost. While Mr. Kelley waited for Vicky to come into season, it was agreed that she could be shown, and she gained five additional Challenge Certificates and a Reserve and was England's Top Challenge Certificate Winning Lab for 1980.

English Show Ch. Bradking Black Charm, W.C., pictured taking her third major in the United States at the Labrador Retriever Club National Specialty in October 1981, where she was Winners Bitch over 177 bitches, then Best of Winners over 125 dogs. Black Charm is owned by Shadowvale Labradors.

These are the Labradors behind the foundation of Shadowvale. Left, yellow female English Show Ch. Bradking Bonny My Gal (the dam of Eng. Sh. Ch. Bradking Black Charm). Center, chocolate female Bradking Cassandra (living in England, a daughter of Black Charm). Right, English Show Ch. Bradking Black Charm, owned by Mr. and Mrs. H.G. Beattie.

English Show Champion Bradking Black Charm was bred in January 1981. The Beatties' delight when she whelped a splendid litter of five males and two bitches is understandable. This was their first litter, and it certainly "wiped away seven years of frustration and tears." From this litter two bitches, Shadowvale's Charm 'n Pride and Shadowvale's Charm 'n Joy, and a male, Shadowvale's Frosty Knight, were kept.

As soon as Vicky had regained her "girlish figure," she was off to the United States for shows. On her first week-end out, she took two majors. October found her owner-handled at the National Specialty where she was Winners Bitch and Best of Winners over 177 bitches and 125 dogs. She also earned her Working Certificate that day.

Shadowvale is now producing Labradors true to the English type, with keen intelligence, good looks, and fine working abilities.

English Show Ch. Bradking Black Charm is the winner of eight Challenge Certificates and three Reserves. By Eng. Ch. Follytower Merrybrook Black Stormer (Eng. Ch. Sandylands Tandy ex Follytower Old Black Magic) ex English Show Ch. Bradking Bonny My Girl (Ch. Sandylands Mark ex Sandylands Carona), this lovely bitch was purchased in England as foundation for Mr. and Mrs. M.G. Beattie's Shadowvale Kennels in Quebec.

Springfield

In Calgary, Alberta, we find the highly successful Canadian kennel known as Springfield (no relation to Springfield Labs in the United States) which is owned by Frank, Shirley, and Joanne Costigan and which was registered with the Canadian Kennel Club on July 10th, 1973. The Costigans became involved in breeding Labradors in England back in 1962. They were living in Hertfordshire at the time and had visited Medburn Farms to buy some fresh eggs. They came away with a dozen eggs *and* a female yellow Lab puppy, Honey of Medburn, line-bred on Sandylands Bob. This bitch subsequently was bred to a Scottish dog from Ballyduff lines, and later the Costigans brought Honey and the pick puppy from her litter of twelve back to Canada with them.

Ch. Springfield's Gi Gi with Shirley Costigan, Springfield Kennels, Calgary, Alberta, Canada.

On arrival at Calgary, the Costigans involved themselves in field trials and obedience with Honey's son, Springfield's Pauline's Peril, C.D. The remark of a seasoned handler concerning their amateurism, overhead at one trial, ("The only trouble with that dog is the handler—he doesn't know what a good dog he's got.") triggered the Costigans to even greater enthusiasm, and they started to show their Labs in the conformation ring, "with the same innocence and a predictable result." They were third out of three Labs in the class.

Not to be discouraged, the Costigans next kept a yellow bitch from Honey's second litter, Springfield's Stubble Jumper, whom they bred to Keith Strader's Sunnyway's Scott of Terregles, the latter out of a Scottish import.

From this breeding came the first of the Costigans' long list of champions, Canadian Champion Springfield's Cleopatra. From "Cleo's" litter-sister, Constant Elsa, came Champion Springfields Fanny Sweet Adams, sired by Champion Redsky's Double Or Nothing, C.D., thus making Fanny line-bred on Canadian, American, and Irish Champion Castlemore Shamus. Fanny has since produced twelve of Springfield's twenty-three champions, among them Champion Springfield's Northern Justice, Number One Canadian Labrador 1979 at two years of age, and Champion Springfield's Uhuru, multiple Best in Show winner and, at 21 months of age and with only five months of showing in 1981, top contender for Number One Lab in Canada.

The Costigans also point with pride to Champion Cyndie Lou of Charleswood, a daughter of Field Trial Champion Flapjack of Duckmaster and granddaughter of Field Trial Champion Chuck of Bracken. The Costigans bought Cyndie at two years of age. She has produced five champions and several pointed progeny from one litter, including Champion Springfield's Dambuster, Number Two Gun Dog, Labrador Retriever Club of Alberta, and winner of the largest Lab Booster in Canada, Calgary 1976; and Champion Springfield's Gigi, Number One Gun Dog, Lab Club of Alberta.

It is due in a large part to the above dogs that the Costigans have been able to maintain a high standard of hunting ability in their Labradors, and they feel it their responsibility as breeders never to forget the fact that the Labrador is first and foremost a gun dog.

Right: Ch. Springfield's Northern Justice, owned by the Costigans, Springfield Labradors, taking Best of Winners under judge Mrs. Marg Patterson.

Below: Ch. Springfield's Uhuru, by Am. Ch. Briary Brendan of Rainell ex Ch. Springfield's Fanny Sweet Adams, is pictured winning his second Best in Show within four weeks, under judge Eve Whitmore; his first Best in Show, at 21 months of age, was from judge William Fetner. This dog is now a top contender for Number One Labrador in Canada in 1981. Bred and owned by Springfield Labradors, the Costigans, and handled by Joanne Costigan.

Ch. Springfield's Under The Red Sky at nine months of age. Frank, Shirley and Joanne Costigan, owners, Springfield Kennels.

Among the famous winners owned or bred by Mr. and Mrs. Costigan are Champion Springfield's Cleopatra, Champion Springfield's Dambuster, Champion Springfield's Fancy Sweet Adams, Champion Springfield's Gorgeous Gussie, Champion Springfield's Gi Gi, Champion Springfield's Hornblower, Champion Springfield's High Country Boy, Champion Springfield's Instant Replay, Champion Springfield's Iron Duke, Champion Springfield's K.G. Five, Champion Springfield's Lifeguard, Champion Springfield's Loco, Champion Springfield's Northern Flight, Champion Springfield's None Such Stalwart, Champion Springfield's Next to Amroth, Champion Springfield's Northern Legend, Champion Springfield's Native Fancy, Champion Springfield's Northern Justice, Champion Springfield's Under The Red Sky, Champion Springfield's Uhuru, Champion Redsky's Double or Nothing, Champion Cyndie Lou of Charleswood, and Champion Springfield's Unsung Hero.

A fine silhouette of Ch. Springfield's Northern Justice. Owned by Springfield Kennels, Frank, Shirley and Joanne Costigan, Calgary, Alberta, Canada.

Teatime for a group of the Springfield champions, Springfield Labs.

Springfields Icebreaker at 3 months. Another lovely show prospect puppy from the Costigans.

These six-and-a-half-week-old babies are by Ch. Springfield's Hornblower ex Springfield's London Pride. Owned by the Costigans, Springfield Kennels.

Ch. Spenrock's Cardigan Bay in a painting by Pamela Edwards of Canada. Photo by owner, Jan Churchill.

CHAPTER SIX

Standards for the Labrador Retriever

Agber's Darlyn, a beautiful profile of a Labrador head. Dennis Livesey owns this bitch who is the foundation of his Amberfield Kennels, Ramsey, New Jersey.

A breed standard is the description of the perfect, or ideal, dog. It is used as a guideline for objectively measuring the appearance (and temperament, to a certain extent) of a given specimen of the breed. The degree of excellence of a particular dog is based on how well the dog meets the requirements described in the standard for its breed, how well the dog approaches the ideal.

The Official A.K.C. Standard

The following standard for the Labrador Retriever was approved on April 9th, 1957, by the American Kennel Club, the governing body for purebred dogs in the United States.

GENERAL APPEARANCE. The general appearance of the Labrador should be that of a strongly built, short-coupled, very active dog. He should be fairly wide over the loins, and strong and muscular in the hindquarters. The coat should be close, short, dense and free from feather.
HEAD. The skull should be wide, giving brain room; there should be a slight stop, i.e., the brow should be slightly pronounced, so that the skull is not absolutely in a straight line with the nose. The head should be clean-cut and free from fleshy cheeks. The jaws should be long and powerful and free from snipiness; the nose should be wide and the nostrils well developed. Teeth should be strong and regular, with a level mouth. The ears should hang moderately close

to the head, rather far back, should be set somewhat low and not be large and heavy. The eyes should be of a medium size, expressing great intelligence and good temper, and can be brown, yellow or black, but brown or black is preferred.
NECK AND CHEST. The neck should be medium length, powerful and not throaty. The shoulders should be long and sloping. The chest must be of good width and depth, the ribs well sprung and the loins wide and strong, stifles well turned, and the hindquarters well developed and of great power.
LEGS AND FEET. The legs must be straight from the shoulder to ground, and the feet compact with toes well arched, and pads well developed, the hocks should be well bent, and the dog must neither be cowhocked nor be too wide behind; in fact, he must stand and move true all 'round on legs and feet. Legs should be of medium length, showing good bone and muscle, but not so short as to be out of balance with rest of body. In fact, a dog well balanced in all points is preferable to one with outstanding good qualities and defects.
TAIL. The tail is a distinctive feature of the breed; it should be very thick towards the base, gradually tapering towards the tip, of medium length, should be free from any feathering, and should be clothed thickly all round with the Labrador's short, thick, dense coat, thus giving the peculiar "rounded" appearance which has been described as the "otter" tail. The tail may be carried gaily but should not curl over the back.

A beautiful example of correct head, front, and feet. Eng., Am. Ch. Lawnwood's Hot Chocolate owned by Janet Churchill, Spenrock Kennels.

MOVEMENT. Movement should be free and effortless. The forelegs should be strong, straight and true, and correctly placed. Watching a dog move towards one, there should be no signs of elbows being out in front, but neatly held to the body with legs not too close together, and moving straight forward without pacing or weaving. Upon viewing the dog from the rear, one should get the impression that the hind legs, which should be well muscled and not cowhocked, move as nearly parallel as possible, with hocks doing their full share of work and flexing well, thus giving the appearance of power and strength.

APPROXIMATE WEIGHTS of dogs and bitches in working condition. Dogs, 60 to 75 pounds; bitches, 55 to 70 pounds.

HEIGHT AT SHOULDERS. Dogs, 22½ inches to 24½ inches; bitches, 21½ to 23½ inches.

COAT. The coat is another very distinctive feature; it should be short, very dense and without wave, and should give a fairly hard feeling to the hand.

COLOR. The colors are black, yellow, or chocolate and are evaluated as follows: (a) *Blacks*: All black, with a small white spot on chest permissible. Eyes to be of medium size, expressing intelligence and good temper, preferably brown or hazel, although black or yellow is permissible. (b) *Yellows*: Yellows may vary in color from foxred to light cream with variations in the shading of the coat on ears, the underparts of the dog, or beneath the tail. A small white spot on chest is permissible. Eye coloring and expression should be the same as that of the blacks, with black or dark brown eye rims. The nose should also be black or dark brown, although "fading" to pink in winter weather is not serious. A "Dudley" nose (pink without pigmentation) should be penalized. (c) *Chocolates*: Shades ranging from light sedge to chocolate. A small white spot on chest is permissible. Eyes to be light brown to clear yellow. Nose and eye-rim pigmentation dark brown or liver colored. "Fading" to pink in winter weather not serious. "Dudley" nose should be penalized.

Gordon W. Sousa, Jr., has sent us this interesting study in head type between the Labrador dog (above) and bitch (below).

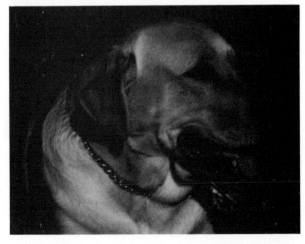

Riverroad's Sand Storm, Best in Sweepstakes 1980 National Specialty. Sired by Am., Can. Ch. Riverroad's Summerstraw, Number Three Lab in 1980. Both owned by Mrs. Frank G. Thomas, Gurnee, Illinois.

Devonwood's Little Miss Broadway going Winners Bitch and Best of Winners at Riverhead in 1978, Janet Churchill judging. Owned by Maryanne and Gene Czerwinski.

An Analysis of the Lab and the Standards

by Janet Churchill

The American standard for Labrador Retrievers, recognized by the English Kennel Club in 1903, is based on the English Standard, and only a few details in the two standards differ.

Any standard is a means for a judge or breeder to evaluate that breed within special limits. The standard should be descriptive enough to give a general picture of the dog and detailed enough to define the limits.

Type specifications that indicate "breed character" are the most important parts of any standard. Type can best be learned from established breeders and from looking at photographs of famous dogs, past and present. Keep in mind that show records and group wins do not indicate a "true" Labrador. We see various types at shows and, in truth, the majority of Labs bred in the United States, some 12,000 per year, are quite far removed from true Lab type. Most Labs are bred for pets, without regard to breeding stock.

Type is what makes a Labrador Retriever look like a Labrador Retriever and not resemble any other breed of dog. Type and conformation are two entirely different things; i.e. a poor type may have good conformation and move very soundly.

Labrador specialties, held at various times of the year throughout the United States, are the best place to observe typical Labradors. The judges selected are usually breed specialists, from well-established lines in the United States or England, and their opinions and placements are of tremendous help to novices.

The Lab has been developed primarily as a hunting dog (called a shooting dog in England). This fact should be taken into consideration by both show and field trial groups as the physical features of the dog should allow it to do its job most effectively. Temperament is as important as physical features. Along with a great willingness to please its master, a Lab should have courage and independence, and the persistence that keeps him out hunting.

The Lab's specialized hunting ability is retrieving. In England he picks up game and pheasants, while in the United States his main job is retrieving ducks and geese. He can also do a good day's work on quail or any upland game birds. Speed is not essential for a gun dog, but field trial competitors admired speed and bred for a streamlined build with lighter bone.

Labs meant to be used for field trials were bred without much regard for conformation, other than sound hips. A typical field trial Lab is tall and rangy and has a rather narrow head, very little depth of body, and a long thin tail. They are bred for qualities that will win field trials, but their appearance does not measure up to the standard description of the ideal Lab. There have been very few dual champion Labs in the United States. On the other hand, Labs of correct type and conformation hunt very well as gun dogs. If their owners don't hunt, at least they train their dogs and get Working Certificates to prove hunting ability.

In 1877, the Earl of Malmesbury said, "the real breed may be known by its close coat, which turns the water off like oil, and, above all, a tail like an otter." These two characteristics, in addition to a good Lab head and a short-coupled substantial body, set the breed apart from other breeds.

Ch. Hornton Delilah (above) was whelped in 1928, sired by the famous Champion Banchory Danilo, and owned by Mrs. M. Anderson. Ch. Drinkstone Nut (below) by Ch. Banchory Danilo ex Ch. Bride of Somersby, born in 1931, was bred and owned by Dr. Monro-Home.

Ch. Sandylands Mona Lisa, English import, littermate to Eng., Am. Ch. Sandylands Midas. Owned by Jim Lewis of Lewisfield Kennels. Handled by Fred Kirkby. Photo courtesy of Janet Churchill.

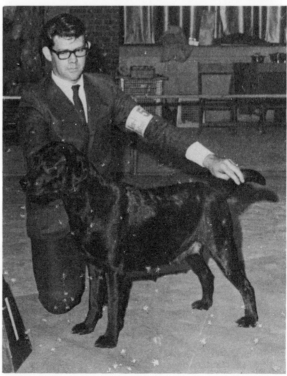

The Lab should present a square picture rather than a rectangular one. It should have ample body of good substance and should have short coupling. At first glance, a Lab should have a typical head, strong level back, and good otter tail and stand nicely balanced (freely, not stacked) on good feet and with properly proportioned forequarters and hindquarters.

Keep in mind that a Lab is expected to do a day's work. Labs which retrieve ducks and Canadian geese will face rough, icy cold water and need every inch of the coat and undercoat called for by the standard. Some duck hunters go to rocky seashores, others to difficult swamps and marshes. Labs used on upland birds may find themselves in rough, rocky, hilly country. A Lab should not shirk its duties no matter where it finds itself with its master.

The typical Labrador Retriever head is well developed and without exaggeration. The stop should be well defined but not dished, and the head should not have a "houndy" look. The plane of the skull should be parallel to the plane of the nose bone. The stop should not be like that of the Pointer, Foxhound, or Flat-coated Retriever.

The muzzle, which is built to lie on the water, should be wide with well-padded lips giving a rounded appearance. The head must be broader overall than it is deep, and the muzzle should be neither too long nor too short. Ears must hang correctly, as flying ears can ruin the expression.

A head long and narrow in muzzle and foreface is faulty, as are large, thin houndy ears. This kind of head does not have a typical Lab expression. At the same time the cheeks must not be "padded" or too coarse. A short, stubby muzzle is wrong at the other extreme.

A correct and typical Lab head is one of the hallmarks of the breed. The eyes should be diamond-shaped rather than round, and they should be protected by a good brow. They should be set fairly wide apart and should be neither full nor deep set. The eyes must impart good temper, kindness, and intelligence. They can be yellow, black, or brown, the latter two being preferred. The eye color needs to be darker in a black Lab than in a yellow Lab. A black-colored eye gives a hard expression while a yellow eye is also harsh; neither of these is desirable. The hazel (however light the hazel) to brown eye color is preferred in a chocolate. In

This beautiful portrait of a yellow Lab bitch was done by the very famous artist, photographer, handler, and breeder Ben Burwell, now living in California. Photo courtesy of Margaret D. Heaney, Ma-Pat-Ma Labradors.

Ch. Banchory Danilo, by Dual Ch. Banchory Bolo ex Modern Scarcity, was born in 1923 and was a winner in England during the mid-1920s. Owned by Lady Howe.

Ch. Witton Ben, grandson of Dual Ch. Titus of Whitmore, became a champion in 1933 for Dr. D.H. Humphrey. Bred by Mrs. H. Blundell.

general, the eye color should blend with the coat. A droopy lower lid with red showing below the eye (haw eye) is undesirable.

The "level mouth" in the American standard means what the British standard says: "teeth sound and strong, the lower teeth just behind but touching the upper." The scissors bite is preferred. The standard does not disqualify for an undershot bite (lower jaw extends past the upper jaw) or overshot bite (upper jaw extends over lower jaw), as do the standards for Chesapeakes and Goldens, but either of these conditions is obviously a fault. The Lab standard also does not mention a level, or pincer, bite (the teeth of both jaws meet exactly even, tip to tip). This sort of bite isn't as serious a fault as a bite which is overshot or undershot, but it is not desirable.

A "swan" neck is correct, but a "ewe" neck, which is found with straight shoulders, is wrong. The Lab's head must flex at the poll to enable him to reach down and pick up game or to balance himself properly when swimming.

The standard calls for "long and sloping" shoulders. If they are straight, the angulation of the hindquarters is also affected. The shoulder blade must be long and well laid back, while the shorter bone, the humerus, is also laid back forming a right angle. A plumb line dropped from the point of the shoulder blade at the withers should fall just behind the dog's elbow.

Often the shoulder is mistakenly thought to be correct when the scapula is well laid back but the humerus upright.

Correct shoulders can be determined by comparing the length from the occiput to the withers to the length from the top of the throat to the point of the shoulder. If the line from the occiput to the withers is shorter than the line from under the head to the point of the shoulders, the shoulder is wrong. A poor shoulder can also be recognized by a foreleg that is set too far forward.

Remember that a Lab is built for swimming; therefore, its shoulders should be slightly narrower than its hindquarters. The shoulders should not be overdeveloped and laden with fat. Too much fat, as opposed to good muscling, causes a loaded front and unbalances the dog.

The typical Labrador Retriever is thick and strong. Tied-in elbows and out at the elbows are serious faults. A good Lab has a deep brisket stemming from the round, barrel-like spring of the ribs from the backbone. In summary, the shoulders and chest must be sturdy and strong but never heavy, loaded, or wider than the quarters. The couplings must be short and the back extra strong with a wide loin muscle. Viewed from the top, the body should not be narrow behind the rib cage over the loin areas.

Ch. Sandylands Spungold going Best of Breed at the Albany Kennel Club in October 1964, Reed Hankwitz judging. This is the dam of Janet Churchill's great bitch Int. Ch. Spenrock Banner, W.C. Photo courtesy of Mrs. Churchill.

The hindquarters are broad, strong, and muscular, with well-turned stifles and well let down to the hocks. The second thigh must be well developed with good hams. The topline is level and the hindquarters do not slope down to the tail. Viewed from the rear, the quarters are wide and rounded, while the hams are thick with muscle, whether viewed from side or rear. Viewed from the side, the hindquarters must not look skimpier than the forequarters. Straight stifles diminish the strength of a working dog. Incorrect hindquarters are a major fault as this is the part of the body that gives the Labrador his thrusting power. Dippy backs or long or weak couplings are also faults.

The legs should be medium long, giving the dog a well-balanced appearance. The Lab needs good bone. Viewed from the front, the legs should be straight with strong carpal joints. The dog must not stand pigeon-toed, and the front feet should not turn out.

The pasterns should be strong; and instead of tapering into a thin wrist, they should carry the bone straight to the feet. The compact, round feet should be cat-like, with well-arched toes and thick pads. Flat, open, splayed feet are a fault.

Toenails must be trimmed to correct length to maintain good, tight feet.

A double-jointed hock is a very serious structural defect. Such a hock bends forward forming a nearly straight line from the stifle joint through the lower thigh and hock to the base of the hock.

Dewclaw removal for neatness and prevention of accidental tearing is advisable when pups are three days old. While removing dewclaws from forelegs is optional, they should, if present, always be removed from hindlegs.

The tail is the most distinctive feature of the Labrador Retriever. The base of the tail is very thick and tapers toward the tip, it is thickly and entirely covered with the Lab's coat and has a rounded appearance ("otter" tail). As for length, the tail should not fall below the point of the hocks, and it should be carried horizontally, completing the balance of the dog by giving a flowing line from the top of the head to the tip of the tail.

Both the American and the English standards require the coat to be "short, very dense and without wave, and should give a fairly hard feeling to the hand." The English standard adds the requirement for a "weather resisting undercoat." This must have been overlooked when the American standard was written. Correct coat in a Lab is one of the components of correct type.

Ch. Spenrock Brown Bess in April 1976, owner-handled by Janet Churchill, Spenrock Kennels. By Ch. Spenrock Heatheredge (England) ex Ch. Wayward of Old Forge (England). Breeder, Madge Dempster.

Eng., Am. Ch. Lawnwood's Hot Chocolate, photographed in England prior to his importation by Mrs. Janet Churchill. "Choc" is the first Lab of this color to have completed championship in England.

The undercoat is soft and fluffy and waterproofs the dog. The undercoat is not visible at a glance, but it can be seen when the top coat is turned back. Even when a Lab is out-of-coat, when he has shed out his undercoat, some of the undercoat is usually detected along the sides of the rib cage. A good undercoat not only waterproofs the dog but it also fills in all the angles and hollows, thus giving the dog a nice rounded appearance which is typical of a true Lab.

A paper-thin, glossy coat is not correct. This is also referred to as a single coat and is not to be confused with an out-of-coat Lab. A Lab will shed his undercoat once or twice a year and it will come out in hunks. A female can be expected to shed after a heat period or a litter. However, the undercoat will come in quickly once it starts to grow back. Any Lab shown out-of-coat is at a disadvantage.

Labradors come in a variety of colors because of the shadings allowed under yellow and chocolate. They are nonetheless considered to be solid colors. A black with brindle marks is incorrect.

Of the three colors, the yellows cover the widest range, going from cream to fox-red. The cream color can be almost white, but the dog must have good pigmentation. Yellows change in appearance as they shed undercoats, and hairs of different shades will be noticed.

Chocolates present the greatest challenge to a breeder. The dark semi-sweet chocolate color is the most desirable. Those who plan to show their chocolates must keep them out of direct sunlight. A sunburned chocolate coat takes on a reddish cast which is unattractive.

Before the recent importation from England of good chocolate Labs or Labs carrying chocolate genes, chocolates found in American kennels lacked consistency in type, substance, and the true Labrador look. Good chocolates now have eyes colored dark golden, rather than baleful topaz.

The registration of Labs in the early days of the breed in England explains the background for genetic mismarks, which are not permitted by today's standard. The English Kennel Club recognized Retrievers under one heading or breed and classified them as "Varieties." Early on one found "Inter-breds" and "Cross-breds" along with Goldens, Labs, Flat-Coateds and Curly-Coateds. Prior to the formation of the English Lab Club in 1916, puppies were registered under the breed of the parent that the puppy most closely resembled. Thus in one litter some may have been registered as Labs and others as Flat-Coated. After 1916 inter-breds were classed separately; and finally, after World War II, they ceased to be of importance.

Ch. Franklin's Ruffian, the last champion out of Ch. Franklin's Tally of Burywood, finishing by going Best of Winners at Chicago International with Dick Cooper handling. Mrs. Bernard W. Ziessow, owner.

Knowing this background of the Labrador, conscientious breeders must avoid characteristics of other breeds which are not typical in Labs, such as Flat-Coated heads. A head with the forehead sloping to the nose in a straight line with a slight or no indentation (stop) between the two is reverting to the Flat-Coated, and this is often found in conjunction with lack of width of head and body in a mature Labrador.

The movement of a Lab is "free and effortless." As a good Lab moves toward you, elbows should not appear to be out. Rather, they should be "neatly held to the body with legs not too close together, and moving straight forward without pacing or weaving." Viewed from the side, the shoulders must move freely and the foreleg must have proper reach and extension. When the length of the stride is not sufficient, the dog takes short, pounding steps; and this sort of choppy movement is incorrect. The hindlegs must be well engaged under the body to provide thrust and drive. Viewed from the rear, the hindlegs should "move as nearly parallel as possible," and the hocks should be well flexed.

A good show dog stands with presence, gaits with power, and transmits his zeal to please. With head, tail, and eyes alert, the animal enjoys showing off and will set himself up properly. A Lab that is properly "stacked," or "set up," must not be stretched out like a Setter. Also his tail should not be held up by the handler. For American shows the whiskers may be trimmed. The tip of the tail may be rounded off. But the hair along the hindquarters should not be cut back to the body like a Terrier. The latter sort of incorrect trimming will give the illusion of a smaller hindquarter than the dog should have.

The standard lists approximate weights of dogs and bitches in working condition, which means well-muscled without excess fat. A Lab does not have to be lean or skinny to work all day. Muscle tone is important for a show dog or a working dog. Flabby fat is unhealthy and has no place in the breed.

Shadowvale's Frosty Knight, by English Show Champion Balrion King Frost ex English Show Champion Bradking Black Charm, is owned by the Shadowvale Labradors in Quebec.

Am., Can. Ch. Powhatan Black Badger, C.D.X., by Eng. Ch. Sandylands Mark ex Powhatan Corn (daughter of Eng. Ch. Braeduke Joyful) finished American Championship with five majors and is the sire of bench and obedience champions. Owned by Michael and Lynn Woods.

Labradors in the show ring should be penalized for the following faults: snipiness of head, overshot or undershot jaws, large or heavy ears, too light or yellow an eye, narrowness between the eyes, lack of stop, straight shoulders, a bad dip in topline, too long and/or narrow in the loins, straight stifles, narrow hindquarters, throaty neck, fat-loaded shoulders, chest not well let down, too much tuck up at the loin, slab sides, legs too long or too short, tail set too low, lack of bone, weak pasterns, splay or hare-shaped feet, long thin tail, too much feathering on tail, curled tail carriage, cowhocks, stickle hocks, no undercoat.

The Labrador in the show ring should be a standout for type and outline. Coat and tail are two of the most distinctive and important char-acteristics of the breed, and they are inter-related. The shape of the head and body are next in importance. It is paramount in our modern day assessment of the Lab that the dog must look like a Lab and not remind one of another breed.

Winning Labs must be typical of the breed, must look like true Labs and must be structural-ly correct. Excellent breeders of Labs produce top quality Labs of good type, and these are the dogs the knowledgeable judge puts up. By and large, the past decade has seen Labradors in the American show ring that are more true to type than ever before, and great numbers of quality Labs are presented at Specialty shows. Judges need not glorify mediocrity by putting up a mediocre dog which is devoid of type over one which is typical of the breed but has a fault.

Middlesex County K.C., June 1969. Judge Isidore Schoenberg awarding Best of Breed in Labs to Ch. Ballyduff Seaman, an English import handled by Robert S. Forsyth for John Martin.

Eng., Am. Ch. Kimvalley Crispin, the first home-bred English champion produced by Kimvalley Labradors, Don and Diana Beckett.

Ch. Whygin John Duck at 16 months of age. One of the many fine Labradors bred by Mrs. Helen Ginnel, Whygin Kennels.

Over 40 years ago, a columnist of the American Kennel Club *Gazette* made a trip to England to study Labradors, and when he returned he said:

> One thing about the Labradors in England at shows, they seem to be more keen and were shown on a loose lead rather than held up by the head and tail on a block the way they are in this country. I wish more Labrador judges in America could go over and see what a *real* Labrador is, for I fear we shall get away from correct type if we go on as we are now; above all, they are short-coupled with an otter tail.

Fortunately since the time the above comment was written, American judges have gone to England to study English dogs, and English Labrador judges have been invited to the United States. On the whole, Americans now have a good conception of what a true Labrador is, and more and more breeders are succeeding in their efforts to breed typical Labradors.

Ch. Heatheredge Myshell, by Eng. Ch. Shadylands Mark ex Heatheredge Seashell, owned by George and Carole Bernier, Bernfield Kennels, Halifax, Nova Scotia. Photo courtesy of Janet Churchill.

Ch. Novacroft Jayncourt Truly Fair belongs to Mrs. D.I. Gardner who has sent us this photograph by Anne Roslin-Williams, England.

Ch. Spenrock Heatheredge Mariner, by Ch. Sandylands Mark ex Seashell of Heatheredge, was bred by Miss M. Ward. Pictured at 14 months of age winning Best of Breed under English judge Viola Wise at Mason-Dixon Kennel Club, Glen Butler handling. Jan Churchill owner, Spenrock Labs.

Int. Ch. Spenrock's Banner, W.C. winning Best of Opposite Sex under English judge Dora Lee at Somerset Hills K.C.

BEST OF WINNERS

ASHBEY PHOTO

The first time in the ring, future champion Spenrock Anthony Adverse, by Ch. Lockerbie Stanwood Granada ex Int. Ch. Spenrock Banner, W.C., takes a major under Diane Beckett, here on a judging trip from England in 1973. Jenny Reynolds handles for Spenrock Kennels, Chesapeake City, Maryland.

Ch. Ardmargha Goldkrest of Syrancot, by Eng. Ch. Sandylands Garry ex Sandylands Komely of Ardmargha. Bred by Mr. and Mrs. H. Clayton of England, owned by Mrs. Robert V. Clark, Jr., and handled by Mrs. Connie Barton.

Ch. MiJan's Corrigan, sire of 11 champions, is by Anderscroft Stalayna Sioux ex Ch. Driftwood's Honeysuckle. Owned by MiJan's Labradors, Joan and Tony Heubel and Mike and Janet Farmilette.

Ch. Springfield's Brodich winning points toward the title. Owned by Mrs. Robert D. Clark, Jr., Springfield Farm, and handled by Mrs. Diana Beckett.

Opposite, above: Chow time for these Lab puppies. A fabulous presentation of the various shades of yellow Labrador, which permissibly range from to snow-white to fox-red. These pups belong to Gordon Sousa, Jr., Shababaland Kennels, Old Tappan, New Jersey. **Below:** The handsome yellow Lab, Ch. Augustin de Gregorio, has won many Group placements. Handled by Robert S. Forsyth for owner Victoria De Palma, Milford, Connecticut.

A lovely Lab puppy. Photo submitted by MiJan Labradors.

Opposite, above: "Here we come!" Nine-week-old Lab puppies from Manora Kennels, Ballston Lake, New York. **Below:** Pups at Spenrock by Tweed ex Banner. Owned by Jan Churchill, Chesapeake City, Maryland.

Left: Where could you possibly find a more adorable puppy than this one? From Riverroad Labradors, Mrs. Frank C. Thomas, Gurnee, Illinois.

Below: Baby Labs learn about water from their own play-pools at an early age. Ch. Scrimshaw Blue Nun is doing so at eight weeks. Barbara Barfield, owner.

Right: The late Mrs. E.P. Taylor enjoying a picnic at Spenrock with her Lab puppy, now Ch. Spenrock Tweed of Windfields. Windfields Farm, owned by Mr. and Mrs. Taylor, is the leading breeding place of thoroughbred race horses in the world. "Harris" was their only Labrador.

Below: Ch. Marbra Guardsman sired this adorable eight-week-old Lab puppy belonging to MiJan's Kennels.

Ch. Spenrock's Bohemia Champagne, left, owned by Chucklebrook Labradors, with two daughters by Ch. Lockerbie Brian Boru, W.C. In the center is Ch. Chucklebrook Black Irish and on the right is Ch. Chucklebrook Champagne Mist. Chucklebrook Labs belong to Mr. and Mrs. Leslie G. Pilbin and are at Burlington, Connecticut.

Best of Breed and Best of Opposite Sex at Old Dominion Kennel Club in 1980. Ch. Marda's Brandlesholme Sam's Song, left, with Diana Beckett; and his daughter, Ch. Springfield's Dinorah, right. Both are owned by the Springfield Kennels of Mrs. Robert D. Clark, Jr., at Middleburg, Virginia.

Right: Ch. Jollymuff Orange Blossom, fourth generation of Jollymuff Labradors owned by Diane B. Jones, Mt. Holly, New Jersey.

Below: Ch. Elden's Elyod The Bear Facts, "Bear Bear," America's Number One Lab for 1981, with his daughter Elden's Stop 'n' Smell The Roses. Both owned by Elden Williams, Portland, Oregon.

Left to right are Ch. The Black Baroness (Moorwood's foundation bitch) and two of her "puppies" by Ch. Somerset Cider of Kimvalley. They are Beaver's Blac Mac of Moorwood and Ch. Beaver's Hillary of Moorwood, W.C. All belong to Moorwood Labs, Rosalind B. Moore, Indian Lake, New York.

Opposite, above: Ch. Scrimshaw Blue Nun at five weeks in the phlox bed. Bred and owned by Barbara Barfield, Scrimshaw Labs. **Below:** Family secrets, or so it seems, being shared by Threepear's Nightshade, C.D., with her daughter Manora's Robin, C.D. (yellow). Two fine representatives of Manora Labs, Ballston Lake, New York.

Right: Ch. Springfield's Fanny Sweet Adams with her hungry brood. Owned by Springfield Kennels, the Costigans, Calgary, Alberta, Canada.

Opposite: A lovely picture of Madge (Mrs. Bernard W.) Ziessow, of Franklin, Michigan, at the Labrador Retriever Club 1981 Specialty show winning the Brace Class with her veterans, Ch. Franklin's Hickory Grove, eleven years old, and Ch. Franklin's Bushwick Rally, nine years old. These are Tally Light Brigade daughters and are now the Ziessows' house dogs.

Below: A breeder's most treasured picture! Ch. Briary Bustle and Ch. Briary Brendan of Rainell Brood Bitch Class and Stud Dog Class (13 and 10 respectively in competition) at the 1981 Labrador Retriever Club of the Potomac Specialty with four different get. Mrs. Janet Bontecue and Mrs. Dede Hepworth (of Poolstead) were the respective judges of dogs and bitches. The Labs are, left to right, Am. Ch. Finchingfield Faith, Bermuda Ch. Finchingfield Indigo, Bustle, Brendan, Can. Ch. Finchingfield Ivan of Oaklea, and Am. Ch. Finchingfield Fantasia. Richard and Marilyn Reynolds, owners, Finchingfield Labradors, Herndon, Virginia.

Three generations of champions owned by Mr. and Mrs. Leslie Pilbin, Chucklebrook Kennels, Burlington, Connecticut. Ch. Spenrock's Bohemia Champagne (yellow), aged twelve years; Ch. Chucklebrook Helen (black), nine years; and Ch. Chucklebrook Fannie Farmer (chocolate), two years.

Campbellcroft's Morag prefers drinking straight from the faucet. Campbellcroft Labradors are owned by Donald and Virginia Campbell, Soquel, California.

A lovely head study of the great Ch. Lockerbie Brian Boru, son of Ch. Lockerbie Kismet ex Lockerbie Tackety Boots (Ch. Lockerbie Sandylands Tarquin ex Ch. Lockerbie Pebblestreet Dinah). This splendid dog was bred by James and Helen Warwick and, with Ch. Lockerbie Shillelagh, was the basis of the Briary line of Marjorie and Ceylone Brainard. By 1982 he had sired 59 champions and is to be found in the background of some of our leading present-day kennels and winners.

CHAPTER SEVEN

Breeding Labrador Retrievers

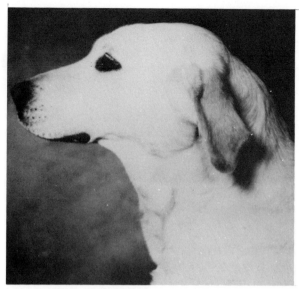

Ch. Franklin Tally of Burywood, the dam of 16 champions, from Franklin Labradors, Mrs. Bernard W. Ziessow, Michigan.

The Stud Dog

Choosing the right stud dog to best complement your bitch is not an easy task. The principal factors to be considered are the stud's quality and conformation and his pedigree. The pedigree lists the various bloodlines involved with the ancestry of the dog. If you are a novice in the breed, I would suggest that you seek advice from some of the more experienced breeders who are old-timers in the Fancy and thus would be able to discuss and tell you about some of the various dogs behind the one to which you are planning to breed your bitch. Many times such people accurately remember the dogs you need to know about, perhaps even having access to photos of them. And do be sure to carefully study the photos in this book as they show representatives of important bloodlines.

It is extremely important that the stud's pedigree be harmonious with that of your bitch. Do not rush to breed to a current winner with no regard for whether or not he can produce well. Take time to check out the stock being sired by the dog, or dogs, you have under consideration. A dog that has sired nothing of quality for other people probably will do no better for you, unless, of course, it is a young stud just starting out; such a stud may not have had the opportunity to produce much of anything thus far. Do you want to waste your bitch's time on an unknown quantity? Wouldn't you prefer to use a dog with a proven, good producing record?

Breeding dogs is not a moneymaking proposition. By the time you pay a stud fee, take care of the bitch during gestation, whelp the litter, and raise and care for the puppies (including shots and food, among other things) until they reach selling age, you will be fortunate if you break even on the cost of the litter. Therefore, it is foolish to skimp on the stud fee. Try to breed to the dog that seems most suited to your bitch and that has the best producing record, regardless of the cost. Remember: raising mediocre puppies is just as expensive as raising good ones, and you will fare better financially if you have some show prospects to sell than if you come up with nothing but pets, which you will probably wind up selling for far less than you had anticipated or you'll end up giving away. Remember, the only excuse for breeding and bringing puppies into the world is an honest effort to improve the breed. So in choosing the stud you use, keep in mind that breeding to the most suitable one which has an impressive producing record is the best investment.

You will have to decide on one of three choices in planning the breeding: inbreeding, line-breeding, or outcrossing. Inbreeding is normally considered to be father to daughter, mother to son, or brother to sister. Line-breeding is combining two dogs belonging originally to the same strain or family of Labradors, descended from the same ancestors, such as half-brother to half-

Croysdales Blue Creek Julie with her grand-sire, Ch. Killingworth's Ben. Both owned by Mrs. Nancy W. Story, Croysdales Labs, Connecticut.

especially until one has acquired considerable experience with the breed and the various blood-lines of which it consists.

Inbreeding should be left for the experienced, very sophisticated breeder who knows the line extremely well and thus is in a position to evaluate the probable results. Outcrossing is nor-mally done when you are trying to bring in a specific feature or trait, such as a shorter back, better head type, more correct bone or action, or better personality or temperament.

Ch. Carefree of Keithray at eight years old. Born in 1976, bred by Mrs. Mary Wilkinson, England, this is a son of Ch. Sandylands Tandy (Australian Ch. Sandylands Tan ex Sandylands Shadow) from Ch. Hollybeaut of Keithray (Ch. Sandylands Tweed of Blaircourt ex Ch. Hollybanks Beauty). Co-owned by Mrs. Robert V. Clark Jr. and Mrs. Eileen Ket-cham.

sister, niece to uncle, granddaughter to grand-sire, and so on. Outcross breeding is using a dog and a bitch of completely different bloodlines with no, or only a few, mutual ancestors, and these far back, if at all.

Each of these methods has advantages and disadvantages; each has supporters and detrac-tors. I would say that line-breeding is probably the safest, the most generally approved, and the most frequently used with the desired results. Thus, I would say, it is perfect for the novice breeder because it is the easiest to figure out,

Can. Ch. Eireannach Irish Grouse, by Timspring Lucky Star ex Powhatan Sable, and Powhatan Sable, by Powhatan Chief ex Powhatan Corn. These two were the foundation of Nancy and Walter Rutter's Eireannach Kennels, now in Ireland.

Everyone sincerely interested in breeding dogs wants to develop a line of their own, but this is not accomplished overnight. It takes at least several generations before you can claim to have done so, during which the close study of blood-lines and the observation of individual dogs are essential. Getting to know and truthfully evaluate the dogs with which you are working will go a long way in helping you to preserve the best in what you have while at the same time to remove weaknesses.

As a novice breeder, your safest bet is to start by acquiring one or two bitches of the finest quality and background you can buy. In the beginning, it is really foolish to own your own stud dog; you will make out better and have a wider range of dogs with which to work if you pay a stud fee to one of the outstanding producing Labs available to service your bitch. In order to be attractive to breeders, a stud dog must be well-known, must have had at least one champion (and usually one that has attracted considerable attention in Specials competition), and must have winning progeny in the ring; this represents a large expenditure of time and money before the dog begins to bring in returns on your investment. So start out by paying a stud fee a few times to use such a dog, or dogs, keeping the best bitch out of each of your first few litters and breeding those once or twice before you consider owning a stud of your own. By that time, you will have gained the experience to recognize exactly what sort of dog you need for this purpose.

A future stud dog should be selected with the utmost care and consideration. He must be of very high standard as he may be responsible for siring many puppies each year, and he should not be used unless he clearly has something to

Two Labs of tremendous importance in quality and contribution to the breed. Left, Ch. Lockerbie Goldentone Jensen, English import owned by Bill Metz and handled by Bob Fisher taking Best of Breed, with Int. Ch. Spenrock Banner, W.C., winning her 97th Best of Opposite Sex, owner-handled by Janet Churchill, at the Eastern Dog Club in 1971. The judge is James Cowie who was so instrumental in the progress of the Lab in its earlier days and who handled Ch. Earlsmoor Moor of Arden throughout his spectacular show career.

contribute to the breed. Ideally, he should come from a line of excellent dogs on both sides of his pedigree, the latter containing good dogs *and good producing dogs* all the way through. The dog himself should be of sufficient quality to hold his own in competition in his breed. He should be robust and virile, a keen stud dog who has proved that he is able to transmit his best qualities to his puppies. Do not use an unsound dog or a dog with a major or outstanding fault. Not all champions seem able to pass on their individual splendid quality and, by the same token, occasionally one finds a dog who never finished but who does sire puppies better than himself *provided that his pedigree is star-studded with top producing dogs and bitches*. Remember, too that the stud dog cannot do it alone; the bitch must have what it takes too, although I must admit that some stud dogs, the truly *dominant* ones, can consistently produce type and quality *regardless* of the bitch

or her background. But great studs like this are few and far between.

If you are the proud owner of a promising young stud dog, one that you have either bred from one of your own litters or have purchased after great thought and deliberation, do not permit him to be used for the first time until he is about a year old. His first breeding should be to a bitch that is a proven matron, experienced at being mated and not likely to give him a bad time. His first encounter should be pleasant and easy, as he could be put off breeding forever by a maiden bitch that fights and resents his advances. His first breeding should help him develop confidence and assurance. It should be done in quiet surroundings, with only you and one other person (to hold the bitch) present. Do not make a circus of it, as this first time will determine his attitude and feeling about breeding from then on.

Ch. Briary Barley winning the Stud Dog Class at the Labrador National Specialty in October 1980 with his progeny, Ch. Hart Lake Moon Magic and Ch. Sinco's Marnee Bee (right and center). Hart Lake Labrador Retriever, Bob and Kaye Peltonen, Illinois.

Left to right: Ch. Spenrock's Cognac, owned by Jerry and Lisa Weiss; Ch. Spenrock's Bohemia Champagne, owned by Diane Pilbin; and Ch. Spenrock's Cardigan Bay, owned by Janet Churchill. All by Ch. Lockerbie Goldentone Jensen ex Ch. Spenrock's Banner, and all pictured at 11 years old.

Your young stud dog must allow you to help with the breeding, as later there will be bitches that will not be cooperative and he needs to develop the habit of accepting assistance. If, right from the beginning, you are there helping and praising him, he will expect and accept this help. Before you introduce the dogs, be sure to have everything which you may need. K-Y Jelly is the only lubricant that should be used, and you should have handy either a stocking or a length of gauze with which to muzzle the bitch should it seem necessary.

The stud fee is due to be paid at the time of breeding. Normally a return service is offered should the bitch fail to produce. Usually one live puppy is considered to be a litter. In order to avoid any misunderstanding regarding the terms of the breeding, it is wise to have a breeding certificate printed up which both you and the owner of the bitch should sign. It should spell out quite specifically all the conditions of the breeding, as well as the dates of the matings.

Sometimes a pick of the litter puppy is taken instead of a stud fee, and this should be noted on the breeding certificate along with such terms as at what age the owner of the sire will select his pup and whether it is to be a dog puppy, a bitch puppy, or just "pick puppy." All of this should be clearly stated to avoid any unpleasant misunderstandings later on.

In almost every case, the bitch must come to the stud dog for breeding. Once the owner of the bitch decides to what stud dog she will preferably be bred, it is important that the owner of the stud be contacted immediately to discuss stud fee, terms, approximate time the bitch is due in season, and whether she will be shipped or brought to the stud owner. Then, as soon as the bitch comes into season, another phone call must follow to finalize the arrangements. I have personally experienced times when the bitch's owner has waited until the last moment to contact the stud's owner, only to meet with disappointment owing to the dog's absence.

Ch. Killingworth's Thunderson with some of his puppies. An unusual photo for a stud dog, most of whom do *NOT* love puppies! Lorraine Robbenhaar, owner, Killingworth Labs, Connecticut.

It is essential that the stud owner have proper facilities to house the bitch while she is there. Nothing can be more heartbreaking than to have a bitch misbred or, still worse, get away and become lost. Unless you can provide safe and proper care for visiting bitches, do *not* offer your dog at public stud.

Owning a stud dog is no easy road to riches, as some who have not experienced it seem to think; making the dog desirably well-known is expensive and time-consuming. Be selective in the bitches which you permit your dog to service. It takes two to make the puppies, and while some stud dogs *do* seem almost to achieve miracles, it is a general rule that an inferior bitch from a nothing sort of background will probably never produce well no matter *how* dominant and splendid the dog to whom she is bred. Remember that those puppies will be advertised and perhaps shown as sired by your dog, and you do not want any puppies around that will be an embarrassment to him—or to you.

A stud fee is generally figured on the price of one show-type puppy and on the sire's record as a producer of champions. Obviously, a stud throwing champions in every litter is worth a greater price than a dog that seldom has sired puppies of this caliber. Thus a young stud, just starting out, is less expensive before proven than a dog with, say, forty or fifty champions in the ring and show stock in every litter an accomplished fact.

I do not feel that we need to go into the actual breeding here, as the experienced breeder already knows and the novice should not attempt to try it for the first time by reading directions in

a book. Plan to have a breeder or handler friend help you until you are accustomed to handling such matters with ease or, if this is not possible, it is very likely that your veterinarian can arrange either to himself help or to get someone on his staff to assist you.

If a complete "tie" is made, that breeding is all that is actually necessary. However, with a maiden bitch, a bitch that has missed in the past, or one that has come a long distance, most people like to give a second breeding, allowing one day to elapse in between the two.

Once the "tie" has been completed, be sure that the penis goes back completely into its sheath. The dog should be allowed a drink of water and a short walk, and then he should be put in his crate or kennel or somewhere alone to settle down. Do not allow him to be with other males for a while, as he will have the odor of the bitch about him and this could result in a fight.

The bitch should not be allowed to relieve herself for at least an hour. In fact, many people feel that she should be "upended" for several minutes after the mating to allow the sperm to travel deeper. In any case, she should be crated and kept quiet.

There are no standard rules governing the conditions of a stud service. They are whatever the owner of the stud dog chooses to make them. The stud fee is paid for the act, not for the litter; and if a bitch fails to conceive, this does not automatically call for a return service unless the owner of the stud sees it that way. A return service is a courtesy, not something that can be regarded as a right. But dog owners, especially those with a stud in which they take pride, are always anxious that their clients get good value for their money. Plus the more winners sired by their stud dogs, the better. Therefore, very few would refuse a return service if the bitch "misses," provided, of course, that the stud dog is still under the same ownership as when the breeding originally took place.

When a bitch has been given one return service and misses again, that ends the stud dog owner's responsibility even among the most lenient stud owners, and it is unreasonable and unrealistic for the owner of a bitch to expect more than one return service. This is particularly true when other bitches are producing normally by him, in which case it is very obvious that the problem is hers, not his, and the stud's owner should feel no further obligation.

The Brood Bitch

One of the most important purchases you will make in dogs is the selection of the foundation brood bitch, or bitches, on which you plan to build your breeding program. You want marvelous bloodlines representing top producing strains; you want sound bitches of basic quality and free of any hereditary problems.

Your bitch should not be bred until her second heat, but if she starts her seasons extra early, coming in at or very little over six months of age and then again right around one year of age, you would be wise to wait until her third heat. This waiting period can be profitably spent carefully watching for the perfect stud to complement her and her background. With this in mind, attend dog shows and watch the males who are winning and, even more important, *siring* the winners. Subscribe to any dog magazines which include Labradors and study the pictures and stories accompanying them to familiarize yourself with dogs in other areas which you may previously have known nothing about. Be sure to watch for a stud dog strong in your bitch's weaknesses, carefully noting his progeny to see if he succeeds in passing along the features you admire. And watch for his offspring from bitches with backgrounds similar to your bitch's; then you can get an idea of how the background fits with his. When you see a stud that interests you, talk with the owner about your bitch and request a copy of his dog's pedigree for your study and perusal.

When a tentative decision has been reached, contact the owner of the stud and make the arrangements regarding stud fee (whether it is to be in cash or a puppy), approximate time she should be ready, and so on. Find out, too, the requirements such as health certificates and tests the stud owner has regarding bitches accepted for breeding. Also find out to which airport you will ship her if you are sending the bitch rather than taking her and which airlines come into that airport.

The airlines have certain requirements such as crate size and type they will accept. Most airlines have their own crates available for sale at a nominal cost, which may be purchased if you do not have a suitable one. These are made of fiberglass and are the safest type for shipping. Most airlines also require that the dog be at the airport two hours before the flight is scheduled to depart.

Highland's Egyptian Queen, by Ch. Groveton's Copper Buck Shot ex Sambeau's Cam, handled by George W. Knobloch, Jr., with her sons: Highland's Bronze Chieftain, 17 months of age, handled by Lillian Knobloch, and Highland's Bronze Starbuck, 17 months. Frank E. Jones, judge. Both young dogs bred and owned by the Knoblochs' Highland Kennels and sired by Groveton's Ko Ko Khalif.

Normally the airline must be notified several days in advance for the bitch's reservation, as they can accommodate only a limited number on each flight. Plan on shipping the bitch on her eighth or ninth day, but be careful to figure on not doing so on a weekend, as some flights do not run then and some freight offices are closed on Saturday and Sunday. Whenever it possibly can be arranged, ship dogs on a direct flight to their destination and thus avoid the danger of one being left behind or transferred with other cargo.

It is simpler if you can plan on bringing your bitch to the stud dog. Some people fear that the trauma of the plane trip may cause the bitch not to conceive. Be sure to allow sufficient time for

Chilbrook Kennels, Virginia, own this beautiful Lab bitch, Ch. Briary Bonnie Brianna. She was Best of Opposite Sex at Westminster and Top Bitch in 1976, and she is the dam of three champions including Ch. Briary Bustle. Photo by Debby Kobilis.

breeding her at the correct time, usually anywhere from the tenth through the fourteenth day, and if you want the bitch bred twice, you must allow a day in between the two services. Do not expect the stud owner to put you up during your stay in his area. Find a good, nearby hotel or motel that welcomes dogs, and make a reservation for yourself there.

Just prior to your bitch's season, you should make a visit to your veterinarian with her. Have her checked for worms, see that she is up to date on all her shots, and take care of any other tests the stud owner has requested. The bitch may act and be perfectly normal up until her second or third week of pregnancy, but it is better to have any tests or shots attended to ahead of time. If she is a little overweight, right now is when you should start getting the fat off her; she should be in good hard condition, neither fat nor thin.

The day you've been waiting for finally arrives, and you notice the swelling of her vulva, followed within a day or two by the appearance of color. Immediately call the stud owner to finalize arrangements, advising whether you will ship or bring her, the exact day she will arrive, and so on. Then, if she goes by plane, as soon as you know the details, advise the stud owner of the flight number, the time of departure, and the time of arrival. If you are shipping the bitch, the check for the stud fee should be mailed *now*. If the owner of the stud dog charges for his trips to the airport, for picking the bitch up and then returning her, reimbursement for this should either be included with the stud fee or sent as soon as you know the amount of the charge.

If you are going to ship your bitch, do not feed her on the day of the flight. But be sure that she has had a drink of water and been well exercised prior to being put in her crate. Place several layers of newspapers, topped with some shredded papers, on the bottom of the crate for a good bed. The papers can be discarded at the end of her trip and then replaced with fresh ones for her return journey. Rugs and towels are not suitable for bedding material as they may become soiled, necessitating laundering when she reaches her destination. Remember to have her at the airport two hours ahead of her flight time.

If you are driving, be sure that you will arrive at a reasonable time of day. If you are coming from a distance and get in late, have a good night's sleep and contact the stud's owner in the morning. If possible, leave the children and relatives home; they will not only be in the way, but also most stud owners definitely object to too many people around during the actual breeding.

Once the breeding has been completed, if you wish to sit for a while and chat, take the bitch out to the car and put her in her crate. Remember that she should not urinate for at least an hour following the breeding. If you have not already done so, pay the stud fee now, and get your copy of the stud certificate and the stud dog's pedigree.

Now all you need to do is to wait in happy anticipation for the puppies to arrive.

Mrs. Helen Ginnel with two of her favorites, Ch. Whygin John Duck, black, and Ch. Whygin Gold Bullion, yellow.

Our readers can only benefit by the words of a breeder so consistently successful as Helen Ginnel:

Looking back over 35 years of breeding Labradors, I am glad I had the opportunity to raise, show, and run dogs during those years.

Today a new exhibitor is going to be confronted with a definite choice: to breed for the show or for the field. During the late 1950s, there appeared a number of English kennels producing a short, stocky, smallish dog that became immensely popular in a country where very few people had the opportunity or interest in shooting. The emphasis was on accenting some of the typical breed characteristics. Short backs were emphasized by breeding dogs with short necks and steep shoulders. Broad heads looked broader by shortening muzzles in length and depth. The heavy otter-tail, a trademark, was emphasized—attractive tail-set ignored. Rear angulation was sought, but front angulation became Terrier-like to create the appearance of short coupling. Over-reaching in the rear thus became a norm.

Today the American show ring is becoming devoted to the new English type of *non*-sporting Lab. It is sad to think that the country that has developed the finest shooting dog the world has ever known, a true athlete where the best specimens could (and did) attain the coveted title of Dual Championship, should see this happen. I am glad that I was on the scene when I could enjoy breeding field trial champions and bench champions from the same animals.

I am proud that every puppy I have ever produced carries the blood of Cedarhill Whygin and Whygin Poppitt. There were good ones, bad ones, and great ones. Reading the list of 42 Top Derby Field Trial Dogs in 1981, 24%, I found, were descended from Poppitt and Dinah.

May I make one last plea for show judges to interpret the standard with an eye to choosing the dog that has the best conformation to do the job in the duck blind and in the shooting field? To pick up a large goose or pheasant. To be able to leap across boggy terrain or shallow water-flats with enough speed to catch that cripple.

Speed, style, brains, and an overcoming desire to please are what make the American Labrador one of the greatest breeds on earth.

Ch. Whygin Copper Coin in 1960. Mrs. Helen Ginnel, owner, Whygin Labradors, New York.

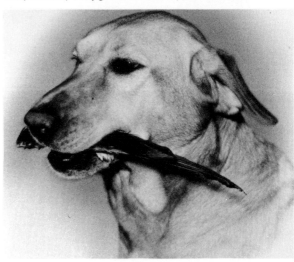

Pedigrees

To anyone interested in the breeding of dogs, pedigrees are the basic tool with which this is successfully accomplished. It is not sufficient to just breed two nice-looking dogs to one another and then sit back and await outstanding results. Chances are they will be disappointing, as there is no equal to a scientific approach in the breeding of dogs, if quality results are the ultimate goal.

We have selected for you pedigrees of Labrador Retriever dogs and bitches that either are great producers or have come from consistently outstanding producing lines. Some of these dogs are so dominant that they have seemed to "click" with almost every strain or bloodline. Others, for best results, need to be carefully line-bred. The study of pedigrees and breeding is both a challenge and an exciting occupation.

Even if you have no plans to involve yourself in breeding and just plan to own and love a dog or two, it is fun to trace back the pedigree of your dog, or dogs, to earlier generations and thus learn the sort of dogs behind your own. Throughout this book you will find a great many pictures of dogs and bitches whose names you will find in these pedigrees, enabling you not only to trace the names in the background of your Lab, but also to see what the ancestors look like.

Ch. Briary Bustle at 17 months of age. A granddaughter of Ch. Lockerbie Shillelagh, Bustle is from the Finchingfield Kennels of Richard and Marilyn Reynolds, Virginia. On the facing page is a certificate of pedigree for a litter produced by Jayncourt Ajoco Justice and Ch. Briary Bustle. See following pages for additional representative pedigrees.

Certificate of Pedigree

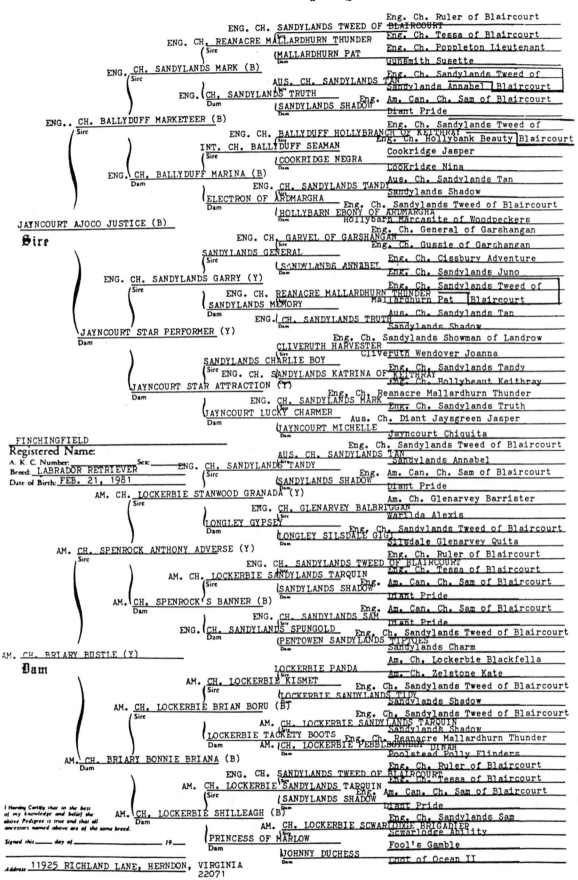

ENG. CH. SANDYLANDS TWEED OF BLAIRCOURT — Eng. Ch. Ruler of Blaircourt
Eng. Ch. Tessa of Blaircourt

ENG. CH. REANACRE MALLARDHURN THUNDER
MALLARDHURN PAT — Eng. Ch. Poppleton Lieutenant
Gunsmith Susette

ENG. CH. SANDYLANDS MARK (B)

AUS. CH. SANDYLANDS TAN — Eng. Ch. Sandylands Tweed of Blaircourt
Sandylands Annabel

ENG. CH. SANDYLANDS TRUTH
SANDYLANDS SHADOW — Eng. Am. Can. Ch. Sam of Blaircourt
Diant Pride

ENG. CH. BALLYDUFF MARKETEER (B)

ENG. CH. BALLYDUFF HOLLYBRANCH OF KEITHRAY — Eng. Ch. Sandylands Tweed of Blaircourt
Eng. Ch. Hollybank Beauty

INT. CH. BALLYDUFF SEAMAN
COOKRIDGE NEGRA — Cookridge Jasper
Cookridge Nina

ENG. CH. BALLYDUFF MARINA (B)

ENG. CH. SANDYLANDS TANDY — Aus. Ch. Sandylands Tan
Sandylands Shadow

ELECTRON OF ARDMARGHA
HOLLYBARN EBONY OF ARDMARGHA — Eng. Ch. Sandylands Tweed of Blaircourt
Hollybarn Marcasite of Woodpeckers

JAYNCOURT AJOCO JUSTICE (B)
Sire

ENG. CH. GARVEL OF GARSHANGAN — Eng. Ch. General of Garshangan
Eng. Ch. Gussie of Garshangan

SANDYLANDS GENERAL
SANDYLANDS ANNABEL — Eng. Ch. Cissbury Adventure
Eng. Ch. Sandylands Juno

ENG. CH. SANDYLANDS GARRY (Y)

ENG. CH. REANACRE MALLARDHURN THUNDER — Eng. Ch. Sandylands Tweed of Blaircourt
Mallardhurn Pat

SANDYLANDS MEMORY
ENG. CH. SANDYLANDS TRUTH — Aus. Ch. Sandylands Tan
Sandylands Shadow

JAYNCOURT STAR PERFORMER (Y)

CLIVERUTH HARVESTER — Eng. Ch. Sandylands Showman of Landrow
Cliveruth Wendover Joanna

SANDYLANDS CHARLIE BOY
ENG. CH. SANDYLANDS KATRINA OF KEITHRAY — Eng. Ch. Sandylands Tandy
Eng. Ch. Hollybeaut Keithray

JAYNCOURT STAR ATTRACTION (Y)

ENG. CH. SANDYLANDS MARK — Eng. Ch. Reanacre Mallardhurn Thunder
Eng. Ch. Sandylands Truth

JAYNCOURT LUCKY CHARMER
JAYNCOURT MICHELLE — Aus. Ch. Diant Jaysgreen Jasper
Jayncourt Chiquita

FINCHINGFIELD
Registered Name:
A. K. C. Number: _____ Sex: _____
Breed: LABRADOR RETRIEVER
Date of Birth: FEB. 21, 1981

ENG. CH. SANDYLANDS TANDY — Aus. Ch. Sandylands Tan
Sandylands Annabel

AM. CH. LOCKERBIE STANWOOD GRANADA (Y)
SANDYLANDS SHADOW — Eng. Am. Can. Ch. Sam of Blaircourt
Diant Pride

LONGLEY GYPSEY — Eng. Ch. Glenarvey Balbriggan
Warilda Alexis

AM. CH. SPENROCK ANTHONY ADVERSE (Y)
LONGLEY SILSDALE GIG — Eng. Ch. Sandylands Tweed of Blaircourt
Silsdale Glenarvey Quita

ENG. CH. SANDYLANDS TWEED OF BLAIRCOURT — Eng. Ch. Ruler of Blaircourt
Eng. Ch. Tessa of Blaircourt

AM. CH. LOCKERBIE SANDYLANDS TARQUIN
SANDYLANDS SHADOW — Am. Can. Ch. Sam of Blaircourt
Diant Pride

AM. CH. SPENROCK'S BANNER (B)

ENG. CH. SANDYLANDS SAM — Am. Can. Ch. Sam of Blaircourt
Diant Pride

ENG. CH. SANDYLANDS SPUNGOLD
PENTOWEN SANDYLANDS TIPTOES — Eng. Ch. Sandylands Tweed of Blaircourt
Sandylands Charm

AM. CH. BRIARY BUSTLE (Y)
Dam

LOCKERBIE PANDA — Am. Ch. Lockerbie Blackfella
Am. Ch. Zelstone Kate

AM. CH. LOCKERBIE KISMET
LOCKERBIE SANDYLANDS TIDY — Eng. Ch. Sandylands Tweed of Blaircourt
Sandylands Shadow

AM. CH. LOCKERBIE BRIAN BORU (B)

AM. CH. LOCKERBIE SANDYLANDS TARQUIN — Eng. Ch. Sandylands Tweed of Blaircourt
Sandylands Shadow

LOCKERBIE TACKETY BOOTS
AM. CH. LOCKERBIE PEBBLES — Eng. Ch. Reanacre Mallardhurn Thunder DINAH
Poolstead Polly Flinders

AM. CH. BRIARY BONNIE BRIANA (B)

ENG. CH. SANDYLANDS TWEED OF BLAIRCOURT — Eng. Ch. Ruler of Blaircourt
Eng. Ch. Tessa of Blaircourt

AM. CH. LOCKERBIE SANDYLANDS TARQUIN
SANDYLANDS SHADOW — Am. Can. Ch. Sam of Blaircourt
Diant Pride

AM. CH. LOCKERBIE SHILLEAGH (B)

AM. CH. LOCKERBIE SCWARLODGE BRIGADIER — Eng. Ch. Sandylands Sam
Scwarlodge Ability

PRINCESS OF MARLOW
JOHNNY DUCHESS — Fool's Gamble
Loot of Ocean II

I Hereby Certify that to the best of my knowledge and belief the above Pedigree is true and that all ancestors named above are of the same breed.

Signed this _____ day of _____ 19 ___

Address 11925 RICHLAND LANE, HERNDON, VIRGINIA 22071

269

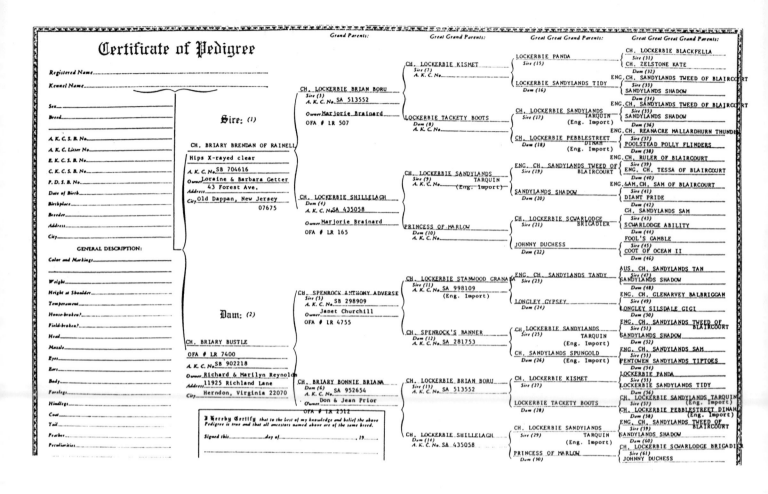

PEDIGREE OF MINDY, MEGAN, MORAG (WOOFIE)

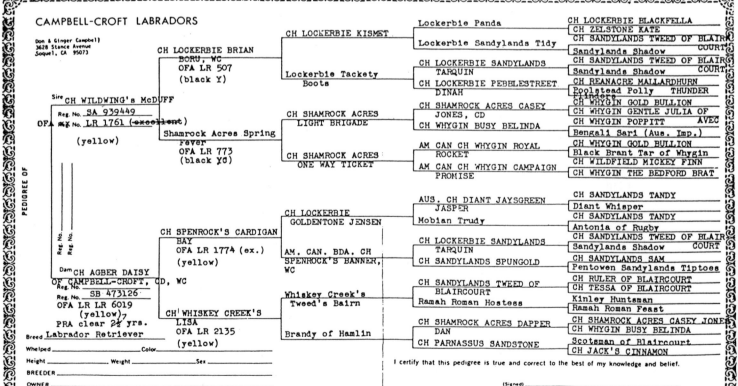

Certified Pedigree

GROVETON KENNELS

P. O. BOX 146

WEST LEBANON, N. Y. 12195

REGISTERED NAME		CALL NAME		REGISTERED NUMBER	
CH. Springfield's Cheshire Cheese		Chessy		SA 425508	
WHELPED	BREED		COLOR		
10/13/66	Lab. Ret		Yellow	Bitch	
BREEDER AND ADDRESS					
Mrs R. V. Clark Jr.					

	GRANDPARENTS (2nd generation)	GREAT GRANDPARENTS (3rd generation)	GREAT GR. GRANDPARENTS (4th generation)
PARENTS			Forbes of Blaircourt
	CH. Sandylands Tweed of Blaircourt	CH. Ruler of Blaircourt	Oliver of Blaircourt
	GRAND SIRE		CH Laird of Lochaber
CH. Harris Tweed of Ide		Sh Ch. Tessa of Blaircourt	CH. Imp of Blaircourt
SIRE			Black Knight of Ide
SA147524		Black Sheik of Ide	Black Bess of Ide
Reg. No. of sire	Cindy Sue of Ide		Black Knight of Ide
	GRAND DAM	Black Sarah of Ide	Black Bess of Ide
			CH. Sandylands Tweed of Blaircourt
	CH Sandylands Tandy	Australian Ch. Sandylands Tan	Sandylands Annabel
	GRAND SIRE		Eng. Am & Can Ch. Sam of Blaircourt
CH. Kimvalley Cinderella		Sandylands Shadow	Diant Pride
DAM			Fld Ch. Whatstandwell Hiwood Brand
Reg. No. of dam	Kimvalley Guildown Cassandra	CH Whatstandwell Coronet	CH. Honey of Whatstandwell
	GRAND DAM		CH. Diant Swandyke Cream Cracker
		Guildown Ecru	Guildown Marcherita

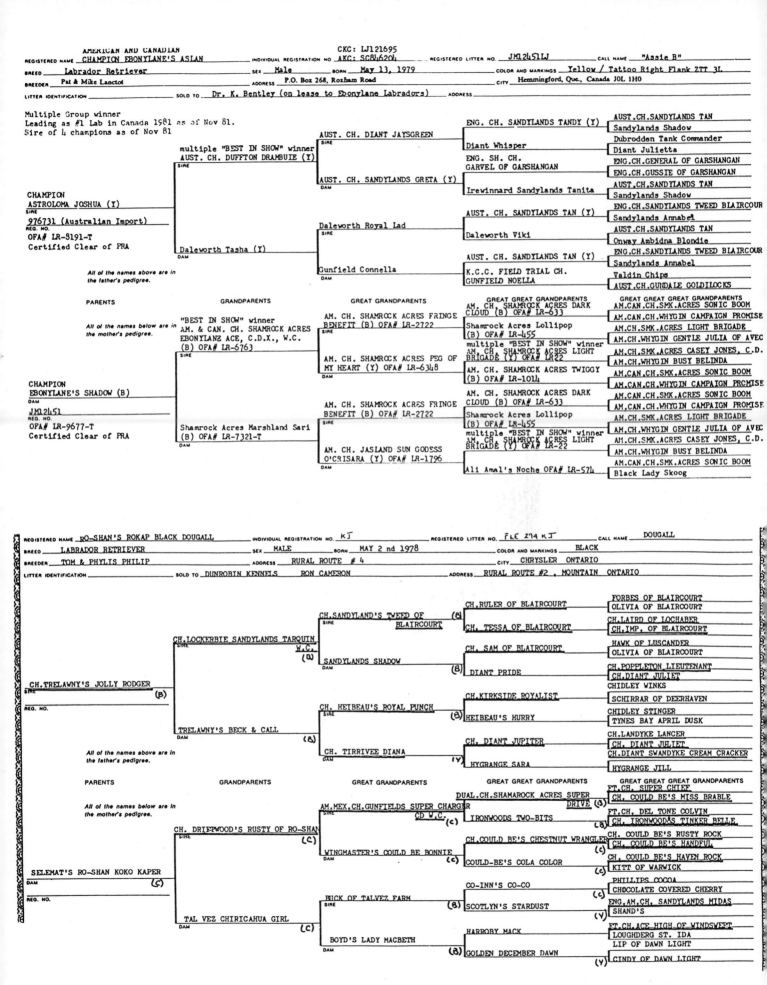

AMERICAN AND CANADIAN
REGISTERED NAME __CHAMPION EBONYLANE'S ASLAN__ CKC: LJ121695 INDIVIDUAL REGISTRATION NO. AKC: SC846204 REGISTERED LITTER NO. JM12451LJ CALL NAME "Assie B"

BREED __Labrador Retriever__ SEX __Male__ BORN __May 13, 1979__ COLOR AND MARKINGS __Yellow / Tattoo Right Flank ZTT 3L__

BREEDER __Pat & Mike Lanctot__ ADDRESS __P.O. Box 268, Roxham Road__ CITY __Hemmingford, Que., Canada J0L 1H0__

LITTER IDENTIFICATION _____ SOLD TO __Dr. K. Bentley (on lease to Ebonylane Labradors)__ ADDRESS _____

Multiple Group winner
Leading as #1 Lab in Canada 1981 as of Nov 81.
Sire of 4 champions as of Nov 81

CHAMPION
ASTROLOMA JOSHUA (Y)
SIRE
976731 (Australian Import)
REG. NO.
OFA# LR-3191-T
Certified Clear of PRA

multiple "BEST IN SHOW" winner
AUST. CH. DUFFTON DRAMBUIE (Y)
SIRE

AUST. CH. DIANT JAYSGREEN
SIRE

ENG. CH. SANDYLANDS TANDY (Y)
- AUST.CH.SANDYLANDS TAN
- Sandylands Shadow

Diant Whisper
- Dubrodden Tank Commander
- Diant Julietta

AUST. CH. SANDYLANDS GRETA (Y)
DAM

ENG. SH. CH.
GARVEL OF GARSHANGAN
- ENG.CH.GENERAL OF GARSHANGAN
- ENG.CH.GUSSIE OF GARSHANGAN

Irewinnard Sandylands Tanita
- AUST.CH.SANDYLANDS TAN
- Sandylands Shadow

Daleworth Tasha (Y)
DAM

Daleworth Royal Lad
SIRE

AUST. CH. SANDYLANDS TAN (Y)
- ENG.CH.SANDYLANDS TWEED BLAIRCOUR
- Sandylands Annabel

Daleworth Viki
- AUST.CH.SANDYLANDS TAN
- Onway Ambidna Blondie

Gunfield Connella
DAM

AUST. CH. SANDYLANDS TAN (Y)
- ENG.CH.SANDYLANDS TWEED BLAIRCOUR
- Sandylands Annabel

K.C.C. FIELD TRIAL CH.
GUNFIELD NOELLA
- Valdin Chips
- AUST.CH.GUNDALE GOLDILOCKS

All of the names above are in
the father's pedigree.

PARENTS	GRANDPARENTS	GREAT GRANDPARENTS	GREAT GREAT GRANDPARENTS	GREAT GREAT GREAT GRANDPARENTS

All of the names below are in
the mother's pedigree.

CHAMPION
EBONYLANE'S SHADOW (B)
DAM
JM12451
REG. NO.
OFA# LR-9677-T
Certified Clear of PRA

"BEST IN SHOW" winner
AM. & CAN. CH. SHAMROCK ACRES
EBONYLANE ACE, C.D.X., W.C.
(B) OFA# LR-6763
SIRE

AM. CH. SHAMROCK ACRES FRINGE
BENEFIT (B) OFA# LR-2722

AM. CH. SHAMROCK ACRES DARK
CLOUD (B) OFA# LR-633
- AM.CAN.CH.SMK.ACRES SONIC BOOM
- AM.CAN.CH.WHYGIN CAMPAIGN PROMISE

Shamrock Acres Lollipop
(B) OFA# LR-455
- AM.CH.SMK.ACRES LIGHT BRIGADE
- AM.CH.WHYGIN GENTLE JULIA OF AVEC

AM. CH. SHAMROCK ACRES PEG OF
MY HEART (Y) OFA# LR-6348

multiple "BEST IN SHOW" winner
AM. CH. SHAMROCK ACRES LIGHT
BRIGADE (Y) OFA# LR-22
- AM.CH.SMK.ACRES CASEY JONES, C.D.
- AM.CH.WHYGIN BUSY BELINDA

AM. CH. SHAMROCK ACRES TWIGGY
(B) OFA# LR-1014
- AM.CAN.CH.SMK.ACRES SONIC BOOM
- AM.CAN.CH.WHYGIN CAMPAIGN PROMISE

Shamrock Acres Marshland Sari
(B) OFA# LR-7321-T
DAM

AM. CH. SHAMROCK ACRES FRINGE
BENEFIT (B) OFA# LR-2722

AM. CH. SHAMROCK ACRES DARK
CLOUD (B) OFA# LR-633
- AM.CAN.CH.WHYGIN CAMPAIGN PROMISE
- AM.CAN.CH.WHYGIN CAMPAIGN PROMISE

Shamrock Acres Lollipop
(B) OFA# LR-455
- AM.CH.SMK.ACRES LIGHT BRIGADE
- AM.CH.WHYGIN GENTLE JULIA OF AVEC

AM. CH. JASLAND SUN GODESS
O'CRISARA (Y) OFA# LR-1796

multiple "BEST IN SHOW" winner
AM. CH. SHAMROCK ACRES LIGHT
BRIGADE (Y) OFA# LR-22
- AM.CH.SMK.ACRES CASEY JONES, C.D.
- AM.CH.WHYGIN BUSY BELINDA

Ali Amal's Noche OFA# LR-574
- AM.CAN.CH.SMK.ACRES SONIC BOOM
- Black Lady Skoog

REGISTERED NAME __RO-SHAN'S ROKAP BLACK DOUGALL__ INDIVIDUAL REGISTRATION NO. KJ REGISTERED LITTER NO. FLE 274 KJ CALL NAME DOUGALL

BREED __LABRADOR RETRIEVER__ SEX __MALE__ BORN __MAY 2nd 1978__ COLOR AND MARKINGS __BLACK__

BREEDER __TOM & PHYLIS PHILIP__ ADDRESS __RURAL ROUTE #4__ CITY __CHRYSLER ONTARIO__

LITTER IDENTIFICATION _____ SOLD TO __DUNROBIN KENNELS RON CAMERON__ ADDRESS __RURAL ROUTE #2, MOUNTAIN ONTARIO__

CH.TRELAWNY'S JOLLY RODGER
SIRE (B)
REG. NO.

CH.LOCKERBIE SANDYLANDS TARQUIN
W.C.
SIRE (B)

CH.SANDYLAND'S TWEED OF
BLAIRCOURT
SIRE (B)

CH.RULER OF BLAIRCOURT
- FORBES OF BLAIRCOURT
- OLIVIA OF BLAIRCOURT

CH. TESSA OF BLAIRCOURT
- CH.LAIRD OF LOCHABER
- CH.IMP. OF BLAIRCOURT

SANDYLANDS SHADOW
DAM (B)

CH. SAM OF BLAIRCOURT
- HAWK OF LUSCANDER
- OLIVIA OF BLAIRCOURT

DIANT PRIDE
- CH.POPPLETON LIEUTENANT
- CH.DIANT JULIET

TRELAWNY'S BECK & CALL
DAM (B)

CH. HEIBEAU'S ROYAL PUNCH
SIRE (B)

CH.KIRKSIDE ROYALIST
- CHIDLEY WINKS
- SCHIRRAR OF DEERHAVEN

HEIBEAU'S HURRY
- CHIDLEY STINGER
- TYNES BAY APRIL DUSK

CH. TIRRIVEE DIANA
DAM (Y)

CH. DIANT JUPITER
- CH.LANDYKE LANCER
- CH. DIANT JULIET

HYGRANGE SARA
- CH.DIANT SWANDYKE CREAM CRACKER
- HYGRANGE JILL

All of the names above are in
the father's pedigree.

PARENTS	GRANDPARENTS	GREAT GRANDPARENTS	GREAT GREAT GRANDPARENTS	GREAT GREAT GREAT GRANDPARENTS

All of the names below are in
the mother's pedigree.

SELEMAT'S RO-SHAN KOKO KAPER
DAM (C)
REG. NO.

CH. DRIFTWOOD'S RUSTY OF RO-SHAN
SIRE (C)

AM.MEX.CH.GUNFIELDS SUPER CHARGER
CD W.C.
SIRE (C)

DUAL CH.SHAMROCK ACRES SUPER
DRIVE (B)
- FT.CH. SUPER CHIEF
- CH. COULD BE'S MISS BRABLE

IRONWOODS TWO-BITS
- FT.CH. DEL TONE COLVIN
- CH. IRONWOODS TINKER BELLE

WINGMASTER'S COULD BE BONNIE
DAM (C)

CH.COULD BE'S CHESTNUT WRANGLER
- CH. COULD BE'S RUSTY ROCK
- CH. COULD BE'S HANDFUL

COULD-BE'S COLA COLOR
- CH. COULD BE'S HAVEN ROCK
- KITT OF WARWICK

TAL VEZ CHIRICAHUA GIRL
DAM (C)

BUCK OF TALVEZ FARM
SIRE (B)

CO-INN'S CO-CO
- PHILLIPS COCOA
- CHOCOLATE COVERED CHERRY

SCOTLYN'S STARDUST
- ENG.AM.CH. SANDYLANDS MIDAS
- SHAND'S

BOYD'S LADY MACBETH
DAM (B)

HARROBY MACK
- FT.CH.ACE HIGH OF WINDSWEPT
- LOUGHDERG ST. IDA

GOLDEN DECEMBER DAWN
- LIP OF DAWN LIGHT
- CINDY OF DAWN LIGHT

SCRIMSHAW LABRADORS
JONTE SCRIMSHAW O' SPINDRIFT

SA-470027	LITTER REG. NO.
INDIVIDUAL REG. NO.	AKC
CALL NAME Merrow	
BREED Labrador Retriever	REGISTERED NAME OF DOG
	DATE WHELPED March 17, 1967	REGISTERED WITH SEX Female

BREEDER Mr.&Mrs. John L. Rockwell   ADDRESS Jonte Kennels, Reg., Littleton, Mass.

OWNER Barbara L. Barfield   ADDRESS "Scrimshaw", RFD 2, Meredith, NH 03253

GENERAL DESCRIPTION Black (Bb). Excellent Gundog. OFA-LR-2675. Eyes Clear 7½ yrs.-Dr. Donovan

SIRE
CH. CHEBACCO SMOKEY JOE (B)
REG. NO. S-778601

- CH. ASHUR DEACON (B)
  - CH. HUGGER MUGGER (B)
    - CH. BANGSTONE BOB OF WINGAN (B)
      - DUAL CH. BRAMSHAW BOB (B)
      - CH. DRINKSTONE PEG (B)
    - Marsh
      - CH. EARLSMOOR MOOR OF ARDEN (B)
      - Wingan's Maid O' The Mist
  - CH. RUPERT DESDEMONA (B)
    - Dauntless of Deer Creek (B)
      - DUAL CH. SHED OF ARDEN (B)
      - Brookstone Burma
    - Lena (B)
      - FTC TIMBERTOWN CLANSMAN (B)
      - Wingan's Primrose
- CH. REDLEDGE WALDO
  - Chidley Blakso (B)
    - Chips
      - Peter of Cookhill
      - Ledgeland's Bridget
    - Marsh
      - CH. EARLSMOOR MOOR OF ARDEN (B)
      - Wingan's Maid O' The Mist
  - CH. HOBBIMOOR'S DONNA
    - Driver of Morespense
      - CH. LEDGELAND'S KULO
      - DUAL CH. GORSE OF ARDEN (B)
    - Queen Patricia
      - Teal Wing of Allen Winden
      - Dunottar Tess

DAM
JONTE'S CAMALA (Bb)
REG. NO. SA-286953
X-Ray Normal

- Aldenholme's Robber (B)
  - CH. KILLER ALCESTER (B)
    - CH. STOWAWAY AT DEER CREEK (B)
      - DUAL CH. SHED OF ARDEN (B)
      - CH. BLOOMA OF ARDEN B
    - Dawn II
      - CH. BANGSTONE BOB OF WINGAN (B)
      - Marsh
  - CH. REDLEDGE WALDO (B)
    - Chidley Blakso (B)
      - Chips
      - Marsh
    - CH. HOBBIMOOR'S DONNA
      - Driver of Morexpense
      - Queen Patricia
- Jonte Bewitched (B)
  - Coatuit Rush (Y)
    - Coatuit Kim
      - Toussaint L'Ouverture
      - Quisiana II of Coatuit
    - Coatuit Sedge (Y)
      - ENG. CH. LANDYKE PATRICK (Y)
      - Rupert Sunlight (Y)
  - CH. ALDENHOLME'S WITCHING HOUR (B)
    - Chidley Robber (B)
      - CH. STOWAWAY AT DEER CREEK (B)
      - Dawn II
    - CH. HOBBIMOOR'S PATRICIA (B)
      - Chidley Blakso (B)
      - Queen Patricia

Certificate of Pedigree

Name Winterset Blakela Camanne   AKC No. SC904671

Breed Labrador Retriever   Color B   Sex F

Breeder Mrs. Enid P. Bloome   Whelped 3/27/80

Sire Eng. Am. CH. Lawnwoods Hot Chocolate   AKC No. SC 276903

- CH. Follytower Merrybrook Black Stormer
  - CH. Sandylands Tandy
    - Aus. Ch. Sandylands Tan
      - Ch. Sandylands Tweed of Blaircourt
      - Sandylands Annabel
    - Sandylands Shadow
      - Int. Ch. Sam of Blaircourt
      - Diant Pride
  - Follytower Old Black Magic
    - Ch. Ballyduff Hollybranch of Keithray
      - CH. Sandylands Tweed of Blaircourt
      - CH. Hollybank Beauty
    - CH. Follytower Silsdale Old Chelsea
      - CH. Braeduke Joyful
      - Silsdale Glenarvey Quita
- Lawnwoods Tapestry
  - CH. Lawnwoods Fame and Fortune
    - Rockabee Tobin
      - CH. Sandylands Tandy
      - Rockabee Cornbunting
    - Spinneyhill Lilac of Lawnwood
      - Mallardhurn Tweed
      - Lawnhollow Dainty of Spinneyhill
  - CH. Poolstead Personality of Lawnwood
    - CH. Reanacre Mallardhurn Thunder
      - CH. Sandylands Tweed of Blaircourt
      - Mallardhurn Pat
    - Braeduke Julia of Poolstead
      - CH. Landyke Stormer
      - Diant Joy of Braeduke

Dam CH. Rupert Caviar   AKC No. SB-943472

- CH. Killingworth's Thunderson
  - CH. Torquay's Scorpio
    - Eng Am CH Sandylands Midas
      - Eng. CH. Renacre Mallardhurn Thunder
      - Eng. Ch. Sandylands Truth
    - Mallow's Fancy Free
      - Can Am CH Annwyn's Jack O'Diamonds
      - CH. Goldsboro Velvet of Mallow
  - Killingworth's Snipe
    - Can Am Ch Annwyn's Jack O'Diamonds
      - Can. Am CH. Annwyn's Shedrow
      - Can Am CH. Lignamallard Tarantella
    - CH. Windrow's Samantha
      - Eng. Am. Can. Ch. Sam of Blaircourt
      - Jat's Peggy of Fire Island
- Rupert Goldylocks
  - Eng. Am. CH. Ardmargha Goldkrest of Syrancot
    - CH. Sandylands Garry
      - Sandylands General
      - Sandylands Memory
    - Sandylands Komely of Ardmargha
      - CH. Kinley Skipper
      - CH. Sandylands Truth
  - Rupert Judicious
    - CH. Glenarvey Barrister
      - CH. Glenarvey Brand
      - Sandylands Goldie
    - Rupert Piccadilly Dame
      - CH. Kinley Yorkshireman
      - CH. Rupert Searchon

Ch. Spenrock's Banner, W.C. taking Best of Breed at Westchester when only 15 months old. Mrs. Helen Warwick is the judge, and Janet Churchill is the owner-handler.

Colors in Your Breeding Program

Although I think that most people can now see good in all three Labrador colors, including the various shade range of the yellows, I guess that there will always be those to whom a Labrador is a black dog, period. To me the chocolates, which are the most recent to achieve popularity, are especially beautiful, so I note with pleasure that some kennels are placing particular emphasis on those. And of course the yellows, especially the deeper shades, are extremely eye-catching, beautiful, and attractive.

From the breeder's point of view, there are two kinds of blacks: those that only produce black no matter how the dog may be bred and those that will produce black and yellow except when bred to a partner with chocolate genes, in which case all three colors are produced. Thus, if you like all three colors, the way to get them is by breeding black to black with the proper genes.

Black is a dominant characteristic in Labrador coat color; yellow is recessive. Black Labradors carry either two genes that are for black or the dominant black gene along with a recessive gene for yellow. If both parents carry only black genes, the puppies will be black. If one carries a recessive gene for yellow, the puppies may be black but half of them will carry recessive genes for yellow; these puppies will, in turn, produce both blacks and yellows.

274

Ch. Sandylands Spungold, the dam of Int. Ch. Spenrock Banner, W.C. Photo courtesy of Janet Churchill.

Yellow may be bred to another yellow (yellow puppies will be produced) or yellow may be bred to black, but yellow should never be bred to chocolate. There is a strong possibility that this combination will result in incorrect pigmentation and light eyes in both colors.

Ch. Spenrock Anthony Adverse finishing his title under Mrs. Clayton, owner of Ardmagha Labs in England, at Ladies Kennel Association. Jan Churchill, owner-handler.

Breeding chocolate to chocolate will give you either all or 85% chocolate. Yellows with brown pigment, as opposed to black, may also be produced. To darken eyes and pigment, breed a chocolate to a black.

These remarks are only general. There are books on genetics and on color breeding of dogs that make fascinating reading if you are inclined to study the subject. This is just a "rule of thumb" guide about what can generally be expected from Lab colors.

Multiple Best of Breed and Group winner, Ch. Ironpride's Band of Gold is owned by Mary Fisher, Bridgeton, Missouri.

Gestation, Whelping, and Litter

When your bitch has been bred and is back at home, remain ever watchful that no other male gets to her until at least the twenty-second day of her season has passed. Prior to that time, it will still be possible for an undesired breeding to take place, which, at this point, would be catastrophic. Remember, she actually can have two separate litters by two different dogs, so *be alert and take care.*

In all other ways, the bitch should be treated quite normally. It is not necessary for her to have any additives to her diet until she is at least four to five weeks pregnant. It is also unnecessary for her to have additional food. It is better to underfeed the bitch this early in her pregnancy than to overfeed her at this point. A fat bitch is not an easy whelper, so by "feeding her up" during the first few weeks, you may only be creating problems for her.

Controlled exercise is good, and necessary, for your pregnant bitch. She should not be permitted to just lie around. At about seven weeks along, the exercise should be slowed down to several sedate walks daily, not too long and preferably on the lead.

In the fourth or fifth week of pregnancy, calcium may be added to the diet, and at seven weeks, the one meal a day may be increased to two meals with some nutritional additives in each. Canned milk may be added to her meals at this time.

A week before she is due to whelp, your Labrador bitch should be introduced to her whelping box, so that she will have accustomed herself to it and feel at home there by the time the puppies arrive. She should be encouraged to sleep there and be permitted to come and go as she pleases. The box should be roomy enough for her to lie down and stretch out in it, but it should not be too large or the pups will have too much room in which to roam, and they may get chilled if they move too far off from their dam.

The highly successful producing bitch Labradese Bluebelle Bouquet with puppies by Ch. Franklin's Golden Mandigo. Dr. and Mrs. William A. Hines, owners, Colorado.

Be sure that there is a "pig rail" for the box, which will prevent the puppies from being crushed against the side of the box. The box should be lined with newspapers, which can easily be changed as they become soiled.

The room where the whelping box is placed, either in the home or in the kennel, should be free from drafts and should be kept at about 70 degrees Fahrenheit. It may be necessary, during the cold months, to install an infrared lamp in order to maintain sufficient warmth, in which case guard against the lamp being placed too low or too close to the puppies.

Keep a big pile of newspapers near the box. You'll find that you never have enough of these when you have a litter, so start accumulating them ahead of time. A pile of clean towels, a pair of scissors, and a bottle of alcohol should also be close at hand. Have all of these things ready at least a week before the bitch is due to whelp, as you never know exactly when she may start.

The day or night before she is due, the bitch will become restless; she'll be in and out of her box and in and out of the door. She may refuse food, and at this point her temperature will start to drop. She will start to dig and tear up the newspapers in her box, shiver, and generally look uncomfortable. You alone should be with the bitch at this time (or one other person who is an experienced breeder, to give you confidence if this is one of your first litters). The bitch does not need an audience or any extra people around. This is not a sideshow, and several peo-

Ch. Sandylands Crystal with her last litter of three. This illustrates the whelping box used at Scrimshaw, with indoor/outdoor carpeting and adjustable sides. The thermometer on the upper right of the rail measures the temperature of the heat provided by the heating lamp over one corner of the box. Ribbon collars on the puppies help to distinguish each puppy for daily weighing and to spot potential problems.

276

ple hovering over the bitch may upset her to the point where she may hurt the puppies. Stay nearby, but do not fuss too much over her. Keep a calm attitude; this will give her confidence. Eventually she will settle down in her box and begin to pant; shortly thereafter she will start to have contractions, and soon a puppy will begin to emerge, sliding out with one of the contractions. The mother immediately should open the sac and bite the cord and clean up the puppy. She will also eat the placenta, which you should permit. Once the puppy is cleaned, it should be placed next to the bitch, unless she is showing signs of having another one immediately. The puppy should start looking for a nipple on which to nurse, and you should make certain that it is able to latch on and start doing so successfully.

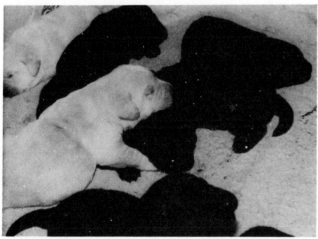

Seven-day-old puppies in a litter owned by Agber Labradors, Agnes Cartier, New Jersey.

If a puppy is a breech birth (*i.e.*, born feet first), then you must watch carefully that it is delivered as quickly as possible and the sac removed very quickly, so that the puppy does not drown. Sometimes even a normally positioned birth will seem extremely slow in coming. Should either of these events occur, you might take a clean towel and, as the bitch contracts, pull the puppy out, doing so gently and with utmost care. If the bitch does not open the sac and cut the umbilical cord, you will have to do so. If the puppy shows little sign of life, make sure the mouth is free of liquid and then, using a Turkish towel or terry cloth, massage the puppy's chest, rubbing back and forth quite briskly. Continue

this for about fifteen minutes. It may be necessary to try mouth-to-mouth resuscitation. Open the puppy's jaws and, using a finger, depress the tongue, which may be stuck to the roof of the puppy's mouth. Then blow hard down the puppy's throat. Bubbles may pop out of its nose, but keep on blowing. Rub with the towel again across the chest, and try artificial respiration, pressing the sides of the chest together slowly and rhythmically, in and out, in and out. Keep trying one method or the other for at least 15 minutes (actual time—not how long it may seem to you) before giving up. You may be rewarded with a live puppy that otherwise would not have made it.

If you are able to revive the puppy, it should not be put back with the mother immediately, as it should be kept extra warm for a while. Put it in a cardboard box near a stove, on an electric pad, or, if it is the time of year for your heat to be running, near a radiator until the rest of the litter has been born. Then it can be put in with the others.

The bitch may go for an hour or more between puppies, which is fine so long as she seems comfortable and is not straining or contracting. She should not be allowed to remain unassisted for more than an hour if she does continue to contract. This is when you should call your veterinarian, whom you should have alerted ahead of time of the possibility so that he will be somewhere within easy reach. He may want the bitch brought in so that he can examine her and perhaps give her a shot of Pituitrin. In some cases, the veterinarian may find that a Caesarean operation is necessary, because a puppy may be lodged in some manner that makes normal delivery impossible. This can occur due to the size of a puppy or may be due to the fact that the puppy is turned wrong. If any of the foregoing occurs, the puppies already born must be kept warm in their cardboard box, which should have been lined with shredded newspapers in advance and which should have a heating pad beneath it.

Once the Caesarean section has been done, get the bitch and the puppies home. Do not attempt to put the pups in with the bitch until she is at least fairly conscious, as she may unknowingly hurt them. But do get them back as soon as possible so that they can start nursing.

If the mother lacks milk at this point, the puppies must be fed by hand, kept very warm, and

Ch. Forecast Atlanta and her hungry brood. Owned by Forecast Labradors, Elizabeth Curtis and Ann and Samuel Cappellina, Connecticut.

held against the mother's teats several times a day in order to stimulate and encourage the secretion of her milk, which should start shortly.

Assuming that there has been no problem, and the bitch has whelped naturally, you should insist that she go outside to exercise, staying just long enough to make herself comfortable. She can be offered a bowl of milk and a biscuit, but then she should settle down with her family. Be sure to clean out the whelping box and change the newspapers so that she will have a fresh bed.

Unless some problem occurs, there is little you need do about the puppies until they become three to four weeks old. Keep the box clean with fresh papers. When the pups get to be a couple of days old, towels should be tacked down to the bottom of the box so that the puppies will have traction when they move.

If the bitch has difficulties with her milk supply, or if you should be so unfortunate as to lose the bitch, then you must be prepared to either hand-feed or tube-feed the puppies if they are to survive. We personally prefer tube-feeding, as it is so much faster and easier. If the bitch is available, it is better that she should continue to clean and care for the puppies in the normal manner, except for the food supplements you will provide. If she is unable to do this, then after every feeding, you must gently rub each puppy's abdomen with wet cotton to induce urination, and the rectum should be gently rubbed to open the bowels.

Newborn puppies must be fed every three to four hours around the clock. The puppies must be kept warm during that time. Have your veterinarian show you how to tube-feed. Once learned, it is really quite simple, fast, and efficient.

After a normal whelping, the bitch will require additional food to enable her to produce sufficient milk. She should be fed twice daily now, and some canned milk should be available to her several times during the day.

When the puppies are two weeks old, you should clip their nails, as they are needle-sharp at this point and can hurt or damage the mother's teats and stomach as the pups hold on to nurse.

Between three and four weeks of age, the puppies should begin to be weaned. Scraped beef (prepared by scraping it off slices of raw beef with a spoon, so that none of the muscle or gristle is included) may be offered in very small quantities a couple of times daily for the first few days. If the puppy is reluctant to try it, put a little on your finger and rub it on the puppy's lips; this should get things going. By the third day, you can mix in ground puppy chow with warm water as directed on the package, offering it four times daily. By now the mother should be kept out of the box and away from the puppies for several hours at a time. After the puppies reach five weeks of age, she should be left in with them only overnight. By the time they are six weeks old, the puppies should be entirely weaned and the mother should only check on them with occasional visits.

Most veterinarians recommend a temporary DHL (distemper, hepatitis, leptospirosis) shot when the puppies are six weeks old. This remains effective for about two weeks. Then, at eight weeks, the series of permanent shots begins for DHL protection. It is a good idea to discuss with your vet the advisability of having your puppies inoculated against the dreaded parvovirus at the same time. Each time the pups go in for shots, you should bring stool samples so that they can be examined for worms. Worms go through various stages of development, and may be present in a stool sample even though the sample does not test positive. So do not neglect to keep careful watch on this.

The puppies should be fed four times daily until they are three months old. Then you can cut back to three feedings daily. By the time they are six months old, two meals daily are sufficient. Some people feed their dogs twice daily throughout their lifetime, while others cut to one meal daily when the puppy reaches one year of age.

The ideal time for puppies to go to their new homes is when they are between eight and twelve weeks old, although some puppies successfully adjust to a new home at six weeks of age. Be certain that they go to their future owners accompanied by a description of the diet you've been feeding them and a schedule of the shots they have received and those they still need. These should be included with a registration application and a copy of the pedigree.

This hungry Lab litter, at Winterset Kennels, is by Ch. Follytower Singalong ex Ch. Killingworth Valiant Lady. Mrs. Enid P. Bloome owner-breeder of the pups.

Puppies by Ch. Scrimshaw Another Deacon ex Ch. Sandylands Crystal at six weeks of age: Scrimshaw Tipsy Parson, Ch. Scrimshaw Blue Nun, Scrimshaw Church Mouse, Ch. Scrimshaw My Sin, and Scrimshaw Holystone. Bred by Barbara L. Barfield, Scrimshaw Kennels, New Hampshire.

CHAPTER EIGHT

Selecting Your Labrador Retriever

Oaklea Fireside Invader at ten weeks of age. A fine young Lab with a bright future owned by the Fireside Labradors of Paula J. Recker, Brecksville, Ohio.

Once you have made the decision that the Labrador Retriever is the breed of dog for you, the next important step for you is to begin your education on the selection of exactly the right Lab to satisfy your needs. Do you prefer to start out with a puppy, with an adult dog, or with a partially mature dog? Do you prefer a male or a female? And what type of dog do you wish: one for show or as a pet and companion, to accompany you or a family member in the field and, perhaps, to work with in obedience? A decision should be reached about these matters prior to contacting breeders; then you can accurately describe your requirements and the breeders can offer you something suitable. Remember, with any breed of dog, (or for that matter with any major purchase), the more care and forethought you invest when planning, the greater the satisfaction and pleasure you are likely to derive.

Referring to a dog as a "major investment" may possibly seem strange to you; however, it is an accurate description. Generally speaking, a sizeable sum of money is involved, and you are assuming responsibility for a living creature, taking on all the moral obligations this involves. Assuming that everything goes well, your Lab will be a member of your family for a dozen or more years, sharing your home, your daily routine, and your interests. The happiness and success of these years depend largely on the knowledge and intelligence with which you start the relationship.

Certain ground rules apply to the purchase of a dog, regardless of your intentions for its future. Foremost among these is the fact that no matter what you will be doing with the dog, the best and most acceptable place at which to make the purchase is at a kennel specializing in the breed you select. Even though pet shops occasionally have Labrador puppies for sale, they are primarily concerned with *pet* stock, puppies without pedigrees. When you buy from a breeder, you are getting a dog that has been the result of parents very carefully selected as individuals and as to pedigree and ancestry. For such a breeding, a dog and a bitch are selected from whom the breeder hopes to achieve show type dogs that upgrade both his own stock and that of the breed generally. Much thought has been given to the conformation and temperament likely to result from the combination of bloodlines and parents involved, for the breeder wants to produce sound, outstanding dogs that will further the respect in which he is held in the Labrador world. A specialist of this sort is eager to raise *better* dogs. Since it is seldom possible to keep all the puppies from every litter, fine young stock thus becomes available for sale. Puppies with flaws which in no way affect their strength or future health are sold as pets. Such flaws may include those which the layman would not even realize exist, but the conscientious breeder will tell you of them, and show them to you, when you are purchasing the puppy. By buying a dog

"Playing with Mom"—five-week-old babies by Ch. Seaward's Adonis of Rupert ex Ch. Killingworth Winterset My Jo, C.D. There were ten in the litter, bred and owned by Mrs. Enid P. Bloome, Winterset Labs, Connecticut.

You also may be able to get information from professional handlers. They have many contacts and might be able to put you in touch with a breeder and/or help you choose a dog.

The moment you even start to think about purchasing a Lab, it makes sense to look at, observe, and study as many members of the breed as possible, prior to taking the step. Acquaint yourself with correct type, soundness, and beauty before making any commitments. Since you are reading this book, you have already started on that route. Now add to your learning by visiting some dog shows if you can. Even if you are not looking for a show dog, it never hurts to become aware of how such a dog appears and behaves. Perhaps there you will meet some breeders from your area with whom you can discuss the breed and who you can visit.

like this from a knowledgeable and reliable breeder, you are getting all the advantages of good bloodlines with proper temperament, careful rearing, and the happy, well-adjusted environment which puppies need to start life in order to be enjoyable, satisfactory adults. And although you do not buy a show dog or show prospect, puppies with such a background have all the odds in their favor to become dogs of excellence in the home and in the field.

If you are looking for a show dog, obviously everything I have said about buying only from a specialized breeder applies with even greater emphasis. Show-type dogs are bred from show-type dogs of proven producing lines and are the result of serious study, thought, and planning. They do *not* just happen.

Throughout the pages of this book are the names and locations of dozens of reliable Labrador breeders. Should it so happen that no one has puppies or young stock available to go at the moment you inquire, it would be far wiser for you to place your name on the waiting list and see what happens when the next litter is born than to rush off and buy a puppy from some less desirable source. After all, you do not want to repent at leisure!

Another source of listings of recognized Labrador breeders is the American Kennel Club, 51 Madison Avenue, New York, NY 10010. A note or phone call will bring you a list of breeders in your area.

This beguiling black Lab puppy, seven weeks old, is a son of the English importation, Am. Ch. Lawnwood's Brands Hatch. Agber Kennels, owner, Agnes Cartier, New Jersey.

A Debby Kobilis photo of the Reynolds' future Ch. Finchingfield Faith at seven weeks of age.

If you wish your Labrador to be a family dog, the most satisfactory choice often is a female. Females make gentle, delightful companions and usually are quieter and more inclined to not roam than males. Often, too, they make neater house dogs, being easier to train. And they are of at least equal intelligence to the males, both in the home and in the field. In the eyes of many pet owners, the principal objection to having a bitch is the periodic "coming in season." Sprays and chlorophyll tablets that can help to cut down on the nuisance of visiting canine swains stampeding your front door are available; and, of course, I advocate spaying bitches who will not be used for show or breeding, with even the latter being spayed when their careers in competition or in the whelping box have come to a close. Bitches who have been spayed remain in better health when they become older, because spaying almost entirely eliminates the danger of breast cancer. Spaying also eliminates the messiness of spotting on rugs and furniture, which can be considerable with a member of a medium-sized or large breed and which is annoying in a household companion.

To many, however, a dog (male) is preferable. The males do seem somehow to be more strongly endowed with breed character. But do consider the advantages and disadvantages of both males and females prior to deciding which to purchase.

If you are buying your Labrador as a pet, a puppy is preferable, as you can teach it the ways of your own household, accustom it to your schedule, and start its training early. Two months is an ideal age to introduce the puppy into your home. Older puppies may have already established habits of which you will not approve and which you may find difficult to change. Besides, puppies are such fun that it is great to share and enjoy every possible moment of the process of growing up.

When you are ready to buy, make appointments with as many Lab breeders as you have been able to locate in your area for the purpose of visiting their kennels, discussing the breed with them, and seeing their dogs. This is a marvelous learning experience, and you will find that the majority of breeders are willing and happy to spend time with you, provided that you have arranged the visit in advance. Kennel owners are busy people with full schedules, so do be considerate about this courtesy and call on the telephone before you appear.

If you have a choice of more than one kennel where you can go to see the dogs and puppies, do take advantage of the opportunity; don't just settle for and buy the first puppy you see and like. You may return to your first choice, but you will do so with greater satisfaction and authority if you have also seen the others that are available. When you look at pet puppies, be aware that the one you buy should look sturdy

Debby Kobilis took this photo of Ch. Finchingfield Faith at six months of age. Owned by Marilyn and Dick Reynolds, this bitch well fulfilled her early promise, growing up to become a Specialty Best of Breed winner from the classes.

and big-boned, bright-eyed and alert, with an inquisitive, friendly attitude. The puppy's coat should look clean and glossy. Do not buy a puppy that seems listless or dull, is strangely hyperactive, or looks half sick. The condition of the premises where the puppies are raised is also of importance as you want a pup that is free of parasites, so don't buy a puppy whose surroundings are dirty and ill kept.

One of the advantages of buying at a kennel you can visit is that you are thereby afforded the opportunity of seeing the dam of the puppies and possibly also the sire, if he, too, belongs to the breeder. Sometimes you can even see one or more of the grandparents. Be sure to note the temperament of these Labs as well as their conformation.

If there are no Labrador breeders within your travelling range, or you have not liked what you have seen on your visits, do not hesitate to contact others which are recommended to you, even if the kennels are at a distance, and to purchase from one of them if you are favorably impressed with what is offered. Shipping dogs is done with regularity nowadays, has become a recognized practice, and is reasonably safe, so this should not present a problem. If you are contacting a well-known, respected breeder, the puppy should be described and represented to you fairly. Breeders of this caliber want you to be satisfied, for both the puppy's sake and for yours. They take pride in their kennel's reputation, and they make every effort to see that their customers are pleased. In this way you are deprived of seeing your dog's parents, but even so you can buy with confidence when dealing with a specialized breeder.

Spenrock Tomahawk being shipped from Philadelphia on TWA to Mrs. William Kobusch, St. Louis, Missouri. This pup, by Eng., Am. Ch. Lawnwood's Hot Chocolate ex Spenrock Citation was bred by Jan Churchill and Janis Butler.

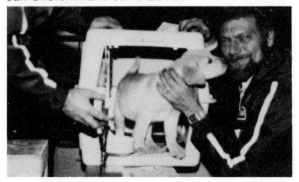

Manora's Annie, one of Nancy Scholz's Labs from New York, after a long trip to new home seems quite relaxed and happy in her "Sky Kennel."

Every word about careful selection of your pet puppy and from where it should be purchased applies twofold when you set out to select a show dog or the foundation stock for a breeding program of your own. You look for all the things already mentioned but on a far more sophisticated level, with many more factors to be taken into consideration. The standard of the Labrador Retriever must now become your guide, and it is essential that you know and understand not only the words of this standard but also their application to actual dogs before you are in a position to make a wise selection. Even then, if this is your first venture with a show-type Labrador, listen well and heed the advice of the breeder. If you have clearly and honestly stated your ambitions and plans for the dog, you will find that the breeders will cooperate by offering you something with which you will be successful.

There are several different degrees of show dog quality. There are dogs that should become top flight winners which can be campaigned for Specials (Best of Breed competition) and with which you can strive for Sporting Group placements. There are dogs of championship quality, which should gain their titles for you but do not have that little extra something to make them potential specials. There are dogs that perhaps may never finish their championships but which should do a bit of winning for you in the Classes:

a blue ribbon here and there, perhaps Winners or Reserve occasionally, but probably nothing too spectacular. Obviously the hardest to obtain, and the most expensive, are those in the first category, the truly top grade dogs. These are never plentiful as they are what most breeders are aiming to produce for their own kennels and personal enjoyment and with which they are loath to part.

A dog of championship quality is easier to find and less expensive, although it still will bring a good price. The least difficult to obtain is a fair show dog that may do a bit of winning for you in the Classes. Incidentally, one of the reasons breeders are sometimes reluctant to sell a really excellent show prospect is that in the past people have bought this type dog from them, then they changed their mind about showing it, and the dog thus became lost to the breed. It is really not fair to a breeder to buy a dog with the understanding that it will be shown and then renege on the agreement. Please, if you select a dog that is available only with this understanding, think it over carefully prior to your decision; then buy the dog only if you will give it an opportunity to prove itself in show ring competition as the breeder expects.

Ch. Amberfield's Beach Boy at three months of age. Amberfield Kennels, owners.

This adorable six-week-old Lab baby was sired by Pleasant Oaks Hopi, son of Eng., Am. Ch. Lawnwood's Hot Chocolate. Bred and owned by Mhyra Staph, Florida.

Obviously, if you want a show dog, you are a person in the habit of attending dog shows. Now this becomes a type of schooling rather than just a pleasant pastime. Much can be learned at the Lab ringside if one truly concentrates on what one sees. Become acquainted with the various winning exhibitors. Thoughtfully watch the judging. Try to understand what it is that causes some dogs to win and others to lose. Note well the attributes of the dogs, deciding for yourself which ones you like, giving full attention to attitude and temperament as well as conformation. Close your ears to the ringside "know-it-alls" who have only derogatory remarks to make about each animal in the ring and all that takes place there. You need to develop independent thinking at this stage and should not be influenced by the often entirely uneducated comment of the ringside spoil-sports. Especially make careful note of which exhibitors are campaigning winning homebreds—not just an occasional "star" but a series of consistent quality dogs. All this takes time and patience. This is the period to "make haste slowly;" mistakes can be expensive, and the more you have studied the breed, the better equipped you will be to avoid them.

Chucklebrook Daisy Mae and Ch. Chucklebrook Fannie Farmer, two very serious looking future show dogs, are owned by Sue E. May and Chucklebrook Kennels respectively.

As you make inquiries among various breeders regarding the purchase of a show dog or a show prospect, keep these things in mind. Show prospect puppies are less expensive than fully mature show dogs. The reason for this is that, with a puppy there is the element of chance, for one never can be absolutely certain exactly how the puppy will develop, while the mature dog stands before you as the finished product—"what you see is what you get" all set to step out and win.

There is always the risk factor involved with the purchase of a show-type puppy. Sometimes all goes well and that is great. But many a swan has turned into an ugly duckling as time passes, and it is far less likely that the opposite will occur. So weigh this well and balance all the odds before you decide whether a puppy or a mature dog would be your better buy. There are times, of course, when one actually has no choice in the matter; no mature show dogs may be available for sale. Then one must either wait a while or gamble on a puppy, but please *be aware that gambling is what you are doing!*

If you do take a show-prospect puppy, be guided by the breeder's advice when choosing from among what is offered. The person used to working with a bloodline has the best chance of predicting how the puppies will develop. Do not trust your own guess on this; rely on the experience of the breeder. For your own protection, it is best to buy puppies whose parents have been certified free of hip dysplasia and eye problems.

Although initially more expensive, a grown show dog in the long run often proves to be the far better bargain. His appearance is unlikely to change beyond weight and condition, which depend on the care you give him. Also to your advantage, if you are a novice and about to become an exhibitor, is that a grown show dog almost certainly will have been trained for the ring; thus, an inexperienced handler will find such a dog easier to manage.

If you plan to have your dog campaigned by a professional handler, have the handler help you locate and select a future winner. Through their numerous clients, handlers generally have access to a variety of interesting show dogs, and the usual arrangement is that the handler buys the dog, resells it to you for the price paid, and at the same time makes an agreement with you that the dog shall be campaigned by this handler throughout the dog's career.

If the foundation of a future kennel is what you have in mind as you contemplate the purchase of a Labrador Retriever, concentrate on

Ch. Spenrock Tweed of Windfields, by Ch. Eireannach Black Coachman ex Ch. Spenrock Winds Aloft, bred and owned by Spenrock Labradors, finishing her championship at Philadelphia 1981 under judge Mrs. Helen Warwick. Mrs. Bonnie Threlfall, handler.

Ch. Shenonvalley Blacksmith finishing at Mid-Kentucky under Ed Kauffman, handled by Jerry Rigden. Photo courtesy of Janet Churchill.

one or two really excellent bitches, not necessarily top show bitches but those representing the finest producing Lab lines. A proven matron which has already produced show type puppies is, of course, the ideal answer here, but, as with a mature show dog, a proven matron is more difficult to obtain and more expensive since no one really wants to part with so valuable an asset. You just might strike it lucky, though, in which case you will be off to a flying start. If you do not find such a matron available, do the next best thing and select a young bitch of outstanding background representing a noted producing strain, one that is herself of decent type and free of glaring faults.

Great attention should be paid to the background of the bitch from which you intend to breed. If the information is not already known to you, find out all you can about the temperament, character, field ability, and conformation of the sire and dam. A person just starting out is wise to concentrate on a fine collection of bitches and to raise a few litters sired by leading *producing* studs. The practice of buying a stud dog and then breeding everything you have to that dog does not always work out. It is better to take advantage of the availability of splendid stud dogs for the first few litters.

In summation, if you want a family dog, buy it young and raise it to the habits of your household. If you are buying a show dog, the nearer it is to being fully mature, the better. If foundation stock for a kennel is the goal, bitches are better than dogs, and proven matrons from top producing bloodlines are best.

Regarding price, you should expect to pay up to a few hundred dollars for a healthy pet Labrador puppy and more than that for a show-type puppy, the price depends on the degree of its potential. A bitch of good background for breeding would probably cost about the same as a show-type puppy. Successful show campaigners or bitches which are proven producers of championship puppies will be priced according to the owner's valuation and can run well into four figures.

When you buy a purebred dog which you are told is eligible for American Kennel Club registration, you must be given an A.K.C. application form that has been properly filled in by the seller. You must then complete this application and submit it, along with the necessary registration fee, to the American Kennel Club. You will, in turn, receive an A.K.C. registration certificate four to six weeks later in the mail. In some cases, the breeder may already have registered the puppy or dog you are buying. Then you will receive a registration certificate at the time of purchase, which must then be signed on the back by both you and the seller in order to transfer the registered dog into your name. *Never* accept a verbal promise that the registration application will follow, and *never* pay for a dog until you are certain that you are getting the registration in exchange. The seller should deliver to you a pedigree of at least several generations at the time of purchase.

Future Ch. Inglenooks Fair Isle Lass at three months of age. A very promising puppy owned by Shirley Costigan, Springfield Kennels, Canada.

Chocolate puppies by Eng., Am. Ch. Lawnwood's Hot Chocolate ex Ch. Meadowrock Fudge of Ayr, C.D.T., W.C. Owned by Mrs. Nancy Martin, Spring House, Pennsylvania. Photo by Will Martin.

Highlands Ebony Elegance, Highlands Ivory Frost Fairy, and Highlands Creme de Coco at four months of age. From the last litter by Ch. Groveton's Lucky Lindy ex Windshire Princess of Bree. Bred by Lillian Knobloch who owns Ivory and Ebony. Coco belongs to Steve Bellows, Marlboro, New Jersey.

Heaney's Ma-Pat-Ma M'Boy Fitzgo with his dam, Heaney's Ma-Pat-Ma Dream Cum Tru. Both owned by Margaret D. Heaney, Ma-Pat-Ma Kennels, New York.

Chucklebrook Daffodil at an early age. Wouldn't you love having a Lab puppy like this one from Chucklebrook Kennels, Reg., owned by Mr. and Mrs. Leslie G. Pilbin of Connecticut?

The Labrador Retriever Club National Specialty of 1981, in Ohio. **Above:** The Open Chocolate Class, an excellent example of the great amount of competition. **Below:** Swedish and American Ch. Puh's Superman, the Best of Breed, accompanied by (left to right) Bruce Hissong, show secretary; Nancy Martin, judge; and Mary Ellen Pfeifle.

Groveton puppies belonging to Mrs. Eileen Ketcham, New York.

CHAPTER NINE

Caring for Your Labrador Puppy

A very nice yellow male puppy owned by Jane Borders of Santa Rosa, California. By Eng., Am. Ch. Lawnwood's Hot Chocolate ex Springfield's Cymbeline, C.D.X.

Advance Preparation

The moment you decide to become the new owner of a Labrador Retriever puppy is not one second too soon to start planning for the new family member in order to make the transition period easier for yourself, your household, and the puppy.

The first thing in need of preparation is a bed for that puppy and a place where you can pen him up for rest periods. I am a firm believer that every dog should have a crate of its own, right from the very beginning. This will solve both of the above requirements, and the puppy will come to know and love this crate as his special haven. It is an ideal arrangement, for when you want him to be free, the crate door stays open. At other times, you securely latch it and know that the puppy is safe from harm, comfortable, and out of mischief. If you plan to travel with your dog, his crate comes along in the car; and, of course, to travel by plane, the dog must be put in a crate. If you show your dog, you will want him to be in his crate at the show a good deal of the day. No matter how you look at it, a crate is a very sensible, sound investment in your puppy's comfort, well-being, and safety—not to mention your own peace of mind!

The crates we prefer are the wooden ones with removable side panels. These wooden crates are ideal for cold weather, with the panels in place; and they work equally well during hot weather when the solid panels are removed, leaving just the wired sides for better air circulation. Crates made entirely of wire are all right in the summer, but they provide no protection from drafts or winter chills. I intensely dislike aluminum crates because aluminum reflects surrounding temperatures. If it is cold, so is the metal of the crate. If it is hot, that too is reflected, sometimes to the point that one's fingers can be burnt when handling it. For this reason I consider them unsuitable.

When you select the puppy's crate, be certain that it is roomy enough not to be outgrown as he matures. He should have sufficient height to stand up comfortably when fully grown and sufficient area to stretch out full length when relaxed. When the puppy is young, give him shredded newspapers as his first bed. In time, the newspapers can be replaced with a mat or turkish towels. Carpet remnants are great for the bottom of the crate, as they are inexpensive and in case of accidents can be easily replaced. Once the dog has matured past the chewing stage, a pillow or a blanket, for something soft and comfortable, is an appreciated luxury in the crate.

Sharing importance with the crate is a safe area where the puppy can exercise and play. If you have a yard of your own (and you should have for a Sporting Dog), then an area should be fenced in so that the dog can be left safely outside. Labs need outdoor activity and, if at all possible, the fenced area should be ready and waiting for your Lab puppy upon his arrival at

The darling blond baby in the middle is future Ch. Briary Barley owned by Hart Lake Labradors, Illinois.

your home. It need not be a vast area, but it needs to be safe and secure and comfortable, with at least some of the area shaded. If you have close neighbors, stockade fencing works out well; then the neighbors are less aware of the dog and the dog cannot see everything passing near the area at which to bark up a storm. If you are in the country with lots of space between you and other families, then regular chain-link fencing is fine. Please do not feel, however, that the fenced area will provide your dog with all the exercise necessary, even if you have just the one dog. A dog alone seldom romps and plays in a fenced yard. Just watch, and you will see him or her roam leisurely around for a while, sniffing and investigating things, and then sit down.

Crate training Highland puppies. Every dog should be raised to enjoy being in a crate and to look upon it as a refuge and his own special place. George and Lillian Knobloch own these babies.

Two or more dogs out together will romp and play, at least to some extent, but even they should have additional exercise. Plan to take your puppy or grown dog for at least one good walk each day (more if you have the time). And also plan on some play periods when you or a member of the family will romp, play ball, or otherwise move the dog about a bit. Play periods with a person are important for both exercise and socialization.

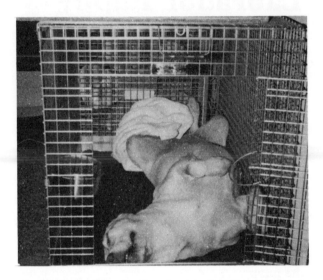

Scrimshaw Clearly An Angel, C.D.X., T.D.X., is hereby putting to rest the assumption that keeping "a dog in a cage" is cruel. If crate training is started at an early age, your Lab will grow to love this safe and comfortable place of his own. Barbara Barfield. Scrimshaw Labs.

Have the fenced area planned and installed *before* bringing home the puppy if you possibly can do so. That is far more sensible than putting it off until perhaps an unfortunate accident occurs. As an absolute guarantee that a dog cannot dig its way out under a fence, an edging of cinder blocks tight against the inside bottom of the fence is very practical protection. If there is an outside gate, a key and padlock are a *must* and should be *used at all times*. You do not want the puppy set free in your absence, either purposely or through carelessness. I have often seen people go through a gate in a fence and then just leave the gate ajar. So for safety's sake, keep the gate *locked* so that only responsible people have access to its opening.

These young Spenrock Labs appear to be asking, "What's going on out there?"

When you go to pick up your Lab, you should take a collar and lead with you. Both of these items should be appropriate for the breed and age of the dog, and the collar should be one that fits him now, not one he has to grow into. Your new Lab also needs a water dish (or two—one for the house, the other for his yard) and a food dish. These should preferably be made from an unbreakable material. You will have fun shopping at your local pet shop for these things, and I am sure will be tempted to add some luxury items of which you will find a fascinating array. For chew things, either Nylabones or real beef bones (leg or knuckle cut to an appropriate size, the latter found for soup bones at most butcher shops or supermarkets) are safe and provide many hours of happy entertainment, at the same time being great exercise during the teething period.

The ultimate convenience, of course, is if there is a door in your house situated so that the fence can be installed around it, thereby doing away with the necessity for an outside gate. This arrangement is ideal, because then you need never be worried about the gate being left unlatched. This arrangement will be particularly appreciated during bad weather when, instead of escorting the dog to wherever in the yard his fenced area may be, you simply open the door and let him directly into his safe yard.

Tug of war! Alex and Arec are nine weeks old. Nancy M. Scholz of New York, owner.

Chocolate Lab puppies at Hywater Kennels, Bob and Brenda Matthews, New York.

Rawhide chews can be safe, too, if made under the proper conditions. There was a problem, however, several years back owing to the chemicals with which some of the rawhide chew products had been treated, so in order to take no chances, avoid them. Also avoid plastic and rubber toys, *particularly* toys with squeakers. If you want to play ball with your Lab, select a ball that has been made of very tough construction for that purpose; Labs have strong jaws. And even then do not leave the ball with the puppy alone; take it with you after every game. There are also some nice "tug of war" toys which are fun when you play with the dog. But again, do not go off and leave them to be chewed.

Stonecrest Lab puppies belonging to George and Louise White, Rhode Island. Photographed by Claire White-Peterson.

Too many changes all at once can be difficult and upsetting for the puppy. Therefore, no matter how you eventually wind up doing it, for the first few days keep him as nearly as you can to the routine he is used to. Find out what brand of food the breeder used, how frequently the puppies were fed and at what times, and start out by doing it that way yourself, gradually over a period of a week or two making whatever changes suit you better.

Of utmost precedence in planning for your puppy is that you select and become acquainted with a veterinarian that you can trust. If the breeder comes from your immediate area, ask him or her for suggestions. If not, discuss it with your dog-owning friends, getting names and comments from them. Then select the one most of the people whose opinion you respect have spoken of favorably and make an appointment to stop in for a moment at his office. If you like him (or her) and feel confident that it is a wise choice, make an appointment to bring the puppy in to be checked over on your way home from the breeder's. Be sure to obtain the puppy's health certificate from the breeder, along with information regarding worming, shots, and so on.

With all of these things in order, you should be nicely prepared for a smooth, happy start when your puppy actually joins the family.

Yellow Lab puppies typical of the quality produced at Stonecrest Kennels, George and Louise White, Rhode Island.

Joining the Family

Remember that as exciting and happy as the occasion may be for you, the puppy's move from his place of birth to your home can be a traumatic experience for him. So very many changes are involved! His mother and littermates will be missed. He will very likely, since he is a baby, be slightly frightened or even awed by the change of surroundings. The person he trusted and upon whom he has depended since birth will be gone. Everything, thus, should be planned to make the move easy for him, to give him confidence, to make him realize that yours is a pretty nice place to be after all.

Never bring a puppy home on a holiday. There just is too much going on, with people and gifts and excitement. If he is honoring "an occasion" (a birthday, for example), work it out so that his arrival will be several days ahead of time or, better still, a day or two after the occasion. Then he will be greeted by a normal routine and will have your undivided attention.

Killingworth's Samian at three months of age sharing a Nylabone® with Caesar. According to the owner, the Lab and the bird became quite friendly. Lorraine Robbenhaar, Connecticut.

Don't you really have to love a Lab puppy? This one belongs to Mary Manuel.

Early in the day is the best time to bring the puppy home, in order to give him a chance to look things over and settle in a bit before bedtime. You will have a more peaceful night's sleep that way, I am sure! Allow the puppy to investigate his new surroundings under your careful eye. If you already have a pet as part of your household, be watchful and be diplomatic. You want them to get on well together, so do not create any jealousy by petting and fussing over the newcomer while ignoring your already established pet. Share your attention between them, so that the relationship gets off to a friendly start. Much of the future attitude of each toward the other will depend on what takes place that first day.

If you have children, again it is important that the relationship start out well. Should this puppy be their first pet, it is assumed that you will have prepared them for it with a firm explanation that puppies are living creatures to be treated with gentle consideration, not playthings to be abused and hurt. One of my friends raised her children with the household rule that should a dog or puppy belonging to the children bite one of the children, the child would be punished, not the dog, as Mother would know that the child had in some way hurt the dog. I must say that this strategy worked out very well, as no child was ever bitten in that household and both daughters grew up to remain great animal lovers. Anyway, on whatever terms you do it, please bring your children up not only to *love* but also to *respect* their pet, with the realization that dogs also have rights. These same ground rules should apply to visiting children, too. I have seen youngsters who are fine with their own pets unmercifully tease and harass pets belonging to other people. Children do not always realize how rough is too rough, and without intending to, they may inflict considerable pain or injury if permitted to ride herd on a puppy.

If you start out by spoiling your pet, your puppy will expect and even demand that you continue to spoil it in the future. So think it out carefully before you invite the new puppy to spend its first night there in bed with you, unless you wish to continue the practice. What you had considered to be a one night stand may be accepted as just great and expected for the future. It is better not to start bad habits which you may find difficult to overcome later.

Treecroft Bamboo with Shannon Nickerson. Both belong to Carole T. Nickerson, Carho Kennels, Canada.

Socializing is important in raising well-adjusted puppies. These six-week-olds belong to Nancy M. Scholz of New York.

Socialization and Training

Socialization and training of your new puppy actually starts the second you walk in the door with him, for every move you make should be geared toward teaching the puppy what is expected of him and at the same time building up his confidence.

The first step is to teach the puppy his name and to come when called. No matter how flowery or long or impressive the actual registered name may be, the puppy should have a short, easily understandable "call name" which can be learned quickly and to which he will respond. Start using this call name immediately, and use it in exactly the same way each time that you address the puppy, refraining from various forms of endearment, pet names, or substitutes which will only be confusing to him.

Using his name clearly, call the puppy over to you when you see him awake and looking about for something to do. Just a few times of this, with a big fuss over what a "good dog" he is when he responds, will teach him to come to you when he hears that name; he knows that he will be warmly greeted and petted.

As soon as he has had a few hours to get acquainted, you can put a light collar on the puppy, so that he will become accustomed to having it on. He may hardly notice it, or he may make a great fuss at first, rolling over, struggling, and trying to rub it off his neck. Have a tasty tidbit or two on hand with which to divert him at this period, or try to divert his attention by playing with him. Soon he will no longer be concerned about the strange new thing around his neck.

The next step in training is to have the puppy become accustomed to the lead. Use a lightweight lead, attached to the collar. Carry him outdoors where there will be things of interest to investigate; then set him down and see what happens. Again, he may appear hardly to notice the lead dangling behind him, or he may make a fuss about it. If the latter occurs, repeat the diversion attempts with food or a toy. As soon as he has accepted the presence of the lead, hold the end of it and follow him about. He may react by trying to free himself, struggling to slip out of the whole thing or trying to bite at the lead. Try to coax him with kind words and petting. In a few moments, curiosity regarding his surroundings and an interesting smell or two should start

What a darling Lab baby! This one is sired by Am., Can. Ch. Riverroad's Summerstraw owned by Mrs. Frank G. Thomas of Illinois.

A little fellow with a very large bone! One of the Spenrock puppies.

diverting him. When this happens, do not try at first to guide his direction; just be glad that he is walking with the lead on and go where he wishes. When he no longer seems to resent the lead, gently try to direct him with a quick, short little tug in the direction you wish him to follow. Never jerk him roughly, as then he will become frightened and fight harder; and never pull steadily, as this immediately starts a battle of wills with each of you pulling in an opposite direction. The best method is a short, quick, and gentle jerk, which, repeated a few times, should get him started off with you. Of course, continue to talk encouragingly to him and offer him "goodies" until he gets started. Repetition of the command "Come" should accompany all of this.

Once he has mastered this step and walks along nicely on the lead, the next step is to teach him to follow on your left-hand side. Use the same process as you used to teach him to respond correctly while on the lead, this time repeating the word "Heel." Of course, all of this is not accomplished in one day, or even in two; it should be done gradually, with lots of encouragement and praise, making him feel that he is having fun and pleasing you. The exact length of time it will take to lead-train a puppy depends largely on the personality and aptitude of the individual puppy.

Am. Ch. Kimvalley Deborah at six months of age. Owned by Diana Beckett, Kimvalley Labradors.

"Share and share alike." Springfield's Family Fetcher at ten weeks of age with his little friend Donna. Fetcher has never snapped or growled at Donna, and she steals food right out of his mouth. Fetcher belongs to A.C. Williams of Fort Nelson, British Columbia, Canada.

Housebreaking a puppy is more easily accomplished by the prevention method than by the cure. Try to avoid "accidents" whenever you can rather than punishing the puppy once they have occurred. Common sense helps a great deal. The puppy will need to be taken out, or to the newspaper, at regularly spaced intervals: first thing in the morning directly from his bed, immediately after meals, after he has napped, or whenever you notice that he is "looking for a spot." Choose roughly the same place outdoors each time you take the puppy out for this purpose, so that a pattern will be established. If he does not go immediately, do not return him to the house as chances are he will go the moment he gets inside the door. Try to remain out with him until you get results; then praise him mightily and both of you can return indoors. If you catch the puppy having an "accident," pick him up firmly, rush him outside, and sharply say, "No!" If you do not see the accident occur, there is little point of doing anything beyond cleaning it up, as once it has happened and been forgotten, the puppy will not likely even realize why you are angry with him.

Your Labrador puppy should form the habit of spending a certain amount of time each day in his crate, even when you are home. Sometimes the puppy will do this voluntarily, but if not, he should be taught to do so. Lead the puppy by the

collar to the crate, and then gently push him inside the crate, firmly saying "Down" or "Stay" as you fasten the door. Whatever command you use, always make it the same word for each act every time. Repetition is the big thing in training, and the dog must learn to associate a specific word or phrase with each different thing he is expected to do. When you mean "Sit," always say exactly that. "Stay" should mean that the dog should remain where he received the command. "Down" means something else again. Do not confuse the dog by shuffling the commands, as you will create a problem for yourself by having done so.

As soon as he has received his immunization shots, take your Lab puppy with you wherever and whenever possible. Nothing can equal this close association for building up self-confidence and stability in a young dog. It is extremely important that you take the time to socialize your puppy properly, particularly if you are planning on the puppy becoming a show dog.

Spenrock Dolphin, shown here at three months of age, is a son of Janet Churchill's Ch. Rivermist Tweed of Spenrock. Mr. and Mrs. William Gosnell, owners, Pittsburgh, Pennsylvania.

An adorable Lab puppy contemplates the world. Owned by Nancy M. Scholz of New York.

Take your Lab in the car, so that he will enjoy riding and not become carsick, as can happen to a dog unused to the motion of riding. Take him everywhere you go, provided you are sure he will not be unwelcome or create any difficulties: visiting friends and relatives (if they do not have house pets of their own that may resent the intruder), to busy shopping centers (always keeping him on the lead), or just walking around the streets of your town. If someone admires him, as

At three-and-a-half months age, Spenrock's Chief Candor sits pensively staring out over the water. By Ch. Rivermist Tweed of Spenrock ex Spenrock Egyptian Candor. Breeder, Susan Powers of Indiana. Owner, Susie Crum of Illinois.

always seems to happen under these circumstances, encourage that person to pet or talk to him. Socialization of this type brings out the best in your puppy, helping him to grow up with a relaxed, outgoing, easy personality, liking the world and its inhabitants. The most debilitating thing for a puppy's self-confidence is excessive sheltering and pampering. Keeping the puppy always away from strange people and strange dogs may well turn him into a nervous, neurotic dog. So don't do it!

Trent, Tiffany, and Tanya, three eight-week-old Labs from Manora Kennels, Nancy M. Scholz.

Going out for their first swim in the ocean at three months of age, Chs. Casadelora's Dream Weaver, Undercover Angel, and Burch Magic with their owners, Mr. and Mrs. W.E. Brown, Casadelora Labs, Canada.

Make obedience training a game with your puppy while he is extremely young. Try to teach him the meaning of and expected response to such basics as "Come," "Stay," "Sit," "Down," and "Heel," along with the meaning of "No" even while he is still too young for formal training, and you will be pleased and proud of the good manners that he will exhibit. Labs are intelligent dogs, so take advantage of that fact right from the beginning.

This is Stonecrest's Sailing Kraft doing his bit for a favorite product. Stonecrest Labs, owners, George and Louise White. Photograph by their daughter, Claire White-Peterson.

Feeding

There was a time when providing nourishing food for our dogs involved a far more complicated routine than people now feel is necessary. The old school of thought was that the daily rations should consist of fresh beef, vegetables, cereal, egg yolks, and cottage cheese as basics, with such additions as brewer's yeast and vitamin tablets.

Spenrock puppies sired by imported son of Eng., Am. Ch. Lawnwood's Hot Chocolate, Lawnwood's Kunta, ex Spenrock Pitts Special. Breeder-owner, Janet Churchill.

During recent years, however, many attitudes have changed regarding this procedure. We still give eggs, cottage cheese, and supplements to the diet, but the basic methods of feeding dogs have changed; and the changes are, in the opinion of many authorities, definitely for the better. The school of thought now is that you are doing your dogs a service and a favor when you feed them some of the fine, commercially prepared dog foods in preference to your own homecooked concoctions.

The reason behind this new outlook is easy to understand. The production of dog food has grown to be a major industry, participated in by some of the best-known and most respected names in the dog fancy. These trusted firms turn out excellent products, so people are feeding dog food preparations with confidence—and the dogs are thriving. What more could one ask?

These Lab puppies, having a drink of milk after their meal, belong to Moorwood Kennels in New York.

300

There are at least half a dozen absolutely top-grade dry foods which can be mixed with water or broth and served to your dog according to the directions given on the package. There is a variety of canned meats, and there are several kinds of "convenience foods," those in a packet which you open and shake out into the dog's dish. It is just that simple. The "convenience foods" are new and are very neat and easy when you are away from home, but generally speaking we prefer to use a dry food mixed with hot water or soup and meat. We also feel that the canned meat, with its added fortifiers, is more beneficial to dogs than fresh meat. However, the two can be used alternately or, if you prefer and your dog does well on it, by all means use ground beef. A dog enjoys variety in the meat part of his diet, which is easy to provide with the canned food. The canned meats available include all sorts of beef (chunk, ground, stewed and so on), lamb, chicken, liver, a blend of five meats, and even such combinations as liver and egg. With new additions to this assortment appearing periodically from one manufacturer or another, your dog can enjoy quite a varied menu.

There also is prepared food geared to every age bracket of your dog's life, from puppyhood to old age, with special additions or modifications to make it especially nourishing and beneficial. The dogs of yesterday never had it so good during the canine dinner hour because these foods are tasty and geared to meet the dog's gastronomic approval.

Additionally, contents and nutritional values are clearly listed on the labels, and careful instructions for feeding just the right amount for the size and weight of each dog are also given.

With the great choice of dog foods available today most people do not feel that the addition of vitamins is necessary; but if you do, there are several excellent vitamin products available at pet shops. These products serve as tasty treats in addition to being beneficial.

Of course, there is no reason not to cook up something for your Lab to eat if you would feel happier doing so, but it seems to us unnecessary when such truly satisfactory rations are available with so much less trouble and expense.

How often you feed is a matter of how a schedule works out best for you. Many owners prefer to feed their dog once a day. I personally think that two small meals are better for the digestion and more satisfying to the dog, particularly if yours is a household member who stands around and watches the preparation of family meals. Do not overfeed; overfeeding is the shortest route to all sorts of problems, and it should be especially guarded against with Labs lest you suddenly find yourself with a very overweight dog.

Full tummies—sleepy pups! Suzie Spencer took this photo of some of the Campbellcroft babies, these from Ch. Leyward Softly Softly at Lawnwood ex Ch. Campbellcroft's Pede, C.D., W.C. Donald and Virginia Campbell, owners, California.

Until they are about twelve weeks old, fully weaned puppies should be fed four times daily. Each morning and evening, a Lab pup would need about one and a half to two cups of puppy kibble soaked in about a cup, or slightly less, of hot water, soup, or broth, mixed with a half can or so of beef or about a quarter pound of ground raw beef. Exact amounts for the age and weight of your puppies will be on the kibble wrapper. At noon and before bedtime, about three-quarters of a can of evaporated milk (up to a full can) mixed with an equal amount of water and an addition of some dry kibble can be given.

As the pups grow older, from three to six months of age, cut to three meals, increasing the size of each accordingly, in keeping with the directions on the package. The amount of meat for each meal now should be doubled. From six months to a year old, the pups can switch to one meal daily if you wish, although most people prefer keeping them on two meals until they are a year old. If you do feed just once daily, do so by early afternoon at the latest and give the dog a snack or biscuit at bedtime.

Remember that fresh, cool water should always be available to your dog. This is of utmost importance to his good health.

Nap-time! These baby Labs belong to Casadelora Kennels, Mr. and Mrs. W.E. Brown, British Columbia, Canada.

Grooming

Keeping your Labrador looking tidy and well groomed is in no way a difficult task to perform. A good brushing every few days (daily, if you have the time) is all that his coat will need. We do not advocate frequent bathing of Labs as this will soften the coat, which is undesirable in the breed. Emergencies may arise, of course, when a bath is a must; but whenever possible, avoid bathing your Lab. Even if he comes home covered with mud, just let the mud dry and it will readily brush or shake off, leaving him quite clean.

First lesson in being groomed—obviously unwelcome from the "I'm not going to like this" expression on the puppy's face. Rosalind B. Moore, Moorwood Labs, owner.

If you do have to bathe your dog, be sure to protect his eyes with a drop of castor oil in each and protect his ears with a small wad of cotton; you want to keep soap and water out of both. Use either a good baby shampoo or, better yet, one of the especially prepared dog shampoos which also contain a flea and tick repellent. Start lathering behind the ears and work to the back of the dog. Be certain to rinse the dog *very thoroughly*, as soap residue can be irritating and cause the dog to scratch and possibly start skin problems.

Nails should be clipped regularly. Just think how uncomfortable or painful walking on long, curled toenails can be, not to mention the damage thus done to the foot structure and the pasterns. If your dog does not exercise regularly on cement or concrete, by which nails are naturally filed down, you must attend to this for him with nail clippers or an electric file, whichever works out best for you.

Ch. Angus of Wayland as a puppy. Sired by Helen Ginnel's Ch. Whygin Poppitt.

For good health and well-being, ears should be checked and cleaned out regularly with a cotton swab. Peroxide is good to use for this purpose. If you notice any indications of an infection or other problem, have your veterinarian recommend a treatment appropriate for the specific condition. An ear problem might also be indicated if your dog continually holds his head to one side or shakes his head a great deal; prompt attention should be given to either of these symptoms.

Ch. Spenrock Skylane as a handsome young puppy. Albert Prest and Janet Churchill, owners.

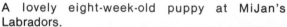
A lovely eight-week-old puppy at MiJan's Labradors.

A chocolate puppy at Groveton Labradors, Mrs. Eileen Ketcham of New York, owner.

These seven-week-old babies were sired by the English import, Am. Ch. Lawnwood's Brands Hatch and were bred by Agber Labradors, Agnes Cartier, New Jersey.

Seven weeks old, by Ch. Lobuff's Seafaring Banner. Lobuff Labs, Jerry and Lisa Weiss, New York.

Another heart-melting puppy picture from Shababaland Labradors, Gordon Sousa, Jr., New Jersey.

Ch. Timmbrland Golden Star, by Ch. Royal Oaks V.I.P. O'Shamrock Acres ex Ch. Starline Mecca of Timmbrland, is the Top Point Winning Yellow Labrador in the history of the breed, having defeated more than 25,000 dogs on the Group and Best in Show level. His grandsire, Ch. Shamrock Acres Light Brigade, remains the Top Best in Show Labrador as well as the Top Producing Labrador Sire. Here Golden Star is pictured winning Best in Show at Cincinnati Kennel Club, May 1978, judged by Mr. Haworth Hoch. Owned by Ambersand Labradors, Janet Stolarevsky, Dexter, Michigan.

Ch. Franklin's Hickory Grove, handled by Dick Cooper, wins the Sporting Group at Ingham County 1972, under judge Peter Knoop. This Top Labrador Bitch and Third Top Labrador for 1973 was sired by Ch. Shamrock Acres Light Brigade ex Ch. Tully of Burywood. Owned by Mrs. Bernard W. Ziessow, Franklin Labradors, Franklin, Michigan.

Opposite, above: Obedience Trial Ch. Shakespeare's Trixie with Jimmy Wilson, her owner's son, then two years old. Owned by Margaret S. Wilson, Damascus, Maryland. **Below:** Moorwood Beaver's Patience, born June 1979, by Ch. Sandylands Markwell of Lockerbie ex Ch. The Black Baroness. Judge, Mrs. Maxwell. Rosalind B. Moore, owner, Moorwood Kennels, Indian Lake, New York.

Am., Can. Ch. Seaward's Adonis of Rupert, Number Four Labrador 1980 and 1981, *Kennel Review* system. Owned by Seaward Kennels, Manchester Center, Vermont; bred by Dorothy B. Howe; handled by Gerlinde V. Hockla.

Opposite: Ch. Coal Creek's Perish of Char-Don, by Ch. Coal Creek's Briary Breakthru ex Ch. Scrimshaw My Sin, taking Best of Breed at age 19 months at Chico Dog Fanciers. Handled by Ellen Lofgaard. Currently Number Five Lab in the U.S., *Canine Chronicle* system. Bred by Debbie Sharpsteen, Coal Creek Kennels. Owned by Janet Schoonover, Char-Don Kennels.

BEST OF
BREED
CHICO
DOG FANCIERS
JUNE 1981
FOX FOTO

Ch. Lobuff's Candy Dancer, reserve at the National just before finishing under Mrs. Mary Roslin-Williams (Mansergh Labs), by Ch. Almar's Bobo Quivari ex Ch. Spenrock's Cognac. Owned by Lobuff Labradors, Jerry and Lisa Weiss, Huntington, New York.

Champion Chebacco J. Robert, doubly descended from Ch. Hugger Mugger, is owned by Mary Swan. Pictured taking Reserve Winners at the Labrador Retriever Club of Potomac Specialty in 1980.

Ch. Mibar's Bonnie I Like Ike won the first Mid-Jersey Labrador Retriever Club Specialty in 1980. A very handsome Labrador owned by Ira and Judy Goldstein.

Ch. Labradese Sundance Kid, handled by Scott Willsey, left, and Ch. Labradese Came the Dawn with owner-breeder Billie Hines. Littermates by Ch. Labradese Lancelot O'Longbow ex Labradese Bluebelle Bouquet, bred by Dr. William A. and Mrs. Billie Hines. Sundance Kid is co-owned by Dr. and Mrs. Hines with Dan and Julie Nuchols of Sundance Labs and Jim and Karen Case of Sunny Labs.

Ch. MiJan's All That Jazz, by Ch. Jayncourt Ajoco Justice ex Ch. Lockerbie MiJan's Britannia, taking Best of Breed at the Potomac Labrador Retriever Specialty. Owned by MiJan's Labradors, Joan and Tony Heubel and Mike and Janet Farmilette of New Jersey.

Opposite, above: Ch. Briary Barley, by Ch. Lockerbie Brian Boru, W.C., ex Briary Allegra, was Winners Dog under Mrs. Winifred Heckmann at the Labrador Retriever Club National Specialty in October 1976. Owned by Hart Lake Labradors, Bob and Kaye Peltonen, McHenry, Illinois. **Below:** Janet Churchill handles her handsome Ch. Spenrock Winds Aloft, by Ch. Spenrock Heatheredge Mariner and Ch. Spenrock Boomerang, to Best of Opposite Sex to Best in Sweepstakes at the Labrador Retriever Club of the Potomac in 1976. Well-known professional handler Mr. Bobby B. Barlow is the judge.

FIRST

Berman

Labrador Retriever Club of the Potomac
Specialty Show April 16th 1976
Judge Mr. Bobby B Barlow

Best of Opposite Sex
to Best
in Sweepstakes

Left: Am., Can. Ch. Rorschach's Royal Flush at 11 months. Bred by Jan and Jay Stielstra, this lovely youngster more than fulfilled the promise he then showed, as he became Number Nine Labrador Retriever in 1974 with six Group placements and 56 Bests of Breed. To date he has sired two champions, with several more pointed. Ambersand Labradors, owners, Jan Stolarevsky, Dexter, Michigan.

Below: Ch. Kimvalley Warrenton taking Best in Show under Anna K. Nicholas at Tampa Bay Kennel Club in 1977. D. Roy Holloway handled for Mrs. Robert D. Clark, Jr., Springfield Farm, Middlebury, Virginia.

Heaney's Ma-Pat-Ma Dream Cum Tru, bred and owned by Margaret D. Heaney, Derby, New York.

Heaney's Ma-Pat-Ma M'Boy Fitzgo, Best of Breed at Kennel Club of Buffalo 1975. M.D. Heaney, owner.

Ch. Amberfield's Beach Boy winning Best of Breed at Ox Ridge in 1980 under breeder-judge Mrs. Janet Churchill. Joy Quallenberg, handler. Amberfield Kennels, owners.

Opposite, above: Am., Can. Ch. Rorschach's Royal Flush, by Shamrock Norton of Burywood ex Ch. Royal Oaks Rorschach's Libido. Number Nine Labrador Retriever in 1974 with six Group placements and 56 Bests of Breed. Bred by Jan and Jay Stielstra and owned by Ambersand Labradors, Jan Stolarvsky. **Below:** Ch. Spenrock's Boomerang winning a five-point major from the Bred-by-Exhibitor Class at her first show. Sired by Ch. Rivermist Tweed of Spenrock ex Int. Ch. Spenrock Banner, W.C. Bred, owned and handled by Jan Churchill, Spenrock Labradors.

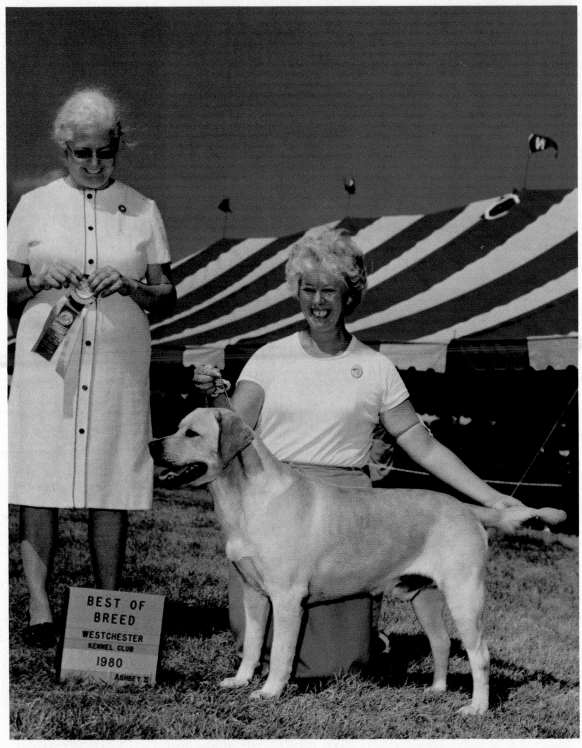

Ch. Poolstead Private Member winning Best of Breed at Westchester 1980. Mrs. Diana Beckett handled for owner Mrs. Robert D. Clark, Jr., Springfield Farm.

Devonwood's You Are My Sunshine, by Ch. MiJan's Corrigan ex Follytower Joy, owned by Lyric Labradors, Dennis and Sue Simon, New Jersey.

Two lovely young hopefuls at Shababaland Labradors owned by Gordon W. Sousa, Jr.

Braunayr's Kimo at Pinerock, seven weeks old. Bruce and Sandra Derby, Ontario, Canada.

Springfield's Family Fetcher, littermate to Ch. Springfield's Fanny Sweet Adams, is owned by A.C. Williams, Fort Nelson, British Columbia, Canada.

An eleven-week-old puppy of exceptional merit. This is Hywind's Yellow W of Windsong, photographed in July 1981, owned by Mrs. Barbara B. Gill, Hywind Labradors, Michigan.

Ch. Jayncourt Follow Mee, yellow male English import by Sandylands Charlie Boy ex Jayncourt Never, bred by Mr. and Mrs. Palmer Without and owned by Barbara Barfield and Richard Oster. Pictured at eight-and-a-half years of age having just won both the Stud Dog and the Veteran Classes at Labrador Retriever Club of Greater Boston, June 1980, under breeder-judge Anne Simoneau. Barbara Barfield handling, Scrimshaw Labradors, New Hampshire.

CHAPTER TEN

Showing Your Labrador Retriever

Frank Jones has loaned us this photo from the 1965 Lab National Specialty. On the left is Ch. Sam of Blaircourt; on the right is Ch. Rupert John Glenn.

The groundwork for showing your Lab has been accomplished with your careful selection and purchase of your future show prospect. If it is a puppy, we assume that you have gone through all the proper preliminaries of good care, which actually should be the same whether the puppy is a pet or a future show dog, with a few extra precautions in the latter case.

General Considerations

Remember that a winning dog must be kept in trim, top condition. You want him neither too fat nor too thin, so do not spoil his figure and his appearance, or his appetite for proper nourishing food, by allowing family members or guests to be constantly feeding him "goodies." The best "treat" of all is a small wad of ground raw beef or the packaged dog "goodies." To be avoided are ice cream, potato chips, cookies, cake, candy, and other fattening items which will cause the dog to gain weight. A dog in show condition must never be fat, nor must he be painfully thin to the point of his ribs fairly sticking through the skin. Remember that with a Lab, what he is is what you see. There are no heavy fringings to cover up any part of his anatomy; thus it is of particular importance that his figure be correct.

The importance of temperament and showmanship cannot possibly be overemphasized. These two qualities have put many a mediocre

dog across, while lack of them can ruin the career of an otherwise outstanding specimen. So, from the day your dog or puppy arrives home, socialize him. Keep him accustomed to being with people and to being handled by people. Encourage your friends and relatives to "go over" him as the judges will in the ring, so that at the shows this will not be a strange, upsetting experience. Practice showing his "bite" (the manner in which his teeth meet) deftly and quickly. It is quite simple to spread the lips apart with your finger, and the puppy should be accustomed and willing to accept this from you or from the judge, without struggle.

Take your future show dog with you in the car, so that he will love riding and not become carsick when he travels. He should associate going in the car with pleasure and attention. Take him where it is crowded: downtown, shopping malls, or, in fact, anywhere you go where dogs are permitted. Make the expeditions fun for him by frequent petting and words of praise; do not just ignore him as you go about your errands or other business.

Do not overly shelter your future show dog. Instinctively you may want to keep him at home, especially while a young puppy, where he is safe from germs or danger, but this can be foolish on two counts. To begin with, a dog kept away from other dogs or other environment builds up no natural immunity against all the things with which he will come in contact at the dog shows. Actually it is wiser to keep him well up-to-date on all protective "shots" and then allow him to become accustomed to being among other dogs and dog owners. Also, a dog who never goes among people, to strange places, or among strange dogs, may grow up with a timidity of spirit that will cause you deep problems when his show career gets under way.

Assuming that you will be handling the dog personally, or even if he will be professionally handled, it is important that a few moments of each day be spent practicing dog show routine. Practice "stacking," or "setting him up," as you have seen the exhibitors do at the shows you've attended, and teach him to hold this position once you have him stacked to your satisfaction. Make the learning pleasant by being firm but lavish in your praise when he behaves correctly. Work in front of a mirror for setting up practice; this enables you to see the dog as the judge does and to learn what corrections need to be made by looking at the dog from that angle.

Spenrock Bearcat at six weeks of age. By Ch. Spenrock Heatheredge Mariner ex Ch. Spenrock Brown Bess. Breeder, Spenrock Kennels, owner Mary Manuel, Bakersfield, California.

Teach your Lab to gait at your side at a moderate rate of speed on a loose lead. When you have mastered the basic essentials at home, then look for and join a training class for future work and polishing up your technique. Training classes are sponsored by show-giving clubs in many areas, and their popularity is steadily increasing. If you have no other way of locating one, perhaps your veterinarian may know of one through some of his clients, but if you are sufficiently aware of the dog show world to want a show dog, you will probably be personally acquainted with other fanciers who will share information of this sort with you.

Accustom your show dog to being in a crate (which you should be doing, even if the dog is to be only a pet). He should be kept in the crate "between times" at the shows for his own well-being and safety.

A show dog's teeth must be kept clean and free of tartar. Hard dog biscuits can help toward this. If tartar does accumulate, see that it is removed promptly by your veterinarian. Bones are not suitable for show dogs once they have their second teeth as they tend to damage and wear down the tooth enamel (bones are all right for puppies, as they help with the teething process).

Grooming for the Show

In preparation for showing your dog, there are a few grooming hints which will enhance his appearance once you have the correct tools and have learned to use them properly.

Campbellcroft's Bardot at ten weeks of age is already doing well on the lead. Donald and Virginia Campbell, owners, California.

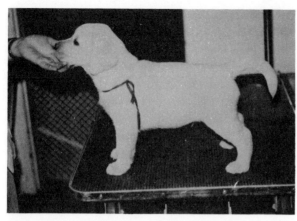

Scrimshaw Gorblimee, seven-week-old yellow male (by Ch. Jayncourt Follow Mee ex Ch. Scrimshaw Blue Nun), is illustrating training for the table and the lightweight ribbon collar that precedes the lead for your puppy. Owned by Clen Kennels, Austin, Texas. Bred and co-owned by Barbara Barfield.

The tools you will need for grooming are a hound glove, or mitt (for "polishing" the coat to look its best), a good quality soft hairbrush, a stripping comb, and both curved scissors (to use on the face) and fairly long straight scissors. You can purchase these from your pet shop. If you are not certain about choosing them, ask a more experienced friend to go with you to make the selection. You will also need nail clippers and/or a file.

Place the dog on a grooming table or on the top of his crate, so that you will be working at eye level. Start at the head by completely remov-

Mary Manuel of Bakersfield, California, owns this seven-week-old puppy, by Spenrock Bearcat ex Killingworth Lady Bug of Ahavahnee's.

ing whiskers with curved scissors made especially for this purpose. If the dog's neck is inclined toward a "throaty," or heavy, appearance, it can be improved a few days before the show by carefully stripping out some of the excess hair, using a special stripping comb which you can purchase for this purpose. Do a little at a time; then brush out and view the results. You can always take out more hair, but no one has yet discovered a way to return any, so do go slowly. If straggly hairs spoil the underline of the dog, they may be evened off neatly, using long scissors. Straggly hairs at the elbow should also be evened off for a tidy look.

Manora's Albert at nine weeks of age learning to pose nicely, "basic training" for future show dogs. Nancy M. Scholz owns this baby at her New York kennel.

With your scissors, very carefully round off the excess hair at the end of the tail.

Great caution and restraint should be exercised in removing hair from the hindquarters. Remember that the standard calls for powerful, muscular development of a Lab's rear, yet lately we have noticed a tendency to strip and/or scissor off far more than is becoming, causing the dog to look weak and underdeveloped behind, thrown out of balance in appearance by a scissors-happy groomer. Keep in mind that the least possible hair is what you wish to remove from the hindquarters, and brush the hair on the hindquarters *out from the dog (never flat for this purpose)*; then tidy up by scissoring off "stragglers."

These puppies are Lobuff's Seafaring Banner and Lobuff's Seagoing Lobo at three months of age. Owned and bred by Jerry and Lisa Weiss, Lobuff Kennels, handled here by Mollie B. Weiss, who is winning Best Brace in Match at the big Mid-Island Kennel Club Match show in February 1977.

Never leave the preparation of your dog for the ring until the last moment. The major portion of the grooming, particularly any stripping or scissoring, should be done four or five days in advance. The final brushing and rubdown should come nearer to the actual day of the show, along with a quick check for isolated whiskers or straggly hair which may have grown in during the short interval and which should be snipped off. You do *not* want the fact that the dog has been stripped out or scissored to be noticeable. You do *not* want the dog to look sculptured. You do *not* want scissors marks. Here is a classic example of "practice makes perfect," so try your hand at doing the dog up a few times well in advance of when he will be shown. Mistakes will grow out and fill in quickly, but obviously you do not want them to occur the night before the dog show.

If you are uncertain, or feel timid, about undertaking the pre-show coat work at first, try taking your dog to a professional handler whose Labs look well in the ring and have him or her do the dog for you a couple of times while you watch and learn how to do it yourself. The comparatively small expenditure will pay off for you should get the hang of it quite quickly; then you yourself can do it with greater confidence.

There is a difference of opinion between English and American fanciers regarding the amount of stripping or scissoring acceptable in Labs. The English prefer that the dogs be shown in an entirely natural state while the Americans do not object to grooming to bring out the best in a dog's appearance. Keep this in mind, however, when it is an English judge under whom you will be showing, as your dog may be penalized if any coat work has been done on it.

A few words of caution are appropriate here. If the Labrador you are planning to show is either chocolate or black, exercise the dog morning and evening rather than midday during the summer. Strong sunlight can fade the chocolate coat, turning it to an unpleasant washed-out color, while black coats can turn rusty as a result of overexposure to the sun's rays.

Your Lab's coat can be kept in immaculate condition by brushing him daily. Baths are seldom necessary under normal circumstances. But when you do bathe your Lab, use a mild baby shampoo or a shampoo especially prepared for dogs. Remember that bathing softens the coat, so should you feel that a bath is necessary, it is best to do it a couple of days ahead of showing your dog, rather than at the last moment. Two wise precautions are to put a drop of castor oil into each eye to prevent soap irritation and to put a wad of cotton in each ear so that no water goes into the ear cavity. Be sure to rinse the dog thoroughly and carefully.

Toenails should be examined and trimmed whenever necessary. It is important not to allow nails to grow long, as they will ruin the appearance of both the feet and pasterns.

Beyond these special considerations, your show prospect will thrive under the same treatment as accorded any other well-cared-for family pet. In fact, most of the above is applicable to a pet Labrador as well as to a show Labrador, for what it boils down to is simply keeping the dog at its best.

Match Shows

The first experience in show ring competition for your Lab puppy should be in match shows. There are several reasons for this. First of all, these events are intended as a learning experience for both the dog and the exhibitor. You will not feel self-conscious or embarrassed no matter how poorly your puppy acts up or how inept your initial attempts at handling may appear. The majority of the exhibitors present will be in the same position. So take the puppy and go, and the two of you can learn the ropes of actually being in competition.

Only on rare occasions is it necessary to make match show entries in advance, and even those with a "pre-entry" policy will usually accept entries at the door as well. Thus, you need not plan several weeks ahead, as is the case with point shows. Also, there is a vast difference in the cost, as match show entries cost less than five dollars, while entry fees for the point shows often cost over ten dollars, an amount none of us needs to waste until we have some idea of how the puppy will behave or how much more "pre-show training" is needed.

Match shows very frequently are judged by professional handlers who, in addition to making

Ambersand Lady Godiva, by Am., Can. Ch. Rorschach's Royal Flush ex Hollidaze Medea of Ambersand, getting off to an early start at ten weeks of age by taking Best Puppy in Match at the Huron River Labrador Retriever Club Specialty Match, September 14th 1980. One of the outstanding Labs from Ambersand Kennels, Jan Stolarevsky, Michigan.

the awards, are happy to help new exhibitors with comments and advice on their puppies, helpful hints on their grooming and preparation as well as their presentation in the ring. So avail yourself of all of these opportunities before heading out to the sophisticated world of the point shows.

Brother and sister at a Labrador Match Show. Highlands Regimental Brass and Highlands Regimental Piper at five-and-a-half months of age. Bred by Highlands Kennels in New Jersey. By Eng. Ch. Lawndale's Hot Chocolate ex Sambeau's Cam.

Winner of Best in Match, Labrador Retriever Club of Long Island, August 1981, was MiJan's Repeat Performance, by Ch. Jayncourt Ajoco Justice ex Ch. Lockerbie MiJan's Britannia. Bred by Anthony Heubel of Little Ferry, New Jersey, and owned by MiJan's Labs, Joan and Tony Heubel and Mike and Janet Farmilette.

Stepping smartly around the ring, two Lab puppies in the 9-12 month Puppy Class at the first Specialty Show of the Mid-Jersey Labrador Retriever Club, August 1980. Photo courtesy of Nancy M. Scholz.

Point Shows

Entries for American Kennel Club championship shows, "Point Shows," must be made in advance. This must be done on an official entry blank of the show-giving club. The entry must then be filed either in person or by mail with the show superintendent in time to reach the latter's office prior to the published closing date or the filling of the advertised quota. These entries must be made carefully, must be signed by the owner of the dog or the owner's agent (your professional handler), and must be accompanied by the entry fee; otherwise, they will not be accepted. Remember, it is not when the entry blank leaves your hands that counts but the date of arrival at its destination. If you are relying on the mails, keep in mind that they are not always reliable, so get the entry form off well in advance of the deadline.

Nancy Martin, the judge, takes a careful look at Spenrock Flying Circus in the Puppy Bitch Class at the Labrador National 1981.

A dog must be entered at a dog show in the name of the actual owner at the time of entry closing. If a registered dog has been acquired by a new owner, it must be entered in the name of the new owner in any show for which entries close after the date of acquirement, regardless of whether the new owner has or has not actually received the registration certificate indicating that the dog is recorded in his name. State on the entry form whether or not transfer application has been mailed to the American Kennel Club. It goes without saying that the latter should be promptly attended to when you purchase a registered dog.

Ch. Scrimshaw Blue Nun on the Cherry Blossom Circuit 1979 at 11 months of age, undergoing the scrutiny of breeder-judge George Bragaw. Bred and owned by Barbara Barfield, New Hampshire.

When you fill out your entry blank, type, print, or write clearly, paying particular attention to the spelling of names, correct registration numbers, and so on. Also carefully check the premium list to find out whether or not the Open Class, if that is what you are entering, is divided into three classes by color (Open, black; Open, yellow, and Open, chocolate) to be sure that your dog is entered in the correct one. All shows do not make this division, but Specialty events and those which draw exceptionally large entries generally do.

National Labrador Specialty 1982 in Mason, Ohio. Photo taken by Jenny Reynolds as her mother, Jan Churchill, flew over the show site in her Skymaster.

The Puppy Class is for dogs or bitches who are at least six months of age and under 12 months, were whelped in the United States, and are not champions. The age of a dog is calculated up to and inclusive of the first day of a show. For example, the first day a dog whelped on January 1st is eligible to compete in a Puppy Class at a show is July 1st of the same year; and he may continue to compete in Puppy Classes up to and including a show on December 31st of the same year, but he is *not* eligible to compete in a Puppy Class at a show held on or after January 1st of the following year.

This is the first class in which you should enter your puppy. In it, a certain allowance is made for the fact that they *are* puppies; thus, an immature dog or one displaying less than perfect showmanship will be less severely penalized than, for instance, in Open. When you enter a puppy, be sure to check the classification carefully, as some shows divide their Puppy Class into a 6 to 9 months old section and a 9 to 12 months old section.

The Novice Class is for dogs six months of age and over, whelped in the United States or Canada, which *prior to* the official closing date for entries have *not* won three first prizes in the Novice Class; any first prize at all in the Bred-by-Exhibitor, American-bred, or Open Classes; or one or more points toward championship. The provisions for this class are confusing to many people, which is probably why it is not more frequently used. A dog may win any number of first prizes in the Puppy Class and still retain eligibility for Novice. He may place second, third, or fourth not only in Novice on an unlimited basis but also in Bred-by Exhibitor, American-bred, and Open and still remain eligible for Novice. But he may no longer be shown in Novice when he has won three blue ribbons in that class, when he has won even one blue ribbon in either Bred-by-Exhibitor, American-bred, or Open, or a single championship point.

In determining whether or not a dog is eligible for the Novice Class, keep in mind that previous wins are calculated according to the official published date for closing of entries, not by the date on which you may actually have made the entry. So if, in the interim between the time you made the entry and the official closing date, your dog makes a win causing it to become ineligible for Novice, change your class *immediately* to another for which the Lab still will be eligible. The Novice Class always seems to have the least entries of any class; and therefore it is a splendid "practice ground" for you and your young Labrador while you both are getting the "feel" of being in the ring.

Bred-by-Exhibitor Class is for dogs whelped in the United States or, if individually registered in the American Kennel Club Stud Book, for dogs whelped in Canada that are six months of age or older, are not champions, and are owned wholly or in part by the person or by the spouse of the person who was the breeder or one of the breeders of record. Dogs entered in this class must be handled in the class by an owner or by a member of the immediate family of the owner. Members of an immediate family for this purpose are husband, wife, father, mother, son, daughter, brother, or sister. This is the class which is really the "breeders showcase," the one which breeders should enter with special pride, to show off their achievements.

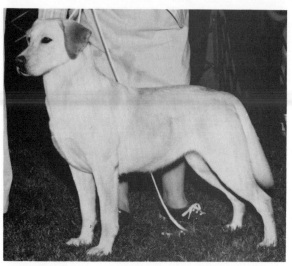

Ch. South Gate's Gator, C.D., an owner-handled homebred belonging to Sally P. Jennings, Connecticut. Gator, by Ch. Winroc Picaro, W.C., ex a daughter of Am., Can. Ch. Sebastian of Anderscroft C.D., gained her title from the Bred-by-Exhibitor Class.

The American-bred Class is for all dogs excepting champions, six months of age or older, that were whelped in the United States by reason of a mating which took place in the United States.

The Open Class is for any dog six months of age or older (this is the only restriction for this class). Dogs with championship points compete in it; dogs which are already champions can do so, dogs which are imported can be entered; and, of course, American-bred dogs compete in it. This class is, for some strange reason, the favorite of exhibitors who are "out to win." They rush to enter their pointed dogs in it, under the false impression that by so doing they assure themselves of greater attention from the judges. This really is not so; and it is my feeling

Ch. Meggin of South Gate W.C., owned by Charles W. Appleton of New Canaan, Connecticut, was handled entirely by her breeder, Sally P. Jennings, to such wins as Best of Breed at the Potomac Labrador Retriever Club Specialty the first time she was ever shown, in an entry of over 350 Labs including 39 champions! Meggin is used extensively in the field for water fowl and upland game birds. She is a thoroughly well-mannered house pet, and she is O.F.A. certified sound.

that to enter in one of the less competitive classes, with a better chance of winning it and then getting a second chance to gain the judge's approval by returning to the ring in Winners Class, can often be a far more effective strategy.

One does not enter for the Winners Class. One earns the right to compete in it by winning first prize in Puppy, Novice, Bred-by-Exhibitor, American-bred, or Open. No dog which has

Harwyn's Deirdre of Winterset at six months of age. By Ch. Spenrock Heatheredge Mariner ex Ch. Killingworth's Valiant Lady.

been defeated in one of these classes is eligible to compete in Winners, and every dog which has been a *blue-ribbon winner* in one of them *must* do so, provided that a dog which has placed first in one class was not entered in more than one class and defeated in another. Following the selection of the Winners Dog or the Winners Bitch, the dog or bitch receiving that award leaves the ring. Then the dog or bitch which placed second in the class, unless previously defeated by another dog or bitch in another class at the same show,

Agber's A Taste of Honey, shown by Joy Quallenberg in the exciting competition of Westminster, wound up taking Reserve Winners Bitch for owner, George W. Sousa, Jr., New Jersey.

Ebonylane's Cupie Doll, C.D.X., with breeder-handler Mike Lanctot winning Best Puppy in Group and Winners Bitch at Montreal.

re-enters the ring to compete against the remaining first-prize winners for Reserve. The latter award means that the dog or bitch receiving it is standing "in reserve" should the one that received Winners be disqualified or disallowed through any technicality when the awards are checked at the American Kennel Club. In that case, the dog or bitch who placed Reserve is moved up to Winners, at the same time receiving the appropriate championship points. So the Reserve award fulfills a definite purpose and is not entirely senseless, as some people evidently believe.

Winners Dog and Winners Bitch are the awards which carry with them points toward championship. The points are based on the number of dogs or bitches actually in competi-

tion; and the points are scaled one through five, the latter being the greatest number available to any one dog or bitch at any one show. Three-, four-, or five-point wins are considered majors. In order to become a champion, a dog or bitch must have won a minimum of two majors under two different judges, plus at least one point from

Ch. Franklin's Tally of Burywood, dam of 16 champions, on the day she became a champion. Top Producing Lab Bitch in the U.S. 1970, 1971, 1976, and 1977. Tally did not like being shown after she had gained three majors and needed just a single point to finish, but she did so for Gary Kingsbury, son of her co-owner. (Mrs. Ziessow and Mr. Kingsbury, owners.)

Can., Am. Ch. Killingworth Squire finishing his American championship with a five-point major. Marion Reid, owner.

When a dog or bitch is adjudged Best of Winners, its championship points are, for that show, compiled on the basis of which sex had the greater number of points. If there are two points in dogs and four in bitches and the dog goes Best of Winners, then *both* the dog and the bitch are awarded an equal number of points, in this case four. Should the Winners Dog or the Winners Bitch go on to Best of Breed, extra points are accorded for the additional Labs defeated by so doing, provided, of course, that there are entries specifically for Best of Breed competition, or Specials, as this is generally called.

If your dog or bitch takes Best of Opposite Sex after going Winners, points are credited accordingly in this case, too, the winner receiving credit for the number of Specials of his or her sex shown in addition to the points already gained by taking Winners. Many a one- or two-point win has turned into a major by this means!

Ch. Kimvalley Swing In going Best of Opposite Sex to Sam's Song at Westminster, with Diana Beckett handling for Springfield Kennels.

a third judge, and the additional points necessary to bring the total to 15. When your dog has gained 15 points as described above, a Certificate of Championship will be issued to you, and your Labrador's name will be published in *Pure-Bred Dogs American Kennel Gazette,* the official publication of the American Kennel Club.

The scale of championship points for each breed is worked out by the American Kennel Club and reviewed annually, at which time the number required in competition may be either changed (raised or lowered) or remain the same, depending on the average number of Labradors in competition at that period in various sections of the United States. The scale of championship points for all breeds is published annually in the May issue of the *Gazette,* and the current ratings for each breed within its area is published in the catalogue of every dog show at which championship points are offered.

Ch. Broad Reach Bittersweet placing in the Sporting Group at Shawnee Kennel Club 1979. Elsworth Howell judging, Roy Holloway handling. Martha Lee K. Voshell, owner, Broad Reach Labs, Virginia.

Moving further along, should your Labrador win its Variety Group from the classes (in other words, if it has received either Winners Dog or Winners Bitch along the way that day), you then receive points based on the greatest number of those awarded to any member of the Sporting Group at that event. Proceeding still further, should this dog or bitch then go on to win Best in Show, the same rule of thumb applies, and you will receive points equal in number to the greatest number awarded to any dog of any breed at that show.

Best of Breed competition consists of the Winners Dog and Winners Bitch, which automatically compete on the strength of those awards, plus whatever dogs or bitches have been entered specifically for this class, for which Champions of Record are eligible. Labs who, according to their owners' records, have completed the required number of championship points for a championship rating, whether or not they have been officially notified at the time entries closed, are eligible. Since July 1980, dogs who, according to their owners' records, have completed the requirements for a championship after the closing of entries for the show, but whose championships are unconfirmed, may be transferred from one of the regular classes to the Best of Breed

competition, provided this transfer is made by the show superintendent or show secretary *prior to the start of judging at the show.*

This has proved an extremely popular new rule, as under it a dog can finish on Saturday, then be transferred to Specials, and compete as such as Sunday. It must be emphasized that the change *must* be made *prior* to the start of the day's judging, which means prior to the start of *any* judging at the show, not only your individual breed.

Best of Breed winners are entitled to compete in the Variety Group which includes them; in the case of Labs, this is the Sporting Group. This competition is not mandatory, but it is a privilege which Lab exhibitors value. The dogs winning *first* in each Variety Group *must* compete for Best in Show.

Ch. Poolstead Purchaser, pictured winning the breed at Carroll Kennel Club in 1980, was imported and handled by Jane K. Forsyth for owners, the Richard Osters.

Non-regular classes are sometimes included at the all-breed shows, and they are almost invariably included at Specialty shows. These include Stud Dog Class and Brood Bitch Class, which are judged on the basis of the quality of the two offspring accompanying the sire and dam. The quality of the latter two is beside the point; it is the youngsters that count, and the qualities of *both* are averaged (two is the usual number of get permitted to compete) in deciding which sire or dam is the better and more consistent producer. Then there is the Brace Class (which, at all-breed shows, moves up to Best Brace in each Variety Group and eventually moves to Best Brace in Show), to be judged on the similarity and evenness of appearance of the two members of the brace. In other words, the Labs should look like identical twins in size, color, and conformation and should move together almost as a single dog, one person handling with precision and ease. The same applies to the Team competition except that four dogs are involved and, if necessary, two handlers.

The Veteran's Class is for the older dog, the minimum age of which is usually seven years. This class is judged on the quality of the dogs, as the winner competes in the Best of Breed com-

Ch. Jayncourt Follow Mee (Sandylands Charlie Boy ex Jayncourt Never Without) shown winning Stud and Veteran Classes at Labrador Retriever Club of Greater Boston Specialty, August 1980, under breeder-judge Anne Morgan Simoneau. Handled by Barbara Barfield, co-owner with Richard Oster. Bred by Mr. and Mrs. Palmer, England.

petition and, on a good number of occasions has been known to win it. So the point is *not* necessarily to pick out the *oldest* dog, as some seem to consider is correct, but the *best specimen of the breed*, exactly as throughout the regular classes.

Then there are Sweepstakes and Futurity Stakes, sponsored by many Specialty Clubs, sometimes as part of their Specialty shows and sometimes as separate events. The difference here is that Sweepstakes entries usually include dogs from 6 to 18 months of age, and entries are made at the usual time as others for that show, while for a Futurity the entries are bitches nominated when bred and the individual puppies at or shortly following their birth.

Junior Showmanship

If there is a youngster in your family between the ages of 10 and 17, I can suggest no better or more rewarding hobby than having a Lab to show in Junior Showmanship competition. This is a marvelous activity for young people. It teaches responsibility, good sportsmanship, the fun of competition where one's own skills are the deciding factor of success, proper care of a pet, and how to socialize with other young folks. Any youngster may experience the thrill of emerging from the ring a winner and the satisfaction of a good job done well.

Int. Ch. Spenrock Banner, W.C., and Ch. Lewisfield Spenrock Ballot, W.C., winning a Brace Class at Pittsburgh. Banner and Ballot were never defeated in Sporting Group Brace, winning this honor nine times. Always owner-handled by Janet Churchill.

Your Lab is an outstandingly satisfactory breed of dog for this purpose. His amiability and desire to please make him cooperative. And his comparatively simple show preparation make him an easy dog for a youngster to keep looking well to take into the ring.

Entry in Junior Showmanship Classes is open to any boy or girl who is at least 10 years old and under 17 years old on the day of the show. The Novice Junior Showmanship Class is open to youngsters who have not already won, at the time the entries close, three firsts in this class. Youngsters who have won three firsts in Novice may compete in the Open Junior Showmanship Class. Any junior handler who wins his third first-place award in Novice may participate in the Open Class, at the same show, provided that the Open Class has at least one other junior

Benched dog shows make for a long day. Jenny Reynolds helps pass the time for Ch. Tweed, owned by Spenrock Kennels.

Young Janet Churchill shows her Lab, Ch. Rivermist Tweed of Spenrock, under judge Ed Squires at the Mason Dixon Kennel Club. Later the same year, Janet and her Lab qualified for Junior Showmanship at the 1974 Westminster Kennel Club event.

handler entered in it. The Novice and Open Classes may be divided into Junior and Senior Classes. Youngsters between the ages of 10 and 12, inclusively, are eligible for the Junior division; and youngsters between 13 and 17, inclusively, are eligible for the Senior division. Any of the foregoing classes may be separated into individual classes for boys and for girls. If such a division is made, it must be indicated on the premium list. The premium list also indicates the prize for Best Junior Handler, if such a prize is being offered at the show. Any youngster who wins a first in any of the regular classes may enter the competition for this prize, provided the youngster has been undefeated in any class at that show.

Junior Showmanship Classes, unlike regular conformation classes in which the dog's quality is judged, are judged entirely on the skill and ability of the junior handling the dog. Which dog is best is not the point—it is which youngster does the best job with the dog that is under consideration. Eligibility requirements for the dog being shown and other detailed information can be found in *Regulations for Junior Showmanship*, issued by the American Kennel Club.

Ch. Spenrock Cognac, by Ch. Lockerbie Goldentone Jensen ex Ch. Spenrock Banner, taking Best of Opposite Sex handled by Mollie B. Weiss for Lobuff Kennels.

Ch. Ro Shan Fusby Sable Mont, a homebred from Canada's Ro-Shan Kennels, Mr. and Mrs. Tom Philip. Samuel Cappellina is handling here.

Ch. Linershwood Kalan, a grandson of Ch. Kimvalley Crispin, handled by D. Roy Holloway for Mrs. Robert V. Clark, Jr., Springfield Farm, Middleburg, Virginia.

Can. Ch. Ranchman's Medicine Man owned by Bert Van Niekirk taking Best of Breed at Trio Kennel Club in 1978.

Ch. Spenrock Baroke Buffet, by Ch. Spenrock Cajun ex Ch. Sandylands Mona Lisa, owned by Agnes Cartier.

Hart Lake Bart Maverick at one year. Bob and Kaye Peltonen, owners, Hart Lake Labs, Illinois.

Two sons of Gold Bullion at the Labrador Retriever Specialty in September 1963: Winners Dog, Ch. Shamrock Acres Sonic Boom, right, and Reserve, Whygin John Goose. Fine representatives of Helen Ginnel's Whygin breeding program at Bedford Hills, New York. Joseph C. Quirk is judging at this event.

Preparing for the Day of the Show

Preparation of the things you will need as a Labrador Retriever exhibitor should not be left until the last moment. They should be planned and arranged for at least several days prior to the show in order for you to be calm, relaxed, and ready for the big occasion when that day dawns.

The importance of the crate has already been mentioned, and we assume that one is already in use by your Lab. A grooming table is a useful commodity, because you can place your Lab on it for last minute touches prior to taking him into the ring and, of course, it is useful for working on your dog at home. If you do not have one already, folding tables with rubber tops are made specifically for the purpose and can be purchased from the concession booths at most dog shows. Then you will need a sturdy tack box

(also available at the show concessions) in which to carry your brush, comb, scissors, nail clippers, whatever you use for last minute clean-up jobs, cotton swabs, first-aid equipment, and anything else you are in the habit of using on the dog, such as a leash or two of the type you prefer and some well-cooked and dried-out liver or any of the small packaged dog treats for use in "baiting," or alerting, your dog in the ring.

Take a large thermos or cooler of ice, the biggest one you can accommodate, for use by "man and beast." Take a jug of water (there are lightweight, inexpensive ones available at all sporting goods shops) and a water dish. If you plan to feed the dog at the show, or if you and the dog will be away from home more than one day, bring food from home so that he will have the type to which he is accustomed.

You may or may not have an exercise pen. Personally, I think having one is a *must*, even if you only have one dog. While the shows do provide facilities for exercise of the dogs, these are among the best places to come into contact with any illnesses which may be going around, and I feel that having one of your own for your dog's use is excellent protection. Such a pen can be used in other ways, too, as a place other than the crate in which to put the dog to relax. And a pen should be used at motels and at rest areas when you wish to exercise the dog during your travels; it makes picking up after him very simple. Exercise pens too, are available at the show concession stands and come in a variety of sizes.

Bring along folding chairs for the members of your party, unless all of you are fond of standing, as these are almost never provided by the clubs. Have your name stamped or painted on the chairs so there will be no doubt as to whom the chair belongs. Bring whatever you and your family enjoy for drinks and snacks in a picnic basket or cooler, as show food, in general, is expensive, and usually not great. You should always have a pair of boots, a raincoat, and a rain hat with you (they should remain permanently in your vehicle if you plan to attend shows regularly), as well as a sweater, a warm coat, and a change of shoes. A smock or big cover-up apron will assure that you remain tidy as you prepare for the ring. Your overnight case should include a small sewing kit for emergency repairs, headache and indigestion remedies, and any personal products or medications you normally use.

In 1967, at Westbury Kennel Association, Mrs. Beatrice Godsol gives the top awards in Labs to Int. Ch. Spenrock Banner, W.C., owner-handled by Janet Churchill, left, and Ch. Lockerbie Kismet, owner handled by Helen Warwick.

In your car you should always carry maps of the area where you are headed and an assortment of motel directories. Generally speaking, we have found Holiday Inns to be the nicest about taking dogs. Some Ramada Inns and some Howard Johnsons do so cheerfully, but some have a "no dogs" policy; this should be checked out ahead of time. Quality Inns usually accept dogs, but Best Westerns generally frown on pets (not all of them, but enough to make it important that you find out which do). Some of the smaller chains welcome pets. The majority of privately owned motels do not.

Have everything prepared the night before the show to expedite your early morning departure. Be sure that your dog's identification and your judging program and other information are in your purse or briefcase. If you are taking sandwiches, have them ready. Anything that goes into the car the night before the show will be one thing less to be concerned with in the morning. Decide upon what you will wear and have it out and ready. If you are undecided about what to wear, try on the possibilities before the day of the show; don't risk feeling you may want to change when you see yourself dressed a few

Bda. Ch. Amanda of Mandalay, by Ch. Harrowby Todd ex Ch. Walden's Blackbird, C.D., handled by Mary Jane Ferguson to a good win at 14 months of age under judge William Spilstead. Julie Brown Sturman, Melrose Park, Pennsylvania, bred this excellent black bitch, by Ch. Harrowby Todd ex Ch. Walden's Blackbird, C.D., and sold her to Mrs. John Faiella.

Northwestern Connecticut, 1978. Mrs. Robert Tongren awarding Best of Breed to Am., Can. Ch. Forecast Witchita, granddaughter of Mallow Fanfare, owned by Forecast Labradors.

moments prior to departure time! Plan to wear a simple outfit, one that will not detract from your Lab. If he is black or chocolate, wear any light color to best show off and enhance his beauty. If he is yellow, then wear a darker color for the same reason. I have noted many well-dressed exhibitors who blend the color of their outfit with that of their dogs, which certainly looks pretty but which does *not* place emphasis on the *dog* as one should do at this time. Sport clothes always look best at a dog show. What you wear on your feet is important, as many types of floor are slippery, and wet grass, too, can present a hazard.

Make it a rule to wear rubber soles and low or flat heels in the ring for your own safety and so that you can move along freely.

Your final step in preparing for the day of the show is to leave yourself plenty of time to reach the show that morning. Traffic can be extremely heavy as one nears the immediate area of the show; parking places are usually difficult to find; and other delays may occur. You'll be in a calmer and better humor if you can take it all in your stride without the pressure of watching every second because you have figured the time too closely.

Highlands Bronze Chieftain is always eager to go off in the van to a dog show. One of the many fine Labs belonging to Lillian and George Knobloch, New Jersey.

Going to the Show

From the moment of your arrival at the dog show until after your Labrador has been judged, keep foremost in your mind that he is your purpose for being there. You will need to arrive in advance of the scheduled judging in order to take your dog out of his crate, play with him, exercise him, and give him time to get fully alert and awake. Be sure that he has a chance to attend to personal matters. A dog arriving in the ring and immediately using it as an exercise pen hardly makes a fond impression on the judge.

When you reach ringside, request your arm card from the steward and anchor it firmly into place on your arm. Make sure that you are where you should be when your class is called. The fact that you have picked up your arm card does not guarantee, as some seem to think, that the judge will wait for you more than a minute or two. Even though you may be nervous, assume an air of cool, collected calm. Remember—this is a hobby to be enjoyed, so approach it with that in mind. The dog will do better, too, because he will be quick to reflect your attitude.

If you make a mistake while presenting the dog, don't worry about it—next time you'll do better. Do not be intimidated by the more expert or experienced exhibitors. After all, they, too, were once newcomers.

Always show your Labrador with an air of pride. An apologetic attitude on the part of an exhibitor does little to help the dog win, so try to appear self-confident as you gait and set up the dog.

The judging routine usually starts when the judge asks that the dogs be gaited in a circle around the ring. During this period, the judge watches each dog as it moves along, forming his initial opinion. During this period, the judge notes style, topline, reach and drive, head and tail carriage, and general balance. While this is taking place, keep your mind and your eye on your dog, moving him at his most becoming gait and holding your place in line without coming up too close to the exhibitor ahead of you. Always keep your Lab on the inside of the circle, between yourself and the judge, so that the judge's view of the dog is unobstructed.

Calmly pose the dog when requested to set up for examination. If you are at the head of the line and many dogs are in the class, go all the way to the end of the ring before starting to stack the dog. Do not stop halfway down and begin setting up the dog. Consideration for others and plain good manners demand that sufficient space be left for the other dogs to be lined up along whatever side of the ring the judge has requested, so do not be a hog about it. The Labs should be spaced so that on all sides of the dog the judge will have room in which to make his examination; this means there must be sufficient space between each for the judge to move around. Time is important when you are setting up your Lab, as you want him to look right when the judge gets there, so practice in front of

Ch. Spenrock Windshift, by Ch. Eireannach Black Coachman ex Ch. Spenrock Winds Aloft, at Labrador Club of Potomac Specialty. Breeder, Jan Churchill. Handler, Jenny Reynolds. Owners, Mr. and Mrs. John Lentz. Also pictured is the judge Ted Eldredge.

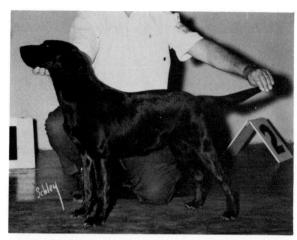

Ch. Whygin Gay Flapper at 13 months of age. Winners Bitch, Best of Opposite Sex for five points at Silver Bay Kennel Club, 1964. Owner, Helen Ginnel, Whygin Labradors.

a full-length mirror at home, as I have suggested, trying to accustom yourself to "getting it all together" correctly in the least possible length of time. When you set up your Lab, you want his forelegs well under the dog, feet directly below the elbows, toes pointed straight ahead, and hindquarters extended *correctly*, not overdone (stretched too far behind) or with the hindfeet further forward than they should be. Hold the dog's head up, with your hand either under the chin or at the back inner corner of the lips. You want the dog to look short-backed with head carried proudly, hindquarters nicely angulated, the front straight and true, and the dog standing firmly on his feet.

Listen carefully as the judge instructs the manner in which the dog is to be gaited, whether it is straight down and straight back; down the ring, across and back; or in a triangle. The latter has become the most popular pattern with most judges. "In a triangle" means down the outer side of the ring to the first corner, across that end of the ring to the second corner, and then back to the judge from the second corner, using the center of the ring in a diagonal line. Please learn to do this pattern without breaking in each corner to twirl the dog around you, a senseless maneuver we sometimes have noted. Judges like to see the dog in an *uninterrupted* triangle, as they get a better idea of the dog's gait.

It is impossible to overemphasize that the gait at which you move your Lab is tremendously important, and considerable thought and study should be given to the matter. At home, have someone move the dog for you at different speeds so that you can tell which shows him off to best advantage. Your Lab should move in a powerful, effortless manner, head up and topline holding. He should not gallop around the ring, and he should not pace or weave. He should move with strength and power, holding a straight line, elbows close to the body, hindquarters parallel. Pick the speed at which he looks best, keeping the above description in mind; then use that speed when you gait him for the judges in the ring and as you work with him for show training at home.

Baiting your Lab, to show expression and alertness, should be done in a manner which does not upset the other Labs in the ring. A tasty morsel of well-cooked and dried-out liver is fine for keeping your own dog interested, but when discarded on the floor, it can throw off the behavior of someone else's dog, who may lunge after it. So, please, if you drop a piece of liver or any other treat, pick it up and take it with you when you leave the ring.

One's right hand in the pocket while in the ring generally spells *l-i-v-e-r* to a show dog. Notice how alertly MiJan's Ain't Misbehavin is "baiting." MiJan's Labradors, Joan and Tony Heubel and Mike and Janet Farmilette.

Above: The National Labrador specialty in Ohio, October 1981, with Winners Dog competition in the ring. **Left:** Best of Breed competition at the same show. Both photos by Jan Churchill.

Ch. Jagersbo Hawk of Broad Reach, by Eng., Am. Ch. Lawnwood's Hot Chocolate ex Ch. Yarrow's Broad Reach Psaphire. Bred by Martha Lee Voshell. Owner-handled by Eric Bergishagen. Nancy Martin judges.

When the awards have been made, accept yours graciously, no matter how you actually may feel about it. To argue with a judge is unthinkable, and it will certainly not change the decision. Be courteous, congratulate the winners if your dog has been defeated, and try not to show your disappointment. By the same token, please be a gracious winner; this, surprisingly, sometimes seems to be even more difficult.

If you already show your Lab, if you plan on being an exhibitor in the future, or if you simply enjoy attending dog shows, there is a book, written by me, which you will find to be an invaluable source of detailed information about all aspects of show dog competition. This book is *Successful Dog Show Exhibiting* (T.F.H. Publications, Inc.) and is available wherever the one you are now reading was purchased.

Ch. Sam of Blaircourt (Dusk of Luscander ex Olivia of Blaircourt), Mrs. Grace Lambert's famed winner on the occasion of his final ring appearance, the Labrador Specialty in 1965.

Moorwood-bred "Rocky" with Joan Nankivell. By Ch. Sorn Sandpiper of Follytower ex Ch. Beaver's Hillary of Moorwood, C.D. This excellent gun dog was trained by his owners, Joan and James Nankivell.

CHAPTER ELEVEN

Obedience and
Working Labradors

An obedience class at the National Labrador Specialty, Mason, Ohio, 1981. Photo by Jan Churchill.

Labradors are all-around dogs. Aside from proving their championship qualities in the show ring, Labradors have shown themselves to be excellent dogs in obedience and multi-talented workers in several specialized fields. Their high degree of intelligence and their willingness to please have made Labrador Retrievers a breed of distinction in many areas.

Obedience

For its own protection and safety, every dog should be taught, at the very least, to recognize and obey the commands "Come," "Heel," "Down," "Sit," and "Stay". Doing so might, at some time, save the dog's life and in less extreme circumstances will certainly make him a better-behaved, more pleasant member of society. If you are patient and enjoy working with your dog, study some of the excellent books available on the subject of obedience and teach your Lab these basic manners. If you need the stimulus of working with a group, find out where obedience training classes are available (usually your veterinarian, your dog's breeder, or a dog-owning friend can tell you) and you and your dog can join up. Alternatively, you could let someone else do the training by sending the dog to class, but this is not very rewarding, because you lose the opportunity of developing the closeness of working with your dog.

If you are going to do it yourself, there are some basic rules which you should follow. You must remain calm and confident in attitude. You must never lose your temper and frighten or punish your dog unjustly. Never resort to cruelty. Be quick and lavish with your praise each time a command is correctly followed. Make it fun for the dog and he will be eager to please you by responding correctly. Repetition is the keynote, but it should not be continued without recess to the point of tedium. Limit the training sessions to ten- or fifteen-minute periods at a time.

Formal obedience training can be followed, and very frequently is, by entering the dog in obedience competition to work toward an obedience degree, or several of them, depending on the dog's aptitude and your own enjoyment. Obedience trials are held in conjunction with the majority of all-breed conformation dog shows and also frequently with or as Specialty events. If you are working alone with your dog, a list of trial dates might be obtained from your veterinarian, your pet supplier, or the breeder of your Lab; or contact the American Kennel Club. If you have been working with a training class, you will find information readily available to you regarding dates and locations of trials.

The goals for which one works in the formal A.K.C. member or licensed obedience trials are

347

the following titles: Companion Dog (C.D.), Companion Dog Excellent (C.D.X.), and Utility Dog (U.D.). These degrees are earned by receiving three "legs," or qualifying scores, at each level of competition. The degrees must be earned in order, with one completed prior to starting work on the next. For example, a dog must have earned C.D. prior to starting work on C.D.X. Then C.D.X. must be completed before U.D. work begins. The ultimate title possible to attain in obedience work is that of Obedience Trial Champion (O.T.C.). To gain this one, dogs must have received the required number of points by placing first or second in Open or Utility after having earned their U.D. There is also a Tracking Dog title (T.D.), to be earned at tracking trials, and a new, more-difficult-to-attain degree, Tracking Dog Excellent (T.D.X.).

When you see the letters "C.D." following a dog's name, you will know that the dog has satisfactorily completed the following exercises: heel on leash, heel free, stand for examination, recall,

Manora's Trent at six months of age carrying his dumbbell. Nancy M. Scholz of New York, owner.

Cedarhill Snow Blaze, Am., Can., Bda. U.D. is owned by James Bennett and was bred by Thomas J. Feneis, New Jersey.

long sit, and long stay. "C.D.X." means that tests have been passed in all of the above plus heel free, drop on recall, retrieve over high jump, broad jump, long sit, and long down. "U.D." indicates that the dog has additionally passed tests in scent discrimination (leather article), scent discrimination (metal article), signal exercises, directed retrieve, directed jumping, and group stand for examination.

On page 349 is a series of pictures showing O.T. Ch. Shakespeare's Trixie, U.D. Margaret S. Wilson of Damascus, Maryland, is owner-trainer-handler.

Stand for Examination, Utility Class, Labrador Retriever Club of the Potomac, April 1980. O.T. Ch. Shakespeare's Trixie, U.D. stands nearest to the judge's table.

Retrieving over the high jump at Hyattsville, 1977.

Going around the outside turn on Figure 8.

Waiting for the placements, Utility Class, Labrador Retriever Club of the Potomac, April 1980.

Going over the bar jump.

Labrador Retriever Club of Potomac Specialty, Leesburg, Virginia, April 1977. Shakespeare's Trixie wins High in Trial under judge Tom Knott with a score of 197½.

The letters "T.D." indicate that the dog has been trained and passed the tests to follow the trail of a stranger along a path on which the trail was laid between 30 minutes and two hours previously. Along this track there must be more than two right-angle turns, at least two of which are well out in the open where no fences or other boundaries exist for guidance of dog or handler. The dog wears a harness and is connected to the handler by a lead 20 to 40 feet in length. Inconspicuously dropped at the end of the track is an article to be retrieved, usually a glove or wallet, which the dog is expected to locate and the handler to pick up. "T.D.X." is a more difficult version of the above, with a longer track and more turns to be worked through.

Labradors have distinguished themselves admirably in obedience work. As you turn the pages of this book, you will note the frequency with which bench show champions also carry one or more of the obedience titles following their names, some in one country, others in two or more. Beauty and brains are well combined in this breed, to be sure!

As an example of what can be accomplished in obedience by an owner working with her dog, we bring you a summary of the career of Obedience Trial Champion Shakespeare's Trixie and her owner, Margaret S. Wilson of Damascus, Maryland. It took Mrs. Wilson a year and a half of patient training to bring her six-year-old Lab bitch to this proud list of achievements, the highest possible honor to be attained in obedience competition.

When Margaret Wilson was pregnant with her son Jimmy, she felt that she was going stir crazy spending so much time at home. She was also concerned over Trixie's rambunctious character, fearing that the enthusiastic Lab, just by her size and activity, might hurt the baby as it grew. If Trixie was to remain a house pet, it would be necessary for her to obey! And so Mrs. Wilson and Trixie enrolled in a training class in Damascus to see what they could do about teaching Trixie the meaning of the basic obedience commands. They did so well that Trixie soon was promoted to an advanced class, seeming to know almost instinctively what was expected of her. Work at home in the yard followed, but little prompting was needed.

Somewhere along the way, Mrs. Wilson decided that, since Trixie was so responsive and had learned the basic rules so quickly, it would be fun to try entering her in formal obedience competition at a dog show. She did, and Trixie topped all scores that day.

Scent discrimination, Utility Class. O.T. Ch. Shakespeare's Trixie, U.D., owned by Margaret S. Wilson of Maryland.

O.T. Ch. Shakepeare's Trixie, T.D., doing the Retrieve Over High Jump exercise. Margaret S. Wilson, owner, Damascus, Maryland.

Trixie lost no time in gaining C.D., C.D.X., U.D., and, finally, Obedience Trial Championship, the grand prize of all. A Tracking Dog title has also been added, and now a roomful of ribbons, trophies, and certificates attest to Trixie's triumphs. In the 1979 regional show sponsored by Gaines, Trixie was named one of the Top Ten dogs on the East Coast. Her owners have had her in competition on an average of about twenty shows annually.

Adding particular interest to the story is the fact that Trixie was the first dog Mrs. Wilson had ever attempted to train, giving emphasis to the fact that *you*, too, can accomplish success with your dog in obedience if you go about it with loving patience and kindness and with the will to achieve.

O.T. Ch. Shakespeare's Trixie, T.D., and Shadow Glen's Autumn Gold, "Little Sister," two-and-a-half months old. Both owned by Margaret S. Wilson.

O.T. Ch. Shakespeare's Trixie, U.D., has brought all the most coveted obedience honors to her owner, Margaret S. Wilson, who personally trained and handled her to her exciting scores.

Way back when the Labrador Retriever Club, with American Kennel Club approval, would not allow regional breed clubs, a group of eight exhibitors organized the Waterland Retriever Club which included *all* retrievers since just Labs were not permitted. That was in 1965. The people involved were Nancy Martin, Marilyn and Ken Stahly, Chris and Ona Noto, Skip Patton, George Millington (now deceased), and Julie Brown (now Julie Sturman). The club is still going strong and doing an excellent job promoting retrievers in obedience, in the field, *and* on the bench.

At the left above is the club patch, designed by Julie Sturman to show the three uses for Waterland members' retrievers. At the right above is the trophy offered by the Waterland Retriever Club for the top-winning owner-handled retriever (all breeds). Jan Churchill won the trophy three times with Eng., Am. Ch. Lawnwood's Hot Chocolate and once with Ch. Spenrock Cardigan Bay.

Champion Ebonylane's Dawn of Rivendell, C.D., is owned by Billy Mauer of Montreal.

F.T. Ch. Timberstone Trigger, at the 1949 National Field Trial, Westhampton, New York, belonged to S.C. Stout of Hinsdale, Illinois.

Mara's Darcy Farm Blaircourt, C.D., T.D., owned by Mhyra Stapf, Pleasant Oaks Labradors, Kissimmee, Florida.

Ch. Groveton's Moon Valley Gwen, C.D., W.C., by Ch. Groveton's Apollo Countdown ex Groveton's Maid Guenevere, innocently asking, "Do I look like the type that would eat three days supply of liver bait?" Owned by Eileen Ketcham.

Ch. Jollymuff Honey Pot, C.D., W.D., third generation of Jollymuff Labradors. Diane B. Jones of New Jersey, owner.

Mother and daughter. Trieven's Happy I'm A Triever, C.D.X., was the first Lab owned by Mr. and Mrs. Tom Philip of Ro-Shan Kennels, and she was also their foundation bitch. She died at 14 years of age in 1978. Her daughter, on the left, is Ch. Ro-Shan's Runhappy Hopper, C.D., sired by Ch. Runroy.

Ch. Casadelora's Shiloh, C.D., by Ch. Bet's Golden Major ex Ch., O.T. Ch. Trollheimen's Golden Sol, taking Best of Breed at Northern Interior Kennel Club, July 1976, judged by Rutledge Gilliland. Mr. and Mrs. W.E. Brown, owners, Casadelora Kennels, British Columbia.

After only six lessons, Ranchman's Sundown Cowboy, C.D., C.D.X., owned by Don Wirth, Redcliff, Alberta, finished C.D. in three shows with scores 193, 193½, and 194.

Ch. Ro-Shan's Canzoo Frisbee C.D., by Ch. Ro-Shan's Kapko Canajun ex Selemat's Ro-Shan Ko Ko Kazoo. Owned by Irene Whiteside, Canada.

Ch. Killingworth's Valiant Lady, C.D., owned by Enid Bloome, Winterset Labradors, Connecticut, pictured taking Best of Opposite Sex at Longshore-Southport, 1980.

Gun Dogs

Developing the natural instinct and talent that a Labrador possesses for retrieving is not at all difficult. The inclination is there, simply waiting to be developed and guided to the proper channels. The big question is whether or not *you* are equipped to train the dog, as it takes knowledge, patience, and kindness to bring this about successfully.

Working with your own dog is far more satisfactory than turning him over to a trainer. The rapport and closeness that develop between man and dog who work together is one of the great pleasures of dog ownership, and if you miss out on it, you will be losing something of great value. So study up on the subject yourself (there are numerous excellent and helpful books on training and on hunting with your dog) and see if you are not able to accomplish the job yourself.

We have already touched upon the importance of early obedience training for your puppy. These commands, with the addition of "fetch," are the first steps in field work which must be learned. Keep the commands short and brisk, always using the same word for the same act, so that the dog will immediately associate what you want with what he is hearing. This part of the training can, and should, be started as soon as the puppy is a few months old, the younger the better. The lessons should be short, pleasant, and lacking in tedium, and they can take place in the house as well as outdoors.

Gradually you will perhaps wish to add whistle or hand signals to the verbal commands. If you decide to use hand signals, do not swing or wave your arms about; this will be confusing to the dog. Hold your arm out straight, moving your hand to indicate "right" or "left," and hold your arm above your head to indicate "back." With repetition and practice, the commands can be learned by the dog faster than you might anticipate.

Pleasant Oaks Hopi after a day of duck hunting in Florida. By Ch. Lawnwood's Hot Chocolate ex Mara's Darcy Farro Blaircourt, C.D., T.D. Owned by Mhyra Stapf, Pleasant Oaks Labradors, Kissimmee, Florida.

Ch. Killingworth's Valiant Lady, owned by Mrs. Enid P. Bloome, is all set to do some fun retrieving.

Through the water to the retrieve. Two of Nancy Scholz's Labs doing what comes naturally to this breed.

Bringing it in! One of Nancy Scholz's Manora Labs from New York.

Manora's Thor and Manora's Trent at six months of age showing how one does a water-retrieve-to-hand. Nancy M. Scholz, owner, Manora Labradors.

Some people prefer to use a whistle or a combination of hand and whistle for signaling. One sharp blast generally means the dog should sit wherever it may be, or one blast can be used to call the dog's attention to the hand signal you are about to give. Three blasts usually mean that the dog is to return to you or come part way back to you.

For training equipment, you will need a dummy, one that will hold up on land and in water. These come in assorted sizes and are made of canvas stuffed with shredded rubber. You will also need a lead with a choke collar, to prevent the dog from roaming too far away during the learning stage. The introduction to feathers is of primary importance and is usually accomplished by way of a chicken or turkey wing from which the feathers have not been removed or by a dummy with feathers tied to it. Any inclination on the part of the dog to go off with the dummy or feathered object upon retrieving same, not bringing it promptly and directly back to you, must be discouraged. Never forget that a Lab's retrieve is to be made to your hand.

Training with a retriever dummy. The chocolate dog, Highlands Sir Lochee, bred and owned by Lillian Knobloch. This dog is a son of Ch. Grovetons Copper Buck Shot (a Ch. Lockerbie Sandylands Tarquin son) ex Sambeau's Cam. Photo by Vince Serbin.

From the very beginning, accustom your Lab puppy to sudden sharp noises. Lots of pan-clattering at meal time and hand clapping are two good ways to help the dog get used to loud noises. The dog's introduction to the gun should start with the gun being fired a considerable distance away from him; then the gun should gradually be fired closer and closer until the sudden loud noise becomes routine. During this step great care is necessary not to frighten the dog, as by so doing you may make him forever gun-shy. Praise him, pet him, and be generally cheerful each time the gun is fired, until he grows to associate the sound with something he enjoys.

Ch. Driftwood's Rusty of Ro-Shan making the retrieve. Mr. and Mrs. Tom Philip, owners, Ro-Shan Labs.

Jollymuff Fly Away with owner, Diane B. Jones of New Jersey.

Diane B. Jones with Jollymuff Fly Away waiting to retrieve.

Jollymuff Fly Away doing a retrieve with owner, Diane B. Jones.

Introduction to the water also should be handled with care. A child's wading pool of shallow water might be a good starting place for him to get the feel of being in water. Be cautious the first time the puppy enters deep water; see that he does not become frightened. It is well to have along his dam or another experienced older dog who enjoys being in the water to set an example for the pup, but be very careful that the baby Lab does not get into difficulty before he learns how to proceed.

If you are starting out with your first Lab, try to get a more experienced friend to come out with you for some of the earlier training sessions. This can be helpful to you and your dog in getting you both off on the right foot.

Scrimshaw The Prodigal, yellow male, by Ch. Jayncourt Follow Mee ex Ch. Scrimshaw Blue Nun, proves that Lab ears *do* float. Bred by Barbara Barfield; owned by Mr. and Mrs. Eugene Philbrick.

Bill Wunderlich when he was training for the Wallaces. These were the days when breeding to field champions produced dogs handsome enough to be show champions besides hunters and field trial dogs. This is the foundation that Mrs. Bernard W. Ziessow believes still makes their descendants outstanding hunters. Photo courtesy of the Ziessows, Franklin, Michigan.

A day's goose hunting on the Eastern Shore at Taylor's Bridge in Delaware. The ladies are Jan Churchill, second from the left, and Lana duPont Wright with her Lab, "Kelly".

Working Certificate
by Janet Churchill

By the late 1930s, members of the Labrador Retriever Club (founded in 1931) became aware that separate strains of Labs were being developed for show and for field, as was happening in many other sporting breeds at that time. Thus Article VII was added to the club's constitution in 1939, and it reads as follows:

ARTICLE VII.

Section 1. No member of the Club shall use the title "Ch." until a dog, having won a bench show Championship, shall receive a Working Certificate or better at a field trial. This rule shall not apply to any dog that has won a bench show Championship prior to June 1st, 1939.

Section II. At the Club's trials dogs may be entered for the purpose of obtaining a Working Certificate and not in the regular classes, and the fee for such test shall not be in excess of $5.00.

Working Certificates are designed to prove that:

1. The dog is not gun-shy.

2. The dog will retrieve a shot bird at approximately 50 yards on land.

3. The dog will retrieve two ducks from water, either as a double or in immediate succession, in order to prove willingness to re-enter the water.

4. Steadiness is not required, so a dog may be held on the line.

The English have similar requirements; and until 1958, the English Kennel Club required tests to prove working ability for all sporting breeds. After 1959, the English Kennel Club decided to use the title Show Champion (Sh. Ch.) for English dogs that were bench champions but had not passed working tests in the field. Thus in reading pedigrees of English dogs, we know that those with "Ch." are full champions that have also passed their field tests, while the others are titled "Sh. Ch."

In the United States, the Working Certificate requirement (Article VII, Section I) is limited to Labrador Retriever Club members, but the W.C. is available to all Labs that have completed A.K.C. championship requirements.

Int. Ch. Spenrock Ballot, W.D., sitting in a blind. Janet Churchill, owner.

There are several ways to gain a Working Certificate title for a Lab. Any Lab entered in an A.K.C. licensed trial who has satisfactorily completed both a land and water series in the same trial is deemed to have earned a W.C. If the dog has completed his A.K.C. championship requirements, it will be awarded a W.C. A dog may complete the requirements for the W.C. prior to finishing his championship requirements, in which case the Working Certificate will be awarded at a later date when the dog becomes eligible for it by gaining his championship. Certificates may be applied for when the A.K.C. championship title is confirmed.

Successful in the field as well as in the show ring, Ch. Spenrock Brown Bess (Ch. Spenrock Heatheredge ex Ch. Wayward of Old Forge) brings in the bird at Spenrock.

Working Certificate tests can also be judged by any director of the Labrador Retriever Club or by any person who has licensed field trial judging experience. Standards of performance are almost the same as required in a field trial test when competing for a Working Certificate, bearing in mind that for the W.C. the dog does not have to be steady, and line manners are not marked, so the bird does not have to be delivered to hand. If the bird is delivered reasonably near to the handler, the test is complete.

These tests can be held with as few as one or two dogs as long as an appropriate location is used. Ducks and pheasants are usually used, although pigeons are acceptable. The land test is a single retrieve in light cover at a distance of 40 to 50 yards. A shooter ("gun") with a 12-gauge shotgun using live ammunition or blanks must stand near the dog and its handler and fire at the same time that an assistant throws the shackled bird or dead pheasant up in the air at the correct distance away. Since the dog need not be steady, the handler may hold its collar. However, when the gun is fired the dog must not be gun-shy. The handler will send the dog, using standard field trial signals. Delivery must be in close proximity to the handler but need not be to hand.

Introducing baby Labradors to the bird at Spenrock, owned by Janet Churchill.

Int. Ch. Spenrock Banner, W.C., in the water with the ducks at Spenrock. Janet Churchill, owner.

The water test consists of two single retrieves to prove a dog's willingness to re-enter the water. Standards of completion are the same as for the land test. Once again, it is important that the gun be fired in close proximity to the dog to detect gun-shyness.

Ch. Lawnwood's Hot Chocolate, Janet Churchill's noted great chocolate Labrador, is teaching his children (out of Spenrock Flying Clipper) about water retrieving.

Training a Lab to a Working Certificate level of performance is not difficult as the tests are designed mainly to prove that the dog has innate hunting ability and is not gun-shy. Many regional Labrador clubs give their own certificates, and many clubs also have advanced levels requiring a higher standard of performance. Advanced Certificates may be awarded by these clubs.

Those who wish to train their Labs can start with a canvas training dummy. Teach your dog to sit at your side while a friend throws the dummy, making a high arch in the air. When the dummy falls, send your dog to fetch it, and call him to return it to you. Soon the dog will realize that the handler is not the thrower, thus preparing the dog for the field tests. Next have another friend fire a blank pistol while the dummy is thrown. Do not do this until the dog is enthusiastic about retrieving. In a short time, the dog will associate the gun shot with something he enjoys doing—retrieving.

Most Labs take to water naturally, but be sure that they are happy about swimming before starting water work.

Remember that in training for a W.C., you are working to prove that your dog has basic hunting instincts and that he can go on to more advanced work. After training with dummies, you should work with shackled ducks, so that your dog becomes used to picking up a live or dead bird.

The owner of a Labrador Retriever that has satisfactorily met the requirements of the Labrador Retriever Club, Inc. Working Certificate may write to Mrs. A.L. Foote, 6146 Mines Road, Livermore, California 94550, requesting a certificate. The following information should be included for entry in the Working Certificate records:

1) The dog's name and registration number.

2) Date dog completed bench title.

3) Sex and date of birth.

4) Owner's name and address.

5) Copy of confirmation of completion of the tests showing judge's or director's signature.

6) Judge's identification, *i.e.*, judge of licensed field trials, director of club, etc.

Working Certificate tests are usually held in conjunction with the National Labrador Retriever Club Specialty and by the regional Lab clubs in various part of the United States. These dates are published in the American Kennel Club's *Gazette*, as are the field trials. At these events, birds and guns are provided by the club sponsoring the tests.

His day's job well done, Ch. Lewisfield Spenrock Ballot, littermate to the great bitch Banner, sits proudly. Janet Churchill, owner.

However, if none of the above is convenient, you may arrange for Working Certificate tests by contacting a Labrador Retriever Club director or properly qualified judge and selecting a mutually convenient place. You will be expected to arrive at the location with the dog, ducks, gun (12-gauge shotgun) and shells, and the appropriate means to re-shackle the duck. You must also arrange for friends to assist with the gun and throwing the birds. The tests will then be conducted just as at a trial and, if satisfactory, the results tabulated and signed by the judge. If your dog is ready, this can be done prior to finishing the bench title, and then the W.C. can be applied for at that time.

Labradors exercising at Spenrock Farm, on the Eastern Shore at Chesapeake City, Maryland.

Caution: while it is good practice to introduce a pup to birds, retrieving and water, one must not overwork the dog while it is growing, especially under the age of a year. Serious joint injuries can be caused by the sudden stops and quick turns associated with retrieving on land. It is less harmful to work your pup in water.

"Just follow Dad, fellows, and you'll be O.K." might be what Ch. Lawnwood's Hot Chocolate is saying to his kids. All belong to Janet Churchill.

To help earn a Working Certificate, this Lab is going through the water tests. Here entering the water. Photo courtesy of Joel Riddel.

Am., Can. Ch. Agber's Daniel Aloysius, W.C., by Ch. Spenrock Cardigan Boy ex Am., Can. Ch. Whiskey Creek's Lisa.

Step 2 of the water test for Working Certificate, the dog swimming out to get the bird.

Obedience Trial Champion Claybank's Black Maria, W.C., owned, trained, and handled by Ebonylane Labradors, Hemmingford, Quebec.

Step 3 of the water test for Working Certificate is retrieving the bird.

This lovely head belongs to Chucklebrook Cassandra, W.C., owned by Christine Kofron, D.V.M.

Working Certificate test, 1977. Young Moorwood-bred dog, born February 1976, by Ch. Somerset Cider of Kimvalley ex Ch. The Black Baroness. Rosalind B. Moore, breeder. Photo by Paul Genthner.

Start them early in the water! Ch. Meggin of South Gate, W.C., thoroughly enjoying her swim, although only four months old! Charles W. Appleton, owner.

Ch. Beaver's Hillary of Moorwood, W.C., as a young Lab taking the Working Certificate tests in 1978. Rosalind B. Moore, owner, Moorwood Labs, New York. Photo by Paul Genthner.

Spenrock Janny, by Ch. Spenrock Cardigan Bay, being told "a good job well done." Elsie Hunteman, owner, St. Michaels, Maryland.

Jim Nankivell praises "Rocky" for a job well done. Moorwood's Hillary Mr. Brown, owner-trained and handled by Jim and Joan Nankivell.

"Rawhide," bred by Moorwood Labs, field-trained and show-handled by owner, Paul Saucier. Officially, "Rawhide" is Moorwood's Drake of Rokin Pas, and he is one of the Markwell-Hillary puppies.

"Tige" doing his thing. Ch. Groveton's Velvet Tiger with owner Robert Page proving that Groveton Labs are good retrievers.

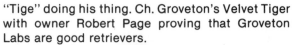

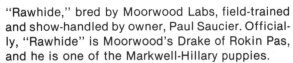

Ch. Agber Doone's Buggy at ten months of age training to retrieve with a pigeon. Agber Labradors, owner, Agnes Cartier, New Jersey.

Ch. Zipper's Hustlin' Wahoo, U.D.T., W.C., owned by Martha Lee K. Voshell, and Ch. Broad Reach's English Muffin, U.D.T., W.C.

This is one of America's first yellow Labrador field trial champions, Beau of the Lark, who holds probably the best record of any yellow field trial champion. Owned by Mahlon Wallace, bred by Bill Wunderlich. Photo courtesy of Mrs. Bernard W. Ziessow.

Ch. MiJan's All That Jazz, by Ch. Jayncourt Ajoco Justice ex Ch. Lockerbie MiJan's Britannia, belongs to MiJan's Kennels, the Heubels and the Farmilettes.

Beaver's Copper of Moorwood after having retrieved and delivered live duck shot over him in mid-January 1978. By Ch. Somerset Cider of Kimvalley ex The Black Baroness. Rosalind B. Moore, owner, Moorwood Kennel.

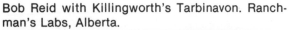

Bob Reid with Killingworth's Tarbinavon. Ranchman's Labs, Alberta.

Casadelora's Sweet Love Bandit, by Ch. Casadelora's Shadrack, C.D., ex Ch. Casadelora's Special Blend, C.D., surveys the spoils of his day's work. Mr. and Mrs. W.E. Brown, owners, Casadelora Labs, British Columbia.

Scrimshaw Clearly An Angel, C.D.X., T.D.X., pictured at ten months old. By Ch. Scrimshaw Another Deacon ex Champion Sandylands Crystal, bred by Barbara Barfield, owned by David and Marilu Meredith, Garland, Texas.

Am., Mex., 1978 World Champion Mandigo's Annabel Lee, C.D.X., W.C., just after a swim. By Am., Can., Mex., 1978 World, and Int. Ch. Franklin's Golden Mandigo, C.D., A.W.C., ex Am., Can. Ch. Chivas Regal, W.C. Bred and owned by Mandigo Labs, John and Laurell Jenny, West Bountiful, Utah.

Right: Ch. Franklin's Golden Mandingo, Am., Can., Mex., 1978 World, and Int. C.D., W.D., and A.W.C. The Ziessows tell us this is the Top Producing Labrador in the United States and that his sperm is being preserved in the bank in Texas. He is a son of Ch. Franklin's Tally of Burywood and Ch. Shamrock Acres Light Brigade. Owned by John and Laurell Jenny of Utah. Photo courtesy of Mrs. Ziessow.

Below: Ch. Broad Reach's English Muffin, U.D.T., W.C., is the *First Champion U.D.T. Labrador Retriever bitch*. Owned by Broad Reach Labradors, Martha Lee K. Voshell, Charlottesville, Virginia.

Off on a retrieve! Manora's Robin, C.D., belonging to Nancy Scholz and her nephew, Steven.

Eleven-month-old Highlands Samantha's Riptide picking up the bird in the water (top left), carrying it carefully in a gentle mouth (top right) on up onto land (bottom left), and delivering it to his master's hand (bottom right). Owned by Samantha Eggertson, whose father is pictured with the dog.

Beaver's Toby of Moorwood, personal gun dog of Barbara Genthner, Tealbrook Labrador Retriever Field Training Kennel, Monticello, Florida. Paul Genthner took this photograph, loaned to us by Toby's breeder, Rosalind B. Moore.

A beautiful head study by owner Charles W. Appleton of his Specialty-winning Lab bitch, Ch. Meggin of South Gate, W.C.

Opposite, above: Ch. Augustin de Gregorio, C.D., by Ch. Killingworth's Thunderson ex Ironpride's Spindrift Misty, has done a great deal of winning for his owner, Victoria K. De Palma, Milford, Connecticut. During his four years in the show ring, "Gus" gained 98 Best of Breed awards, and four Group firsts, becoming Number Six Labrador, *Kennel Review* system, in 1977 and 1978. **Below:** Ch. Spenrock Cardigan Bay at 13 years old at Spenrock Farm with English Corgi friend in the cart. Janet Churchill, owner.

Ch. Yarrow's Broad Reach Psaphire, U.D.T., W.C.; Ch. Broad Reach's English Muffin, U.D.T., W.C.; and Ch. Zipper's Hustlin' Wahoo, U.D.T., W.C.; owned by Martha Lee K. Voshell, Broad Reach Labs, Charlottesville, Virginia. These are three of only eight Ch. U.D.T. Labrador Retrievers in the United States at the close of 1981, of which only five are alive at the present time.

Am., Can. Ch. Campbellcroft's Angus, C.D., W.C., taking Best of Breed at the Golden Gate Labrador Retriever Club Specialty in April 1981. Donald and Virginia Campbell, owners, Soquel, California.

Am., Can. Ch. Sunnybrook Acres Ace O'Spades, C.D., W.C. From the Sunnybrook Acres Labradors, Dr. and Mrs. John H. Ippensen, Springfield, Missouri.

Left: "Jake" is the second Lab to have gone to The Seeing Eye from Dennis and Sue Simon's Lyric Kennels. He is a son of Ch. Caballero Brand of Devonwood.

Below: These two puppies are future guide dogs at Guiding Eyes for the Blind, Patterson, New York.

Am., Can. Ch. Seaward's Dr. Watson of Rupert, C.D., owned by Seaward Kennels, bred by the late Dorothy Howe and handled in the show ring by Phyllis Wright.

This exquisite head study of Ch. Beaver's Hillary of Moorwood, W.C., was made in 1978 by Paul Genthner. Hillary, whelped February 1976, is by Ch. Somerset Cider of Kimvalley ex Ch. The Black Baroness. Owned by Rosalind B. Moore, Moorwood Labs, Indian Lake, New York.

Opposite, above: Ch. Cedarhill Sundance Kid, one of the Champion Lockerbie Goldenstone Jensen ex Champion Cedarhill Amber Dawn progeny, bred, owned, and handled by Thomas J. Feneis, Freehold, New Jersey. **Below:** Ch. Cedarhill Amber Dawn, Am. and Bda. C.D., and Binta's Stellar Honey, C.D., are two important bitches in the breeding program at Cedarhill Labradors, Tom and Barbara Feneis, Freehold, New Jersey.

Ch. Driftwood's Gypsy at nine years of age. Owned by Pam Kelsey, Bayville, New Jersey.

Field Ch. Cork of Oakwood Lane. "Behind almost all the great field trial Labs of today. He was unusual in that he was so large, weighing over 100 pounds." Photo courtesy of B.W. Ziessow.

On the track. Ch. The Black Baroness at work in the field. Moorwood Kennels, owner, Rosalind Moore.

Scrimshaw Mother Carey, black bitch, by Chebago Walter R. and Jonte Scrimshaw O'Spindrift, pictured at ten months of age. Bred and owned by Barbara Barfield of New Hampshire.

Ch. The Black Baroness, Moorwood's foundation bitch, retrieving at two years age in 1974.

Ch. Scrimshaw Another Deacon at three months of age retrieving a bird brought in by his mother earlier in the day. Barbara and John Barfield, owners, Meredith, New Hampshire.

Tracking Dog
by Mhyra Stapf

Tracking is a sport that can be enjoyed with all breeds. However, it is one in which the Labrador excels.

The Lab was used quite extensively in Vietnam as a tracking dog because of the breed's reliability and enthusiasm. They were easily trained and could adapt themselves to all kinds of terrain. Because of their innate ability in the field, the Labrador is a natural tracker.

Mara's Darcy Farro Blaircourt, C.D., T.D., is shown here following the track and in other pictures on this page with owner-trainer-handler Mhyra Stapf of Kissimmee, Florida. All four photos by Joel Riddell.

I remember the first time that I decided it would be fun to train my Lab for tracking. I went to a seminar for police dogs, and I immediately became interested in tracking when my little Lab picked up the scent much faster than any of the German Shepherds. I then started to read up on the subject, finding some wonderfully helpful and instructive books which give insight into training a dog for tracking.

My next step was to puchase a harness and a 40-foot lead, and with these in hand, I was up bright and early the following morning to "teach my dog to track." Much to my amazement, it was totally unnecessary for *me* to teach my *dog* anything! Rather, it was the other way around, and my little Lab taught me what the wind will do to a scent, twisting and turning it, and all the other things we never think of until we have experienced them. At the same time, I became elated by watching a dog follow a track, picking up each turn as he went, so that all I, the trainer,

Coming to the glove.

Picking up the glove.

Back to the finish line, glove in mouth.

had to do was to follow! This is one thing you can do with your dog in which you can put all of your trust in his or her senses. All you need to teach, or at least so it was with me, are the two words "Go find." Once those are understood, the dog will almost certainly do the rest.

You work with your dog until *you* learn the signals. The dog's head will lift up when the scent is in the air, circling to make sure of that turn, nose down with determination when absolutely certain that the track is being followed correctly. If you are lucky, you can impose on someone in your family, or a nice neighbor, to be the tracklayer for you. You practice until you are quite sure you and the dog are ready; then you contact a tracking judge who will come and watch you and the dog work. When the judge is satisfied that you and your Lab both are quite proficient, you become certified and then you are ready for your tracking test.

I well remember my first tracking test. All of the participants were up and out in the field early one foggy morning. After three cups of coffee and meeting with the judges and the other tracking enthusiasts, we drew numbers to determine which track we would work. Mine was later in the day so I had plenty of time to sit back and wait, becoming increasingly nervous as the time slowly passed. By the time my number was called, the wind had picked up to a crisp 35 miles per hour, and I was becoming even more apprehensive. The judges pointed out the stake, and after showing it to Darcy and making sure she had the scent, she was left on her own. She took off like a streak of lightning, with me hanging on to her lead for dear life. You have no way of knowing whether she is right or wrong, so you just put all your trust, as I did, into your dog. At the same time, you listen for the judges' whistles, which will tell you she is "off the track and will have to try again another day." But the whistle never blew! I guess the biggest thrill of my life was seeing my dog, with her nose down and tail wagging, pick up my sought-after glove at the end of her trail. While I was busy being congratulated by the judges, we looked up to see Darcy running across the field as fast as her legs would carry her toward the small group of spectators watching the event. Much to my chagrin, she ran right up to a nice man standing in the crowd and handed him the glove! Why? We found out later that he was the man who had laid the track!

That day, Darcy received her T.D. (Tracking Dog title) from the A.K.C. The next step will be T.D.X. (Tracking Dog Excellent), which means that the dog must pass an even more extensive test on far more difficult terrain, a longer track with cross tracks, and with several articles placed on the track along the way.

Pleasant Oaks Hopi at 23 months of age, son of Eng., Am. Ch. Lawnwood's Hot Chocolate, bred and owned by Mhyra Stapf, Kissimmee, Florida.

I shall never cease to be amazed at the ability of a tracking dog. We do not know how or why an animal tracks, but I guess that must be one of the six senses we hear about. A Labrador can follow a duck that has been downed and floated downstream, coming back with it in mouth each time, or find a wounded bird that has limped off into the brush. That's what makes Labs such versatile hunting dogs and such excellent tracking dogs. Whether on land or in the water, or even merely scented in the air, they never fail to find and retrieve that bird.

This magnificent Labrador is F.C., A.F.C., C.F.C., and C.A.F.C. Franklin's Tall Timber owned by Roger and Pat Magnusson, bred by Mrs. Bernard W. Ziessow.

briskly without undue commotion, delivering the bird gently to hand. After the retrieve, he awaits further orders. Accurate marking of the "fall" is of enormous importance, as is the ability of the dog to take and follow directions.

Some owners hire professional trainers to instruct their dogs and handle them in these events. This is a good idea especially for beginners, although many owners, once they learn the ropes, prefer doing it themselves.

Hundreds of field trials are held each year, and a great many of them are for retrievers. Highlight competition takes place at the National Open Championship Stake and the National Amateur Championship Stake.

To gain full information on the subject, a request to the American Kennel Club, 51 Madison Avenue, New York, NY 10010, will bring you a copy of the booklet, *Rules and Regulations Applying to Field Trials.*

F.C., A.F.C., C.F.C., and C.A.F.C. Franklin's Tall Timber, pictured here with Roger Magnusson.

Field Trial Dogs

Field trials are competitions in which dogs of the sporting breeds, and some hounds, compete to test their hunting ability. These trials come under four different categories: hounds, pointing breeds, retrievers and spaniels. Obviously it is the retriever category which is of interest to Labrador owners.

The dogs participating in a retriever trial are expected to retrieve any type of game bird under any and all conditions. Retriever field trials simulate as closely as possible the natural conditions met on an ordinary day's hunting.

It is the retriever's job to find and retrieve fallen game upon order. The dog should sit quietly in line or in the blind, follow at heel or assume whatever position is designated by his handler until sent to retrieve. When that order is given, the dog is then to retrieve promptly and

Guide Dogs for the Blind

The intelligence, reliability and steady, even temperament of our Labrador have made this breed one of the most popular and desirable for the important work of serving as eyes for the blind. Hundreds of Labs are now involved in this wonderful program, to the justifiable pride of the entire Labrador Fancy!

Highlands Onyx, by Ch. Groveton's Lucky Lindy ex Betty Lou, was bred by Lillian Knobloch and trained and is owned by the Guide Dog Foundation for the Blind, "Second Sight," at Smithtown, Long Island, New York. Onyx is guiding her owner through Law School. She is pictured with her present owner, her second, having previously guided an earlier owner through a Canadian blizzard, saving her life, when that owner was hopelessly lost. After suffering a heart attack, this first owner had to return Onyx; but Onyx is working beautifully with her second owner. It is interesting that the Guide Dog Foundation retains ownership on all of the dogs it places and thus has control over their future should one no longer be needed by the person with whom the dog was placed.

A Guiding Eyes Lab puppy from Guiding Eyes for the Blind, Patterson, New York.

I have received permission to tell the story of Guiding Eyes for the Blind (GEB), whose headquarters are at Yorktown Heights, New York, with breeding kennels at Patterson, New York, knowing that it will be of interest to the readers of this book. Guiding Eyes does a magnificent job, as anyone who has seen their trained dogs at work can attest.

A non-profit organization, GEB's sole mission is to help blind people achieve mobility, and thus their independence, through the proper use of highly trained, quality guide dogs. It has a program of controlled breeding, the goal of which is to produce dogs with the essentials to qualify for their work. Labradors, Golden Retrievers and German Shepherds are bred at the kennel. Boxers, Bouvier des Flandres and Collies have also proven acceptable, although they are not raised there.

The intensive training of each dog at GEB begins when the dog is still a puppy. The dogs live one year at home with volunteer puppy raisers, who provide them with the love they need and the family setting to prepare them for a lifetime of human companionship. Then, each future guide dog embarks on a minimum of 12 weeks of training with expert instructors. When the dog has learned obedience and the proper sense of leadership, he then is teamed with a blind student.

Next follows a 26-day course of intensive training, student and dog learning to work as a unit. Together they face the hazards they are likely to encounter in normal living, under all types of conditions, from country roads where no sidewalks exist to busy city streets filled with people and traffic. Training includes how to travel safely on escalators and stairs, through revolving doors, in and out of elevators, through stores, on buses and even on New York City subways.

Along with the mobile training, students receive instruction on the care, feeding, grooming and general maintenance of their dogs. Following the student's graduation, GEB continues to keep in touch with the student. In some instances, the latter may find it necessary to call upon the school with requests for special help should exceptional situations or unexpected problems arise. This, however, happens only occasionally.

One of the Labradors from Guiding Eyes for the Blind at work.

Guide dogs in training with blind students from Guiding Eyes for the Blind at Patterson, New York.

Highland's Heed Destiny, the dam of these puppies, was bred and donated by Lillian Knobloch to Guide Dog Foundation for the Blind at Smithtown, New York. Sired by Odin of Fifty Acres, the pups were born July 15th 1981. This is Destiny's first litter for "Second Sight," and it is hoped that all will serve well the purpose for which they were bred.

A future guide dog at Guiding Eyes for the Blind.

Guiding Eyes for the Blind breeding farm is the home of this inquisitive Lab puppy inspecting a harness.

Bright and sunny, the puppy section of the breeding kennel at Guiding Eyes for the Blind, Patterson, New York.

In its first 25 years of operation, since its beginning in 1956, Guiding Eyes for the Blind has graduated more than 2,300 students from all over the United States. At the present time, GEB has more than 860 active guide dog users throughout the country, a fact of which they are extremely proud.

Any qualified person is eligible for guide dog training. The minimum age is 16 years, but there is no maximum age and many people over 60 years old have found a new life opening up to them by this means.

The total cost of providing one guide dog, including breeding, raising, a three-month minimum training period, student transportation to and from the school, room and board for the month-long stay and the follow-up to ensure that the graduate and guide dog are functioning correctly, is in the area of $8,000.

The only cost to the student is a voluntary tuition fee of $150. However, no qualified applicant is ever denied a guide dog for financial reasons. It is the aim of GEB to make absolutely certain that no qualified blind person will ever have to live without a needed guide dog.

Prior to 1958, all Guiding Eyes' dogs were acquired from outside sources. In 1966, the first GEB puppies from the original breeding facilities, which were in Mahopac, New York, were placed with local 4-H clubs, which provided foster homes for them as youngsters. Now the continued assistance of 4-H clubs is augmented by many other volunteer puppy raisers from Maine to all parts of New York State.

Many leading Labrador breeders regularly contribute puppies to be used as future guide dogs and for the breeding program at Guiding Eyes and at other major non-profit organizations for breeding and training dogs for the blind. These other organizations include Second Sight, in Smithtown, New York; Guide Dogs for the Blind in San Rafael, California; The Seeing Eye in Morristown, New Jersey; Leader Dog in Rochester, Michigan; and Pilot Dog in Columbus, Ohio.

The training school and kennel facilities at Guiding Eyes for the Blind.

Moorwood-bred "Minnie," now guiding her blind mistress. Given to and trained by Guiding Eyes for the Blind. Born in March 1980, "Minnie" is a daughter of Ch. Sandylands Markwell of Lockerbie ex Ch. Beaver's Lavinia of Moorwood, W.C. Two other bitches from this same litter, which included twelve puppies all successfully raised by their dam, have graduated from Guiding Eyes for the Blind and are now serving blind owners. Bred by Moorwood Kennels, Mrs. Rosalind B. Moore, Indian Lake, New York.

This is Campbellcroft's Morag, known as "Woofie," listening attentively. Campbellcroft Labradors are owned by Donald and Virginia Campbell, California.

CHAPTER TWELVE

You and Your Labrador

Two of Mrs. Richard C. du Pont's Labs, Gussie and Pistol, formerly owned by Janet Churchill.

When a breed of dog continually remains near the top of the list of popular dog breeds, you can be sure that this breed has some very special qualities to recommend its ownership. The Labrador Retriever is such a breed, and people from all walks of life enjoy sharing their home with this intelligent, adaptable, even-tempered dog.

Labradors as Family Companions

The Labrador Retriever, with his calm, even disposition, his intelligence, and his eagerness to please those he loves, makes an exceptionally fine family dog.

He is sensitive and devoted and has a friendly, outgoing personality. He has keen hearing and thus is quick to sense danger. He is instinctively clean, making him pleasant as a household member; and he is very adaptable to the ways of his family, anxious to be with them and adjusting himself quite readily to their lifestyle and routine.

Although basically an outdoor dog, Labs love the comforts of home and thrive well in city, suburbs, or country.

The Labrador's retrieving instinct makes him easy to train for the field if you wish him as a gun dog, to accompany you on shooting expeditions. His love of children makes him a patient, devoted companion to them. He is an all-'round dog of versatility—a good worker and a good friend.

Responsibilities of Labrador Breeders and Owners

The first responsibility of a person breeding Labs nowadays is to do so with care, forethought, and deliberation. It is inexcusable to breed more litters than you need to carry on your show program or perpetuate your bloodlines. A responsible breeder should not cause a litter to be born unless there are definite plans for disposition of the puppies and unless the breeder has a waiting list to assure that each healthy puppy will be welcomed to a good home and happy future. Overpopulation is the dog world's most heartbreaking tragedy. Those of us who truly love and are involved with dogs should not add to it. Breeding programs should be planned so that no Labrador bitch ever whelps a litter without a definite purpose. If you have any reason to feel that placing the puppies may become a problem, wait for a more propitious moment before bringing them into the world. Certainly, no Lab owner wants to find himself running frantically around in search of someone to take some of the puppies off his hands, even if he has to give them away (the latter frequently is not a good idea anyway). I am a firm believer that people getting a Lab should *buy* that Lab, paying a fair price for it. Any dog demands *proper care*, even so easy a breed to keep as a Labrador, and I have found that a lot of people in the world cannot resist "something for nothing," accepting anything that is free regard-

Ch. Lawnwood's Tamstar Trust and Int. Ch. Spenrock Banner, W.C., with Janet Churchill on the lawn at Spenrock. Trust now is owned by Mrs. Richard du Pont.

Ch. Spenrock Brown Bess obviously enjoys life at Woodstock Farm, Chesapeake City, Maryland. Now owned by Jan Churchill and Mrs. Richard C. du Pont, she is Mrs. du Pont's constant companion. Mrs. du Pont shares her affections for animals between her horses and her Labs. She is the owner of the famous racehorse Kelso.

less of whether or not they *really* want it—this can, and often does, lead to lack of care, if not downright neglect, for the unfortunate dog.

A responsible Lab breeder makes absolutely certain, so far as is humanly possible, that the home to which one of his puppies will go is a *good* home from the dog ownership point of view. I have tremendous admiration for those people who carefully check out the credentials of prospective purchasers, and I firmly believe that all breeders should do likewise, as it is a most important issue. If possible, visit the prospective owners to see if they have suitable facilities for keeping a dog, that they understand the responsibility involved, and that all of the members of the household are in accord regarding the desirability of owning one.

I am certain that no breeder ever wants to find a Lab puppy, or grown dog, winding up in an animal shelter, in an experimental laboratory, or as a victim of a speeding car. While complete control of such a situation may be impossible, it is at least our responsibility to make every effort on behalf of the dogs we bring into the world. When selling a puppy, it is a good idea to do so with the understanding that should it become necessary to place the dog in other hands, the purchaser will contact you, the breeder, before taking any steps. You may want to help in some way, possibly by taking or buying back the dog or placing it elsewhere. It is not fair to just sell our puppies and then never again give a thought to their welfare. Family problems arise, or people grow bored with a dog or with the care of it, and thus the dog becomes a victim.

As a Labrador breeder, the future of these lovely dogs is in your hands. Guard it well and with conscience!

The final obligation every dog owner shares, be there just one dog or an entire kennel involved, is that of making detailed, explicit plans for the future of our dearly loved animals in the event of the owner's death. Far too many of us are apt to procrastinate and leave this very important matter unattended to, feeling that everything will work out all right or that "someone will see to them." The latter is not too likely, at least not to the benefit of the dogs, unless you have done some advance planning which will assure their future well-being.

This handsome portrait of "Gussie" and "Debbie" was done by talented artist Pamela Edwards of Canada. The two beautiful Labs are owned by Mrs. Richard C. du Pont, Woodstock Farm, Chesapeake City, Maryland.

Life is filled with the unexpected, and even the youngest, healthiest, most robust of us may be the victim of a fatal accident or sudden illness. *One never knows.* The fate of our dogs, so entirely in our hands, should never be left to chance. If you have not already done so, please get together with your lawyer and set up a clause in your will saying exactly what you want done with each of your dogs, to whom they will be entrusted (after first making absolutely certain that the person selected is willing and able to assume the respon-

Barbara Gill's son with his Labrador, Windsong's Patrick, pictured helping to raise money for multiple sclerosis. These two run marathons together for various charities in Nashville, Tennessee.

sibility), and telling the locations of all registration papers, pedigrees, and kennel records. Just think of the possibilities of what might happen otherwise! If there is another family member who shares your love of the dogs, that is good and you have less to worry about. But if your heirs are not dog-oriented, they will hardly know how to proceed or how to cope with the dogs themselves, and they may wind up disposing of or caring for your dogs in a way that would break your heart were you around to know about it.

In our family, we have specific instructions in each of our wills for each of our dogs. A friend, also a "dog person" who regards her own dogs with the same esteem as we do ours, has agreed to take over their care until they can be placed accordingly and will make certain that all will work out as we have planned. We have this person's name and telephone number prominently displayed in our van, in our car, and in our wallets. Our lawyer is aware of this fact. It is all spelled out in the wills. The friend has a signed check of ours to be used in case of an emergency or accident when we are travelling with the dogs, for her expenses to come and take over their care should anything happen to make it impossible for us to do so. This, we feel, is the least any dog owner should do in preparation for the time our dogs suddenly find themselves without us. There have been so many sad cases of dogs unprovided for by their loving owners, left to heirs who couldn't care less and who disposed of them in any way at all to get rid of them or who kept and neglected them under the misguided idea that they were providing them "a fine home with lots of freedom." *All* of us *must* prevent any of these misfortunes befalling our own dogs who have meant so much to us.

Ch. Spenrock Anthony Adverse with Jenny Reynolds at Spenrock.

Children and Labs make wonderful companions. These two pals are peeking through the guardrail when caught with her camera by Mrs. Nancy W. Story.

The registration certificates of all our dogs are enclosed in the envelope with our wills. The person who will be in charge knows each one of them, and one from the other, so that there will be no confusion about identification. These are points to be considered, for which provision should be made.

We also owe an obligation to our older dogs who too often are disregarded. It disgusts me that there are people in the world, supposed dog fanciers, who are only interested in getting an older dog out of the way once its show career has ended, in order to make room for new litters. The people I like, and consider to be genuine dog lovers, are the ones who permit their dogs to live out their lives in happy comfort. How quickly some of us seem to forget the thrill and happiness that dog has brought with exciting wins!

Illustrating the slogan "Save Water—Bathe With A Friend" are Tanya Philbrook and Sheba's Chivas Regal, yellow Lab female, at four months of age, by Scrimshaw Tipsy Parson ex Sheba's Midnight Dream. Both belong to Mr. and Mrs. Eugene Philbrook, New Hampshire.

Travelling with Your Labrador

When you travel with a dog, you must always remember that everyone does not necessarily share your love of dogs and that those who do not, strange creatures though they may seem, have their rights too. These rights, on which we should not infringe, include not being disturbed, annoyed, or made uncomfortable by the presence and behavior of other people's pets. Labrador owners, since theirs is an intelligent and easily trained breed, should have their dog well schooled in proper canine behavior by the time maturity is reached. Your dog should not jump enthusiastically on strangers, no matter how playful or friendly the dog's intentions. A sharp "Down" from you should be quickly obeyed, as should be "Come," "Sit," and "Stay."

Captain Jabaez Bloch helping celebrate Samantha Eggertson's fourth birthday. Owned by Samantha's Dad, Ted Eggertson.

If you expect to take your dog on many trips, he should have, for your sake and for his, a crate of appropriate size for him to relax in comfortably. In any emergency or accident, a crated dog is far more likely to escape injury than one riding loose in a car. Dogs quickly become accustomed to being in their crates (particularly if started, as they should be, at an early age) and are far better off when this precautionary measure has been taken. If you do permit your dog to ride loose in a car, do *not* permit him to hang out the window, ears blowing in the breeze. He could become overly excited over something he sees and jump out; he could lose his balance and fall out; and he could suffer an eye injury induced by the strong wind generated by the moving car.

Never, ever, under any circumstances, should a dog be permitted to ride uncrated in the back end of an open pick-up truck. I have noted, with horror, that some people do transport their dogs in this manner, and I think it cruel and shocking. How easily such a dog can be thrown out of the truck by sudden jolts or an impact! And I am sure that many dogs have jumped out at the sight of something exciting along the way. Some unthinking individuals tie the dog, probably not realizing that if he were to jump under those circumstances, his neck might be broken, he could be dragged alongside the vehicle, or he could be hit by another vehicle. If you are for any reason taking your dog in an open-back truck, *please* have sufficient regard for that dog to provide a crate. Also please remember that a dog riding exposed to the sun in hot weather can really suffer and have his life endangered by the heat.

If you are staying at a hotel or motel with your dog, *please* exercise him somewhere other than in the flower beds and parking lot of the property. People walking to and from their cars really are not thrilled at "stepping in something" left by your dog, so try to avoid it. Should an accident occur, pick it up with tissues or a paper towel and deposit it in a proper receptacle; don't just let it remain there. Usually there are grassy

Highlands Samantha's Riptide at one year is towing the boat to shore. Sired by Highlands Ace of Aries, bred by the Knoblochs and owned by Samantha Eggertson.

areas on the sides or behind motels where dogs can be exercised. Use those rather than the more conspicuous, usually carefully tended areas. If you are becoming a dog show enthusiast, you will eventually need an exercise pen to take with you to the show. Exercise pens are ideal to use when staying at motels, too, as they permit you to limit the dog's roaming space and pick up after him more easily.

Spenrock Skylane enjoying the company of his young friends. Owned by Janet Churchill and Albert Prest, he shares many happy hours with Mr. Prest's children.

Groveton's Mocha Mariner has climbed 4 of 40 "Adirondack 46" mountains over 4000 feet high. He has both majors and is being shown by his owner, Kay Van Woert. Bred by Eileen Ketcham, by Ch. Groveton's Copper Adventurer ex Groveton's Amber Promise.

Never leave your dog unattended in the room of a motel unless you are absolutely, positively certain that he will stay quietly and not destroy anything. You do not want a long list of irate complaints from other guests, caused by the annoying barking of a lonesome dog in strange surroundings or an overzealous watch dog barking furiously each time a footstep passes the door. And you certainly do not want to return to torn curtains or bedspreads, soiled rugs, or other embarrassing evidence of the fact that your dog is not really house-reliable!

If yours is a dog accustomed to traveling with you and you are positive that his behavior will be acceptable when left alone, that is fine. But if the slightest uncertainty exists, the wise course is to leave him in the car while you go to dinner or whatever and then bring him into the room when you are ready to retire for the night.

When you travel with a dog, it is often simpler to take along his food and water from home rather than buying food and looking for water while you travel. In this way he will have the rations to which he is accustomed and there will be no fear of problems due to different drinking water. Feeding on the road is quite easy now, at least for short trips, with all the splendid dry prepared foods and high quality canned meats available. And many types of lightweight, handy water containers can be bought at many types of stores.

If you are going to another country, you will need a health certificate from your veterinarian for each dog you are taking with you, certifying that each has had rabies shots within the required length of time preceding your visit.

Be careful always to leave sufficient openings to ventilate your car when the dog will be alone in it. Remember that during the summer, the rays of the sun can make an inferno of a closed-up car within only a few short minutes, so leave sufficient windows open. Again, if your dog is in a crate, this can be done more safely. The fact that you have left the car in a shady spot is not always a guarantee that you will find conditions the same when you return. Don't forget that the position of the sun changes in a matter of minutes, and the car you left nicely shaded half an hour ago can be getting full sunlight far more quickly than you may realize. So, if you have a dog in the car, leave sufficient ventilation and check back frequently to ascertain that all is well.

The importance of teaching your dog the basic commands of obedience before you travel with him can not be overemphasized. Teach him the meaning of "Come," "Stay," "Sit," "Down," "Heel," and "No" even while he is still too young for formal obedience training classes; and with this head start, you will be pleased and proud at the nicely mannered Lab you thus will raise, the sort of dog that can accompany you and be welcome wherever your travels may take you.

Brig. General William W. Spruance of Marathon, Florida with his Lab, Spenrock Phantom, known as "Nacho," a son of Eng., Am. Ch. Lawnwood's Hot Chocolate ex Spenrock Cricket, bred by Charlotte Williams and Jan Churchill.

Ch. Killingworth Thunderson with a Siamese friend. Mrs. Lorraine Robbenhaar of Connecticut, owner.

A Spenrock Lab puppy with one of the Rottweilers. The two breeds get on very amiably at Janet Churchill's Spenrock Farm.

Ch. Winterset Hot Tar takes 3 points to finish at Riverhead in 1981, handled by Joy Quallenberg for B.J. Chubett III, Waccabuc, New York.

Croysdales Sadie gets a big hug from her young mistress! One of Mrs. Nancy W. Story's Labs snapped informally with her daughter.

Ch. Spenrock Bohemia Champagne at 11 years of age. Chucklebrook Labradors, the Pilbins.

CHAPTER THIRTEEN

Veterinarian's Corner

by Joseph P. Sayres, D.V.M.

Frank Jones has sent us this photo of Thunder, illustrating that weather conditions seldom bother a Lab.

By way of introduction to this chapter concerning the medical aspects of the care of your Labrador Retriever, I think we should devote a few paragraphs to how to choose your veterinarian.

Until recent years, there has been a lot of misunderstanding and even animosity between veterinarians and breeders. Some distrust arose on the breeder's part because most veterinarians were not familiar with, or even interested in learning about, purebred dogs. Some of the problems encountered were peculiar to certain breeds and some would crop up at inconvenient times. Veterinarians were then beset by breeders who thought that they knew more about the medical problems of their dogs than the vets did. The veterinarians very often were called only for emergencies or when it was too late to save a sick dog that had been treated too long by people in the kennel. Another problem was that many breeders had never included veterinary fees in their budgets and were slow to pay their bills, if indeed they paid them at all.

Fortunately, these problems, to a large extent, have been solved. Education and better communication between breeders and veterinarians have eliminated most areas of friction.

Today, veterinary education and training have advanced to a point paralleling that of human standards. This resulted from advances in the field of Veterinary Science in the last two decades. Sophisticated diagnostic procedures, new and advanced surgical techniques, and modern well-equipped hospitals all make for improved medical care for our dogs.

Educated breeders now realize that, while they may know more about the general husbandry of their dogs and the unique traits of the Labrador Retriever, they should not attempt to diagnose and treat their ailments.

In choosing your veterinarian, be selective. He or she should be friendly, should be interested in your dogs, and, in the case of breeders, should be interested in your breeding programs. Veterinarians should be willing to talk freely with you. Such things as fees, availability for emergencies, and what services are and are not available should be discussed and understood before a lasting relationship with your veterinarian can be established.

You can expect your veterinarian's office, clinic, or hospital to be clean, free of undesirable odors, well equipped, and staffed by sincere, friendly personnel who willingly serve you at all times. All employees should be clean, neat in appearance, and conversant with whatever services you require. You may also expect your dog to be treated carefully and kindly at all times by the doctor and his staff.

Your veterinarian should participate in continuing education programs in order to keep up with changes and improvements in his field. He should also be aware of his limitations. If he doesn't feel confident in doing certain procedures, he should say so and refer you to qualified individuals to take care of the problem. Seeking second opinions and consultation with specialists on difficult cases is more the rule than the exception nowadays. That is as it should be.

The breeding farm kennel at Guiding Eyes for the Blind, Patterson, New York.

You will know that if your veterinarian is a member of the American Animal Hospital Association, he and his facility have had to measure up to high standards of quality and are subjected to inspections every two years.

Another of Claire White-Peterson's fantastic puppy photographs. Again the subjects are from Stonecrest Kennels belonging to George and Louise White, Charlestown, Rhode Island.

Many excellent veterinarians and veterinary hospitals by choice do not belong to the American Animal Hospital Association. You can satisfy your curiosity about these places by taking guided tours of the facilities and learning by word of mouth about the quality of medicine practiced at these hospitals.

So far, we have discussed only what you should expect from your veterinarian. Now, let's discuss what the veterinarian expects from his clients.

Puppies by Can., Am., Mex, 1978 World and Int. Ch. Franklin's Golden Mandigo, C.D., W.C., and Labradese Bluebelle Bouquet. Owned by Dr. and Mrs. Wm. A. Hines, Labradese Labradors.

Would you believe that the owner of these very comfortable Labs is the author of a book entitled, *Dogs Don't Belong on Beds?* It's true, though, and she is Mrs. Enid P. Bloome, Winterset Labs.

If you are dissatisfied with the services or fees, then ask to discuss these things in a friendly manner with the doctor. If his explanations are not satisfactory or he refuses to talk to you about the problem, then you are justified in seeking another doctor.

The veterinarian expects to provide his services for your animals during regular hours whenever possible. But he also realizes that in a kennel or breeding operation, emergencies can occur at any time, and his services will be needed at off hours. You should find out how these emergencies will be handled and be satisfied with the procedures.

Killingworth Tarbinavon (black), Killingworth Squire (center) and Ranchman's Snap -n- Tickle. All owned by Ranchman's Labradors, Marion and Bob Reid.

Most of all, he expects his clients to be open and frank in their relations with him. He doesn't like to be double-checked and second-guessed behind his back. He also wants you to handle your pet so that he, in turn, can examine him. He also expects you to leash your dog, to control him, and to keep him from bothering other pets in the room. He expects to be paid a fair fee and to be paid promptly for services rendered. Fees in a given area tend to be consistent, and variations are due only to complications or unforeseen problems. Medicine is not an exact science; therefore, things unpredictable can happen.

"Puppy Raisers Day" at Guiding Eyes for the Blind, Patterson, New York.

No veterinarian can be on duty 24 hours of every day. Today, cooperative veterinarians group together to take turns covering each other's emergency calls. Some cities have emergency clinics that operate solely to take care of those catastrophes that seem usually to happen in the middle of the night or on weekends.

My conclusion, after thirty years of practice, is that most disagreements and hard feelings between clients and veterinarians are a result of a breakdown in communication. Find a veterinarian that you can talk to and can be comfortable with, and you'll make a valuable friend.

In using veterinary services to their best advantage, I believe that you will find that prevention of diseases and problems is more important than trying to cure these things after they occur. In other words, an ounce of prevention is worth a pound of cure.

Congenital Defects

Labrador Retrievers have their share of congenital defects. From the publication *Congenital Defects in Dogs* published by Ralston Purina Company, as well as other reliable sources, the following conditions are listed as congenital defects in Labrador Retrievers:

a. Cataracts, Bilateral—Opaque lenses

b. Retinal Dysplasia—Abnormally formed layers of the retina with detachment, causing blindness, more frequently found in England and Sweden.

c. Central Progressive Retinal Atrophy—Mottling and increased reflectivity in retina resulting in loss of central vision affecting dogs three to five years old. Difficulty in seeing still objects. Affected individuals can see best in dim light.

d. Cystinuria—Excess cystine in the urine predisposing to calculi or stones.

An exciting day in the ring as Ch. Lobuff's Seafaring Banner takes Best of Breed and Ch. Lobuff's Tequila Sunrise takes Best of Opposite Sex, both by Ch. Spenrock Heatheredge Mariner ex Ch. Spenrock Cognac. Lobuff Labradors, owned by Jerry and Lisa Weiss.

e. Hemophilia A—Prolonged bleeding episodes.

f. Myopathy—A disorder of the muscles, seen at age six months or younger. The dogs are stiff-legged, have a hopping gait and hold their head and neck abnormally. They also have poor muscle development.

g. Craniomandibular Osteopathy—Abnormal boney proliferation of jaw bone and its joints. Causes discomfort from chewing and opening mouth. Bouts of fever starting at four to seven months old to about one year old. Then may regress.

h. Carpal Subluxation—Partial dislocation of pastern joints.

i. Cryptorchidism—Non-descent of testicles.

Two young puppies, bred by Jan Churchill, at Spenrock Kennels on the Bohemia River. Their sire is Ch. Spenrock Heatheredge Mariner and their dam is Spenrock Brandy Snifter, C.D.

Eight-week-old Labs happily amuse themselves at Nancy M. Scholz's Manora Kennels.

A litter of six-week-old yellow puppies at Spenrock Kennels, sired by Ch. Rivermist Tweed of Spenrock and owned by Janet Churchill.

Ch. Scrimshaw Blue Nun as a six-week-old puppy with the family Whippet, Ballykelly Kevin. Can't you just hear the canine version of "Hi there! I'm your new cruise director. How about a little shuffleboard? Bingo? Ping-pong? Disco dancing?" These two belong to Barbara Barfield, Scrimshaw Labs.

Vaccines

By proper and vigilant vaccination programs, the following contagious diseases can be eliminated: distemper, hepatitis, parainfluenza, leptospirosis, rabies, and parvovirus enteritis.

The following vaccination schedule should be set up and strictly followed to prevent infectious diseases:

Disease:	*Age to Vaccinate:*
Distemper	Six to eight weeks old; second inoculation to be given at 12 to 16 weeks of age. Revaccinate annually.
Hepatitis (Adenovirus)	Same as distemper.
Parainfluenza (Kennel cough)	Same as distemper.
Leptospirosis	Give first vaccine at nine weeks old. Revaccinate with second DHLP (distemper, hepatitis, leptospirosis, parainfluenza) at 12 to 16 weeks of age. Revaccinate annually.
Rabies	First inoculation at three to four months old; then revaccinate when one year old, and at least every three years thereafter. If dog is over four months old at the time of the 1st vaccination, then revaccinate in one year and then once every three years thereafter.
Parvovirus	Give first vaccine at seven to eight weeks old; second vaccine four weeks later; third vaccine four weeks later. Duration of immunity from three injections established at one year at the time of this writing. See explanation below. Revaccinate annually.

Vaccines used are all modified live virus vaccines except for leptospirosis, which is a killed bacterium. New and improved vaccines to immunize against parvovirus have appeared recently. The long-awaited modified live virus vaccine of canine origin was made available recently. It is safe and will produce immunity lasting one year.

408

Other communicable diseases for which no vaccine has been perfected as yet are: canine coronavirus, canine rotavirus, and canine brucellosis.

Infectious and Contagious Diseases

Distemper

Distemper is caused by a highly contagious, airborne virus. The symptoms are varied and may involve all of the dog's systems. A pneumonic form is common, with heavy eye and nose discharges, coughing and lung congestion. The digestive system may be involved as evidenced by vomiting, diarrhea, and weight loss. The skin may show a pustular type rash on the abdomen. Nervous system involvement is common, with convulsions, chorea, and paralysis as persistent symptoms. This virus may have an affinity for nerve tissue and cause encephalitis and degeneration of the spinal cord. These changes, for the most part, are irreversible and death or severe crippling ensues.

We have no specific remedy or cure for distemper; and recoveries, when they occur, can only be attributed to the natural resistance of the patient, good nursing care, and control of secondary infections with antibiotics.

That's the bad news about distemper. The good news is that we rarely see a case of distemper in most areas today because of the efficiency of the vaccination program. This is proof that prevention by vaccination has been effective in almost eradicating this dreaded disease.

Hepatitis

Hepatitis is another contagious viral disease affecting the liver. This is not an airborne virus and can only be spread by contact. Although rarely seen today because of good prevention by vaccination programs, this virus is capable of producing a very acute, fulminating, severe infection and can cause death in a very short time. Symptoms of high temperature, lethargy, anorexia, and vomiting are the same as for other diseases. Careful evaluation by a veterinarian is necessary to confirm the diagnosis of this disease.

The old canine infectious hepatitis vaccine has been replaced by a canine adenovirus type 2 strain vaccine which is safer and superior. The new vaccine seems to be free of post-vaccination complications such as blue eyes, shedding of the virus in the urine and some kidney problems.

Shababaland Labrador puppies, owned by Gordon Sousa.

These three are representative of the high quality demanded by Mrs. Enid P. Bloome in her Winterset Labradors.

Exceptional head studies. On the left is "Chip," sired by Highlands Sir Lochee ex Velvet of Ebb Tide, and on the right is Highlands Serenity, by Highlands Ace of Aries ex Sambeau's Cam. "Chip" was bred by Joshua Moriarity, owner of Ebb Tide Labradors, who took this lovely photo. Serenity was bred by Lillian Knobloch.

Para influenza

This is commonly called kennel cough. It is caused by a throat-inhabiting virus that causes an inflammation of the trachea (wind pipe) and larynx (voice box). Coughing is the main symptom and fortunately it rarely causes any other systemic problems. The virus is airborne and highly contagious, and it is the scourge of boarding kennels. A vaccine is available that will protect against this contagious respiratory disease and should be given as part of your vaccination program, along with the distemper, hepatitis, leptosperosis, and parvo virus shots. Pregnant bitches should not be vaccinated against para influenza because of the possibility of infecting the unborn puppies. As there may be more than one infectious agent involved in contagious upper respiratory diseases of dogs, vaccination against para influenza is not a complete guarantee to protect against all of them.

This marvelous photo of baby Labs was taken by Claire White-Peterson, daughter of the George Whites of Rhode Island, who own the puppies.

Leptospirosis

This is a disease that seriously affects the kidneys of dogs, most domestic animals, and man. For this reason, it can become a public health hazard. In urban and slum areas, the disease is carried by rats and mice in their urine. It is caused by a spirochete organism which is very resistant to treatment. Symptoms include fever, depression, dehydration, excess thirst, persistent vomiting, occasional diarrhea and jaundice in the latter stages. Again, it is not always easy to diagnose so your veterinarian will have to do some laboratory work to confirm it.

We see very few cases of leptospirosis in dogs and then only in the unvaccinated ones. The vaccine is generally given concurrently with the distemper and hepatitis vaccinations.

A group of the Novacroft Labradors owned by Mrs. D.I. Gardner, Sambrook, Shropshire, England.

Rabies

This is a well-known virus-caused disease that is almost always fatal and is transmissible to man and other warm-blooded animals. The virus causes very severe brain damage. Sources of the infection include foxes, skunks, and raccoons, as well as domesticated dogs and cats. Transmission is by introduction of the virus by saliva into bite wounds. Incubation in certain animals may be from three to eight weeks. In a dog, clinical signs will appear within five days. Symptoms fall into two categories, depending on what stage the disease is in when seen. We have the dumb form and the furious form. There is a change of personality in the furious form; individuals become hypersensitive and overreact to noise and stimuli. They will bite any object that moves. In dumb rabies, the typical picture of the loosely hanging jaw and tongue presents itself. Diagnosis is confirmed only by a laboratory finding the virus and characteristic lesions in the brain. All tissues and fluids from rabid animals should be considered infectious and you should be careful not to come in contact with them. Prevention by vaccination is a must because there is no treatment for rabid dogs.

Labradors make great chin-rests! Rosalind B. Moore, owner, Moorwood Labs.

This is Diana Beckett's father with some of the Kimvalley Labradors.

Canine Parvovirus (CPV)

This is the newest and most highly publicized member of the intestinal virus family. Cat distemper virus is a member of the same family but differs from canine parvovirus biologically, and it has been impossible to produce this disease in dogs using cat virus as the inducing agent; and conversely canine parvovirus will not produce the disease in a cat. However, vaccines for both species will produce immunity in the dog. The origin of CPV is still unknown.

Canine parvovirus is very contagious and acts rapidly. The main source of infection is contaminated bowel movements. Direct contact between dogs is not necessary, and carriers such as people, fleas, and medical instruments may carry and transmit the virus.

The incubation period is five to fourteen days. The symptoms are fever, severe vomiting and diarrhea, often with blood, depression, and dehydration. Feces may appear yellowish gray streaked with blood. Young animals are more severely affected, and a shock-like death may occur in two days. In animals less than six weeks old, the virus will cause an inflammation of the heart muscle, causing heart failure and death.

Five generations of Labradese ladies. Dr. and Mrs. Wm. A. Hines, owners.

These pups may not have diarrhea. A reduction in the number of white blood cells is a common finding early in the disease.

The virus is passed in the feces for one to two weeks and may possibly be shed in the saliva and urine also. This virus has also been found in the coats of dogs. The mortality rate is unknown.

Dogs that recover from the disease develop an immunity to it. Again, the duration of this immunity is unknown.

Control measures include disinfection of the kennels, animals and equipment with a 1 to 30 dilution of Clorox and isolation of sick individuals.

Treatment is very similar to that for coronavirus, namely: intravenous fluid therapy, administration of broad spectrum antibiotics, intestinal protectants, and good nursing care.

Transmission to humans has not been proven.

Trent and Teak, two playful Lab youngsters from Nancy Scholz's Manora Kennels, enjoying a game with the typical enthusiasm of eight-week-olds.

Clinical studies have proven that vaccination with three injections of the new modified live virus vaccine of canine origin, with four weeks between injections, will be over 90% effective. Recent work at the James A. Baker Institute for Animal Health at Cornell University has shown that maternally derived antibodies can interfere with the immunizing properties of our vaccines for as long as 15 to 16 weeks. This means that some of our puppies, especially those from dams with good immunity, will not become susceptible to successful vaccination until they are 16 weeks old. It is also known that the maternal protection afforded these puppies, while enough to prevent successful vaccination, may not be enough to protect them from an exposure to the virus. The best advice is to give our puppies three inoculations of a canine origin modified live virus vaccine four weeks apart, starting when they are eight weeks old. Then, hope for the best and revaccinate annually.

411

Ch. Ironpride's Delta Dignity, out of Ch. Franklin's Delta Dignity, is owned by Mrs. Bernard W. Ziessow, Franklin Labs, Franklin, Michigan.

Below, Ch. Rivermist Tweed of Spenrock poses with an English Foxhound puppy at Spenrock. Janet Churchill, owner. At the right, Tweed (with the rope in his mouth) pulls his young owner on a raft in the Bohemia River. A German Shepherd puppy completes the trio.

Canine Coronavirus (CCV)

This is a highly contagious virus that spreads rapidly to susceptible dogs. The source of infection is through infectious bowel movements. The incubation period is one to four days, and the virus will be found in feces for as long as two weeks. It is hard to tell the difference sometimes between cases of diarrhea caused by coronavirus and parvovirus. Coronavirus generally is less severe or causes a more chronic or sporadic type of diarrhea. The fecal material may be orange in color and have a very bad odor; occasionally, it will also contain blood. Vomiting sometimes precedes the diarrhea, but loss of appetite and listlessness are consistent signs of the disease. Fever may or may not be present. Recovery is the rule after eight to ten days, but treatment with fluids, antibiotics, intestinal protectants, and good nursing care are necessary in the more severe watery diarrhea cases. Dogs that survive these infections become immune but for an unknown length of time.

To control an outbreak of this virus in a kennel, very stringent hygienic measures must be taken. Proper and quick disposal of feces, isolation of affected animals, and disinfection with a 1 to 30 dilution of Clorox are all effective means of controlling an outbreak in the kennel.

There is no vaccine yet available for prevention of canine coronavirus. Human infections by this virus have not been reported.

Canine Rotavirus (CRV)

This virus has been demonstrated in dogs with a mild diarrhea but again with more severe cases in very young puppies. Very little is known about this virus.

A milder type of diarrhea is present for eight to ten days. The puppies do not run a temperature and continue to eat. Dogs usually recover naturally from this infection. There is no vaccine available for this virus.

Canine Brucellosis

This is a disease of dogs that causes both abortions and sterility. It is caused by a small bacterium closely related to the agent that causes undulant fever in man and abortion in cows. It occurs worldwide.

Symptoms of brucellosis sometimes are difficult to determine, and some individuals with the disease may appear healthy. Vague symptoms such as lethargy, swollen glands, poor hair coat, and stiffness in the back legs may be present. This organism does not cause death and may stay in the dog's system for months and even years. The latter animals, of course, have breeding problems and infect other dogs.

Poor results in your breeding program may be the only indication that brucellosis is in your kennel. Apparently, normal bitches abort without warning. This usually occurs 45 to 55 days after mating. Successive litters will also be aborted. In males, signs of the disease are inflammation of the skin of the scrotum, shrunken testicles, and swollen tender testicles. Fertility declines and chronically infected males become sterile.

The disease is transmitted to both sexes at the time of mating.

Other sources of infection are aborted puppies and birth membrane and discharge from the womb at the time of abortions.

Humans can be infected, but such infections are rare and mild. Unlike in the dog, the disease in humans responds readily to antibiotics.

What Labs like best! These two beauties belong to Mrs. Enid P. Bloome, Winterset Kennels.

Diagnosis is done by blood testing, which should be done carefully. None of the present tests are infallible and false positives may occur. The only certain way that canine brucellosis can be diagnosed is by isolating the B. canis organism from blood or aborted material and for this, special techniques are required.

Treatment of infected individuals has proven ineffective in most cases. Sterility in males is permanent. Spaying or castrating infected pets should be considered as this will halt the spread of the disease and is an alternative to euthanasia.

At present, there is no vaccine against this important disease.

Manora's Tiffany making a retrieve in water. Owned by Kathy Finneson. Photo courtesy of Nancy M. Scholz.

Our best hope in dealing with canine brucellosis is prevention. The following suggestions are made in order to prevent the occurrence of this malady in your dogs.

a. Test breeding stock annually and by all means breed only uninfected animals.

b. Test bitches several weeks before their heat periods.

c. Do not bring any new dogs into your kennel unless they have two negative tests taken a month apart.

d. If a bitch aborts, isolate her, wear gloves when handling soiled bedding, and disinfect the premises with Roccal.

e. If a male loses interest in breeding or fails to produce after several matings, have him checked.

f. Consult your veterinarian for further information about this disease; alert other breeders and support the research that is going on at the James A. Baker Institute for Animal Health at Cornell University.

External Parasites

The control and eradication of external parasites depends on the repeated use of good quality insecticide sprays or powders during the warm months. Make a routine practice of using these products at seven day intervals throughout the season. It is also imperative that sleeping quarters and wherever the animal habitates be treated also.

Shababaland Ike's Candy Apple, a typical Shababaland puppy, playing hide and seek. Gordon W. Sousa, Jr., owner.

Fleas

These are brown, wingless insects with laterally compressed bodies and strong legs, and they are bloodsuckers. Their life cycle comprises 18 to 21 days from egg to adult flea. They can live without food for one year in high humidity but die in a few days in low humidity. They multiply rapidly and are more prevalent in the warm months. They can cause a severe skin inflammation in those individuals that are allergic or sensitive to the flea bite or saliva of the flea. They can act as a vector for many diseases and do carry tapeworms. Control measures must include persistent, continual use of flea collars or flea medallions, or sprays or powders. The dog's bedding and premises must also be treated because the eggs are there. Foggers, vacuuming, or professional exterminators may have to be used. All dogs and cats in the same household must be treated at the same time.

Winterset Tamess Primros, by Ch. Lawnwood's Hot Chocolate ex Ch. Rupert Caviar, is owned by Eric Johnstone, Millbrook, New York.

Ticks

There are hard and soft species of ticks. Both species are bloodsuckers and at times cause severe skin inflammations on their host. They act as a vector for Rocky Mountain Spotted Fever, as well as other diseases. Hibernation through an entire winter is not uncommon. The female tick lays as many as 1000 to 5000 eggs in crevices and cracks in walls. These eggs will hatch in about three weeks and then a month later become adult ticks. Ticks generally locate around the host's neck and ears and between the toes. They can cause anemia and serious blood loss if allowed to grow and multiply. It is not a good idea to pick ticks off the dogs because of the danger of a reaction in the skin. Just apply the tick spray directly on the ticks which then die and fall off eventually. Affected dogs should be dipped every two weeks. The premises, kennels, and yards should be treated every two weeks during the summer months, being sure to apply the insecticide to walls and in all cracks and crevices. Frequent or daily grooming is effective in finding and removing ticks.

Killingworth's Tarbinavon, owned by Marion and Bob Reid, Ranchman's Labradors.

Lice

There are two kinds of lice, namely the sucking louse and the biting louse. They spend their entire life on their host but can be spread by direct contact or through contaminated combs and brushes. Their life cycle is 21 days, and their eggs, known as nits, attach to the hairs of the dog. The neck and shoulder region, as well as the ear flaps, are the most common areas to be inhabited by these pesky parasites. They cause itchiness, some blood loss, and inflammation of the skin. Eradication will result from the dipping or dusting with methyl carbonate or Thuron once a week for three to four weeks. It is a good idea to fine-comb the dogs after each dip to remove the dead lice and nits. Ask your veterinarian to provide the insecticides and advice or control measures for all of these external parasites.

Scrimshaw Gorblimee, at four months of age, took Best Puppy in Match, San Antonio Labrador Retriever Club, spring 1981. Bred by Barbara Barfield, co-owned by Mrs. Barfield and Jo Clendening, Clen Kennels, Austin, Texas.

This handsome fellow, Highlands Barrister Brown, was bred by Lillian Knobloch, Highland Kennels.

Internal Parasites

The eradication and control of internal parasites in dogs will occupy a good deal of your time and energy.

Puppies should be tested for worms at four weeks of age and then six weeks later. It is also wise to test them again six weeks following their last worm treatment to be sure the treatments have been successful. Annual fecal tests are advisable throughout your dog's life. All worming procedures should be done carefully and only with the advice and supervision of your veterinarian. The medicants used to kill the parasites are, to a certain extent, toxic, so they should be used with care.

Ch. The Black Baroness is sprinting over the countryside. Rosalind B. Moore, owner, Moorwood Labs.

Mites

Less commonly occurring parasitic diseases such as demodectic and sarcoptic mange, caused by mites, should be diagnosed and treated only by your veterinarian. You are wise to consult your doctor whenever any unusual condition occurs and persists in your dog's coat and skin. These conditions are difficult to diagnose and treat at best, so that the earlier a diagnosis is obtained, the better the chances are for successful treatment. Other skin conditions such as ringworm, flea bite allergy, bacterial infections, eczemas, hormonal problems, etc., all have to be considered.

A Royal Flush puppy owned by Ambersand Kennels.

Hookworms

Hookworms are bloodsuckers and also cause bleeding from the site of their attachment to the lining of the intestine when they move from one site to another. They can cause a blood-loss type of anemia and serious consequences, particularly in young puppies. Their life cycle is direct and their eggs may be ingested or pass through the skin of its host. Treatment of yards and runs where the dogs defecate with 5% sodium borate solution is said to kill the eggs in the soil. Two or

Ascarids

These include roundworms, puppy worms, stomach worms, and milk worms. Puppies become infested shortly after birth and occasionally even before birth. Ascarids can be difficult to eradicate. When passed in the stool or thrown up, they look somewhat like cooked spaghetti when fresh or like rubber bands when they are dried up. Two treatments at least two weeks apart will eliminate ascarids from most puppies. An occasional individual may need more wormings according to the status in its system of the life cycle of the worm at the time of worming. Good sanitary conditions must prevail and immediate disposal of feces is necessary to keep down the worm population.

Scrimshaw Mother Brown, chocolate daughter of Ch. Scrimshaw Another Deacon, at the age of six weeks. Barbara Barfield, owner, Scrimshaw Labs.

Ch. Ro-Shan's Canzoo Chieftain, by Ch. Ro-Shan's Kapko Canajun, chocolate male owned by Ro-Shan Labradors.

three worm treatments three to four weeks apart may be necessary to get rid of hookworms. New injectable products administered by your veterinarian have proven more effective than remedies used in the past. Repeated fecal examinations may be necessary to detect the eggs in the feces. These eggs pass out of the body only sporadically or in showers, so that it is easy to miss finding them unless repeated stool testing is done. As is true with any parasite, good sanitary conditions in the kennel and outside runs will help eradicate this worm.

Can., Am. Ch. Casadelora's All Spice taking the jumps with ease. Mr. and Mrs. W.E. Brown, owners, Casadelora Labs.

Whip worms

These are a prevalent parasite in some kennels and in some individual dogs. They cause an intermittent mucousy type diarrhea. As they live only in the dog's appendix, it is extremely difficult to reach them with any worm medicine given by mouth. Injections seem to be the most effective treatment, and these have to be repeated several times over a long period of time to be effective. Here again, repeated fresh stool samples must be examined by your veterinarian to be sure that this pest has been eradicated. Appendectomies are indicated in only the most severe chronic cases. The fact that cleanliness is next to Godliness cannot be emphasized too often; it is most important in getting rid of this parasite.

Manora's Amber at six weeks of age sees something interesting in the grass. Nancy M. Scholz, owner.

Tapeworms

They are another common internal parasite of dogs. They differ in the mode of their transmission as they have an indirect life cycle. This means that part of their cycle must be spent in an intermediate host. Fleas, fish, rabbits, and field mice all may act as an intermediate host for the tapeworm. Fleas are the most common source of tapeworms in dogs, although dogs that live near water and may eat raw fish and hunting dogs that eat the entrails of rabbits may get them from those sources. Another distinguishing feature of the tapeworm is the suction apparatus which is the part of the head which enables the tapeworm to attach itself to the lining of the intestine. If, after worming, just the head remains,

Looking eagerly expectant, Highlands Tasse is a nine-week-old chocolate bitch by Highlands Ace of Aries ex Highlands Sweet Toffee. Bred by Lillian Knobloch and owned by Jody Hetchka, Elmwood Park, New Jersey.

it has the capability of regenerating into another worm. This is one reason why tapeworms are so difficult to get rid of. It will require several treatments to get the entire parasite out of a dog's system. These worms are easily recognized by the appearance of their segments which break off and appear on top of a dog's feces or stuck to the hair around the rectal area. These segments may appear alive and mobile at times, but most often they are dead and dried up when found. They look like flat pieces of rice and may be white or brown when detected. Elimination of the intermediate host is an integral part of any plan to rid our dogs of this worm. Repeated wormings may be necessary to kill all the adult tapeworms in the intestine.

Heartworms

Heartworm disease is caused by an actual worm that goes through its life cycle in the blood stream of its victims. It ultimately makes its home in the right chambers of the heart and in the large vessels that transport the blood to the lungs. They vary in size from 2.3 inches to 16 inches. Adult worms can survive up to five years in the heart.

By its nature, this is a very serious disease and can cause irreversible damage to the lungs and heart of its host. Heart defect and lung pathology soon result in serious problems for the dog.

The disease is transmitted and carried by female mosquitoes that have infected themselves after biting an infected dog; they then pass it on to the next dog with which they come in contact.

The disease has been reported wherever mosquitoes are found, and cases have been reported in most of the United States. Rare cases have been reported in man and cats. It is most prevalent in warmer climates where the mosquito population is the greatest, but hotbeds of infection exist in the more temperate parts of the United States and Canada also.

Concerted effort and vigorous measures must be taken to control and prevent this serious threat to our dog population. The most effective means of eradication I believe will come through annual blood testing for early detection, by the use of preventive medicine during mosquito exposure times, and also by ridding our dogs' environment of mosquitoes.

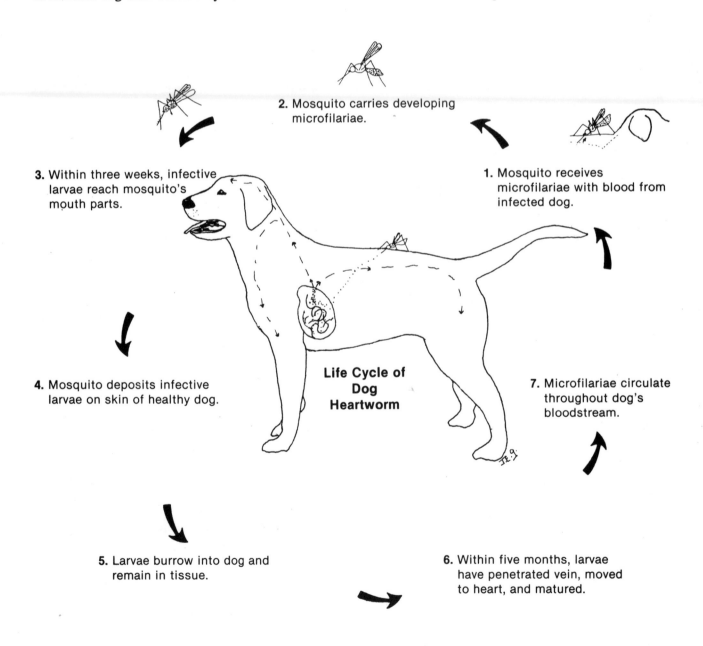

2. Mosquito carries developing microfilariae.

3. Within three weeks, infective larvae reach mosquito's mouth parts.

1. Mosquito receives microfilariae with blood from infected dog.

Life Cycle of Dog Heartworm

4. Mosquito deposits infective larvae on skin of healthy dog.

7. Microfilariae circulate throughout dog's bloodstream.

5. Larvae burrow into dog and remain in tissue.

6. Within five months, larvae have penetrated vein, moved to heart, and matured.

Annual blood testing is necessary to detect cases that haven't started to show symptoms yet and thus can be treated effectively. It also enables your veterinarian to prescribe safely the preventive medicine to those individuals that test negative. There is a 10 to 15% margin of error in the test, which may lead to some false negative tests. Individuals that test negative but are showing classical symptoms of the disease such as loss of stamina, coughing, loss of weight, and heart disease should be further evaluated with chest X-rays, blood tests, and electrocardiograms.

Serious consequences may result when the preventive medication is given to a dog that already has heartworm in his system. That is why it is so important to have your dog tested annually before starting the preventive medicine.

In order to be most effective, the preventive drug diethylcarbamazine should be given in daily doses of 2.5 mg. to 3 mg. per pound of body weight or 5 mg. per kilogram of body weight of your dog. This routine should be started 15 days prior to exposure to mosquitoes and be continued until 60 days after exposure. Common and trade names for this drug are Caricide, Styrid-Caricide, and D.E.C. It comes in liquid and tablet forms.

This drug has come under criticism by some breeders and individuals who claim that it affects fertility and causes some serious reactions. Controlled studies have shown no evidence that the drug produces sterility or abnormal sperm count or quality. Long-term studies on reproduction, when the drug was given at the rate of 4.9 mg. per pound of body weight (two times the preventive dose level) for two years, showed no signs of toxic effects on body weight maintenance, growth rate of pups, feed consumption, conception rate, numbers of healthy pups whelped, ratio of male to female pups, blood counts, and liver function tests. It is reported to be a well-tolerated medication, and many thousands of dogs have benefitted from its use. From personal experience, I find only an occasional dog who will vomit the medicine or get an upset stomach from it. The new enteric coated pills have eliminated this small problem.

However, if you still don't want to give the preventive, especially to your breeding stock, an alternative procedure would be to test your dogs every six months for early detection of the disease, so that it can be treated as soon as possible.

It's been a busy day for Croysdales Sadie and her young mistress. Mrs. Nancy W. Story sent this cute photo of her daughter with her Lab.

Heartworm infestation can be treated successfully. There is a 1 to 5% mortality rate from the treatment. It can be expected that treatment may be completed without side effects if the disease hasn't already caused irreversible problems in the heart, lungs, liver, kidneys, or other organs. Careful testing, monitoring, and supervision is essential to success in treatment. Treatment is far from hopeless these days and if the disease is detected early enough, a successful outcome is more the rule than the exception.

In conclusion, remember that one case of heartworm disease in your area is one too many, especially if that one case is your dog. By following the steps mentioned here, we can go a long way in ridding ourselves of this serious threat to our dogs.

Highlands Samantha's Riptide with owner Samantha Eggertson waiting for the school bus on the first day of school.

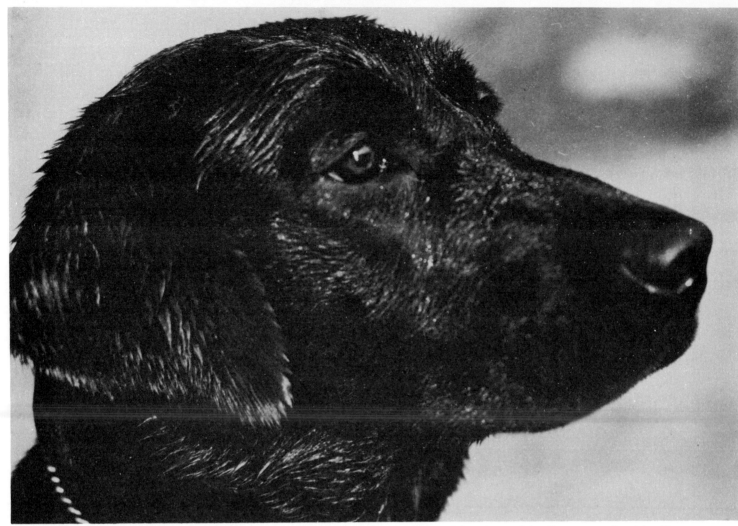

Croysdales Ma-Pat-Ma Tru Chanc, by Ch. Killingworth Ben ex Croysdales Sara of Ludlowe, was bred by Nancy Story of Connecticut. This bitch has points toward her title and is owned by Margaret D. Heaney, Ma-Pat-Ma Labradors, New York.

Home Remedies and First Aid

You have repeatedly read here of my instructions to call your veterinarian when your animals are sick. This is the best advice I can give you. There are a few home remedies, however, that may get you over some rough spots while trying to get professional help.

I think it is a good idea to keep on hand some medical supplies in a first aid kit. The kit should contain the following items: a roll of cotton, gauze bandages, hydrogen peroxide, tincture of metaphen, cotton applicator swabs, BFI powder, rectal thermometer, adhesive tape, boric acid crystals, tweezers, and a jar of petroleum jelly.

A word here on how to take a dog's temperature may be in order. Always lubricate the thermometer with petroleum jelly and carefully insert it well into the rectum. Hold it in place for two to three minutes and then read it. The thermometer should be held firmly so that it doesn't get sucked up into the rectum.

To administer liquid medicines to dogs, simply pull the lips away from the side of the mouth, making a pocket for depositing the liquid. Slightly tilt the dog's head upward and he will be able to swallow the liquid properly. Giving liquids by opening the mouth and pouring them directly on the tongue is an invitation to disaster because inhalation pneumonia can result. Putting it in the side of the mouth gives the dog time to hold it in his mouth and then swallow it properly.

Tablets are best administered by forcing the dog's mouth open, and pushing the pill down over the middle of the tongue into the back of his mouth. If put in the right place, a reflex tongue reaction will force the pill down the throat and thus be swallowed. There is no objection to giving the pills in favorite foods as long as you carefully determine that the medicine is surely swallowed with the food.

Vomiting

To stop vomiting, mix one tablespoon of table salt to one pint of water and dissolve the salt thoroughly; then give one tablespoonful of the mixture to the patient. After waiting one hour, repeat the procedure and skip the next meal. The dog may vomit a little after the first dose, but the second dose works to settle the stomach. This mixture not only provides chlorides but also acts as a mild astringent and many times in mild digestive upsets will work to stop the vomiting.

Diarrhea

In the case of adult Labradors, give three or four tablespoons of Kaopectate or Milk of Bismuth every four hours. Use one-fourth of this dosage for puppies. Skip the next meal, and if diarrhea persists, then start a bland diet of boiled ground lean beef and boiled rice in the proportions of half and half. Three or four doses of this medicine should suffice. If the diarrhea persists and, particularly, if accompanied by depression, lethargy and loss of appetite, your veterinarian should be consulted immediately. With all these new viral-caused diarrheas floating around, time is of the essence in securing treatment.

Mild Stimulant

Dilute brandy half and half with water, add a little sugar, and give a tablespoonful of the mixture every four to five hours. For puppies over three months old, reduce the dosage to a teaspoonful of the mixture every four to five hours.

Mild Sedative

Dilute brandy half and half with water, add a little sugar, and give a tablespoon of the mixture every 20 to 30 minutes until the desired effect is attained. For puppies over three months old, reduce the dosage to a teaspoonful of the mixture every 20 to 30 minutes.

Using brandy for both sedation and stimulation is possible by varying the time interval between doses. Given every four to five hours, it's a stimulant; but given every 20 to 30 minutes it acts as a sedative.

Laurell Jenny's Mandigo, a great show dog and a talented working retriever.

Minor Cuts and Wounds

Cleanse them first with soap and water, preferably Tincture of Green Soap. Apply a mild antiseptic such as Bactine or Tincture of Metaphen two or three times daily until healed. If the cut is deep, and fairly long and bleeding, then a bandage should be applied until professional help can be obtained.

Whenever attempting to bandage wounds, first apply a layer or two of gauze over the cleaned and treated wound. Then apply a layer of cotton and then another layer or two of gauze. The bandage must be snug enough to stay on but not so tight as to impair the circulation to the body part. Adhesive tape should be applied over the second layer of gauze to keep the bandage as clean and dry as possible until you can get your dog to the doctor.

Tourniquets should be applied only in cases of profusely bleeding wounds. They are applied tightly between the wound and the heart, in addition to the pressure bandage that should be applied directly to the wound. The tourniquets must be released and reapplied at 15 minute intervals.

Burns

Application of ice or very cold water and compresses is the way to treat a skin burn. Apply cold packs as soon as possible and take the dog immediately to your vet.

Frostbite

Frostbite is a rarely occurring problem. The secret in treating this condition is to restore normal body temperature gradually to the affected parts. In other words, use cold water, then tepid water, to thaw out the area slowly and restore circulation. In cases of severe freezing or shock due to bitter cold temperature, take the animal to the veterinarian as soon as possible.

Abscesses and Infected Cysts

Obvious abscesses and infected cysts that occur between the toes may be encouraged to drain by using hot boric acid packs and saturated dressings every few hours until professional aid can be secured. The boric acid solution is made by dissolving one tablespoon of crystals to one pint of hot water. Apply frequently to the swollen area. Further treatment by a veterinarian may involve lancing and thoroughly

Spenrock Lantern on an autumn day. Ruth and Ed Brooking, Wilmington, Delaware, own this handsome Lab by Ch. Spenrock Cardigan Bay ex Ch. Lawnwood's Tamstar Trust, bred by Janet Churchill.

Out for a swim! Some of the Labs from Agnes Carter's Agber Kennels in New Jersey.

draining and cleaning out the abscess cavity. As most abscesses are badly infected, systemic antibiotics are generally indicated.

Heatstroke or Heat Exhaustion

A word about the serious effects of heat on a dog is timely. It never ceases to amaze me how many people at dog shows have to be warned and advised not to leave their dogs in cars or vans on a warm day.

A dog's heat regulating mechanism is not nearly as efficient as ours. Consequently, dogs feel the heat more than we do. Keep them as cool and as well ventilated as possible in hot weather. Another inducement for shock is taking your dog out of a cool air-conditioned vehicle and exposing him immediately to the hot outdoors. Make that change as gradual as you can because a rapid change can cause a shock-like reaction.

In cases of suspected heatstroke, which manifests itself with very high body temperatures (as high as 106° to 108°F. sometimes), severe panting, weakness, shaking and collapse, act quickly to get him into a cold bath or shower or put ice-cold compresses on his head. Then, again without delay, rush him to the nearest veterinarian

for further treatment. Prevention is the key here and with a little common sense, heatstroke and exhaustion can be avoided.

Poisons

Many dogs are poisoned annually by unscrupulous people who hate dogs. Many others are victims of poisoning due simply to the careless use of rat and ant poisons, insecticides, herbicides, anti-freeze solutions, drugs, and so forth. Dogs also frequently eat poisonous plants, either in the house or outdoors, which can lead to serious consequences. Common sources of these toxic products are named below.

Plants that can be a source of poison for dogs include the following (this list contains only the most common ones): daffodils, oleanders, poinsettas, mistletoe, philodendron, delphiniums, monkshood, foxglove, iris, lilies of the valley, rhubarb, spinach, tomato vines, sunburned potatoes, rhododendron, cherry, peach, oak, elderberry, black locust, jack-in-the-pulpit, Dutchman's-breeches, water hemlock, mushrooms, buttercups, poison hemlock, nightshade, jimson weed, marijuana, locoweed, and lupine.

O.T. Ch. Wimberway the Winning Sue, W.C., is owned by the Okkak Kennels of John and Alanna Downton in Newfoundland.

Poisonous animals include such snakes as vipers, rattlesnakes, copperheads, water moccasins, and the coral snake. Lizards like the Gila monster and Mexican beaded lizard are bad. Some toads, spiders, insects, and fish also are potential sources of trouble.

Chemicals comprise perhaps the largest and most common source of poisoning in our environment. These are hazards that our dogs may be exposed to everyday. Careful handling and awareness of these products are essential.

Toxic materials are found in arts and crafts supplies, photographic supplies, and automotive and machinery products and include such things as antifreeze and de-icers, rust inhibitors, brake fluids, engine and carburetor cleaners, lubricants, gasoline, kerosene, radiator cleaners, and windshield washers. Cleaners, bleaches and polishes, disinfectants, and sanitizers all contain products that potentially are dangerous.

Even health and beauty aids may contain toxic materials if ingested in large enough quantities: some bath oils, perfumes, corn removers, deodorants, anti-perspirants, athlete's foot remedies, eye makeup, hair dyes and preparations, diet pills, headache remedies, laxatives, liniments, fingernail polish removers, sleeping pills, suntan lotions, amphetamines, shaving lotions, colognes, shampoos, and certain ointments.

Paints and related products also can be dangerous. Caulking compounds, driers, thinners, paints, paint brush cleaners, paint and varnish removers, preservatives, and floor and wood cleaners all fit into the category.

Pest poisons for the control of birds, fungi, rats, mice, ants, and snails all can be toxic and sometimes fatal to dogs.

Miscellaneous items like fire extinguishers and non-skid products for slippery floors can be unsafe. Almost all solvents like carbon tetrachloride, benzene, toluene, acetone, mineral spirits, kerosene, and turpentine are bad.

The previous paragraphs serve only to illustrate how many products in our everyday environment exist which can be hazardous or fatal to our dogs.

In cases of suspected poisoning, be aware of what to do until professional help can be obtained:

a. Keep the animal protected, quiet, and warm.

b. If a contact is on the skin, eye, or body surface, cleanse and flush the area with copious amounts of water. Do this also if the dog gets something in his eye. Protect him from further exposure.

c. Inducing vomiting may be dangerous and should be done only on the advice of a veterinarian. Giving peroxide may induce vomiting in some cases. It is better to allow the animal to drink as much water as he wants. This will dilute the poison. Giving milk or raw egg whites is helpful many times to delay absorption of the toxic products.

Do not attempt to give anything by mouth if the patient is convulsing, depressed, or unconscious.

Do not waste time getting veterinary service. Take any vomited material and suspected causative agents, and their containers with you to the vet. When the suspected product is known, valuable time can be saved in administering specific treatment.

A word to the wise should be sufficient. Keep away from your dog all products that can harm him in any way.

Bloat

One of the most serious and difficult problems and real emergency situations that can occur is that of bloat. Other names for this condition are torsion and acute indigestion. This condition generally occurs in larger breeds after the consumption of a large meal (usually dry feed) and then the drinking of a lot of water immediately after eating. If this is followed by a vigorous exercise period, the stage is set for bloat. The stomach, being pendulous and overloaded at this point, can become twisted or rotated. This, of course, cuts off the circulation to the stomach and spleen and may also interfere with the large blood vessels coming to and from the liver. A shock-like syndrome follows and death may ensue shortly if heroic measures are not undertaken to save the stricken animal. If ever there was an emergency, this is truly one. Dry heaves, painful loud crying, and abdominal enlargement, take place in a very short time. Relief of the torsion requires immediate surgery to right the stomach to its normal position and to keep it there. Circulation may then return to normal.

Moorwood Toby retrieving, summer 1980. Barbara Genthner, owner, Tealbrook Labrador Retriever Training Kennel, Monticello, Florida. Bred by Rosalind B. Moore.

In cases of acute indigestion without torsion, the distress and bloat may be relieved by passing a stomach tube to allow the gas to escape. At the risk of being redundant, it must be said that this condition is very acute and requires immediate and heroic action to save the victim.

Preventive measures for bloat include dividing the normal diet of these dogs into three or four meals a day. Water should not be given for one hour before and one hour after each meal, and no exercise is advisable for an hour or two after eating.

With breeders and veterinarians becoming more aware of the bloat syndrome, I feel that more of these cases will be saved than were in the past.

Scrimshaw Ocean Born Mary, black bitch whelped February 9th, 1969. By Chebacco Walter R. ex Jonte Scrimshaw O'Spindrift. An excellent gun dog who at nine years of age brought in 40 pheasants. Bred by Barbara Barfield and owned by Paul Soboloewski, Wareham, Massachusetts.

A lovely pose of Stonecrest's Quissex Riptide, from the kennels of the George Whites at Charlestown, Rhode Island.

Claire White-peterson

Ch. Spenrock Winds Aloft, by Ch. Spenrock Heatheredge Mariner ex Ch. Spenrock Boomerang, a daughter of Ch. Spenrock Banner, owned and bred by Spenrock Kennels, Janet Churchill.

Whelping

We cannot leave the subject of emergencies without considering the subject of whelping. Most bitches whelp without any problems. It is wise, however, to watch them closely during this time. I feel that no bitch should go more than two hours in actual labor without producing a puppy. This includes the time before the first one as well as between puppies. If more than two hours elapse, then the dam should be examined by a veterinarian. It will then be determined if she is indeed in trouble or is just a slow whelper. This rule of thumb gives us time to find out if there is a problem, what it may be, and have time to save both dam and puppies in most cases.

It is good practice to have your bitches examined for pregnancy three and a half to four weeks after mating, as well as at term around the 58th or 59th day. These procedures will enable the veterinarian to discover any troubles that may occur during pregnancy, as well as alerting him as to when the whelping is going to take place. Knowing this, he can plan to provide service, if needed during off hours.

Bitches that are difficult to breed, miss pregnancies, or have irregular reproductive cycles should have physical exams including laboratory tests to determine the cause of the trouble. These tests may be expensive, but a lot of breeding and sterility problems due to sub-par physical condition, hormonal imbalances, or hypo-thyroidism can be corrected. If a valuable bitch is restored to her normal reproductive capacity, the reward more than offsets the medical costs.

Another important thing to remember about whelping and raising puppies is to keep them warm enough. This means a room temperature of 75° to 80°F. for the first ten days to two weeks until the puppies are able to generate their own body heat. Be sure the dam keeps them close; leave a light burning at night for the first week so she won't lose track of any of them or accidentally lie on one of them. Chilling remains the biggest cause of death of newborn puppies. Other causes are malnutrition, toxic milk, hemorrhage, and viral and bacterial infections. Blood type incompatibilities have been understood lately as causes of trouble.

Consultation with your veterinarian concerning these and any other breeding problems you've had in the past may result in the solution of these problems. This may result in larger litters with a higher survival rate.

At 11 months old, Highlands Regimental Piper, a chocolate bitch by Eng., Am. Ch. Lawnwood's Hot Chocolate ex Sambeau's Cam, bred and owned by Lillian Knobloch, Highland Kennels.

A promising four-week-old show-prospect puppy from the Shababaland Kennels, Gordon W. Sousa, Jr.

Manora's Annie, one of the excellent Labs of Nancy Scholz's breeding, illustrates style at eight weeks of age.

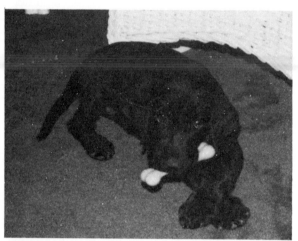

Highlands Samantha's Riptide at nine weeks of age with his first Nylabone® . By Highlands Ace of Aries. Bred at Highland Kennels, owned by Samantha Eggertson.

Ch. Stonecrest's Swift Currant at eight weeks of age. Stonecrest Labradors, George and Louise White, Rhode Island.

Am., Can. Ch. Rorschach's Royal Flush is the sire of this darling puppy. Ambersand Kennels, owner, Jan Stolarevsky.

Spenrock Tailwind owned by Betty Dumaine, Pinehurst, North Carolina.

This is how a future champion Lab looks at three months of age! Ch. Amberfield Sugar Magnolia owned by Amberfield Labradors.

Ranchman's Rustic Rustler at five weeks of age. Owned by Janet Murdock of Ontario.

Spenrock Flying Cloud at six weeks of age. Bred by Spenrock Kennels and Thomas E. Reynolds, this promising young show prospect is by Eng., Am. Ch. Lawnwood's Hot Chocolate ex Spenrock Flying Clipper. Owned by Patsy Morrow, Wilmington, Delaware.

Scrimshaw Call Me Madam learning to pose nicely, as a future show dog should do, at only four weeks of age. This yellow bitch, by Ch. Jayncourt Follow Mee ex Scrimshaw Church Mouse, was bred by Barbara Barfield and belongs to Dennis Livesey.

A typical puppy from Groveton Labradors. Owned by Eileen Ketcham of New York.

A Finchingfield puppy, Mr. and Mrs. Richard Reynolds of Virginia, owners.

Ch. Kimvalley Kenbara Mr. Softee is one of the fine Labs at Kimvalley Kennels owned by Don and Diana Beckett.

Romillar's Silence Is Golden, by Can. Ch. Wimberways Cutty Sark ex Can. Ch. Romillar's September Velvet. Walter and Helen Millar of Ontario, owners.

Care of the Older Dog

Providing medical services from cradle to grave is the slogan of many veterinarians, and rightly so. The average life expectancy for our dogs these days is about 13 years. Sad to say, this is a short time compared to our life span. Larger breeds historically do not live as long as the medium-sized or smaller breeds. However, I think that with proper care your Labradors should be expected to reach this expectancy.

Probably the most common ailments in older dogs are arthritis, kidney disease, heart problems, and cataracts; hip dysplasia may also become evident as the dog ages.

Kimvalley Guildown Cassandra, famous ancestor of many important winners, owned by Don and Diana Beckett, Kimvalley Labradors.

Arthritis

When your pet has trouble getting up in the morning, jumping up, or going upstairs, you can bet that some form of a joint problem is starting. Giving two enteric coated aspirin tablets three times a day for five days very often will help these individuals. This dosage is for adult dogs. It is relatively free of side effects and as long as nothing else is wrong, your dog will get a bit of relief.

Kidney Disease

Signs of kidney weakness are excessive drinking, inability to hold urine through the night, loss of weight, lack of appetite, and more than occasional bouts of vomiting and diarrhea. If any of these signs present themselves, it would be worthwhile to have a checkup. Very often corrective measures in diet and administering some medicine will prolong your dog's life.

Ch. Labradese Misty Morn at the kennel gate. Labradese Labs belong to Dr. and Mrs. Wm. A. Hines of Colorado.

Heart Problems

Some form and degree of heart problems exist in a lot of older animals. Symptoms of chronic congestive heart failure consist of a chronic cough, especially after exercise, lack of stamina, lethargy, abdominal enlargement, and labored breathing at times. If diagnosed and treated early in the disease, many heart patients live to a ripe old age.

Cataracts

Cataracts form in the lenses of most, if not all, old dogs. They are a part of the normal aging process. Total blindness from cataracts generally does not result for a long time. Distant and peripheral vision remain satisfactory for the expected life span of the dog. Rarely is total blindness produced by these aging cataracts before the dog's life expectancy is reached. There is no effective treatment for cataracts other than their surgical removal which is not recommended in the older patient that has any vision at all left.

Spenrock Dynamo in June 1973. By Champion Sandylands Midas ex Am., Can. Ch. Spenrock Banner, W.C. Bred by Janet Churchill and owned by Jane Babbitt.

Hip Dysplasia

It is becoming more evident that most of the arthritis in older dogs in large breeds is the result of problems in bone growth and development when the individual was very young. Problems such as panosteitis, hip dysplasia, elbow dysplasia, and osteochondrosis dessicans all are often precursors of arthritis. In Labradors, according to information from the Orthopedic Foundation for Animals, hip dysplasia is found in 15.5% of the cases presented to them.

Can. Ch. Chilbrook Brannigan at two years of age. Photo by Debby Kobilis.

At any rate, hip dysplasia seems to be a developmental condition and not a congenital anomaly. It is thought to be an inherited defect, with many genes being responsible for its development. Environmental factors also enter into the severity of the pathology in the hip joints. Nutrition during the growth period has been an important factor. Overfeeding and over-supplementation of diets have caused an abnormal growth rate with overweight puppies. These individuals, if they were susceptible to hip dysplasia in the first place, show more severe lesions of hip dysplasia. Restricted feeding of growing dogs is necessary for normal bone growth and development.

431

Ch. Sandylands Markwell of Lockerbie, co-owned by Helen Warrick and Diane B. Jones. His pedigree is shown below.

Signs of hip dysplasia vary from one dog to another, but some of the more common ones are difficulty in getting up after lying for awhile, rabbit-like gait with both rear legs moving forward at the same time when running, lethargy, and walking with a swaying gait in the rear legs. In many cases, a period of pain and discomfort at nine months to one year of age will resolve itself; and even though the dysplasia is still there, most of the symptoms may disappear.

It is recommended that dysplastic individuals not be bred, that they not be allowed to become overweight, and that they have moderate exercise.

The selection of dysplastic-free individuals for breeding stock eventually will result in the production of sounder hip joints in affected breeds. This factor, of course, is only one consideration in the breeding and production of an overall better Labrador Retriever.

Hips x-rayed-rated excellent at age 3 yr
eyes clear of all hereditary defects at 6 yr
owners : Helen Warwick & Diane B. Jones
Crispin Rd., Mt. Holly, NJ 08060

CH Sandylands Markwell
Name of Lockerbie (Eng Imp)   AKC No. SC148602
Breed Labrador Retriever   Color (byc) Black Sex Male
Breeder G. Broadley & G. Anthony Whelped March 21, 1975

		ENG CH RULER OF BLAIRCOURT	Forbes of Blaircourt
	ENG CH SANDYLANDS TWEED OF BLAIRCOURT		Olivia of Blaircourt
		ENG CH TESSA OF BLAIRCOURT	ENG CH LAIRD OF LOCHABER
ENG CH REANACRE MALLARDHURN THUNDER			ENG CH IMP OF BLAIRCOURT
		ENG CH POPPLETON LIEUTENANT	Poppleton Beech Flight
	Mallardhurn Pat		Poppleton Golden Sunray
		Gunsmith Susette	Gunsmith Silver Flight
ENG CH SANDYLANDS MARK		ENG CH SANDYLANDS TWEED	Gunsmith Sugar
Sire AKC No.		OF BLAIRCOURT	ENG CH RULER OF BLAIRCOURT
	AUS CH SANDYLANDS TAN		ENG CH TESSA OF BLAIRCOURT
		Sandylands Annabel	ENG CH CISSBURY ADVENTURE
ENG CH SANDYLANDS TRUTH			ENG CH SANDYLANDS JUNO
		ENG AM CAN CH SAM OF BLAIRCOURT	Hawk of Luscander
	Sandylands Shadow		Olivia of Blaircourt
		Diant Pride	ENG CH POPPLETON LIEUTENANT
		ENG CH SANDYLANDS TWEED	ENG CH DIANT JULIET
		OF BLAIRCOURT	ENG CH RULER OF BLAIRCOURT
	AUS CH SANDYLANDS TAN		ENG CH TESSA OF BLAIRCOURT
		Sandylands Annabel	ENG CH CISSBURY ADVENTURE
ENG CH SANDYLANDS TANDY			ENG CH SANDYLANDS JUNO
		ENG AM CAN CH SAM OF BLAIRCOURT	Hawk of Luscander
	Sandylands Shadow		Olivia of Blaircourt
		Diant Pride	ENG CH POPPLETON LIEUTENANT
ENG CH SANDYLANDS WAGHORN HONESTY			ENG CH DIANT JULIET
Dam AKC No.		Cliveruth Harvester	CH SANLYLANDS SHOWMAN OF LANDRO
	AUS CH PINCHBECK NOKEENER HARVEST HOME		Cliveruth Wendover Joanna
		Nokeener Novelblack	Cliveruth Black Knight
ENG CH SANDYLANDS HONOUR			Nokeener Novelty
		AUS CH SANDYLANDS TAN	CH SANLYLANDS TWEED OF BLAIRCOURT
	ENG CH SANDYLANDS TRUTH		Sandylands Annabel
		Sandylands Shadow	INT CH SAM OF BLAIRCOURT
			Diant Pride

Certificate
of Pedigree

I Hereby Certify to my knowledge and belief, this Pedigree is true and correct

Date 4-26-78

STONEHEDGE, POCASSET MA 02559

432

Canine Nutrition

After mentioning the problem of overfeeding and oversupplementation of puppies' diets with vitamins and minerals in the discussion of hip dysplasia, a few words about canine nutrition are in order.

It is generally agreed that great strides have been made in canine nutrition in the past few years and that most of our well-known commercial dog foods provide all the essential ingredients of a well-balanced diet for our dogs. Probably the greatest problem is providing good quality protein in proper proportions. It behooves us to read dog food labels and to know what we are feeding and how much is necessary to provide the requirements for a lean healthy individual. The tendencies in our society today are to overfeed and under exercise both our dogs and ourselves.

We must know the energy content or caloric value of the foods we are feeding. Then we must determine the energy requirements of our dogs. These will vary with time and circumstances. Your adult Labrador requires about 25 calories per pound of body weight daily for maintenance.

Generally speaking for the average adult Labrador house dog, a diet consisting of 16% high quality protein, 10% fat, and 44% carbohydrates is a good mix. For the working dogs, dogs being shown, or pregnant bitches, increase the protein and fat percentages by about 25% and decrease the carbohydrate proportion by 25%. To meet the needs of the increased stress

A full view of Ch. Sandylands Markwell of Lockerbie.

Ch. Briary Bell Buoy of Windsong. Owned by Betty Dunlap, Goodrich, Michigan. Photo courtesy of Janet Churchill.

of growth in young puppies and nursing bitches, the protein and fat components should be increased yet another 10 to 15% and the percentage of carbohydrates should be decreased by the same percentage. Any stress situation means a rise in caloric requirement. For example, in the case of pregnancy, it is advisable to increase the amount of food intake by 20% after four weeks of gestation and by 75% after six weeks of gestation, and so forth.

We are assuming that the vitamins and minerals in the foods used are complete and balanced.

You may have to combine, mix, and juggle various types and brands of food to attain the desired diet, but don't despair; it can be done. Prescription and special diet foods are available through your veterinarian. These probably cost more initially but may pay off in the long run.

As to exactly how much to feed each individual dog, no one can give you a magic formula that works in all cases. My best advice is to use common sense and a scale. The guidelines on dog food containers have a tendency to be overinflated. It is better to err on the low side than to overfeed. Remember, keep your dog slim and fit with a proper diet and plenty of exercise. That's not a bad idea for your own well-being also.

433

This puppy is South Gate's Quiche Lorraine at about six months old. Owned by Sally P. Jennings, South Gate Labradors, Connecticut.

Jollymuff Fly Away, 15 months old, is owned by Diane B. Jones of New Jersey.

This young Lab is making a name for himself in Bogota, Colombia. He is a litter-brother to Ch. Winterset Hot Tar and Ch. Winterset High Jinks, by Janet Churchill's Ch. Lawnwood's Hot Chocolate ex Ch. Rupert Caviar, and is from Enid Bloome's Winterset Kennels.

Beach-Ayrs Sand Mark at 11 months of age. Owned by Patsy Morrow, Wilmington, Delaware.

Mrs. Helen Ginnel's Ch. Whygin Gold Bullion.

Ocular Disease in Retrievers*

Two major classes of ocular disease occur in Labradors: retinal abnormalities and abnormalities of the lens (cataract). Of the retinal diseases, retrievers suffer from three main genetic types. Each type is quite distinct in its appearance and in its early signs. In all of the retinal abnormalities, the clinical signs are determined best by ophthalmoscopic examination of the retina and its adjacent structures. The continuing source of confusion about the diseases in retrievers stems from the unfortunate similarity in the names of the diseases. Another cause for confusion is the disparity in geographic distribution of the diseases.

Central Progressive Retinal Atrophy

The most widely publicized retinal disease and the one which has been the best studied is central progressive retinal atrophy (CPRA). This is the most common type of retinal disease in retrievers in the United Kingdom, but it is extremely rare in the United States. CPRA may be detectable ophthalmoscopically at two years of age, and it has been stated that all potentially affected animals can be detected ophthalmoscopically by four years of age. In the studies performed in English dogs, the conclusion of the researchers was that CPRA was transmitted as a dominant factor but that the dominance was not always evident. Pedigrees in which CPRA exists show an overall high incidence and a similar high incidence within affected litters, often about half being affected. Normal by normal breedings generally produce all normals, and affected by affected breedings can produce normals as well as abnormals. The investigations into the pedigrees indicate that there are a proportion of animals which possess the gene for central progressive retinal atrophy but which do not show the disease; these animals will, however, transmit the disease. Recent experimental work has indicated that a disease which has some of the ocular signs of CPRA can be produced in dogs deficient in Vitamin E. Retrievers are not the only type of dog affected with CPRA (others such as Briards, Border Collies, and Shetland Sheepdogs have been diagnosed); but again, the incidence of diagnosis is far higher in the United Kingdom than it is in the United States.

*This section written by Dr. Lionel F. Rubin, University of Pennsylvania School of Veterinary Medicine.

"Gussie" in her favorite chair. Mrs. R.C. du Pont owns this lovely Lab at Woodstock Farms in Maryland.

Ranchman's Thundercrest just sitting and watching. Owned by Carol Mia of Barrie, Ontario.

Ch. Spenrock Heatheredge Mariner making a perfect retrieve. Owned by Janet Churchill.

Ch. Spenrock Heatheredge Mariner, one of the great Labs at Spenrock Kennels owned by Janet Churchill.

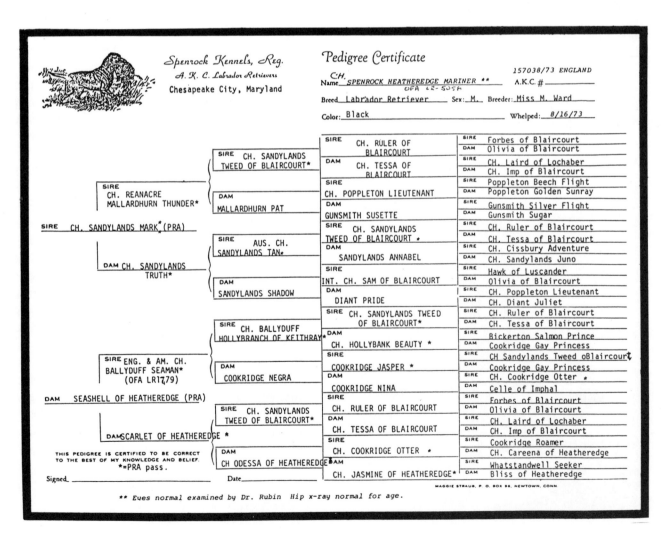

Spenrock Kennels, Reg.
A. K. C. Labrador Retrievers
Chesapeake City, Maryland

Pedigree Certificate

157038/73 ENGLAND

CH.
Name _SPENROCK HEATHEREDGE MARINER **_   A.K.C. # _____
      OFA LR-505A

Breed _Labrador Retriever_   Sex: _M._   Breeder: _Miss M. Ward_

Color: _Black_   Whelped: _8/16/73_

			SIRE	SIRE	Forbes of Blaircourt
		SIRE CH. SANDYLANDS	CH. RULER OF BLAIRCOURT	DAM	Olivia of Blaircourt
		TWEED OF BLAIRCOURT*	DAM	SIRE	CH. Laird of Lochaber
	SIRE		CH. TESSA OF BLAIRCOURT	DAM	CH. Imp of Blaircourt
	CH. REANACRE		SIRE	SIRE	Poppleton Beech Flight
	MALLARDHURN THUNDER*	DAM	CH. POPPLETON LIEUTENANT	DAM	Poppleton Golden Sunray
		MALLARDHURN PAT	DAM	SIRE	Gunsmith Silver Flight
SIRE CH. SANDYLANDS MARK* (PRA)			GUNSMITH SUSETTE	DAM	Gunsmith Sugar
		SIRE AUS. CH.	SIRE CH. SANDYLANDS	SIRE	CH. Ruler of Blaircourt
		SANDYLANDS TAN*	TWEED OF BLAIRCOURT *	DAM	CH. Tessa of Blaircourt
	DAM CH. SANDYLANDS		SANDYLANDS ANNABEL	SIRE	CH. Cissbury Adventure
	TRUTH*			DAM	CH. Sandylands Juno
		DAM	SIRE	SIRE	Hawk of Luscander
		SANDYLANDS SHADOW	INT. CH. SAM OF BLAIRCOURT	DAM	Olivia of Blaircourt
			DAM	SIRE	CH. Poppleton Lieutenant
			DIANT PRIDE	DAM	CH. Diant Juliet
		SIRE CH. BALLYDUFF	SIRE CH. SANDYLANDS TWEED	SIRE	CH. Ruler of Blaircourt
		HOLLYBRANCH OF KEITHRAY*	OF BLAIRCOURT*	DAM	CH. Tessa of Blaircourt
	SIRE ENG. & AM. CH.		DAM	SIRE	Bickerton Salmon Prince
	BALLYDUFF SEAMAN*		CH. HOLLYBANK BEAUTY *	DAM	Cookridge Gay Princess
	(OFA LR17,79)	DAM	SIRE	SIRE	CH Sandylands Tweed oBlaircourt
		COOKRIDGE NEGRA	COOKRIDGE JASPER *	DAM	Cookridge Gay Princess
DAM SEASHELL OF HEATHEREDGE (PRA)			DAM	SIRE	CH. Cookridge Otter *
			COOKRIDGE NINA	DAM	Celle of Imphal
		SIRE CH. SANDYLANDS	SIRE	SIRE	Forbes of Blaircourt
		TWEED OF BLAIRCOURT*	CH. RULER OF BLAIRCOURT	DAM	Olivia of Blaircourt
	DAM SCARLET OF HEATHEREDGE *		DAM	SIRE	CH. Laird of Lochaber
			CH. TESSA OF BLAIRCOURT	DAM	CH. Imp of Blaircourt
		DAM	SIRE	SIRE	Cookridge Roamer
		CH ODESSA OF HEATHEREDGE*	CH. COOKRIDGE OTTER *	DAM	CH. Careena of Heatheredge
			DAM	SIRE	Whatstandwell Seeker
			CH. JASMINE OF HEATHEREDGE*	DAM	Bliss of Heatheredge

THIS PEDIGREE IS CERTIFIED TO BE CORRECT
TO THE BEST OF MY KNOWLEDGE AND BELIEF.
*=PRA pass.

Signed _____   Date _____

MAGGIE STRAUB, P. O. BOX 98, NEWTOWN, CONN.

** *Eyes normal examined by Dr. Rubin Hip x-ray normal for age.*

The signs of central progressive retinal atrophy are detectable only ophthalmoscopically in the early stages. Using the ophthalmoscope, one can see heavy pigmentation in the central area of the retina. As the disease progresses, the pigmentation increases and the retinal deterioration, which accompanies it, becomes more widespread. The main behavioral sign associated with central progressive retinal atrophy is inability to mark a stationary object and/or difficulty with vision in bright daylight. Dogs with central progressive retinal atrophy generally retain fairly good peripheral vision and get about well even in the late stages of the disease. Only those dogs whose performance depends on acute central vision show visual abnormalities early. Most affected dogs never go completely blind.

Ch. Spenrock Heatheredge Mariner, by Ch. Sandylands Mark ex Seashell of Heatheredge, bred by Miss Margaret Ward, England. Owner, Janet Churchill; handler, Glen Butler.

← At the bottom of page 436 is the pedigree for Ch. Spenrock Heatheredge Mariner. In addition to listing the background for several generations, the form carries the notation that eyes have been examined by Dr. Rubin and were found to be normal.

Progressive Retinal Atrophy

The second major inherited disease is progressive retinal atrophy (PRA or Generalized PRA). Despite the similarity of the name to CPRA, this is an entirely different and much more devastating problem. Dogs with PRA generally go blind at an early age. The first behavioral sign of PRA is night blindness. Animals affected have difficulty maneuvering at night or in twilight. There are generally no behavioral abnormalities under conditions of bright light. Later, as the disease becomes more widespread in the eyes, day vision will be lost as well. The ophthalmoscopic signs of PRA (GPRA) are generally found slightly before or coincident with the earliest indications of night blindness. In the retina the blood vessels are narrowed and there is increased reflection from the back of the eye (making the dog's eye seem to glow in daytime as well as night). In the breeds in which it has been carefully studied (Irish Setters, Norwegian Elkhounds, and Poodles) PRA is a disease inherited as a recessive trait. However, the disease seems to be inherited by a different gene in each of the breeds in which it has been studied. Irish Setters with PRA, when bred to Norwegian Elkhounds with PRA, do not produce PRA affected dogs, although the breeding runs true within each breed. It is not possible, therefore, to state definitively that PRA is recessively inherited in retrievers. While this remains to be proven, PRA has been shown to be recessive in all the breeds in which it has been studied carefully. If PRA is inherited as a recessive in retrievers, the implication is that the parents of affected animals are carriers of the disease and while they may not show signs of it, they are capable of transmitting the potential for the disease to their offspring. There is no way to determine which animal is a carrier and which is not, except when a case shows up within the litter.

Generalized PRA in the Labrador is a rare condition in the United Kingdom, but it is far more common in the United States than is CPRA. Only research will tell us how early the disease can be clinically detected, when an animal can be considered clinically free of the disease, and whether it is in fact recessively inherited completely. If it is recessively inherited, it carries a much more devastating impact on the breed since the numbers of carrier animals can be many, and these will go undetected throughout the general population.

Retinal Dysplasia

The third retinal disease, retinal dysplasia, is a localized failure in the development of the retina. This disease is present at birth and can be detected as soon as the animal's eyes are clear enough to examine. Retinal dysplasia in the mildest form causes no visual difficulty and may never do so. In some animals, however, the failure of development is sufficient so that the retina becomes liable to detach from its blood supply, and the retinal detachment which ensues causes blindness. This happens in only a small number of cases. Retinal dysplasia is generally seen more among field retrievers than in bench types. It is generally prudent to avoid breeding affected animals. Once the dog affected with retinal dysplasia reaches two years, the likelihood of blindness occurring from the presence of localized retinal dysplasia is small.

Spenrock Corsair, C.D., by Ch. Spenrock Heatheredge Mariner ex Spenrock Egyptian Candor, was bred by Susan Powers and belongs to Susan Crum and Spenrock Kennels.

A less common but more serious form of retinal dysplasia is one in which the abnormal ocular development is very severe. In this type the pups are born blind as a result of complete retinal detachment. At least one form of this total retinal dysplasia is thought to be inherited as a simple recessive trait, but there remain some questions whether this condition is a subtype of a less severe form or whether it represents yet another independent disease.

Cataract

Cataract, an opacity of the lens, is a second major class of ocular disease in Labradors. Many types of insult (other than hereditary) can produce cataract, and sometimes it is possible to differentiate between those caused by genetic defects and those caused by other insults.

The major type of cataract in Labradors occurs at the back of the lens forming a triangular, Y, or circular shape. It generally occurs between the ages of six and 18 months, though some instances of later development are known. The cataract is slowly progressive but rarely blinding, although under some field conditions the presence of cataract may result in poor marking ability. Complete visual loss, if it occurs, does not come until late. However, in some retrievers (the Chesapeake notably), visual impairment has been found early. The hereditary form of cataract in Labradors is presumed to be dominantly inherited (as it is in Goldens and Chesapeakes), but there may be some instances in which a genetically affected dog does not manifest the disease (incomplete penetrance).

There remains a great deal of research to be done on all of the ocular diseases in retrievers. Recommendations for detection and elimination of these diseases can only be made on the basis of specific data which in most cases we now lack. At the very least, retriever breeders are urged to submit their dogs for regular ophthalmoscopic examination and should refrain from breeding from affected animals and their offspring. Examination and certification should reduce the incidence of all types of PRA in the breed, but one must bear in mind a certificate of freedom from a disease is much more valuable when the disease is a dominantly inherited one than if it is recessively inherited. Retrievers should be examined annually until about six years of age, so as to eliminate the possibility of late onset of the disease.

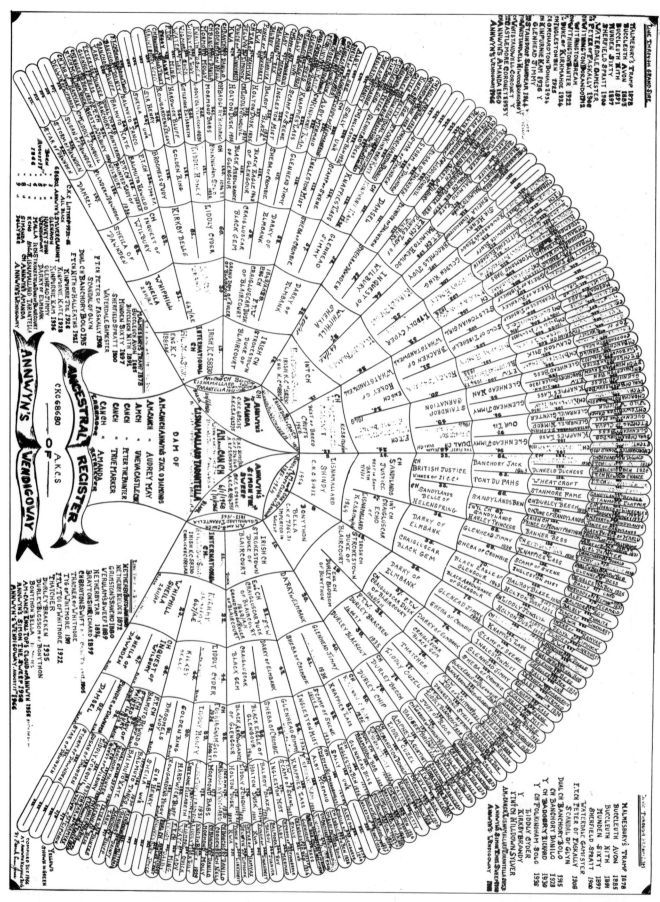

This is one of the extremely interesting ten generation pedigrees that Frank Evans Jones has done. Mr. Jones has researched and recorded numerous similar pedigrees of other important Labs. Additional samples of pedigrees, in the more traditional format, may be found on the following pages.

PEDIGREE CERTIFICATE
THE AMERICAN KENNEL CLUB

Name of Dog __Pitch of Franklin__ Sex __Female__ Stud-Book No. __S488,255__

Breed __Labrador Retriever__ Vol. __69__ Color __Black__

Date Whelped __June 5, 1949__

Breeder __Carey Rogers__

				Thatch of Whitmore
			(Ch) Raffles of Earlsmoor	
			Sire 957536	Task of Whitmore
		(Bench and Fld Ch) Shed		**Dam**
		of Arden		Odds On
		Sire A330767	(Fld Ch) Decoy of Arden	**Sire** 811077
	(Fld Ch) Pickpocket for		**Dam** 965611	Peggy of Shipton
	Deer Creek			**Dam** 873808
	Sire S104594			Blenheim Scamp
			(Ch) Banchory Trump of Wingan	**Sire**
			Sire 917271	Lady Daphne
		Peggy of Pheasant Lawn		**Dam**
		Dam A338118		(Fld Ch) Banchory Varnish of Wingan
			Laquer	**Sire** A61030
			Dam A156298	Cheverells Dina
				Dam A95496
				Thatch of Whitmore
			(Ch) Raffles of Earlsmoor	**Sire**
			Sire 957536	Task of Whitmore
		(Ch) Earlsmoor Moor of		**Dam**
		Arden		Odds On
		Sire A159966	(Fld Ch) Decoy of Arden	**Sire** 811077
	Wardwyn Warbler		**Dam** 965611	Peggy of Shipton
	Dam A816280			**Dam** 873808
				Jericho Paul
			Fife of Kennoway	**Sire** A59366
			Sire A234882	Judy of Kennoway
		(Ch) Buddha of Arden		**Dam** A127379
		Dam A557014		Elwood Risk
			Pitch of Arden	**Sire** 868031
			Dam A210253	Peggy of Shipton
				Dam 873808

The foregoing is a true copy from the records of the American Kennel Club.

440

Registered Name **Mallow's Fanfare Mallow**

AKC Reg. No. **SA-45219**

Sex **F**

Date of Birth **Jan. 29, 1967**

Color **Black**

Bred by **Constance Hennessy**

LABRADOR RETRIEVERS
MR. AND MRS. R. J. HENNESSY
LYONS PLAIN RD. • WESTON, CONN.

PARENTS	GRAND-PARENTS	G.G.-PARENTS	G.G.G.-PARENTS	G.G.G.G.-PARENTS
SIRE CAN & AM CH. JACK O'DIAMONDS B	**SIRE** CAN & AM. CH. ANNWYN'S SHEDIROW	**SIRE** CAN. DUAL CH. BLYTHE'S ACE OF SPADES	**SIRE** CEDAR BRAE BLACK TARGET	HOLLAND MARSH WATCHMAN
				LANSDOWN BLACK GYPSY
			DAM CAN. CH. GYPSY QUEEN	GUARDSMAN OF TIMBERTOWN
				AFRICAN OF AVONDALE
		DAM CAN. CH. NASCOPIE NEEDLE ANN	**SIRE** CAN. CH. WATERLAND DAN DUBH	CAN. CH. SIMON THE SAGAN?
				BRETHLANDS BARONESS
			DAM CAN DUAL CH. BLYTHE'S QUEEN OF SPADES	CEDAR BRAE BLACK TARGET
				CAN. CH. GYPSY QUEEN
	DAM CAN. & AM CH. LISNAMALLARD TARANTELLA	**SIRE** ENG. CH. STROKESTOWN DUKE OF BLAIRCOURT	**SIRE** DARKY OF ELMBANK	GLENHEAD JIMMY
				SHEBA OF CROMBIE
			DAM CRAIGLUSCAR DUSK OF BLAIRCOURT	DARKY OF ELMBANK
				CRAIGLUSCAR BLACK GEM
		DAM ENG. CH. HILLDOWN SYLVER	**SIRE** KIRKBY BRANDY	LIDDLY CYDER
				KIRKBY BELLE
			DAM WHIPHILL SHIELA	ENG F.T.C. GUEST OF WHAICRT?
				SHIELA OF DARNDEN
DAM CH. GOLDSBORO VELVET OF MALLOW	**SIRE** CH. HARRIS TWEED OF IDE	**SIRE** ENG. CH. SANDYLANDS TWEED	**SIRE** ENG. CH. RULER OF BLAIRCOURT	FORBES OF BLAIRCOURT
				OLIVIA OF BLAIRCOURT
			DAM TESSA OF BLAIRCOURT	ENG. CH. LAIRD OF LOCHABER
				ENG. CH. IMP. OF BLAIRCOURT
		DAM CINDY SUE OF IDE	**SIRE** BLACK SHIEK OF IDE	BLACK KNIGHT OF IDE
				ENG. CH. BLACK BESS OF IDE
			DAM BLACK SARAH OF IDE	BLACK KNIGHT OF IDE
				ENG. CH. BLACK BESS OF IDE
	DAM CH. KIMVALLEY DEBORAH	**SIRE** CORNLANDS WESTELM FLIGHT	**SIRE** POPPLETON LIEUTENANT	ENG. CH. POPPLETON BLACK FLIGHT
				POPPLETON GOLDEN SUNRAY
			DAM WESTELM WHISPER	TRACER OF TREESHOLM
				HIGH MEADOWS MAYFLY
		DAM KIMVALLEY GUILDOWN CASSANDRA	**SIRE** ENG. CH. WHATSTANDWELL CORONET	ENG FTC WHITSTANDWELL HUERD BRAND
				ENG. CH. HONEY OF WHATSTANDWELL
			DAM GUILDOWN FERU	ENG. CH. DIANT SCHNAPPS (CAIRNCROSS LIN)
				GUILDOWN RINGLEADER?

Seaward Kennels, Reg. Johnnycake St., Box 700, Manchester Center, Vt. 05255

SIRE

Eng.Ch. Sandylands Tandy (Y)

Eng.Ch.Follytower Merrybrook Black Stormer

Follytower Old Black Magic (B)

Eng.SH.Ch.Sandylands Storm-Along (B)

Eng.Ch.SH Sandylands Garry (Y)

Eng.SH.Ch. Sandylands Girl Friday (Y)

Trewinnard Sandylands Tanita (Y)

Ch. Ardmargha So Famous (By)Eng. imp.

SC 108458 (9/77)

Aus.Ch. Sandylands Tan (Y)

Eng. Ch. Sandylands Tandy (Y)

Sandylands Shadow (By)

Eng. Ch. Faith of Ardmargha

Aus.Ch.Diant Jaysgreen Jasper(Y)

Eng. Ch. Kilree of Ardmargha

Sandylands Komerly of Ardmargha

Pedigree of: Am.& Can. Ch. Seaward's Adonis of Rupert- SC 235432 (Yellow) 4/26/77
Am.& Can. Ch. Seaward's Dr.Watson of Rupert, C.D.-SC 259413 (Y)" " "
Owner: SEAWARD KENNELS, REG.   Breeder: DOROTHY B. HOWE

DAM

Sandylands General (Y)

Eng.Sh.Ch Sandylands Garry (Y)

Sandylands Memory (B)

Am.& Eng.Ch.Ardmargha Goldkrest of Syrancot-Eng.imp.

Eng.Ch. Kinley Skipper (Y)

Sandylands Komely of Ardmargha

Eng.Ch. Sandylands Truth (B)

Rupert Goldylocks (Y)

SB 499160 (7/76)

Eng.Ch. Glenarvey Brand

Ch. Glenarvey Barrister (Y)-Eng.imp.

Sandylands Goldie

Rupert Judicious (Y)

Ch. Kinley Yorkshireman(Y)
(Eng.imp.)

Rupert Piccadilly Dame (Y)

Ch. Rupert Searchon (Y)

442

Am. and Can. Ch. Dark Star of Franklin

Int. Ch. Dark Star of Franklin
(Whelped April 22, 1953)

- **Ch. Labcroft Mister Chips**
  - Labcroft Game Boy
    - Dual Ch. Shed of Arden
      - Ch. Raffles of Earlsmoor
      - Fld. Ch. Decoy of Arden
    - Muellers Judy
      - Fld. Ch. Gun of Arden
      - Duchess of Hickory Hurst
  - Labcroft North Winds
    - Fld. Ch. Chief of Oldbridge
      - Fld. Ch. Oldbridge Boy
      - Fld. Ch. Glenravel Tryst
    - Black Meg of Avandale
      - Dual Ch. Lile Larry
      - Meg of Greeymar
- **Int. Ch. Pitch of Franklin**
  - Fld. Ch. Pickpocket for Deer Creek
    - Dual Ch. Shed of Arden
      - Ch. Raffles of Earlsmoor
      - Fld. Ch. Decoy of Arden
    - Peggy of Pheasant Lawn
      - Ch. Banchory Trump of Wingan
      - Laquer
  - Wardwyn Warbler
    - Ch. Earlsmoor Moor of Arden
      - Ch. Raffles of Earlsmoor
      - Fld. Ch. Decoy of Arden
    - Ch. Buddha of Arden
      - Fife of Kennoway
      - Pitch of Arden

Am. K. C. Reg. No. S-604058

Can. K. C. Reg. No. 333880

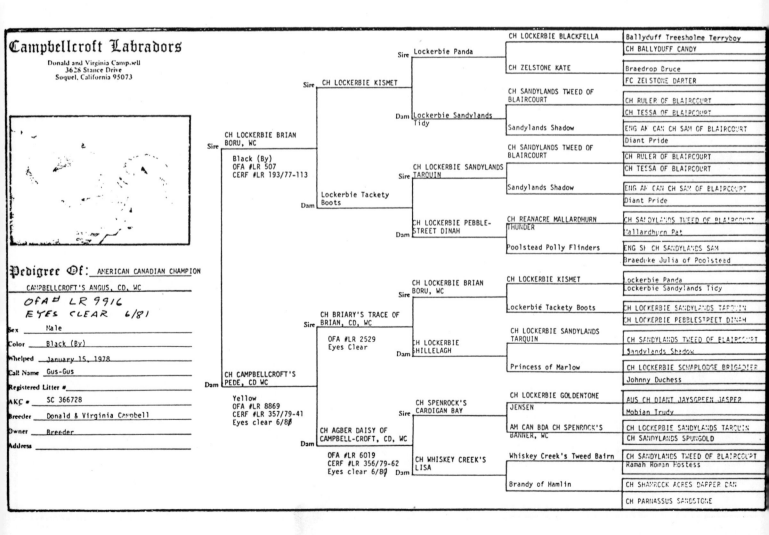

Campbellcroft Labradors

Donald and Virginia Campbell
3628 Stance Drive
Soquel, California 95073

Pedigree Of: AMERICAN CANADIAN CHAMPION

CAMPBELLCROFT'S ANGUS, CD, WC

OFA# LR 991G
EYES CLEAR 6/81

Sex _____ Male
Color _____ Black (By)
Whelped _____ January 15, 1978
Call Name _____ Gus-Gus
Registered Litter # _____
AKC # _____ SC 366728
Breeder _____ Donald & Virginia Campbell
Owner _____ Breeder
Address _____

443

Waiting to fly! Alongside Janet Churchill's airplane is Ch. Spenrock Cardigan Bay, whose pedigree is shown below.

An informal pose of Ch. Spenrock Cardigan Bay. Janet Churchill, breeder-owner, Chesapeake City, Maryland.

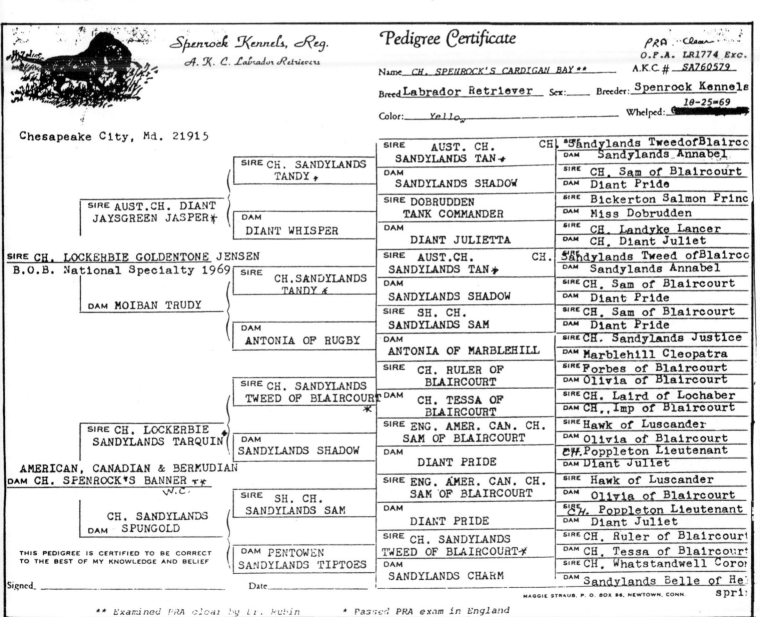

Spenrock Kennels, Reg.
A. K. C. Labrador Retrievers

Pedigree Certificate

PRA Clear
O.P.A. LR1774 Exc.

Name *CH. SPENROCK'S CARDIGAN BAY ** *   A.K.C.# *SA760579*

Breed **Labrador Retriever**   Sex:____   Breeder: Spenrock Kennels

Color: *Yellow*   Whelped: 10-25-69

Chesapeake City, Md. 21915

SIRE CH. LOCKERBIE GOLDENTONE JENSEN
B.O.B. National Specialty 1969

SIRE AUST.CH. DIANT JAYSGREEN JASPER*

SIRE CH. SANDYLANDS TANDY*

SIRE AUST. CH. SANDYLANDS TAN* CH. Sandylands Tweed of Blairco — Sandylands Annabel

DAM SANDYLANDS SHADOW — CH. Sam of Blaircourt — Diant Pride

DAM DIANT WHISPER

SIRE DOBRUDDEN TANK COMMANDER — Bickerton Salmon Princ — Miss Dobrudden

DAM DIANT JULIETTA — CH. Landyke Lancer — CH. Diant Juliet

DAM MOIBAN TRUDY

SIRE CH.SANDYLANDS TANDY*

SIRE AUST.CH. SANDYLANDS TAN* CH. Sandylands Tweed of Blairco — Sandylands Annabel

DAM SANDYLANDS SHADOW — CH. Sam of Blaircourt — Diant Pride

DAM ANTONIA OF RUGBY

SIRE SH. CH. SANDYLANDS SAM — CH. Sam of Blaircourt — Diant Pride

DAM ANTONIA OF MARBLEHILL — CH. Sandylands Justice — Marblehill Cleopatra

AMERICAN, CANADIAN & BERMUDIAN
DAM CH. SPENROCK'S BANNER **
W.C.

SIRE CH. LOCKERBIE SANDYLANDS TARQUIN*

SIRE CH. SANDYLANDS TWEED OF BLAIRCOURT*

SIRE CH. RULER OF BLAIRCOURT — Forbes of Blaircourt — Olivia of Blaircourt

DAM CH. TESSA OF BLAIRCOURT — CH. Laird of Lochaber — CH. Imp of Blaircourt

DAM SANDYLANDS SHADOW

SIRE ENG. AMER. CAN. CH. SAM OF BLAIRCOURT — Hawk of Luscander — Olivia of Blaircourt

DAM DIANT PRIDE — CH. Poppleton Lieutenant — Diant Juliet

CH. SANDYLANDS SPUNGOLD

SIRE SH. CH. SANDYLANDS SAM

SIRE ENG. AMER. CAN. CH. SAM OF BLAIRCOURT — Hawk of Luscander — Olivia of Blaircourt

DAM DIANT PRIDE — CH. Poppleton Lieutenant — Diant Juliet

DAM PENTOWEN SANDYLANDS TIPTOES

SIRE CH. SANDYLANDS TWEED OF BLAIRCOURT* — CH. Ruler of Blaircourt — CH. Tessa of Blaircourt

DAM SANDYLANDS CHARM — CH. Whatstandwell Coro — Sandylands Belle of He

THIS PEDIGREE IS CERTIFIED TO BE CORRECT TO THE BEST OF MY KNOWLEDGE AND BELIEF

Signed _____   Date _____

MAGGIE STRAUB, P. O. BOX 96, NEWTOWN, CONN.   spri

** Examined PRA clear by Dr. Rubin   * Passed PRA exam in England

444

Right: Ch. Spenrock Cardigan Bay in 1971 taking Best of Winners at Pittsburgh on the way to his title. **Below:** Int. Ch. Spenrock's Banner, Cardigan Bay's dam, shown winning her 85th Best of Breed under judge Dr. John Gordon at Bucks County in May 1969. Mrs. Churchill is owner-handling.

Ch. Yarrow's Pendragon, by Ch. Poolstead Peer ex Yarrow Astarte of Windfall, is one of a litter of three champions including the Group winner Ch. Yarrow's Broad Reach Peer and Ch. Yarrow's Broad Reach Psaphire, U.D.T. Handled by owner, Beth Sweigart.

Broad Reach Rolls Royce, second litter offspring of Ch. Lawnwood's Hot Chocolate ex Ch. Yarrow's Broad Reach Psaphire, U.D.T., W.C., is owned by Mrs. Joan Lyons, Silver Spring, Maryland and is handled here by breeder, Martha Lee K. Voshell.

Brig. General William W. Spruance of Marathon, Florida, with his Lab, Spenrock Phantom, by Eng., Am. Ch. Lawnwood's Hot Chocolate ex Spenrock Cricket. Charlotte Williams and Jan Churchill, breeders.

Ch. Lawnwood's Hot Chocolate snapped informally with his owner Jan Churchill.

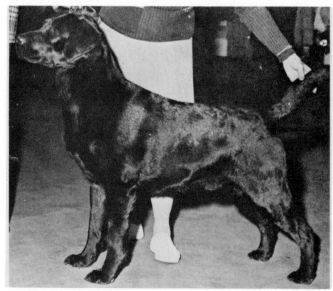

Ch. Briary Brendan of Rainell, Best of Winners at Westminster, is owned by Lorraine Getter.

Mr. and Mrs. Richard M. Oster of Barrington, Rhode Island, are owners of this beautiful Lab, Ch. Ajoco's Damn Yankee, handled to Group first at Framingham District Kennel Club by Jane K. Forsyth.

Ch. Agber's Daniel Aloysius, son of Ch. Spenrock's Cardigan Bay, won four Sporting Groups and three Bests in Show. Pictured here taking Best Puppy in Show early in his career.

Highlands Bronze Chieftain pictured taking his first Best of Winners at 11 months of age. Paul Slaboda handling for breeder-owner George Knobloch, Jr. Mrs. Dona Hausman is the judge.

Above: Shababaland's Creme Puff, a very lovely Labrador, full of promise of a good show future. **Below:** Creme Puff being admired after a big win. Gordon W. Sousa, Jr., owner.

Above: Am., Can. Ch. Forecast Skidmore, C.D.X., a daughter of Mallow's Fanfare. **Below:** Ch. Forecast Beloit, born in September 1968, was one of Fanfare's first two champions. Both Labs owned by Elizabeth K. Curtis and Ann and Samuel Cappellina.

Ch. Carho's Chip Off The Old Block winning a Group placement at Pictou County Kennel Club, September 1980. Owner, Carole Nickerson of Nova Scotia.

Forecast Princeton (pointed) is another fine Lab produced by Ch. Blockmar's Buckie ex Mallow's Fanfare. Elizabeth K. Curtis and Ann and Samuel Cappellina, owners.

Ch. Kemlen Delta Dawn, by Ch. Timmbrland Golden Star ex Franklin's Kemlen Sunshine, taking Best of Breed under judge Glen Sommers. Jan Stolarevsky, Ambersand Labradors.

Ch. Spenrock Sans Souci winning Best of Breed at the National Labrador Specialty in 1970. This daughter of Ch. Sandylands Midas ex Int. Ch. Spenrock Banner, W.C., was bred by Janet Churchill and is owned by John Valentine.

Spenrock Citation, by Ch. Spenrock Heatheredge Mariner ex Spenrock Egyptian Candor, co-owned by Janis Burler with breeder Janet Churchill.

Ch. Briary Allegra, by Ch. Spenrock Anthony Adverse ex Ch. Briary Floradora, is owned by Marjorie Brainard, Briary Labradors. Photo courtesy of Janet Churchill.

Spenrock Moontide, Best of Breed at Penn Treaty 1979, is a son of Ch. Spenrock Cardigan Bay ex Spenrock Alpha and was bred by Janet Churchill. Owner-handled by Joanne Skeie.

Ch. Rivermist Tweed of Spenrock, a son of Ch. Lockerbie Kismet ex Ch. Goldsboro Kim, winning Best of Breed at Salisbury, Maryland. Handled by Jenny Reynolds; owned by Spenrock Kennels.

Ch. Lobuff's Tequila Sunrise, bred and owned by Jerry and Lisa Weiss, is taking Best of Breed in the supported entry the day following the Specialty in August 1980. By Ch. Spenrock Heatheredge Mariner ex Ch. Spenrock Cognac.

Ch. Lewisfield Spenrock Ballot, W.C., winning a major at Devon under judge Ted Eldredge. Owner-handler, Janet Churchill. By Ch. Lockerbie Sandylands Tarquin ex Ch. Sandylands Spungold.

451

Dual Ch. Blyth's Ace of Spades, litter-brother to Dual Ch. Blyth's Queen of Spades, sire of Am., Can. Ch. Annwyn's Shedrow.

Ch. Agber's Excalibur C.D., W.C., training for Open work. Mary Stuart, owner. Photo courtesy of Agber Labradors.

Gun dog in action! Scrimshaw Holystone, by Ch. Scrimshaw Another Deacon ex Ch. Sandylands Crystal, was bred by Barbara Barfield and is owned by Steve Hodges, Meredith, New Hampshire.

Ch. Driftwood's Limited Edition, a daughter of Ch. Mijan's Corrigan ex Ch. Driftwood's Gypsy, takes Best of Opposite Sex, at Boardwalk Kennel Club 1977, over 32 class bitches and two other Specials. Mrs. Pam Kelsey, owner, Driftwood Labradors.

Moorwood Hillary's Mr. Brown, or "Rocky," bringing in the bird. This splendid son of Ch. Sorn Sandpiper and Ch. Beaver's Hillary of Moorwood, W.C., was trained and is handled by his owners, James and Joan Nankivell.

Ch. Agber's Excalibur, by Am., Can. Ch. Agber's Daniel Aloysius, W.C., ex **Ch**. Spenrock Barolce Buffet, is owned by Mary Stuart; breeder, Agnes Cartier.

Ch. Marbra Guardsman, by Waltham Galaxy of Condor ex Marbra Rhapsody, belongs to MiJan Labradors, Joan and Tony Heubel and Mike and Janet Farmilette of New Jersey.

Rainell's Darktown Strutter, by Ch. Lockerbie Sandylands Tarquin ex Ch. Ruslyn's Tugboat Annie, C.D., was bred by Lorraine Getter and is owned by Bonnie and Frank Foyt. Jan Churchill judging, Penn Treaty 1974.

Stonecrest's Quissex Riptide, one of the outstanding Labs belonging to George and Louise White.

Ch. Ro-Shan's Jondy Lucas, owned by Mr. and Mrs. Tom Philip.

Simerdown's Charlie Brown at 22 months of age. Owned by Margee Patton.

Ch. Hillsboro Wizard of Oz. Jack Funk handling for owner, Mrs. Robert V. Clark, Jr., Springfield Farm.

Ch. Ludlow's Topaz Pride winning under Miss Virginia Sivori at the Windham County Kennel Club, May 9th 1976. Handled by Robert S. Forsyth for owner, Nancy Edmonds.

Handler-breeder Sally P. Jennings pictured winning with Charles W. Appleton's lovely yellow bitch, Ch. Meggin of South Gate, W.C.

This pensive Lab puppy is Manora's Tanya at eight weeks of age. Nancy M. Scholz, owner.

Ch. Oscar of Lockwood enjoying his favorite "bath in a barrel."

Stonecrest Alexander, a splendid young Lab owned by the George Whites, photographed by Claire-White Peterson.

Merry Christmas from Romillar's Paddlefoot Tawny, bred by the Walter Millars, now owned by John McDermitt, Picton, Ontario.

Ambersand's Vin Blanc at nine weeks of age. Jan Stolarevsky owner, Ambersand Kennels.

This young Shababaland show-prospect puppy sits outside the stable—maybe waiting for a friend? Gordon W. Sousa, Jr., owner.

456

Ch. Oscar of Lockwood receiving his first points, a three-point major, the first time ever shown. Owner-handler, Edward A. Jennings.

Can., Am. Ch. Casadelora's All Spice at Cariboo Kennel Club, July 1980. Judge, W.P. Bowden; handler, G. Ted Luke; owners, Mr. and Mrs. W.E. Brown, Casadelora Labs.

Ch. Spenrock Ambassador, by Ch. Lockerbie Stanwood Granada ex Int. Ch. Spenrock Banner, W.C. at ten months of age. Bred by Spenrock Kennels; owned by Patty Ramey who is handling.

Ch. Ralston of Shamrock Acres, by Ch. Whygin Poppitt ex Ch. Whygin Campaign Promise, one of the beautiful Labs for which Helen Ginnel's Whygin Kennels are so famous.

Ch. South Gate's Beau Geste waiting his turn. Owned by South Gate Kennels, Sally and Edward A. (Ted) Jennings.

Sandylands Nimbus, by Ch. Sandylands Newinn Columbus ex Show Ch. Longley Come Rain, at 14 months of age. Owned by Mrs. Gwen Broadley and Mr. Garner Anthony. Photo by Fall, courtesy of Mrs. Broadley, Sandylands Labradors, England.

Ch. Spenrock Winds Aloft wins Best of Breed at Harford County in April 1976. William L. Kendrick is the judge. Janet Churchill owns this daughter of Ch. Spenrock Heatheredge Mariner ex Ch. Spenrock Boomerang.

Ch. Whygin Royal Rocket, a fine representative of Whygin Labradors, Mrs. Helen Ginnel.

Ch. South Gate's Beau Geste was mostly owner-handled to his title by Ted Jennings.

Angelica of Harsen's Isle, bred and owned by John A. and E. Carol Horenz of Michigan.

John Lawreck awarding first in the Sporting Group to Jan Stolarevsky's great winner, Ch. Timmbrland Golden Star, Top Winning Yellow Labrador in the history of the Breed.

Christmas at Amberfield.

Can. Ch. Romillar's Ace of Spades, C.D., born February 1980, by Am., Can. Ch. Shamrock Acres Ebonylane Ace, C.D.X., W.C., ex Can. Ch. Romillar's Chelsea, C.D. Bred and owned by Helen and Walter Millar, Carrying Place, Ontario. Gained championship during 1981 in four shows going Best of Breed over Specials and also has Group placements. Earned his C.D. with high scores at three shows in one weekend.

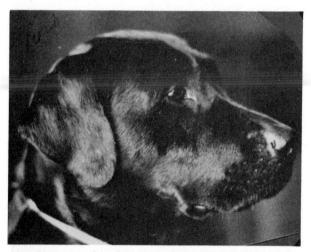

Head study of a Groveton Lab. Eileen Ketcham, owner.

Ranchman's Slap -n- Tickle belongs to the Reids' Ranchman's Kennels in Alberta.

Labradese Sweet Georga, by Ch. MacGeorge's Baron Zena of Dija, W.C., ex Labradese Misty Morn, looks out through the kennel run. Owned by Labradese Labradors, Dr. and Mrs. William A. Hines.

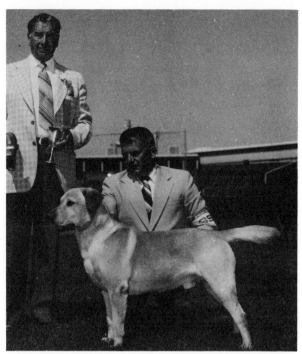

Can., Am. Ch. Casadelora's All Spice taking a Group second in 1980 under Robert Waters. Owners are Mr. and Mrs. W. E. Brown, British Columbia.

Scrimshaw Tipsy Parson taking a three-point major under Phil Marsh, Norman Grenier handling. Bred by Barbara Barfield, co-owner with John Barfield.

Agber's Daisy of Campbell Croft, C.D., Taking Winners Bitch and Best of Opposite Sex in 1975 under Bernard Ziessow. Handler, Terry Hubbs; breeder-owners, Donald and Virginia Campbell.

Ch. Ebonylane's Tiger, C.D., is owned by Stan and Karen Albert of Montreal, Quebec.

Mid-Jersey Labrador Club Specialty 1980. Left is Jenny Reynolds with Spenrock Windshift.

Two of the Moorwood Labradors in Indian Lake, July 1977.

Scrimshaw The Prodigal, by Ch. Jayncourt Follow Mee ex Ch. Scrimshaw Blue Nun, with seven-year-old Tanya Philbrick. Bred by B.L. Barfield; owned by the Philbricks of Barnstead, New Hampshire.

Manora's Aric, eight-week-old Lab puppy belonging to Nancy M. Scholz, Manora Kennels.

Ch. Spenrock Windshift, by Ch. Eireannach Black Coachman ex Ch. Spenrock Winds Aloft, taking Best of Winners on the way to the title at Wallkill Kennel Club, 1981. Bonnie Threlfall, handler.

Ch. Yarrow's The Magus, by Ch. Sandylands Midas ex Ch. Springfield's Ondine, C.D., W.C., winning under Mrs. Arlene Thompson. Bred and owned by Beth Sweigart of Virginia.

Eastern Dog Club 1959. Ch. Whygin Poppitt and Ch. Whygin Eager Nerissa, Best of Breed and Best of Opposite Sex, owned by Mrs. Helen Ginnel, Whygin Labradors.

Ch. Driftwood's Celebration, by Ch. Sandylands Markwell of Lockerbie ex Ch. Driftwood's Limited Edition. The first male Labrador owned by Driftwood Kennels, Mrs. Pam Kelsey, New Jersey. Photo by Vince Serbin.

Glossary

To the uninitiated, it must seem that fanciers of purebred dogs speak a special language all their own, which in a way we do. The following is a list of terms, abbreviations, and titles which you will run across through our pages which may be unfamiliar to you. We hope that this list will lead to fuller understanding and that it will additionally assist you as you meet and converse with others of similar interests in the world of purebred dogs.

A.K.C. The commonly used abbreviation of American Kennel Club.

Albino. A deficiency of pigmentation causing the nose leather, eyerims, lips to be pink.

Almond eye. The shape of the tissue surrounding the eye, which creates the almond shaped appearance required by some breed standards.

American Kennel Club. The official registry for purebred dogs in the United States. Publishes and maintains the Stud Book, handles all litter and individual registrations, transfers of ownership, and so on. Keeps all United States dog show, field trial, and obedience trial records; issues championships and other titles in these areas as they are earned; approves and licenses dog show, obedience trial, and field trial judges; licenses or issues approval to all championship shows, obedience trials, and recognized match shows. Creates and enforces the rules, regulations and policies by which the breeding, raising, exhibiting, handling, and judging of purebred dogs in the United States are governed. Clubs, not individuals, are members of the American Kennel Club, each of which is represented by a delegate selected from the club's own membership for the purpose of attending the quarterly American Kennel Club meetings as the representative of the member club, to vote on matters discussed at each meeting, and to bring back a report to the individual club of any decisions or developments which took place there.

Angulation. The angles formed by the meeting of the bones, generally referring to the shoulder and upper arm in the forequarters and the stifle and hock in the hindquarters.

Apple head. An exaggerated roundness of the topskull.

Apron. Frill of longer hair below the neck.

Bad bite. Can refer to a wryness or malformation of the jaw, or to incorrect dentition.

Bad mouth. One in which the teeth do not meet correctly according to the specifications of the breed standard.

Balance. Symmetry and proportion. A well-balanced dog is one in which all of the parts appear in correct ratio to one another: height to length, head to body, skull to foreface, and neck to head and body.

Beefy. Describes overmusculation or over-development of the shoulders or hindquarters or both.

Best in Show. The dog or bitch chosen as the most representative of any dog in any breed from among the group winners at an all-breed dog show. (The dog or bitch that has won Best of Breed next competes in the group of which its breed is a part. Then the first prize winner of each group meets in an additional competition from which one is selected the Best in Show.)

Best of Breed. The dog that is adjudged best of any competing in its breed at a dog show.

Best of Opposite Sex. The dog or bitch that is selected as the best of the opposite sex to the Best of Breed when the latter award has been made.

Best of Winners. The dog or bitch selected as the better of the two between Winners Dog and Winners Bitch.

Bitch. A female dog.

Bite. The manner in which the upper and lower jaws meet.

Bloom. Coat in healthy, lustrous condition.

Blue ribbon winner. A dog or bitch that has won first prize in the class for which it is entered at a dog show.

Bone. Refers to the girth of a dog's leg bones. A dog called "good in bone" has legs that are correct in girth for its breed and for its own general conformation. Well-rounded bone is round in appearance, flat bone rather flattish. Light bone is very fine and small in diameter, almost spindle-like in appearance; legs are extremely slender. Heavy bone refers to legs that are thick and sturdy.

Brace. Two dogs, or a dog and a bitch, closely similar in size and markings, color and general appearance, moving together in unison.

Breed. Purebred dogs descended from mutual ancestors refined and developed by man.

Breeder. A person who breeds dogs.

Breeding particulars. Name of the sire and dam, date of breeding, date of birth, number of puppies in the litter, their sex, and name of the breeder and of the owner of the sire.

Brisket. The forepart of the body between the forelegs and beneath the chest.

Brood bitch. A bitch used primarily for breeding.

CACIB. A Challenge Certificate offered by the Federation Cynologique Internationale towards a dog's championship.

Canine. Dogs, jackals, wolves, and foxes as a group.

Canine teeth. The four sharp pointed teeth at the front of the jaws, two upper and two lower, flanking the incisors; often referred to as fangs.

Carpals. Pastern joint bones.

Castrate. To neuter a dog by removal of the testicles.

Cat foot. The short-toed, round tight foot similar to that of a cat.

Ch. Commonly used abbreviation of champion.

Challenge certificate. A card awarded at dog shows in Great Britain by which championship there is gained. Comparable to our Winners Dog and Winners Bitch awards. To become a British champion a dog must win three of these Challenge Certificates at designated championship dog shows.

Champion. A dog or bitch that has won a total of fifteen points, including two majors, the total number under not less than three judges, two of which must have awarded the majors at A.K.C. point shows.

Character. Appearance, behavior, and temperament considered correct in an individual breed of dog.

Cheeky. Cheeks which bulge out or are rounded in appearance.

Chest. The part of the body enclosed by the ribs.

Chiseled. Clean-cut below the eyes.

Choke collar. A chain or leather collar that gives maximum control over the dog. Tightened or relaxed by the pressure on the lead caused by either pulling of the dog or tautness with which it is held by the handler.

Chops. Pendulous, loose skin creating jowls.

Cloddy. Thickset or overly heavy or low in build.

Close-coupled. Compact in appearance. Short in the loin.

Coarse. Lacking in refinement or elegance.

Coat. The hair which covers the dog.

Condition. A dog said to be in good condition is one carrying exactly the right amount of weight, whose coat looks alive and glossy, and that exhibits a general appearance and demeanor of well-being.

Conformation. The framework of the dog, its form and structure.

Coupling. The section of the body known as the loin. A short-coupled dog is one in which the loin is short.

Cow-hocked. When the hocks turn inward at the joint, causing the hock joints to approach one another with the result that the feet toe outward instead of straight ahead.

Crabbing. A dog moving with its body at an angle rather than coming straight at you; otherwise referred to as side-wheeling or side-winding.

Crest. The arched portion of the back of the neck.

Crossing action. A fault in the forequarters caused by loose or poorly knit shoulders.

Croup. The portion of the back directly above the hind legs.

Cryptorchid. An adult dog with testicles not normally descended. A disqualification. A dog with this condition cannot be shown and is subject to disqualification by the judge.

Cynology. A study of canines.

Dam. Female parent of a dog or bitch.

Dentition. Arrangement of the teeth.

Derby. Field trial competition for young novices, generally a year to two years of age.

Dewclaws. Extra claws on the inside of the legs. Should generally be removed several days following the puppy's birth. Required in some breeds, unimportant in others, and sometimes a disqualification—all according to the individual breed standard.

Dewlap. Excess loose and pendulous skin at the throat.

Diagonals. The right front and left rear leg make up the right diagonal; the left front and right rear leg the left diagonal. The diagonals correctly move in unison as the dog trots.

Dish-faced. The condition existing when the tip of the nose is placed higher than the stop.

Disqualification. A fault or condition designated by the breed standard or by the American Kennel Club. Judges must withhold all awards at dog shows from dogs having disqualifying faults, noting in the Judges Book the reason for having done so. The owner may appeal this decision, but a disqualified dog cannot again be shown until it has officially been examined and reinstated by the American Kennel Club.

Distemper teeth. A condition so-called due to its early association with dogs having suffered from this disease. It refers to discolored, badly stained, or pitted teeth.

Divergent hocks. The condition in which the hock joints turn outward, creating the condition directly opposite to cow-hocks. Frequently referred to as bandy legs or barrel hocks.

Dock. Shortening of tail by cutting it.

Dog. A male of the species. Also used to describe collectively male and female canines.

Dog show. A competition in which dogs have been entered for the purpose of evaluation and to receive the opinion of a judge.

Dog show, all-breeds. A dog show in which classification may be provided, and usually is, for every breed of dog recognized by the American Kennel Club.

Dog show, specialty. A dog show featuring only one breed. Specialty shows are generally considered to be the showcases of a breed, and to win at one is a particularly valued honor and achievement, owing to the high type of competition one usually encounters at these events.

Domed. A top-skull that is rounded rather than flat.

Double coat. A coat consisting of a hard, weather resistant protective outer covering over soft, short close under layer which provides warmth.

Down-faced. A downward inclination of the muzzle toward the tip of the nose.

Down in pastern. A softness or weakness of the pastern causing a pronounced deviation from the vertical.

Drag. A trail having been prepared by dragging a bag, generally bearing the strong scent of an animal, along the ground.

Drawing. The selection by lot to decide in which pairs dogs will be run in a specific field trial.

Drive. The powerful action of the hindquarters which should equal the degree of reach of the forequarters.

Drop ear. Ears carried drooping or folded forward.

Dry head. One exhibiting no excess wrinkle.

Dry neck. A clean, firm neckline free of throatiness or excess skin.

Dual champion. A dog having gained both bench show and field trial championship.

Dudley nose. Flesh-colored nose.

Elbow. The joint of the forearm and upper arm.

Elbow, out at. Elbow pointing away from the body rather than being held close.

English champion. In the case of a Lab means that the dog has gained a show championship in conformation classes plus a Working Certificate.

English show champion. A Lab that has gained championship in the conformation classes in England but not a Working Certificate.

Even bite. Exact meeting of the front teeth, tip to tip with no overlap of the uppers or lowers. Generally considered to be less serviceable than the scissors bite, although equally permissible or preferred in some breeds.

Ewe neck. An unattractive, concave curvature of the top area of the neckline.

Expression. The typical expression of the breed as one studies the head. Determined largely by the shape of the eye and its placement.

Eyeteeth. The upper canine teeth.

Faking. The altering of the natural appearance of a dog. A highly frowned upon and unethical practice which must lead, upon recognition by the judge, to instant dismissal from the show ring with a notation in the Judges Book stating the reason.

Fancier. A person actively involved in the sport of purebred dogs.

Fancy. Dog breeders, exhibitors, judges, and others actively involved with purebred dogs as a group comprise the dog fancy.

Fangs. The canine teeth.

F.C.I. Abbreviation of the Federation Cynologique Internationale.

Feathering. The longer fringes of hair that appear on the ears, tail, chest, and legs.

Federation Cynologique Internationale. A canine authority representing numerous countries, principally European, all of which consent to and agree on certain practices and breed identification.

Feet east and west. An expression used to describe toes on the forefeet turning outward rather than directly forward.

Fetch. Retrieving of game by a dog, or the command for the dog to do so.

Fiddle front. Caused by elbows protruding from the desired closeness to the body, with the result that the pasterns approach one another too closely and the feet toe outward. Thus, resembling the shape of a violin.

Field champion. A dog that has gained the title field champion has defeated a specified number of dogs in specified competition at a series of American Kennel Club licensed or member field trials.

Field trial. A competition for specified Hound or Sporting breeds where dogs are judged according to their ability and style on following a game trail or on finding and retrieving game.

Finishing a dog. Refers to completing a dog's championship, obedience title, or field trial title.

Flank. The side of the body through the loin area.

Flat bone. Bones of the leg which are not round.

Flat-sided. Ribs that are flat down the side rather than slightly rounded.

Fld. Ch. Abbreviation of field champion, used as a prefix before the dog's name.

Flews. A pendulous condition of the inner corners of the mouth.

Flush. To drive birds from cover. To spring at them. To force them to take flight.

Flyer. An especially exciting or promising young dog.

Flying ears. Ears correctly carried dropped or folded that stand up or tend to "fly" upon occasion.

Flying trot. The speed at which you should *never* move your dog in the show ring. All four feet actually briefly leave the ground during each half stride, making correct evaluation of the dog's normal gait virtually impossible.

Forearm. The front leg from elbow to pastern.

Foreface. The muzzle of the dog.

Front. The forepart of the body viewed head-on. Includes the head, forelegs and shoulders, chest and feet.

Futurity. A competition at shows or field trials for dogs that are less than twelve months of age for which puppies are nominated, at or prior to birth. Highly competitive among breeders, usually with a fairly good purse for the winners.

Gait. The manner in which a dog walks or trots.

Gallop. The fastest gait. Never to be used in the show ring.

Game. The animals or wild birds which are hunted.

Gay tail. Tail carried high.

Goose rump. Too sloping (steep) in croup.

Groom. To bathe, brush, comb, and trim your dog.

Groups. Refers to the variety groups in which all breeds of dogs are divided.

Gun dog. One that has been specifically trained to work with man in the field for retrieving game that has been shot and for locating live game.

Guns. The persons who do the shooting during field trials.

Gun-shy. Describes a dog that cringes or shows other signs of fear at the sound or sight of a gun.

Hackney action. High lifting of the forefeet in the manner of a hackney pony.

Ham. Muscular development of the upper hind leg. Also used to describe a dog that loves applause while being shown, really going all out when it occurs.

Handler. A person who shows dogs in competition, either as an amateur (without pay) or as a professional (receiving a fee in payment for the service).

Hard-mouthed. A dog that grasps the game too firmly in retrieving, causing bites and tooth marks.

Hare foot. An elongated paw, like the foot of a hare.

Haw. A third eyelid or excess membrane at the corner of the eye.

Heat. The period during which a bitch can be bred. Also referred to as being in season.

Heel. A command ordering the dog to follow close to the handler.

Hie on. A command used in hunting or field trials, urging the dog to go further.

Hindquarters. Rear assemblage of the dog.

Hock. The joint between the second thigh and the metatarsus.

Hocks well let down. Expression denoting that the hock joint should be placed quite low to the ground.

Honorable scars. Those incurred as a result of working injuries.

Incisors. The front teeth between the canines.

International champion. A dog awarded four CACIB cards at F.C.I dog shows.

Jowls. Flesh of lips and jaws.

Judge. Person making the decisions at a dog show, obedience trial, or field trial. Must be approved and licensed by A.K.C. if residing in the United States in order to officiate at events where points toward championship titles are awarded, or in another country if a resident there whose governing body is recognized by A.K.C., in which case special permits to officiate here may be granted.

Kennel. The building in which dogs are housed. Also used when referring to a person's collective dogs.

Knee joint. Stifle joint.

Knitting and purling. Crossing and throwing of forefeet as dog moves.

Knuckling over. A double-jointed wrist, or pastern, sometimes accompanied by enlarged bone developement in the area, causing the joints to double over under the dog's weight.

Layback. Used in two different ways. 1) As description of correctly angulated shoulders. 2) As description of a short faced dog whose pushed-in nose placement is accompanied by undershot jaw.

Leather. The ear flap. Also the skin of the actual nose.

Level bite. Another way of describing an even bite, as teeth of both jaws meet exactly.

Level gait. A dog moving smoothly, topline carried level as he does so, is said to be moving in this manner.

Lippy. Lips that are pendulous or do not fit tightly.

Loaded shoulders. Those overburdened with excessive muscular development.

Loin. Area of the sides between the lower ribs and hindquarters.

Lumber. Superfluous flesh.

Lumbering. A clumsy, awkward gait.

Major. A win of either Winners Dog or Winners Bitch carrying with it three, four, or five points toward championship.

Match show. An informal dog show where no championship points are awarded and entries can usually be made upon arrival, although some require pre-entry. Excellent practice area for future show dogs and for novice exhibitors as the entire atmosphere is relaxed and congenial.

Mate. To breed a dog and a bitch to one another. Littermates are dogs which are born in the same litter.

Milk teeth. The first baby teeth.

Miscellaneous class. A class provided at A.K.C. point shows in which specified breeds may compete in the absence of their own breed classification. Dogs of breeds in the process of becoming recognized by A.K.C. may compete in this class prior to the eventual provision of their own individual breed classification.

Molars. Four premolars are located at either side of the upper and lower jaws. Two molars exist on either side of the upper jaw, three on either side below. Lower molars have two roots; upper molars have three roots.

Monorchid. A dog with only one properly descended testicle. This condition disqualifies from competition at A.K.C. dog shows.

Non-slip retriever. A dog not expected to flush or to find game, one that merely walks at heel, marks the fall, then retrieves upon command.

Nose. Describes the dog's organ of smell, but also refers to his talent at scenting. I.e., a dog "with a good nose" is one adept at picking up and following a scent trail.

Obedience trial. A licensed obedience trial is one held under A.K.C. rules at which it is possible to gain a "leg" towards a dog's obedience title or titles.

Obedience trial champion. Denotes that a dog has attained obedience trial championship under A.K.C. regulations by having gained a specified number of points and first place awards.

Oblique shoulders. Shoulders angulated so as to be well laid back.

Occiput. Upper back point of skull.

Occipital protuberance. A prominent occiput noted in some of the Sporting breeds.

O.F.A. Commonly used abbreviation for Orthopedic Foundation for Animals.

Orthopedic Foundation for Animals. This organization is ready to read the hip radiographs of dogs and certify the existence of or freedom from hip dysplasia. Board-certified

469

radiologists read vast numbers of these files each year.

O.T. Ch. An abbreviation of obedience trial champion.

Out at elbow. When the elbows are held away from the body rather than in close.

Out at shoulder. A loose assemblage of the shoulder blades.

Oval chest. Deep with only moderate width.

Overshot. Upper incisors overlap the lower incisors.

Pacing. A gait in which both right legs and both left legs move concurrently, causing a rolling action.

Paddling. Faulty gait in which the front legs swing forward in a stiff upward motion.

Pads. Thick protective covering of the bottom of the foot. Serves as a shock absorber.

Paper foot. Thin pads accompanying a flat foot.

Pastern. The area of the foreleg between the wrist and the foot.

Pigeon chest. A protruding, short breastbone.

Pile. Soft hair making a dense undercoat.

Plume. A long fringe of hair on the tail.

Poach. To trespass on private property when hunting.

Point. The position assumed by a hunting dog indicating the discovery and location of game.

Pointed. A dog that has won points toward its championship is referred to as "pointed."

Police dog. Any dog that has been trained to do police work.

Put down. To groom and otherwise prepare a dog for the show ring.

Quality. Excellence of type and conformation.

Racy. Lightly built, appearing overly long in leg and lacking substance.

Rangy. Excessive length of body combined with shallowness through the ribs and chest.

Reach. The distance to which the forelegs reach out in gaiting, which should correspond with the strength and drive of the hindquarters.

Register. To record your dog with the American Kennel Club.

Registration Certificate. The paper you receive denoting that your dog's registration has been recorded with A.K.C., giving the breed, assigned name, names of sire and dam, date of birth, breeder and owner, along with the assigned Stud Book number of the dog.

Reserve Winners Bitch or **Reserve Winners Dog.** After the judging of Winners Bitch and Winners Dog, the remaining first prize dogs (bitches or dogs) remain in the ring where they are joined by the bitch or dog that placed second in the class to the one awarded Winners Bitch or Winners Dog, provided she or he was defeated only by that one bitch or dog. From these a Reserve Winner is selected. Should the Winners Bitch or Winners Dog subsequently be disallowed due to any error or technicality, the Reserve Winner is then moved up automatically to Winners in the A.K.C. records, and the points awarded to the Winners Bitch or Winners Dog then transfer to the one which placed Reserve. This is a safeguard award, for although it seldom happens, should the winner of the championship points be found to have been ineligible to receive them, the Reserve dog keeps the Winners' points.

Roach back. A convex curvature of the topline of the dog.

Rocking horse. An expression used to describe a dog that has been overly extended in forequarters and hindquarters by the handler, *i.e.*, forefeet placed too far forward, hind feet pulled overly far behind, making the dog resemble a child's rocking horse. To be avoided in presenting your dog for judging.

Rolling gait. An aimless, ambling type of action correct in some breeds but to be faulted in others.

Saddle back. Of excessive length with a dip behind the withers.

Scissors bite. The outer tips of the lower incisors touch the inner tip of the upper incisors. Generally considered to be the most serviceable type of jaw formation.

Second thigh. The area of the hindquarters between the hock and the stifle.

Septum. The vertical line between the nostrils.

Set up. To pose your dog in position for examination by the judge. Same as "stack."

Shelly. A body lacking in substance.

Shoulder height. The height of the dog from the ground to the highest point of the withers.

Sire. The male parent.

Skully. An expression used to describe a coarse or overly massive skull.

Slab sides. Flat sides with little spring of rib.

Soundness. Mental and physical stability. Sometimes used as well to denote the manner in which the dog gaits.

Spay. To neuter a bitch by surgery. Once this operation has been performed, the bitch is no longer eligible for entry in regular classes or in Veterans Class at A.K.C. shows.

Special. A dog or bitch entered only for Best of Breed competition at a dog show.

Specialty club. An organization devoted to sponsoring an individual breed of dog.

Specialty dog show. *See* **Dog show, specialty.**

Spring. To flush game.

Stack. *See* **Set up.**

Stake. A class in field trial competition.

Stance. The natural position a dog assumes in standing.

Standard. The official description of the ideal specimen of a breed. The Standard of Perfection is drawn up by the parent specialty club, usually by a special committee to whom the task is assigned, approved by the membership and by the American Kennel Club, and then serves as a guide to breeders and to judges in decisions regarding the merit, or lack of it, in evaluating individual dogs.

Stifle. The joint of the hind leg corresponding to a person's knee.

Stilted. Refers to the somewhat choppy gait of a dog lacking correct angulation.

Stop. The step-up from nose to skull. An indentation at the juncture of the skull and foreface.

Straight behind. Lacking angulation in the hindquarters.

Stud. A male dog that is used for breeding.

Stud book. The official record kept on the breeding particulars of recognized breeds of dogs.

Substance. Degree of bone size.

Swayback. Weakness in the topline between the withers and the hipbones.

Tail set. Manner in which the tail is placed on the rump.

T.D. An abbreviation of Tracking Dog.

T.D.X. An abbreviation of Tracking Dog Excellent.

Team. Generally consists of four dogs.

Thigh. Hindquarters from the stifle to the hip.

Throatiness. Excessive loose skin at the throat.

Topline. The dog's back from withers to tailset.

Tracking dog. A title awarded dogs that have fulfilled the A.K.C. requirements at licensed or member club tracking tests.

Tracking Dog Excellent. An advanced tracking degree.

Trail. Hunt by following a trail scent.

Trot. The gait at which the dog moves in a rhythmic two-beat action, right front and left hind foot and left front and right hind foot each striking the ground together.

Tuck-up. A natural shallowness of the body at the loin creating a small-waisted appearance.

Type. The combination of features which make a breed unique, distinguishing it from all others.

U.D. An abbreviation of Utility Dog.

U.D.T. An abbreviation of Utility Dog Tracking.

Undershot. The front teeth of the lower jaw reach beyond the front teeth of the upper jaw.

Upper arm. The foreleg between the forearm and the shoulder blade.

Utility Dog. Another level of obedience degree.

Utility Dog Tracking. A double title indicating a dog that has gained both utility and tracking degrees.

Walk. The gait in which three feet support the body, each lifting in regular sequence one at a time off the ground.

Walleye. A blue eye, fish eye, or pearl eye caused by a whitish appearance of the iris.

Weedy. Lacking in sufficient bone and substance.

Well let down. Short hocks, hock joint placed low to the ground.

Wet neck. Dewlap or superfluous skin.

Wheel back. Roached back with topline considerably arched over the loin.

Winners Bitch or Winners Dog. The awards which are accompanied by championship points, based on the number of dogs defeated, at A.K.C. member or licensed dog shows.

Withers. The highest point of the shoulders, right behind the neck.

Wry mouth. Lower jaw is twisted and does not correctly align with the upper jaw.

Ch. Ebonylane's Kim, C.D., a fine representative of Canada's Ebonylane Labradors owned by Mike and Pat Lanctot of Quebec.

INDEX

This index is composed of three separate parts: a general index, an index of kennels, and an index of names of persons mentioned in the text.

General Index

A

Abscesses, 422-3
A.K.C., *see American Kennel Club*
American-Bred Class, 330
American Kennel Club, 282, 332, 361, 363, 387, *see also glossary*
American Kennel Gazette, 236, 282, 386
Arthritis, 430
Ascarids, 416
Awards, accepting, 345

B

Baiting, 339, 343
Baltimore Sun, 155
Bath, bathing, 302, 326
Bed (for puppy), 291
Best Brace, 334
Best Junior Handler, 335
Best of Breed, 332, 333
Best of Opposite Sex, 332
Best of Winners, 332
Bite, 230, 323
Bloat, 425-6
Brace Class, 334
Bred-by-Exhibitor Class, 330
Breech birth, 277
Breeding, 259-67
    inbreeding, 259, 260
    line-breeding, 259
    outcrossing, 259, 260
Brood bitch, 265-7
Brood Bitch Class, 224
Brucellosis, 409, 413
Brushing, 302, 326
Burns, 422

C

Caesarean section, 277
"Call name," 297
Car rides, 299, 323
Carpal subluxation, 407
Cataracts, 406, 431, 438

Central progressive retinal atrophy, 407, 435, 437
Certificate of
    Championship, 332
    Health, 294
    Pedigree, 269-73
Championship points scale, 332
Coat, 226, 233-4
Collar, 293, 296
Color, 226, 233, 274-5
Commands, 297, 298, 300, 357, 363
Companion Dog, 364
Companion Dog Excellent, 364
Congenital defects, 406-7
Coronavirus, 409, 412
Craniomandibular osteopathy, 407
Crate, 238, 265, 291, 325, 399
Cuts, minor, 422
Cystinuria, 406
Cysts, 422-3

D

Dewclaws, 232
Diarrhea, 421
Diseases, 409-10
Distemper, 408, 409
Dog food, 300-1
Dog World, 145, 168, 208, 213

E

Ears, 203, 225
Exercise pen, 339
Eye color, 230
Eyes, 225, 231

F

Family dog, 283
Feeding, 301-2
    newborn, 278
    while travelling, 400
Feet, 225, 232
Field trial dogs, 386

Field trials, 386
First aid, 420-5
Fleas, 414
Frostbite, 422
Futurity stakes, 334

G

Gaiting, 324, 343
Gestation, 275-6
Greatest Sports Legends, 159
Grooming, 324-6, 338
    tools, 325
Groton Hunt, 155
Guide dogs, 389-92
Guiding Eyes For The Blind, 389-92
Gun dogs, 356-9

H

Head, 225, 230
Heart problem, 431
Heartworms, 418, 419
Heat exhaustion, 423
Heatstroke, 423
Hemophilia, 407
Hepatitis, 408, 409
Hip dysplasia, 431-2
Home remedies, 420-5
Hookworms, 416
Housebreaking, 298

I

Inbreeding, 259, 260
Infected cysts, 422-3
Infectious diseases, 409-10

J

Judging routine, 342
Julie Brown's Directory to Labrador Retriever Pedigrees, 59
Junior class, 335
Junior showmanship, 334-5

Index of Kennels

Index of People